Dallas —
What a pleasure
it's been knowing You
and training together all
these years! Best wishes alw

Tom Clements

THE KING AIR BOOK

A TREASURY OF THIRTY-SEVEN YEARS OF FLYING AND TEACHING
EXPERIENCE IN THE WORLD'S MOST POPULAR EXECUTIVE AIRCRAFT

TOM CLEMENTS

Published by **Flight Review, Inc.**

8245 E. Juan Tabo Road, Scottsdale, Arizona 85255

602-625-9132

Third Printing, January 2010

ISBN 978-0-578-04534-4

Printed by Lulu.com

Cover Design & Illustrations by the author

To Pam,

My bright, beautiful, talented, and supportive wife

and

To My Hundreds of King Air Students,

Who taught me as I taught them

TABLE OF CONTENTS

Part 3 – Bonus Extras

INTRODUCTION

I learned to fly in 1962 in New Castle, Indiana, between my Junior and Senior years of High School. My parents, Bill and Ruth Clements, were generous enough to offer to pay for my lessons if I retained my record of good school grades through my Junior year. I guess I met their goals, since they did indeed fund my Private Pilot rating. As you will read in the last chapter of this book, I always loved airplanes and flying…even though my first experiences aloft usually left me sick! As I took the lessons from Larry Barker, my first instructor, never did I think that aviation would wind up being my career. In my family, being a pilot wasn't a high enough aspiration. One had to be a banker, doctor, lawyer, engineer, or other "professional"…and being a pilot, in their ignorance, wasn't on that list. So, to me at the time, getting the Private Pilot license was simply a fun thing to do and something that would allow me to enjoy a neat hobby as I pursued my "real" career.

After graduating from Carnegie Institute of Technology – it changed its name to Carnegie-Mellon University on my graduation day – with a BS in Mechanical Engineering in 1967, I knew that Uncle Sam was eagerly awaiting young men like me for duty in Vietnam. "Let's see now: Being drafted into the Infantry or enlisting in the Navy: Which is the more advantageous route?" I opted for the Navy. I enlisted and was sent to Officer Candidates' School in Newport, Rhode Island, in August, 1967. A lucky break had me selected to interview with Admiral Hyman Rickover himself for the Navy's Nuclear Power Program as an instructor of Thermodynamics and Heat Transfer at their school in Vallejo, California. Even though I told the Admiral that I'd prefer to be on a ship, he selected me as one of his officer cadre.

In January of 1968 I reported for duty at the Nuclear Power School at Mare Island Naval Shipyard in Vallejo, at the north end of San Francisco Bay. The job was challenging and educational, both for the students as well as myself, and I was proud to spend four years there, leaving the service with a rank of Lieutenant. However, I had a lot of free time on evenings and weekends and I used that time to extend my flying avocation with Commercial, Instrument, Multiengine, and Instructor ratings earned from Navajo Aviation, in Concord. With sufficient ratings, I started instructing on a part-time basis for John Thompson at Sonoma Skypark a small 2,500 foot strip, a little west of Napa. What fun!

As my four years and four months of Navy commitment neared its end as 1971 came to a close, I debated what the future would hold: Would I accept the offer to pursue an MBA at Harvard or would I follow my heart into an aviation career?

Crazy? You bet! I went with aviation. Maybe it was rebellion against my folks, maybe it was the "Do your own thing" mentality of the San Francisco hippies of the '70s, or maybe it was God's leading hand…I chose the path less travelled, and I have never regretted the decision.

Sending resumes to any entity that might consider a 1,500-hour pilot with most of the ratings, I started considering the replies. I was very near-sighted and thus knew that airline flying – as well as military flying – was not in the equation. I concentrated instead on instruction, demonstration flying, and corporate aviation.

Wonder of wonders, Beech Aircraft Corporation replied and wanted me to come to Wichita for an interview! Why would they consider a newbie like me? Well, because the instructors at the Beechcraft Training Center (BTC) taught both ground school as well as did flight training and Beech liked the fact that I'd survived four years of classroom teaching at Nuke School.

I passed the interview process and showed up for work on January 3, 1972. At that time, the Beechcraft Training Center was comprised of only five instructors, plus our boss, C. Don Cary, and JoAnn Louie, our fantastically-capable secretary. All of Beech's training at the time was done in the classroom and in the airplane, no simulators. We covered the King Air models – at that time, only the 90, A90, B90, C90, 100, and A100 – as well as the Duke, or Beech model 60. "Look, Ma, a month ago I didn't know what a King Air instructor was, and now I are one!"

I feel sorry in retrospect for my first few students…I was barely a page ahead of them in the book! I had great mentors there, however – Don Cary, Bob Dunfee, Alan Roberts, Bud Small, Mike Unsane, to name a few – and soon I was staying a good step or two ahead of our attendees.

The sales of general aviation airplanes entered a robust period at that time, following a slump in the late '60s, and soon the BTC was humming with activity, forcing the instructors to work overtime and leading to a rapidly-expanding staff. I was assigned the C90 program and was the first instructor for the E90 that made its appearance that year, 1972. In late 1972 the prototype model 200 – then known as the model 101 – made its maiden flight, that I was thrilled to watch, and it went on to receive certification the next year. I was assigned to be the lead instructor on that new model and was trained in serial number BB-1 by Bud Francis, the chief test pilot on the program, and in BB-2 by Mike Preston, his number two man. What a huge step-up in performance the Super King Air 200 offered! What a joy to fly! Want to know what good airplane handling qualities are? Fly a BE-200. The military version of the model 200 – the C-12A – made its appearance in 1976 and that program was also my training responsibility.

In 1974 I was promoted to the lead Instructor Pilot position and a year later I was appointed head of the entire BTC, both pilot and mechanic training. When I decided to accept a position in the

Beech sales organization in California in late 1976, our staff totaled eighteen people…a lot of growth in five years!

Being a salesman was not my cup of tea. For those who can successfully make the required hundreds of cold calls, follow-up with the few demonstrations, close the deal, deliver the airplane, and support the customer after the sale, my hat is off to them! I did not enjoy it nor did I do well at it. I missed the flying and instructing side of things.

My boss at the time, Larry Hall, head of the Beechcraft West distributorship in Fresno and Hayward, California, sensing my discomfort, offered me a leave-of-absence while I delivered BB-294 to the government of the Malaysian state of Sabah, on the island of Borneo, and where I then remained for four months, flying the plane while training the Malaysian crews.

That Asian sojourn was a real treat…fun, challenging, learning about a new location and culture, and getting paid a lot, too! During those months, I reached the inevitable conclusion that I did not wish to remain as a salesman but instead wanted to get back into active flying. Mr. Hall advised me that Beacon Oil Company, in Hanford, California – to which he and I had sold a model 200 – had their pilot leave unexpectedly and that they were wondering if I'd consider flying for them upon my return from Sabah. Yes!

My first wife was not willing to leave the Bay Area where we were living, so I commuted by car the four hours down to Visalia, where Beacon had their hangar, and remained there for most of each week, living in a cheap motel, while I decided whether or not to commit to a long-term relationship with this fine company. Had it been just myself, I would probably have accepted a full-time job there. As a married man, however, I decided to stay in the Bay Area.

What to do now? Some of us BTC instructors had made numerous trips away from Wichita to larger customers – General Motors, Marathon Oil, IBM, to name a few – to provide on-site training at their facilities, since it was cost-beneficial for those companies to pay for one instructor's travel and expenses to their location instead of paying for ten or twenty of their pilots to travel to and stay in Wichita during training. Yet, when the demands for training grew so rapidly in the heydays of the '70s, we no longer had enough staff to both meet our demands at the factory as well as to offer the on-site training option.

Beech's decision to no longer provide on-site training planted the germ of an idea in my head…why not fill that niche? Thus, in January of 1979, *Flight Review, Inc.,* was incorporated in Hayward, California, for the express purpose of providing on-site King Air and Duke Initial and Recurrent pilot training. Thanks to the contacts made through Beech, my services were rather readily accepted and my little company met with quick success. I think it was 1981 when I spent 232 nights in hotel rooms! I needed help!

David Yount – another ex-BTC employee – was the first instructor I hired to help me and I have been very blessed to have had two other absolutely marvelous, highly-talented, instructors give me their extremely loyal and competent service through the years: Eric Berger and Al Hancock. Also, Dianne Grollemond and Kathleen Reese, who served successively as my administrative assistants, provided invaluable service to me and to our clients. Without these capable and hard-working employees, *Flight Review* would not have enjoyed the success that it did.

Traveling to conduct training for twenty-one years was enough for me. I was becoming burnt out. In 1998, I contacted SimCom's president and founder, Wally David, to see if he'd be interested in discussing a possible merger or buy-out. The outcome was that, in January of 2000, while I retained the *Flight Review* company name and the rights to sell my GPS and King Air training videos, SimCom received all of my training materials and my customer list. I signed a five-year, no-compete, contract. I spent three years working for SimCom in Scottsdale while the transition took place, then entered a semi-retired phase of my life, doing occasional flying, flight training, and aircraft management of some Phoenix-based King Airs.

In the early '90s I was approached by Bob Goff and then Paul Neuda, asking me to write some technical articles concerning King Air operation for their respective magazines: *Twin and Turbine* and *King Air Operators Group,* that soon became *Affiliated Aircraft Operator Groups* (AAOG). I have always enjoyed writing – my college minor was English! – and I had written extensively at the BTC, creating most of the factory's written handouts. I jumped at this chance to write on a regular basis. Both magazines paid me nothing – they did provide some free advertising – but I believed that the exposure would help my company grow.

Right? Wrong? Who knows. It's what I chose to do.

My articles were met with appreciation from lots of my King Air pilot customers and later on I often heard the question, "When are you going to compile all of that information into a book?"

The answer is: Now. At last I have decided to expend the time and effort to make this book a reality.

Keeping in mind that these articles were written over nearly a fifteen-year period, not all of the information contained within them is current. For example, VOR/ILS navigation was the only way to go back before Loran and then GPS hit the scene. There are also topics that are discussed more than once. However, I have included nothing that I feel will be wasted on the readers.

Part 1 of this book, *Flying Tips,* includes the articles that, although written for King Air pilots, often contain suggestions and techniques that could be applied to almost any pilot in any airplane. Part 2, *Technical Topics,* definitely is meant solely for King Air operators. Reading this part should expand the pilots' knowledge about how the airplane works and what can be done to maximize enjoyment, comfort, and safety while minimizing abuse to any system. Part 3, *Bonus Extras,* as the title implies, is where I have included additional material that I think the readers will find interesting, worthwhile, and fun.

When I started working for the Beech Aircraft Company it was still family-owned and the Chairman of the Board was that icon of American aviation, Olive Ann Beech, widow of the company's founder, Walter Beech. (Flying Mrs. Beech in her King Air on some of the company's business is a highlighted memory that I'll always cherish!) Later, the company was sold to Raytheon and even later to an entity that calls itself Hawker Beechcraft. Some of the articles contain references to these *other* factory owners but, being an ex-"Beechcrafter" myself, **Beech** and **Beechcraft** are still my preferred methods of designating the manufacturer of the King Air series of airplanes.

I have now logged over 21,000 hours of flight time and over 15,000 of these have been in King Airs. If there is a higher-time, more experienced, King Air pilot out there, I am not aware of whom it may be. I have been truly fortunate to experience the career that I have in this workhorse of a flying machine. Probably no other executive transport would have provided me the depth and breadth of a customer base that would have allowed me to succeed in the same manner.

The King Air has been very good to me. It is my ardent hope that this book will be good to those pilots who operate King Airs now and those who will do so in the future.

Tom Clements

Westcliffe, Colorado

August 2009

PART 1

FLYING TIPS

Your Four Friends

No, I am not talking about Bob, Ted, Carol, and Alice. The four friends are not people, they are PT6 powerplant and aircraft controls: Power Levers, Propeller Levers, Flap Handle, and Gear Handle. Repeat after me: "Power, Props, Flaps, Gear." Say it again: "Power, Props, Flaps, Gear." One more time: "Power, Props, Flaps, Gear." Attaboy! If you will truly embrace these four items, in this order, and make them your good friends, it will improve your King Air flying immensely, I can guarantee it. How? Read on.

When you got your multi-engine rating in the Travel Air or Seminole or whatever piston twin you used, I am sure that your instructor taught you the common mantra to recite and follow when confronted with a suspected loss of power in flight. Namely, it usually goes, "Mixtures – Full forward, Props – Full forward, Throttles – Full forward (or as required by conditions), Flaps – Up (or at least considered), Gear – Up (or at least considered)." Then, if in fact there was a Dead Foot, Dead Engine confronting you, you continued with "Identify, Verify, and Feather."

When we truly do lose power in one of our engines, the most critical thing we will need to do – well, after we take a few breaths, relax, and don't do anything too rash! – is to compensate for the loss by adding more power on the remaining engine, if available. If we don't, obviously we are going to lose airspeed, altitude, or maybe even both…not good unless we are ready to land, eh? The "Mixtures, Props" start of the procedure that we just cited is only necessary because it prepares the engines to accept the Throttles being added without worry about possible detonation or overboosting. The acts of pushing up the Mixture and Propeller levers, by themselves, don't really do much for us except set the stage so that the important levers – the Throttles – can be safely advanced.

In a PT6, however, no harm can ever be caused by going straight for the important levers, the Power Levers, *first*. If we go to the maximum torque limit while the propellers are still governing at cruise RPM, so what? The engine is as happy as a clam at high tide in this situation. However, the only way to achieve *full* rated power is to be at *both* maximum torque and maximum propeller speed *simultaneously*. (Power = Torque x Propeller Speed, remember?)

If you are enjoying the help of a competent and properly-trained additional pilot in the right seat, he or she can be given the command "Props – Full Forward" as you are advancing the Power levers and – bingo! – maximum power can be achieved basically in one step. Neat! However, there are three reasons why this cool method of achieving full power in one smooth operation is usually *not* the way it's done. (1) A lot of King Airs are flown single-pilot or with a real newbie in the right seat

The King Air Book

who couldn't even *find* the propeller levers, much less push them forward expeditiously, on the pilot's command. (2) Rarely is 100% power really needed, even with an engine failure. By leaving the propellers back at cruise speed, you have given up fifteen percent or less of available power. Do you need that last 15%? Except when maximum climb performance is critical, the answer is No. (3) For the less-powerful King Air models – I am thinking of the A90s, B90s, and early C90s powered by their original PT6A-20s, or the 100 and A100 with their -28s – there are relatively few cases in which full rated power can be enjoyed. Why? Because they're ITT-limited first, they cannot get full torque. Unless it is quite cool at Sea Level, those fine machines just cannot perform to their maximum abilities since their available power is less than their rated power.

In summary, if a competent right-seater can get the props forward while you add power, wonderful! But don't sweat it at all if that option does not exist. Instead, just push the propeller levers fully forward *after* you've moved the power levers up. After all, the four friends are Power, *Props*, Flaps, and Gear.

"Doggone it, Tom! Now you've got me confused! You just gave three reasons why advancing the propeller levers wasn't very critical but now you're telling me to do it regardless. What's up with that?!"

Sorry. You're absolutely right: In many cases, advancing the propeller levers to the stops is unnecessary. **But because it gives certain advantages, I want it to be the rule, not the exception. It can never hurt and it might help.** Let me explain further.

First, single-engine climb performance is better with the propellers turning at maximum speed, *even if it gives you no more horsepower.* There's this obscure little consideration of *propeller efficiency.* Unless you've actually seen this demonstrated in flight – or demonstrated it to yourself, as I will soon describe – then what I am saying may be hard to accept but it's nevertheless true. Unless you have the propellers at maximum RPM, you are giving up optimal climb performance.

To see this phenomenon yourself, go up some calm morning to, say, 5,000 feet, and extend gear and full flaps. Slow down to 100 knots or even less. (I usually use 80.) Now, leaving the propellers at your normal cruise RPM, add as much power as you can *comfortably* achieve. That is, you will stop adding power when you either hit the torque limit or the ITT value that you use as your routine, conservative, limit. Pitch up to hold your slow target airspeed. Take your time. Let things stabilize. After all is stable, make note of what rate-of-climb you are achieving and also what pitch attitude is being held to hold the low airspeed constant.

Now reach over and push the propeller levers fully forward. Of course, torque will drop. Don't regain it! Leave the power levers where they were. Realize that power has not changed. The drop in torque is merely a reflection of the flatter blade angle necessary to achieve the higher RPM.

(Power = Torque x Propeller Speed. Propeller Speed went up, torque went down, power did not change.)

Now keep patiently holding your target airspeed. Well, son of a gun, look there: The pitch attitude is now a couple of degrees higher and the rate of climb went up a couple hundred feet per minute, or even more. What you are seeing is the better efficiency of the propellers when they are turning at high RPM while flying at a relatively low IAS.

(This demonstration is probably most impressive in the F90-series, where the rate of climb may double! The 200- and 300-series also yield very obvious differences. The 100-series and A/B/C/E90s will definitely show a noticeable climb improvement, but it won't be a huge change.)

So, even though it may not provide us with a *huge* performance gain, to "stack the deck" in our favor always push those propeller levers fully forward if and when you truly want to maximize climb performance, *after* you've advanced the Power levers. Keep in mind that although we did not regain the lost torque in the demonstration – so that we could look solely at the effect of propeller speed change, not power change – in a real world situation you would return to the power levers and get more torque unless you were already ITT-limited or N1-limited.

There is another reason for always advancing both propeller levers fully forward when dealing with a suspected loss of power. This one is an obscure technical detail. (If your eyes glaze over reading this paragraph just ignore it and move on to the next one!) There is a third propeller speed protection device you learned about in initial Ground School: the Fuel Topping Governor, sometimes known as the Power Turbine (Nf) Governor. This is the one that deals with an overspeeding propeller not by increasing blade angle but by decreasing fuel flow, giving you a power loss. For PT6-powered King Airs (except those early ones with the PT6A-6 or -20 model) whenever the propeller levers are set for cruise speed, the Fuel Topping Governor (FTG) will operate at a speed that is less than the speed setting of the Overspeed Governor. In the event of a propeller overspeed there is a possibility – very slight indeed, but possible – that the FTG will activate before the Overspeed Governor starts increasing blade angle. If you knew what was coming and could calmly examine all of the engine instruments, you would observe an increase in propeller speed immediately followed by a decrease in everything else: ITT, torque, N1, and fuel flow...power, in other words. In the real world, however, who is going to be able to observe and comprehend all of that? Instead, you're going to be dealing with the yaw caused by the power reduction on one side...suspected power loss. If and when you move both propeller levers fully forward, not only are you stacking the deck in favor of the good engine, but you are also moving that pesky FTG up out of the way. In a moment, power may be restored! That's another reason why our second "Friend" is ***Props.***

The King Air Book

Let's suppose that you are flying one of the King Air models that is hardly ever temperature-limited at low altitude, such as a C90B, E90, C90GT, Blackhawk conversion, B200, etc. Down low, you can almost always get maximum torque without ITT ever getting near the redline. When you are starting through your Four Friends by adding Power, don't be timid! Go right to the torque redline! If you go over a tad, who cares?! You see, first of all, there is a lot of excess torque available for short durations that we never use. A brief exceedance of a torque redline will never harm a PT6. Second, as soon as you push the props forward, torque is going to drop back below the redline anyway, right? When ITT is not a factor, if you carefully stop adding power at the torque limit, then add props, you'll need to come right back to the power levers to regain that lost torque…if and when you want or need 100% of rated power.

To get back to the big picture, I have introduced this concept of our Four Friends as a way to easily remember what to begin doing when we suspect a power loss in one of our engines: "Power, Props." Push Power up first, Props second. In a light piston twin, single-engine performance is so darn meager even under the best of conditions that there was hardly ever a doubt as to how much throttle we wanted to add: We wanted all and even more! Often that's not so in the King Air. If you are stabilized on an ILS in the soup or on a visual final, with approach flaps and gear already extended, you are probably using only about a third or even less of available power. For example, a C90, in light winds, will typically be at about 500 ft-lbs of torque to stabilize the ILS at 120 KIAS. When it comes to the "Power" step in the King Air, an excellent rule-of-thumb is to **Double the Torque,** if you can. In our C90 example, when we lost the engine on the ILS, take both power levers and push them up until the responsive one shows 1,000 ft-lbs, double the 500 ft-lbs we had previously. Voila! We have regained all of the lost power and the airplane keeps plodding down the ILS or visual final pretty much like it had been doing a moment ago.

As for the "Flaps, Gear" portion of our four friends, that's just like in the piston twin trainer. If you want to maximize climb performance, you'd best make sure they are retracted. On the other hand, you'd be silly on the ILS or visual final to change their position. The airplane can easily follow a 3 degree glidepath angle with approach flaps and landing gear extended, even on one engine.

"Shouldn't our Four Friends then be Seven Friends?" you ask. "Power, Props, Flaps, Gear, then Identify, Verify, and Feather?" Well, yes and no.

You are absolutely right – again! – if *all* we are using our Four Friends for is dealing with a suspected loss of engine power. But there is more to come, as you will shortly see. Giving credit where credit is due, however, you are of course correct that if you are using your Four Friends in response to a sudden loss of power, and the power is not restored when you pushed *both* power levers and *both* propeller levers forward, then you would continue with Identify, Verify, and Feather. But you know what's really great? For those of you who have the marvelous Autofeather system installed and its switch in the Arm position, those last three steps will already be done! It is pretty darn easy to identify which engine is dead when its propeller is already standing still in the feathered position!

Before I continue to discuss the other situations in which our Four Friends are so helpful, allow me to harangue you for a moment for the purpose of emphasizing that the "Power" step involves *both*, not just one, lever. Have you noticed that I have been using the phrase "Suspected Power Loss" instead of "Engine Failure?" Although, unfortunately, most manufacturers' checklists still title the procedure "Engine Failure in Flight" or something similar, there have been and are going to be *thousands* of cases of *Power Loss* for every single case of *Engine Failure!* What?! That can't be so! Oh, but it is!

King Air power levers have a natural, built in, tendency to spring back toward Idle. There is a spring out in the cowling doing just that! (Why? So that, if a power cable breaks, the engine won't damage itself by going to full N1 speed. Instead, it will benignly wind up at Idle.) The only thing keeping this from happening all the time is the proper setting of the Power lever's friction mechanism. I would estimate that thousands of King Air pilots have had one or both power levers migrate a little or a lot toward idle after takeoff when the pilot took his hand off of the levers to reach for the gear handle. If it weren't so potentially dangerous it would be quite comical: The poor sucker looking for a third hand to keep the power levers up while he retracts the gear and tightens up the friction knob and flies the airplane.

The importance of pushing *both* power levers forward, not just one, is not just limited to King Airs. A Swearingen Metroliner met its demise during an ILS to Raleigh-Durham because the crew thought they had an engine failure when the only problem was that they had reduced power to idle themselves due to being high and fast. Since one engine's idle setting was misadjusted too low, they then assumed the engine was out, added power *only* on the other side, got low and slow, stalled, and died...along with a lot of passengers. Had *both* power levers been advanced, all would have been well.

Even an Air Force C-5A in Delaware came to grief during a three-engine approach that got too high and fast when the crew, after reducing all four thrust levers to Idle to get back in the groove, then moved three levers, not four, back forward to stabilize the approach but one of the three they moved was the wrong one, the one for the dead engine! Thus, they now had only two engines making power and did not make the runway.

Another reason for advancing both power levers in the King Air is that Autofeather is not truly armed until *both* levers are advanced, activating their respective switches inside the pedestal. Also, after you've secured a dead engine, where should the power lever be positioned? I strongly suggest that fully forward, not at idle, is the better choice. (Had the C-5 crew done that I venture they would not have lost the airplane.) **Don't even *think* about which engine may or may not be giving you problems!** Whenever there is suspected engine trouble, advance all the throttles you have! Comprende, amigo?!

OK, enough of that important rant. I have introduced our Four Friends as the method to start dealing with a suspected loss of power in flight but there are *four more* scenarios in which the Four Friends will help, help, help you.

Of the four scenarios, three are very alike: IFR missed approaches, VFR balked landings or Go Arounds, and stall recoveries. Let's start with the balked landing.

Just about the time you are preparing to close the Power Levers in the flare – Son of a ...! – there's that Cherokee at the intersection pulling out on the runway. What to do?! Relax. Use your Four Friends:

Power. Of course. Move both levers to the torque or ITT limits. Don't be timid! You wouldn't takeoff with half power, would you? And for takeoff the most flaps you have extended are Approach, not Full. So why do I see so many pilots timidly start the Balked Landing by going to only half torque or a little more? Slow, dirty, near the ground…and you add only half power? Are you nuts?!

Props. Yep, get them fully forward. Give yourself optimal efficiency and the potential for even more power, if required.

Flaps. Approach or Up. If you are flying a later model with the three-position flap system, going up just one notch to Approach is best here. With the earlier models, moving the flap handle up one notch to Approach won't achieve anything. The flaps remain extended until the handle goes all the way to Up. In that case, to keep it simple and to prevent having to divert your eyes for too long to the flap indicator, bring them all the way up at this time. As the flaps retract the airplane will naturally want to pitch up. As the flaps start retracting, pull gently on the wheel to start a rotation to about +10 degrees – typical takeoff rotation attitude – but then be immediately ready to *push* to prevent the nose from exceeding the 10 degree target. Now trim as needed to remove the push forces.

Gear. Of course. Up, when a positive climb is confirmed. Why is gear always last, after flaps? There are three reasons: First, the drag the gear provides is less than the drag of full flaps. Second, when the flaps retract, if we don't positively rotate to a 10 degree nose up attitude, we will almost surely sink a bit…so let's bounce off of the tires, not hit the fuselage's bottom skin! Third, for most models, if we retract the gear while the flaps are still extended to a position greater than Approach, the landing gear warning horn will be triggered with no way of silencing it except by retracting the flaps.

Very similar to this balked landing is the IFR missed approach. The difference is that, in most cases, this maneuver is initiated a bit higher above the ground and rarely, if ever, with Full flaps, only with Approach. Again: *Power*. Go for it. *Props*. Well, do you want absolutely *maximum* power and efficiency potential? If so, or if there's any doubt in your mind, *you are never wrong by pushing the propeller levers smoothly forward to the stops.* On the other hand, you've still got both motors, right? You're not at gross weight, right? You're not at Aspen in August, right? You're only going to climb a few thousand feet or so before being vectored for another attempt, right? If this is the situation, your conscious decision to leave the props alone, at cruise RPM, is justified and makes a lot of sense. It keeps the airplane less noisy both inside and out. *Flaps*. Leave them at Approach? Retract them to Up? It really makes no significant difference. For consistency of habit patterns, I would retract them now in most cases – certainly airspeed is high enough that stalling is of no concern – but if you'd prefer to leave them at Approach and only retract them after the gear comes up, be my guest. *Gear*. Sure. With a positive climb, up it comes.

For stall recovery, it's the same thing: Power, Props, Flaps, then Gear. As with the balked landing, whether you bring the flaps up in one or two steps depends greatly upon which flap system your airplane contains and whether you have a competent copilot working the flap handle for you. It's really no big deal because – unless you over-rotate far too much before you start the flaps up – your airspeed will be well above even clean stall speed after you've done Power and Props.

(When they know that they are intentionally going to execute stall *practice* for recurrent training, many pilots move the propeller levers to maximum RPM even before they start slowing towards stall speed. Great idea! It shows that they know the importance of that step. However, since a stall is never going to hurt you unless it's an unexpected one near the ground – Geez! How did I let the airspeed get so slow here at MDA in this awful weather?! – I suggest that in this real-world situation your prop levers would probably not yet be full forward as you recognize the impending stall. That is why I prefer practicing the recovery with the props still at the cruise setting as we begin.)

There is one more, somewhat unrelated, procedure in which your four steps are indeed your friends: Emergency Descent. "Oh my God! A passenger is having a medical emergency, I need to land ASAP, I am right over Little Rock, but I'm at FL 250." (See? An Emergency Descent is not only the reaction to an explosive decompression, is it?) What to do?!

Simple: *Power*. Idle. *Props*. Smoothly full forward. *Flaps*. Approach, when the speed gets slow enough but, in the vast majority of cases, your IAS will already be below the little white triangle at this time. *Gear*. Down it comes at the proper limiting speed. Now pitch the nose over to about 15 degrees down and then fine-tune it to maintain the landing gear extended speed limit.

The King Air Book

When you next show up on SimCom's or FlightSafety's or whomever else's doorstep for your annual recurrent training and that evil instructor hits you with engine failure, decompression, a balked landing, an IFR missed approach, or some stall practice, just relax and remember that your Four Friends are ready, willing, and able to help you successfully and properly handle the situation. *Power, Props, Flaps, and Gear.* What very fine friends they are!

IFR Approaches – The Basics

In the course of my work as an active flight instructor, mostly in King Air and Duke airplanes, I have a chance to observe a *lot* of different techniques used in conducting instrument approach procedures. The majority of the professional aviators with whom I work exhibit an excellent grasp of the entire IFR flight environment. They can fly the airplane both accurately and smoothly, plan ahead well, follow the published Instrument Approach Procedure (IAP) precisely, and communicate with ATC in a concise, correct, and yet friendly manner. Some of the owner-pilots I observe have nearly the same high level of skill as their full-time-pilot colleagues.

But, oh my, I have seen some really bad flying, too! Yes, more of these cases come from the owner-pilot ranks than from the professional ranks. Is that surprising? Of course not! These are folks who spend the bulk of their time thinking about their various businesses, not about the details of flying. Yet it is surprising and quite distressing that I often observe some really amateurish flying skill demonstrated by people who earn their livelihood as professional pilots. This isn't right!

So let's forget about details of new whiz-bang GPS navigators and Flight Management Systems for now and get back to a review of the basic procedures that are a necessary ingredient of any IAP. Whether it is a GPS approach to a small airport in west Texas or an ILS to Teterboro or a VOR approach to Tallahassee, some things never change. Let's review them.

Stabilized Approaches. Airlines have embraced the concept of the "Stabilized Approach" for eons. When jets began replacing propeller-driven airliners, virtually all airlines decided that being in the landing configuration and near landing speed at a point significantly above the runway – typically no less than 1,000 feet – offered many benefits. The extra drag of landing flaps required the engines to operate at higher power settings and thus there was less spool up delay in the event of a missed approach. Furthermore, without the drag of windmilling propeller blades in the flare, the jets were generally more difficult to land accurately since they tended to keep on floating past the touchdown aiming point. Again, being stabilized in the full landing configuration at a speed near Reference Speed (Vref, 1.3 times stall speed in the landing configuration) made touchdown control easier. I believe that very few jet pilots would argue with the merits of the stabilized approach.

Yet how about the myriad of airplanes that are still propeller-driven? These airplanes – especially turboprops – can slow down very rapidly near the runway due to their big, flat, propellers. Also, the "little guys" in the Cessna 182s and Piper Archers, flying at 70 knots or so for the last three to five miles during their stabilized approaches, would surely make themselves a sore nuisance for the pilots in the 737 trying to stay behind them!

So do we abandon the stabilized approach idea for the recips and turboprops? No, not *abandon* it, but *modify* it. Because the light singles need comparatively little runway length after touchdown, they can easily scoot down final at cruise speed when the jet is breathing down their neck, yet still land and make the midfield turnoff in most cases. They can also reply "Unable!" when the controller asks for "Maximum forward speed as long as possible!" and accept a vector to try the approach when it is less busy. Not a bad plan at all!

For turboprops and recip cabin-class twins, the major drawback of a truly stabilized approach often is not the "skateboard on the freeway" speed incompatibility issue, but revolves instead around the possibility of an engine failure and the likely inability to continue to the runway without a configuration change. (Damn those windmilling props and the lack of jet power!) Hence, the most typical modifications to the stabilized approach for these types of airplanes are (1) using only some intermediate "Approach" flap setting while still in Instrument Meteorological Conditions (IMC), and (2) carrying a bit of excess speed, such as 120 knots indicated.

In King Airs, the two most commonly utilized speeds for the final segment of IAPs are 140 or 120 knots. I usually use and teach 120, but I have no problem at all with those who feel more comfortable at 140 *if* – and it is a big *if!* – the airplane touches down near the fixed distance markers without excess speed at that point. This implies that power must be reduced early enough so that 140 is not still being seen when the runway threshold is crossed.

Let's face it: The speed, airplane configuration, descent angle, and height – these four variables – *at the threshold* most heavily determine the landing outcome! What came before that is basically unimportant! Bob Hoover could probably do a loop, an eight-point roll, shut an engine down, and extend the gear by hand between the outer marker and the threshold, and yet still be at the perfect Vref speed at 50 feet above the threshold with an absolutely perfect 3 degree descent angle at that position!

But I can't, and you can't, and most pilots can't! That is why it is so important to be stabilized early enough so that hitting that magic combination over the threshold is a done deal.

What I am trying to say is this: Few pilots have the skills required to make consistently safe landings unless preceded by some semblance of a stabilized approach. Get in the groove early and stay in it. In the last 200 feet or so before touchdown there shouldn't be much more to do than turning off the yaw damper and reducing power as you continue the descent so as to touchdown near the fixed distance markers on the runway.

IFR APPROACHES – THE BASICS

Precision versus Non-Precision Approaches. No matter what approach we request or what approach is assigned by ATC, it will be one of two basic types: Precision or Non-Precision. Precision approaches provide vertical glidepath guidance, non-precision approaches do not. Although there is a lot of work being done to add vertical guidance to non-precision approaches, for now the foremost type of precision approach that most civilian pilots will likely conduct is the ILS approach. With enough planning and forethought, any pilot can compute that rate of descent required during a non-precision approach so that MDA will be reached at a location that will allow a normal, 3 degree, descent to be continued to the runway's touchdown zone. However, it is still perfectly acceptable and correct to conduct every non-precision approach by descending rapidly to MDA (or some intermediate step-down altitude restriction) and then to fly level until we reach the point at which further descent can be made or at which we execute the missed approach procedure. "Dive and Drive" it has been called, and that sums it up nicely.

Too often, I find that pilots forget the "Dive" portion of the non-precision approach. Perhaps because they typically execute so many more ILS approaches compared to non-precision approaches, they fall into the trap of descending at ILS-type rates. In some cases, this works; they still reach MDA early enough so that they can make a normal descent for landing. However, in many cases the ILS descent rate is not great enough to ensure timely arrival at MDA. Hence, one must remember that the power setting and descent rate that works for an ILS will probably not be appropriate and correct for a non-precision approach.

Magic Numbers. At Flight Review, we emphasize the use of "Magic Numbers." What are they? Simple power settings that provide guidelines for use during both precision and non-precision approaches. The concept certainly did not originate at Flight Review. A lot of other training providers through the years have preached the benefits of learning and using the numbers to help fly precisely.

Don't know your magic numbers? Never had a training provider or instructor spell them out for you? Well, in a fun couple of hours of flying by yourself, you can find the ones that work in your airplane. Here's how.

Go out some morning when the air is smooth. Climb up to about 5,000 feet AGL and configure your airplane as you would for a normal ILS approach: Gear down, flaps in the Approach position, propeller levers at the typical RPM setting you would be using now. Establish a 3 degree descent profile and really nail the speed and rate of descent accurately. (How to estimate a 3 degree slope? The rate of descent should be five times the airspeed. For example, at 120 knots, descend at 600 feet per minute. 100 knots, 500 fpm.) How much manifold pressure (piston engines) or torque (turboprop engines) is required? Write it down, then go back up to the starting altitude and try it again a time or two. Average out the power settings to arrive at your magic number for an ILS approach.

Next, starting at the original altitude and in the approach configuration, find what power setting works for a 1,000 fpm descent rate at approach airspeed. Level off without changing gear and flap position, and discover what power setting is required to hold level flight and constant airspeed. Be patient on this. Lots of airplanes exhibit enough momentum that it takes quite a while – at least one full minute – to really find the magic number that works.

Let's say you've done these tests in a King Air C90 with the propellers turning at the normal 1,900 RPM cruise and approach value. I suspect you will find that the magic number for the ILS is about 500 ft-lbs and the two numbers for the non-precision approach are about 300 ft-lbs for the "dive" portion and about 800 ft-lbs for the "drive" portion. Remember them! Use them! Will they always be perfect? Of course not! But will they ever be very far off? Never! (Oh! The flaps didn't extend! That's why the numbers are not yielding the expected results on this approach!)

You can also repeat these tests with one engine set at zero thrust and discover what one-engine-inoperative numbers are appropriate. Don't be surprised if you discover that you cannot fly level at approach airspeed with the landing gear down. Hence, it is a good idea to fly the *non-precision* single-engine approach with the gear remaining retracted until the runway is in sight and you are in a position to make a normal descent to it. For the single-engine ILS, however, it is almost always best to extend the gear when established on the glideslope.

An interesting experience. Two or three years ago I was conducting Super King Air 200 recurrent training for an operator based in northern California. Their chief pilot was an older, highly experienced airman, with tons of time logged in everything from DC-3s through 747s, and he also had considerable experience in corporate airplanes such as King Airs and Citations. What a pair of hands he had! He was smooth, accurate, always very much in control of the situation and way ahead of the airplane.

After observing him fly both a precision and a couple of non-precision approaches under the IFR training hood, I was deeply impressed by his performance and complimented him on the wonderful job he was doing. I made reference to the fact that the magic numbers I teach for use in the BE-200 were exactly the power settings he had been using and the outcome was just perfect. "Good job on studying and learning those numbers!" I said.

"What numbers?" was his sheepish reply. "I just used the power I needed to achieve the airspeed and rate of descent that I wanted!"

His comment really impressed me with two things. First, that he was not only an excellent pilot, but a *natural* pilot as well, with an innate feel for the airplane he was flying. Second, that magic numbers – whether set first as an aid in achieving the desired performance, or found experimentally as the power that is needed to make the airplane fly at the specified airspeed on the desired profile – really do work.

For those of us who are not as gifted as he in flying skill, taking the time to learn the magic numbers pays great benefit in accurate instrument approach flying.

Approach Preparation and Briefing. A well-executed instrument approach procedure must be preceded by a thorough briefing, even if the briefing is done silently and only to oneself. What's the weather we'll be facing? Are all of the radios tuned and identified properly, with proper courses set? What is the MDA or DA and how about other important altitudes? Is timing involved and, if so, at what point to we start the clock? What is the missed approach procedure, and am I prepared to execute it? Any special remarks or notes of interest? Have I checked out the airport diagram and considered the runway of intended landing?

Unless these types of items have been considered *before* the approach begins, then too much attention must be diverted to checking them *during* the approach, and that gets in the way of accurately *flying* the approach.

And speaking of being prepared, please don't enter the cockpit with me during an instrument training session unless you have something upon which to write. I don't think I could fly without my trusty clipboard! Clearances, holding instructions, a good place to put charts...the more organized we are, the easier it is to stay prepared and professional.

Excuses. I watched in amazement as a professional pilot, type-rated in the Super King Air 300 we were flying, crossed the Final Approach Fix (FAF) of a VOR approach over 1,000 feet above the published altitude, in clean configuration, and indicating over 200 knots. During this recurrent training session, he had been told this approach would be made when we were still over 30 miles away from the FAF. Certainly there was time available to become briefed and prepared. Furthermore, the nut kept on trying to make the approach! We crossed the Missed Approach Point (MAP) about 1,200 feet above MDA and still going like a bat out of hell. Why, dear lord, was he so far behind the airplane?!

I am not sure that I will ever truly know the answer, but here are some of the contributing factors that make this pilot and others like him such poor instrument flyers: (1) Laziness. (2) Complacency. (3) Too much VFR flying. (4) "Realworlditis."

Unfortunately, some pilots are just lazy people who are unwilling to devote the time and mental effort to learn good flying techniques. That these people can successfully get through the flight training process, receive their ratings, and make a living of flying people for pay is a negative reflection on our training and certification processes. Similarly, complacency – a feeling of contentment and self-satisfaction – at times creeps into the make-up of nearly everyone who flies, even the good pilots. If not recognized and nipped in the bud, this obnoxious weed yields the same results as laziness…a careless, dangerous, approach to flying.

I wonder what percentage of landings in business, personal, and corporate flying follow an approach in IMC (Instrument Meteorological Conditions) as compared to those that are conducted totally in VMC (Visual Meteorological Conditions)? I would guess it is a small percent. By never having to go through the steps of briefing, setting up for, and executing an instrument approach much of the time, the skills necessary for successfully flying an IAP are easily eroded away. Of course you may request a practice approach from ATC, but even without doing that, nothing says you cannot tune and follow the localizer and glideslope or set up for a GPS approach to the landing runway. Even if no landing navaid exists, striving for accurate speed and configuration control on a visual final helps in maintaining the skills necessary for instrument flight.

Often I hear the excuse that stabilized approaches are not what happens in the "real world." It appears this "realworlditis" disease affects a lot of pilots. Hey, I am the first to try and make ATC happy. If they want 210 knots to the marker, I'll sure try my best to give it to them. But I know this: When the weather is really down, they won't be making many requests like this. Why do you think traffic backs up all over the country when Chicago or New York or Atlanta has bad weather? Because ATC cannot accommodate as many airplanes and one contributing factor in this is that the airline captains are saying "Unable" to those high speed, slam dunk, approach requests.

In training, I presume that any pilot who is flying twin-engine or turbine equipment can make quite a nice landing when the weather is good. Why waste time training for that? Instead, it is better to pretend that the weather is really poor…*that's* what we need to practice.

Circling approaches. Some of the basics of executing a landing from a circling approach are these: Don't let the bank angle exceed 30 degrees. Don't leave MDA until on a normal descent angle to the landing runway. Stay within the circling distance limits appropriate for the circling speed you are using, but don't crowd the runway unnecessarily. If you need to execute a missed approach while in the process of circling, start climbing toward the airport's center first, then decide which way to turn to comply with the missed approach instructions.

By the way, here's another fun and educational thing to do someday in your airplane if it is GPS-equipped. Find a not-too-busy, uncontrolled airport and either call up a GPS approach that has a missed approach waypoint at one of the airport's runway ends or else create a "present position waypoint" while sitting on a runway's threshold. Go out and fly a rough "turn about a point" by maintaining the GPS distance at 1.5 or 1.7 nautical miles from this point while maintaining the published circling MDA. Those are the maximum allowable circling distances when circling at speeds up to 120 and 140 knots respectively. I bet you will be surprised at how far out you appear to be! Also, realize that you have this much space from the thresholds of *all* the airport's runways not just the one on which you are planning to land.

Missed approaches and rejected landings. How many good pilots would intentionally choose to takeoff with flaps in a landing position and then use no more than cruise power during the takeoff? Not too many, I hope. Yet these same pilots will start a missed approach or rejected landing by timidly adding much less than takeoff power, even while the gear is still down and the flaps are Approach or Down – not a smart plan!

In aviation, there are times to "Do it, damn it!" A dirty multiengine airplane, near the ground, with less than full power applied, sets up a recipe for disaster if an engine failure occurs at this time. Even in a single-engine plane, gaining as much altitude right away improves the chances of a successful forced landing if the powerplant should quit running. So let's stop babying those engines in the missed approaches and rejected landings that we so rarely do. If you wouldn't be happy with the power setting for a takeoff, please don't use it for these situations either.

I hope your taking the time to read this review of IFR approach basics has been a worthwhile use of your time. Now go out and do some fun practicing!

WHEN AN ENGINE QUITS

Over the 40-plus years of instructing I have conducted with multi-engine pilots in twins, I have reached this conclusion: Most of us can do significantly better in the area of one-engine-inoperative flying in twins. Accident statistics show clearly that many pilots and their passengers have come to grief following the loss of one engine in a twin. Unless flown by a professional crew in a corporate or airline environment, the presumption that "two is safer than one" is a patent falsehood. I hope this review of some basic procedures will allow each of us to improve our performance is this area during our next recurrent training session or – Heaven forbid! – when the real thing next occurs.

"Take two aspirins and call me in the morning," was the old country doctor's way of giving his patients a cheap and often successful way of dealing with a late-night emergency. By morning, the symptoms will have passed and the seeming emergency turns out to be a minor inconvenience. I am reminded of this adage when I see pilots try to react too fast when they suspect an engine failure during training.

My instructor voice says, "Take three or four deep breaths, fly the aircraft, and call me in the morning." Let's break this down into its elements.

Don't Overreact

"Take three or four deep breaths." Try to relax and don't do anything so quickly as to increase the chance of making a big mistake. Look around the cockpit and airplane, both inside and outside. Loosen your death grip on the wheel. Wiggle your toes; flex your elbows. Don't take me verbatim here and do everything I am saying, but do *some* of it. Do whatever forces you to slow down and think about what you are seeing. I think the old World War II Army Air Corps directive was to "Wind your watch." Same thing! Don't go off half-cocked.

A Flight Review instructor once had a student spend over two minutes trying to reset a generator that had failed, the whole time not realizing that the generator quit because the instructor had just failed the engine! The student fixated on the red "Generator Out" annunciator totally, to the exclusion of everything else. Meanwhile, the aircraft lost over 3,000 feet of altitude and drifted hopelessly out of the assigned holding pattern it had been flying.

In a similar manner, I have observed numerous pilots during training turn off the avionics master switch following an Inverter failure that I gave them and thus gave themselves even more lost equipment. Why? Because they acted too fast. You see, the inverter switch and the avionics master switch sit side-by-side on the pilot's left subpanel in most King Airs and the order is not always the same. Sometimes the Inverter switch is to the left and sometimes to the right. What the pilot *thought* he did was switch inverters from Number 1 to Number 2 by moving the inverter switch from up to down. What he *actually* did was move the wrong switch! Haste really and truly does make waste!

Fly the Airplane

To me, "Make the aircraft do what it was last doing correctly," is a more complete description of what most of us mean when we repeat the overused "Fly the Airplane!" Before you got your wakeup call, before the engine sputtered and missed, before you yawed off of your heading or lost some altitude…what was the aircraft doing then? Was it simply cruising straight and level? Maybe it was in the turn to base leg? Perhaps it was between the markers on an ILS, with the needles rather well centered, you were pleased to notice? Whatever it was, make the aircraft keep doing it.

That is so easy to say, and so darn hard to do! I think this is what most instructors mean when they yell, "Fly the airplane!" My frustrated plea to "Fly the airplane!" could easily be stated in reverse: "Don't let the airplane fly you!" When I observe a pilot drift off of his or her last straight and level heading and altitude, or when the pilot allows those nicely centered ILS needles to peg against the case sides, or when the runway that was so easily reachable a moment ago gets too far out of whack, I am seeing concrete evidence of weak handling skill and, sometimes, poor previous training.

Forget power management for a moment; that will be addressed later. Unless you happen to be flying very slowly when the engine failure occurs, I contend that most twins will have enough momentum for a few moments that they can be made to "do what they were last doing correctly" with proper control inputs in the three axes. The ailerons, elevators, and rudder, correctly applied, are what allow us to make the airplane do what we want. I know that very few of us have the skills of a Patty Wagstaff or a Bob Hoover, and hence we cannot make the airplane do *all* of which it is capable. However, straight and level, climbs and turns, an ILS for an instrument-rated pilot…these types of maneuvers are definitely within our comfort zone. If not, they surely should be!

I remember reading of a DC-8 freighter that crashed near Toledo, Ohio, many years ago during a missed approach procedure in which the captain's ADI (Attitude Director Indicator) rolled over and died. Before the first and second officers recognized the failure, bank angle had exceeded 90 degrees. The captain gave the flight controls to the copilot who had a good ADI, but the airplane lost altitude and hit the ground, killing all aboard, before recovery from the unusual attitude was accomplished. The really sad thing here is that maneuvers flown in a DC-8 simulator duplicating these conditions showed that recovery was easily accomplished with room to spare when strong control inputs were made. But the flight data recorder indicated that tentative, smooth, minor control inputs were all that the copilot ever made!

Why? My speculation is that *smoothness* was one of the copilot's high priorities – as it is, and should be, for most pilots – but that he momentarily forgot that smoothness must be quickly sacrificed if it interferes with precision and control. I wonder what percentage of full control travel is ever used during a typical cross-country flight? Ten percent? Probably not much more than that. To ever rotate the wheel one-third of the way to the stops? Unheard of! Pull back to the stops? Be serious! You remember what your first flight instructor told you, don't you? "Use pressure, not motion, on the controls." Hogwash!

For a new student who is over-controlling badly, this "use pressure" mantra has great merit. But once the over-controlling stops, it may well be more harmful than productive. There are times that we must *aggressively* use the controls, pulling, pushing, or turning with much more than normal force and causing some relatively massive control deflections. I think the DC-8 copilot forgot this fact. If he had wrenched that wheel fully to the right until the wings were level and then sucked that yoke into his gut to get out of the dive, the outcome would likely have been success, not tragedy.

(A little side note: One of my pet peeves is seeing a student do the before takeoff checklist's "Controls – Free and Correct" step by tentatively wiggling the wheel and rudder pedals a little bit. Maybe this verifies that the control lock isn't still installed, but not much else. My usual response upon seeing this is to ask the question, "Is that all the control travel you are planning to use?" If it is, then let me out of here! We never know when massive control input may be required. So let's always check that the controls are free all the way to the stops in all directions! Let's hear an "Amen!")

Let me get back on track. The point we were presenting is "Fly the Airplane," or "Make the airplane do what it was last doing correctly." This is almost always achievable, but rarely is it easy. Now is not the time for timid, minor, control pressures. Large forces and control wheel and rudder pedal displacement may well be required to achieve our goal. You must work to hush that little nagging voice in your mind that says, "Careful! You are pushing too hard. Something will break!" Not if we are below maneuvering speed, it won't! (And if we are *above* maneuvering speed? Then keep on relaxing and taking those deep breaths, because we are in fat city with lots of energy to spare. At that high speed, it won't take a whole lot of control input to keep on keeping on.)

How about letting Otto, the autopilot, "Make the airplane do what it was last doing correctly?" I will probably raise some hackles here, because literally every autopilot's Aircraft Flight Manual (AFM) Supplement clearly states that old Otto should be switched off until after the engine failure procedure has been completed and the aircraft is trimmed for single-engine flying – but I believe that good cockpit resource management (CRM) skill would dictate letting Otto do what Otto *can* do to help us out!

The King Air Book

Here is what I have found in the myriad of autopilots I have flown in a lot of twins when an engine suddenly quits: They do a fine job of controlling the ailerons and elevators, bank and pitch, and a horrible job of controlling the rudder, yaw. You see, the yaw axis is designed for one job...*damping* yaw. In no way is it designed to actually apply the needed rudder force to compensate for non-centerline thrust. (The Bendix/King KFC-400 system is an exception here. It actually operates the rudder trim and, by so doing, can apply significant rudder force as needed when confronted with asymmetrical thrust. Amazing!) If we, the pilot, help ol' Otto by pushing on the appropriate rudder pedal -- "Step on the ball!" "Step on the heading!" – then Otto is a heckuva fine and helpful friend at this stressful time. Try it. You'll see.

Speaking of "trying it," here is a homework assignment for you. On your next training flight, in the real aircraft or in the simulator, have the instructor or safety pilot or even yourself, apply some massive and somewhat unexpected inputs to the trims in all three axes...presuming you have three-axis trim, which most of you do. As you are taking those deep breaths, fly the airplane: Make the airplane do what it was last doing correctly. See what it takes? It's rather hard to stop the roll, but it can be stopped, can't it? It's rather hard to keep the nose from dropping, but it can be held up, can't it? It's rather hard to center the ball, but it can be centered, can't it? Now, go ahead and re-establish the proper trimmed condition, in all three axes, and while you do so, keep making the airplane do what you want it to do. This practice can be invaluable in teaching you to be comfortable when you are forced to make control inputs that are rather rare. It will build your confidence and let you see that "flying the airplane" can be accomplished throughout some quite unusual situations requiring a lot more than gentle, typical, forces.

Call me in the Morning

"Take three or four deep breaths, fly the airplane, and call me in the morning." The "Don't Overreact" explained the first part of this. The "Fly the Airplane" addressed the second. Now? Uh oh! How do I make aeronautical sense out of the last part?

When the old-time doc gave the "Take two aspirins and call me in the morning" advice, he probably got very few calls the next day. Likewise, I think once pilots have learned to truly "Fly the Airplane," the battle is mostly won and I won't need to return many phone calls either.

But let's pretend that I do get the call. Someone I've trained had an engine failure, handled it less perfectly than he or she would have liked, and has called me for advice. What do I say? Nothing new. Just a rehash of what is already in most multi-engine training manuals. What I would say goes something like this.

In the course of "making the airplane do what it was last doing correctly," there probably came a time that additional power was needed, right? After all, if we were in a relatively steady state condition and did in fact lose one-half of our power, we probably need more power on the "good" side. For you piston twin drivers, the old "mixtures, props, throttles" should have come into play as you advanced both mixture and both propeller levers fully forward, and then moved both throttle levers forward until you had sufficient power to get the job done.

I'm going to get on my soapbox and orate for a moment; please indulge me.

Too many pilots haven't yet embraced the concept of leaving the "identify dead engine" step to its rightful place near the very end of the engine-out procedure.

I am going to take some of the blame here, because I haven't raised enough ruckus through the years in pressuring the checklist-writers to stop labeling the procedure "Engine Failure in Flight," or something similar. They should be saying something like "Suspected Power Loss in Flight" instead. Compared to fouled plugs, bad magnetos, or a mixture setting that is so lean as to cause engine roughness, how likely is it really for a piston engine to catastrophically fail? And when the catastrophic failure does in fact occur, maybe there should be a different checklist procedure to turn to…something like "Piston Through Cowl!" or, for a King Air, "Shrapnel From Exhaust Stacks!"

Please, folks, don't try to identify the dead engine first, even if it is obvious. Feathering the dead engine's propeller won't contribute nearly as much to your successful handling of the emergency than "flying the airplane" and adding power on the remaining engine. **Here's the thing: Since you are often not yet 100 percent sure which powerplant may be acting up, you must advance power on both engines.** That is why *both* mixtures, *both* props, and *both* throttles are usually the first "memory steps" of an Engine Failure – oops, "Suspected Power Loss in Flight" – procedure.

There was a commuter crew in a BAE Jetstream approaching Raleigh-Durham, N.C., who brought both engines to idle power because they were high and fast. This was a perfectly normal and correct reaction in this turboprop. But one engine's idle fuel flow setting was so low that it got the crew confused and made them believe they had lost the engine. Actually, the problem was that it was at a lower-than-normal idle setting. Because they never once added power on the "dead" engine, and because they didn't do a good enough job of flying-the-airplane, they killed themselves and all on board! See why we instructors scream about adding power using BOTH sets of controls! Don't identify first! Please!

Okay, I'm off of the soapbox. You can relax.

Once you've gotten the power taken care of, the next step is to verify the aircraft's configuration and change it as necessary. This is the "flaps" and "gear" portion of most checklists.

When in doubt, a clean airplane will out-perform a dirty airplane, so retract flaps and gear if you are uncertain of your situation. However, on an ILS or visual approach in the pattern, this rarely, if ever, is the best choice. Even the most under-powered of the twins most of us fly can still continue down a three-degree glide path quite nicely with the gear down and the flaps in the recommended approach position.

Finally, it is time to verify the dead engine (if there truly is one!) and feather its propeller.

For you piston-twin pilots, your memory steps should probably go something like: mixtures, props, throttles, flaps, gear, identify, verify, feather. For you PT6-powered twin pilots, your memory steps probably go something like: power, props, flaps, gear, identify, verify, feather. For you Garrett/AlliedSignal/Honeywell TPE331 pilots, your memory steps probably go something like: power levers, speed levers, flaps, gear, identify, verify, feather.

Wait a minute! My AFM's checklist doesn't say this! It basically says to cut off the fuel on the dead engine and feather its propeller. Oh you poor, misguided, soul!

Let me tell you a sad but true story. When I worked for Beech Aircraft Corporation in the 1970s in their King Air training department, our checklists handled an engine failure by directing pilots to basically do what we have been discussing: Add power, check configuration, then identify, verify, and feather. For those few models (back then!) that had the optional and marvelous propeller Automatic Feathering system installed, the last three steps were done for you! It's pretty easy to figure out which engine is dead when its propeller is already stopped!

But then a nasty little fact emerged: Some PT6s were prone to failing by giving *too much power*, not too little! When this malfunction in the Fuel Control Unit (FCU) occurred, the device sent maximum fuel flow to the engine causing tremendous overtorque and overtemp situations...too darn much power! The only way to deal with this runaway successfully was to cut the fuel off with the condition lever...like a mixture lever, for you piston pilots.

The Beechcraft committee that met to review checklist procedures and to write new ones decided that the solution to this nasty new discovery was to *start* the engine failure procedure by cutting off the fuel with the condition lever. By doing that, the "bad" engine would be shutdown, even when its power lever was ineffective in reducing the runaway power. Some of us instructors in the Beechcraft Training Center vehemently disagreed with this new procedure. It is just too darn risky, we said, to have the very first step being the killing of an engine! How about "Flying the Airplane" first? How about adding power and verifying configuration before shutting the bad one down?

As an alternative, we suggested that cutting off the fuel *first* should only be done when the engine failure is totally obvious: A *confirmed* engine fire in flight; an engine catastrophic failure or explosion, shown by shrapnel out the exhaust pipes; low oil pressure; severe vibration.

We lost the argument. The King Air engine-failure procedure got re-written with no vestige remaining of "Flying the Airplane" first.

Here's the kicker. One of the flight test engineers made this comment to me to show that the new procedure was okay: "Tom, we have to assume that the pilots are well-trained enough to never start an engine failure procedure without flying the airplane first. Of course they will already have added power as required and altered the flap and gear configuration to meet their needs. Otherwise, how will they know that the engine is 'unresponsive to power lever movement' which is part of this checklist procedure's title?"

If only he had been 100 percent correct! Please, friends, regardless of what your exact AFM procedure may say, realize that you must have a plan to fly the airplane first! Commit the following procedural steps to memory and use them religiously! For piston twin pilots: Mixtures-Props-Throttles-Flaps-Gear-Identify-Verify-Feather. For PT6 twin pilots: power levers-prop levers-flaps-gear-identify-verify-feather. For TPE331 pilots: power levers-speed levers-flaps-gear-identify-verify-feather.

Additional Comments

Few light twins can fly level, much less climb, with an engine out and the landing gear down. Some high-performance turboprop twins are the exception here, but generally, a light twin with an engine out has quite horrid performance. What can we conclude from this?

First, when an engine is secured, don't put the gear down until you can continue an uninterrupted descent to the landing runway.

Are you flying a visual traffic pattern, abeam the numbers and number one to land? Then the gear should be extended now. Don't wait until short final. Keep things as routine as possible under the circumstances. Are you on the glideslope at the outer marker? Then it is time for gear extension. Do you see red over white on the VASI or PAPI on final? Gear down!

On the other hand, what if you are doing a VOR or non-WAAS GPS approach because no ILS is available nearby? Then hold off on the gear! Wait until you break out and see the proper VASI indications before you commit yourself to a descent.

On takeoff, a complete engine failure in a light piston engine twin (as well as on some earlier King Air models) while the landing gear is still extended, is almost always handled best by landing straight ahead. Until the gear is retracted and VYSE is attained, it is usually best to land, regardless of what may be ahead. After VYSE is attained, in the piston twin, you may wish to move your hands from the throttles and place them on the propeller levers. After all, mixtures and props are already full forward and throttles are already at maximum. The flaps are up, 99.9 percent of the time, and you have just raised the gear. So you are ready to identify, verify, and feather. Well, identification is usually best done by the old standard: Dead foot, Dead engine. Verification? One method is pulling the throttle halfway back. Another is looking carefully at EGT, TIT, and Fuel Flow. So, since there is no 100 percent requirement to verify with the throttle, you can be poised to proceed with the feathering step since your hand is already on the prop levers.

Why pull the throttle just halfway back when verifying the dead engine? Two reasons. First, when you pull all the way back you close the throttle plate on the piston engine all the way and the resultant restriction to the induction air will cause a drop in manifold pressure, even if the engine is windmilling with no power. This can lead a pilot to believe that the engine is somewhat useful and should be left in operation. No way!

Second, pulling all the way back will trigger the landing gear warning horn in a retractable twin. We don't need this distraction now. If you don't observe some major power changes in the first half of throttle reduction, then that engine is toast. It's OK to shut it down. Do it!

Finally, don't expect the impossible. It is beyond the scope of this article to explain why the loss of 50 percent power leads to a loss of performance *much* greater than 50 percent, but it is true. If you have advanced full power on both levers, have "flown the airplane" but watched the airspeed decay to blue line (VYSE), and the airplane is clean with the propeller feathered, then that is the best you can do! Can't hold altitude? Accept the fact! Don't try the impossible! Start descending before your speed deceases below blue line. In some cases, finding something cheap and soft to hit – while under full control – is the only option available.

USING CHECKLISTS

Oh no! Not another article about checklists! How many more times must we be subjected to this mundane agony?

Sorry, but I guess the answer is, "One more time." Like most pilots and instructors, I have some relatively strong thoughts on the topic and want to pass along my observations to you. As I write this in June of 1999, follow-up reports on the American Airlines MD-82 crash in Little Rock are still in the news. The cockpit voice recorder has been reviewed and the initial conclusion is that activation of spoilers was overlooked, or else the crew covered the item using non-verbal (Pointing? Nodding?) communication. Was the checklist being used properly? We don't know yet.

Within the last few weeks I instructed a student in a Beechcraft Duke, providing his initial ground and flight training in this unique airplane. He was quite experienced, a multi-engine CFI and CFII with over 4,000 hours of flight time logged. Had he learned how to use checklists? Not yet. Not in my opinion.

Why do I say this? Because he preferred to "wing it" rather than truly back up all of his actions with the written list. Was he a safe pilot? The answer is a qualified "Yes." I never saw him make a glaring error. He always remembered to put the gear down for landing and put the mixtures and props up for rejected landings and IFR missed approaches. As is true with anyone who is new to a particular machine, I expected to see some hesitation in actions, some searching for the correct switch or lever, some minor confusion about procedures, and these I saw. However, numerous little procedural steps were being missed. Furthermore, all of the errors were occurring during the airborne phase of operation. The Before Start, Start, After Start, and Before Takeoff procedures were being conducted very well, but once we left the ground it was as if we left the checklist on the runway.

To be better seen during the takeoff roll, I teach to use landing and taxi lights for every takeoff, day or night, and that is what is in our Duke's checklist procedure. As the gear is retracted, the lights need to be turned off. Not a critical thing, but why have the brightest wheel wells in the state and the hottest bulbs? This step was being consistently overlooked and I had to remind the pilot numerous times about it.

In the Duke, it is correct to turn on the left and right electric boost pump switches for landing. In the unlikely event that the engine-driven fuel pump quits on the approach near the ground, the electric pump would keep things operating relatively normal. This step, too, was being consistently skipped.

The conclusion my mind reached was, "Here's another pilot who has never grasped the concept of why a checklist exists!"

He, like many others, had viewed checklists as something for neophytes. "Real pilots don't need checklists!" was the attitude his in-flight actions conveyed.

In a way, he's right! There are certainly times when well-ingrained proper procedures will suffice. Let me offer two examples. First, what "real pilot" of piston-powered, multiengine airplanes, when confronted with a sudden and unexpected loss of power, cannot do the following procedure by memory? Mixtures! Props! Throttles! Flaps! Gear! Identify! Verify! Feather! Pretty basic, right? Correct for almost everything from a PA-23 Apache to a DC-3 Gooney Bird, isn't it?

Another example: What "real pilot" cannot get by fairly well in landing even a complex twin by using GUMP? Gas. Undercarriage. Mixture. Prop.

But these procedures are not enough. As the complexity of the airplanes we fly increases, the procedures get more lengthy. Although there is nothing wrong with conducting the basic steps by memory and/or cockpit flow patterns, the risk of missing something important increases if we don't follow-up our actions with reference to the written list. We are not perfect; we *will* make mistakes.

I believe that there are two different types of checklists, or checklist philosophies, that pilots need to understand. There are CHECK-lists, and there are DO-lists. Checklists are used to crosscheck that normal procedures *have already been done,* and checklists are used to verify that emergency (memory or bold face) procedures *have already been done.* Dolists cover everything else. All abnormal procedures fall into this category. The generator quits. What do we do? We consult the appropriate checklist procedure and do it step-by-step as we slowly and carefully read the steps, one-by-one. The fuel is not transferring from the aux tank to the main tank normally. What do we do? Same thing. We consult the appropriate checklist procedure and do it step-by-step as we slowly and carefully read the steps, one-by-one. The cabin is not pressurizing properly. What do we do? Same thing. We consult the appropriate checklist procedure and do it step-by-step as we slowly and carefully read the steps, one-by-one. Get the idea?

Why guess? Why wing it? Do pilots avoid using the DO-list because they think it makes them look better? Because it is more macho? Because they cannot find it? Because they think it wastes precious time? I don't know the reasons. Maybe it is a little of all of these reasons and more. But let me tell you, friends, when you guess it or wing it or assume it in most cockpits of professional flight operations, you are definitely *not* making yourself look good. In fact, the exact opposite is true. You are making yourself look very, very, bad by appearing that you have an attitude of infallibility or invincibility, traits that can kill people in airplanes. You appear that either you think you are infallible or else you merely don't care to do things right.

USING CHECKLISTS

It is a competitive world out there in aviation. At long last, there truly does seem to be a pilot shortage and many jobs are available. *(Remember, this was first written in 1999!)* Still, each position, especially the good ones, have numerous applicants. Each and every thing a pilot can do to present himself in the best light improves his chances for advancement into the cream of the flying jobs. When the chief pilot takes you out to the Thunderfire VII for a quick check of your flying skills, your being unable or unwilling to follow the checklist carefully and thoroughly is not going to impress her or him. "But we didn't do it that way in the Airblazer 601," is not an acceptable excuse.

There is danger in becoming a slave to checklists. I have observed pilots who are rendered nearly inert if they can't find the written procedure for the situation they face. I have also seen pilots lose situational awareness as they belabor a checklist too much. This is obviously not good.

Some of our readers will recall my concept of *Judicious Suspicion*...a trait that every pilot who aspires to a long and safe career should have. Judicious Suspicion leads to thoughts like these: Today is the day that when I look left outside before turning left, there *will* be another aircraft over there! Today is the day the landing gear motor will run only 90% of the way and leave the gear only partially extended. Today is the day the FBO will not have properly completed my refueling request. Today is the day the VOR I have so carefully tuned will be down for maintenance.

Finally, today is the day that I am going to make a real boner of a mistake and forget a really obvious step of a critical procedure...but I hope like crazy that my strict follow-up with the checklist will allow me to find and correct the error!

My Duke student started missing procedural steps after we tookoff, not on the ground prior to departure. I cannot help but think that the business at hand – flying the airplane, scanning for traffic, following the instructor's and ATC directions – played a big role in distracting him from proper completion of the checklist steps. As I said before, I never expect a newcomer to do all steps correctly or in the proper order right away. Also, I want the pilot to be giving most of his attention to the "business at hand" of flying the airplane and all that entails. Nevertheless, there comes a time when each phase of the flight is completed, when the book is closed on that particular chapter. If the checklist has not been consulted by that time, such that some steps have been omitted or done incorrectly, then we are not operating as thoroughly, safely, nor defensively as we can.

This means that perhaps we don't really have time to carefully read the After Takeoff Checklist until we are climbing through 5,000 or even 10,000 feet AGL. Fine! Do it then. If we have leveled off at our final cruise altitude, however, and not once have peaked at the After Takeoff list yet, we are screwing up.

The most difficult of all checklists to use properly is one of the most important ones: Before Landing. If checklists are used to crosscheck that normal procedures *have already been done,* as stated earlier, does that mean we consult the Before Landing procedure after we have already touched down? Hmmm. There may be a problem here!

The newer the pilot, the less-experienced the pilot, then the earlier he or she needs to get the airplane in landing configuration so as to have time to crosscheck with the checklist. Invariably, there will be a step or two in the procedure that will come *after* the checklist has been viewed and set aside. This may be the setting of final flaps, perhaps, or the clicking off of the yaw damper.

As more experience and familiarity is gained, the crosscheck with the checklist can be done quite close to landing, after the gear has been extended.

Most of this discussion has been directed to the single-pilot operator who is doing his or her own checklists, not to the two-pilot crew. Anything the single-pilot can do to make the task easier, so much the better. I have seen the "Heads Up" verbal checklist machine perform very well for pilots. Putting the list on some type of multifunction display tube works well for some. Mounting a paper scroll checklist device in a conspicuous place is another option. Modifying the factory checklist so that it best fits your habit patterns, keeping it short and sweet and simple while at the same time including all "killer items," is another way in which the checklist can become more of a help and less of a hindrance. Letting the autopilot attend to the flying tasks while you carefully review the checklist – with your attitude of judicious suspicion at the forefront – is a great way to go.

The two-pilot crew has it easier when it comes to checklists. The Pilot-Flying (PF) should call for the initiation of each checklist phase and the Pilot-Not-Flying (PNF) should read the steps. Must this always be done verbally, aloud? Not in my opinion. Must both crewmembers crosscheck each and every step? Not in my opinion. Both crewmembers must, however, be fully cognizant of what flight phase is being checked, and they both need to know when the checklist is completed, to know that the book is closed on that chapter of the flight.

One last request: Realize that there is usually a big difference between a **Control** and an **Indicator**. Just because you moved the landing gear control handle to the Up position, did the gear retract? Just because you moved the flap handle to the Approach position, did the flaps extend? Just because you set the pressurization controller prior to departure, is the airplane pressurizing properly during the climb? When using a checklist properly – to crosscheck that an action has already occurred – don't fall into the trap of checking just the controls. Yes, the gear *handle* is down, but is the gear *itself* down?! Only the proper *indications* will tell, and they are the things that should be examined before that step of the checklist can be considered complete.

Thanks for taking the time to read my little tirade; now you have one more take on checklists to file away and mull over. The proper use of checklists is one skill that separates *mere* pilots from *good* pilots. Let's all be careful out there!

WHOA, BIG FELLA!

SLOWING TO TAXI SPEED AFTER LANDING...THE BEST WAY

I observe a lot of King Air pilots using improper slowing techniques after landing. Since King Airs require such relatively short landing distances, almost any technique that the pilot uses will get the job done in most cases, but unnecessary propeller blade erosion and brake wear can be minimized when the correct procedures are used and the passengers may be provided a more pleasant ride thanks to a consistent deceleration force. That's what this article will discuss.

The first item I wish to mention is the use of proper approach and touchdown speeds. The landing distance charts in your Pilot's Operating Handbook (POH) provide a table showing "Approach Speed" as a function of airplane weight. In most cases, the speed decreases with weight, as one would expect if we are trying to maintain the same margin above stall speed. What is unclear – unless the Associated Conditions fine print is read carefully or a knowledgeable instructor explains the chart correctly – is that this Approach Speed is neither the actual speed on final approach nor the touchdown speed. Instead, it is the speed at 50 feet height above touchdown (HAT) as the initial flare is initiated. This number is correctly referred to as VREF, and it is almost always calculated as 1.3 times power off stall speed.

If the final approach was flown in a truly stabilized condition – a technique that is great for jets but not very needed nor desirable in turboprops – then this speed was not only the one at 50 feet HAT but would have been maintained all the way from 500 or 1,000 feet HAT down to that point. For most of us, the actual speed on final is probably closer to 120 knots or so, and only when full flaps are selected at about 500 feet HAT in visual conditions do we then slow so as to reach the proper 50 foot speed. I think this is a great technique, but it is important that we do indeed reach VREF no later than the 50 foot mark.

By the way, if your airplane has been modified – such as a 200-series model with the Raisbeck Enhanced Performance Leading Edges – make certain that you are targeting the correct, slower, VREFs that are shown in the proper POH Supplement, not the standard, unmodified numbers.

The flight test engineers and test pilots plan their landing tests so that VREF is the 50 foot speed at the runway threshold, with power at idle, and with a touchdown point usually about 1,000 feet further down the runway. I am not sure if anyone has ever made an attempt to truly calculate the speed when the mains touch the runway, since this figure is difficult if not impossible to accurately control and since varying it a few knots either way will likely have no appreciable effect on the overall landing distance from 50 feet. I heard some of my old mentors at Beech suggest that the touchdown speed was probably about 15 knots below VREF and my experience throughout these many years of King Air flying makes me think that's a very realistic number.

There is no question that a little excess speed at touchdown is easily handled on most runways due to the King Air's reversing propellers and good brakes, so strict adherence to VREF usage is not as critical as in the jets. However, don't be content with sloppy control of speed. Strive to stay on the VASI or PAPI until the threshold, really nail VREF before the flare begins, and then touch down on those big fixed distance paint markers 1,000 feet down the runway. To discuss proper slowing techniques on the runway is a rather fruitless exercise if we begin the slowing process from a speed many knots faster than it needs to be.

Before continuing, let me review some important definitions. "Beta" is the region of the Power Lever aft of Idle and before Reverse in which the propeller blades' low pitch stop is being flattened while there is no change in idle Ng speed. (Ng means Gas Generator Speed, also known as N1 speed.) "Reverse" is the region behind Beta in which the blades' low pitch stop continues decreasing – now going negative – while at the same time Ng is increasing. For newer King Airs, the separation between Beta and Reverse is "Ground Fine," where another lift of the power lever is necessary before entering Reverse. For the earlier models, the separation is less obvious, merely being the point at which Ng starts to increase as the power lever continue aft.

Why are so many pilots reluctant to *fully* utilize propeller reverse? I am sure there are lots of reasons for this reluctance and probably a lot of them come from past instruction that was misguided. Well, here you go: With my blessing, I authorize your use of Maximum Reverse after touchdown anytime you want it! Pull those power levers *all* the way back and down until they won't go any further!

Although all of the arguments that I've heard explaining why *not* to use maximum reverse are easily refuted, the one that perhaps carries the most weight is the idea of being nicer to the engines by having one less ITT cycle. I agree that one less rise and fall of ITT is an admirable goal when it can be done in the context of safe flying. However, to use this as an excuse for avoiding reverse is faulty reasoning. Do you know how little power is actually developed in maximum Reverse? Since the engine's Ng speed only reaches 88%, maximum, in full reverse – it should be 85 ± 3% – that means that no more than 50% power is being produced. The rise in ITT is nowhere like the one that occurs when takeoff or go around power is applied. In fact, realize that the official logging of engine cycles has no correction factor whatsoever reflecting whether none, some, or maximum Reverse was used in the landing. Giving up the proven benefits of using maximum Reverse for the non-proven benefit of reducing an engine temperature cycle is a very poor tradeoff.

WHOA, BIG FELLA!

The best way to utilize reverse thrust is to do it *completely* right after touchdown. Of course, the propeller levers should be placed fully forward before going into reverse, as you've been taught. This takes a moment to achieve, leading to a nearly imperceptible delay. For passenger comfort more than anything else, the *normal* landing in a King Air is made with the propeller levers in the cruise position until after touchdown. However, the instant the landing becomes *abnormal* in any way – landing without flaps, or while single-engine, or on a very short runway, or in extremely gusty winds, or from a very low visibility ILS – then forget about keeping the noise level down and go ahead and push those props smoothly up early in the approach. That way, there won't be *any* delay before you can select maximum Reverse at touchdown.

Why is it important to use maximum Reverse so quickly? Most things we do in flying are done at a deliberate, slow, pace. Why am I telling you to lift and slam those power levers back once you've touched down and pushed the prop levers forward?

There are two reasons why this is the right way to do it. First, the drag of the propeller blades in maximum Reverse depends not only upon blade angle and Ng speed but also upon forward speed. Remember that parasite drag depends upon both the characteristic of the item – a thin antenna gives less drag than a big flap panel – and on velocity, squared. That is, the drag increases four times when speed is doubled (2 x 2 = 4) and nine times when speed is tripled (3 x 3 = 9). If maximum Reverse can be obtained by, say, 80 knots, it will be four times as effective as that available at 40 knots.

The second reason for getting to maximum Reverse immediately at touchdown is because it's the only time we can use it with no worries about blade erosion and engine FOD. Due to the twist of the propeller blade, when we have a normal, small, positive blade angle when taxiing on the ground, the angle at the blade tip is nearly flat. Because of this, little wind is blown off the blade tip and debris on the ramp or taxiway surface is relatively unaffected. On the other hand, when the blade angle is in Reverse, the angle at the tip is even *further* into reverse and now the swirling air off the tip sucks debris up like a vacuum cleaner! The only way we can have this large negative blade angle while still being safe to the propeller blades and engine inlet is to be going fast enough to outrun the junk getting sucked up. Beech states in the POH that the minimum speed for Reverse is 40 knots. I say this: When the airspeed indicator shows 60 knots *start* coming out of maximum Reverse and *be back into Beta* by the time it reads 40 knots. Notice that you don't come to Idle by 40 knots, a very common mistake. No, the limitation does not apply to Beta, just to Reverse. By 40 knots the goal is to have a *flat* blade angle, not the positive bite that exists at Idle.

How I cringe when I see what so many misguided pilots do! They slowly and tentatively select a little Reverse after landing. Since they don't select enough of it, it is rather ineffective and they aren't slowing rapidly enough to make the turnoff they were aiming for. So, with the airspeed coming up on 50 knots or so, *now* they decide to use more Reverse! They pull back all the way and hold it there until making the turn. Ouch! I feel sorry for the powerplants when I see this.

For those of you who have three-blade propellers and thus have your Low Idle Ng speeds set near 50%, you will experience such a delay in spooling up from 50% to about 85% that by the time maximum Reverse is actually achieved you'll be close to 60 knots already and need to immediately start coming out of Reverse. This is fine when you don't need to make the early turnoff. To avoid the spool up delay, the correct procedure is the Short Field one in which the condition levers are positioned to High Idle early in the approach so that the Ng speeds never drop below 70% while flaring, touching down, and selecting maximum Reverse. Is there a downside to this Short Field technique?

Yes, there is one, but it is a minor one that can be readily handled. The problem is that, with 70% Ng idle during the flare, the plane won't decelerate like it will with only 50% idle. Unless the speed and the flare are managed correctly, the plane will float in ground effect well past the touchdown aiming spot. So either learn to not be fast and not to over-flare when you want to use High Idle to minimize spool up delay, or else accept the fact that achieving maximum Reverse will be a rather slow process from Low Idle.

All of the four-blade equipped models have their Low Idle speeds set closer to 60%. Now the difference in spool up times when using Low or High Idle in the flare will not be nearly as pronounced. With the exception of the 300-series – They are real floaters in the flare, even at Low Idle – the other King Air models that have four-blade propellers tend to "fall out of the sky" much more rapidly than their three-blade cousins during the landing flare. Because of this, lots of pilots of the four-blade models *prefer* landing with High Idle almost all of the time. Go ahead and experiment a little and see what works best for you. Remember, too, that the condition levers are continually variable: If you don't like Low Idle or High Idle, there are intermediate settings you can use if you want.

I want to make one last comment about landing at Low Idle for you folks with three-blade propellers. Namely, even if you like the feel of this idle setting the best of all, you shouldn't even *be* at Low Idle if the generator load exceeds 50%. Doing so is in violation of generator load limits and leads to both excessive generator temperatures as well as very large ITT transient spikes when adding power. On those summer days when the air conditioning is running, you shouldn't be landing with a 50% Idle, period! Often, a compromise setting of about 60% works wonderfully well.

What about brakes? Just as Reverse is most effective and desirable at high speed, the brakes are best at slower speeds. If we stomp on the pedals soon after a high speed touchdown, we are asking for a scuffed or blown tire, especially in the 200- and 300-series with their dual tires and long wings giving lots of ground effect. I teach that brakes shouldn't be used until you hit 60 knots, when you start moving the power levers out of maximum Reverse. Now is the time to get on the brakes, aggressively if needed. By 60 knots or less, the wing will be producing hardly any lift, the weight will be solidly carried by the tires, and therefore the chance of locking up a wheel and scuffing a tire is quite small. Flying with a copilot? At touchdown, have that person push your propeller levers forward for you and also retract the flaps. It makes it easier for you and virtually guarantees being very solidly on the mains before braking is used.

Don't get me wrong. I am not trying to advocate the use of maximum Reverse and aggressive braking on *every* landing. There will be plenty of times when we want the plane to keep rolling rapidly down some long runway to reach the exit at the far end closer to the FBO. In those cases, leaving the power levers at Idle or lifting them back just a tad into Beta is well-advised and makes sense. However, when you want to make the closer turnoff, I hope that now you are better-educated about how to do it efficiently and safely while being gentle to your equipment.

Let me close with a reminder that perhaps brings us back full circle to the item I covered initially in this discussion….the importance of being at the correct speed as the flare begins. More than one King Air has overshot a landing runway and gone off into the dirt beyond. Often, the pilot admits to excess speed during the approach: A few extra knots for the gusts, a few extra because full flaps weren't selected, a few extra for the spouse and kids, a few extra because ATC requested keeping the speed up. "But, heck, I knew I could get it stopped. I've got those big reversing props to use! I don't know what happened but it seemed like I had no reverse!" *With too much speed, you won't have Reverse.*

Take a close look back at my definition of Beta and Reverse: "Beta" is the region of the Power Lever aft of Idle and before Reverse in which the propeller blades' low pitch stop is being flattened while there is no change in idle Ng speed. "Reverse" is the region behind Beta in which the blades' low pitch stop continues decreasing – now going negative – while at the same time Ng is increasing.

Please notice that my definition doesn't say that the propeller's *blade angle* is being flattened. The power lever controls the *Low Pitch Stop.* Only if we have a low enough *power* as well as a low enough *airspeed* will the propeller speed drop below the governor's setting into an underspeed condition, causing the blade angle to be on the low pitch stop.

We know that power will be low in the flare so long as we get the power levers to Idle. But airspeed? That's a variable that, if too high, will nullify any attempt to enter Reverse. In a nutshell, that's the whole reason why we push the propeller levers forward before lifting the power levers: We are setting the governing speed as high as possible, making it more likely that the props will be underspeeding and thus will follow the moving low pitch stop back into Beta and Reverse. Even with maximum governing speed selected, however, excessive speed can windmill the propellers so strongly that they won't ever reach an underspeed condition.

In the F90 POH, among others, there is a statement stating that "Propellers will not Reverse at airspeeds in excess of 95 knots." The F90 may be the worst offender here, since it has relatively high published Approach speeds and yet a maximum governing RPM of only 1,900, but if we increased the number from 95 knots up to perhaps 120 knots, this statement would be universally applicable to every King Air.

The bottom line here is that Reverse cannot always salvage a totally messed up, too fast, approach and touchdown. Rest assured, however, that there is a very, very, easy way to handle this poorly flown approach. "Uh, tower, King Air 90S is going around. We got a little behind it there." See how easy that was?

STEEP TURN TIPS

One of the training maneuvers most of us will be asked to practice and demonstrate many times in our flying careers is the steep turn. There are many variations in how this maneuver is executed. Most of the time a 45-degree bank angle is specified but it may be as high as 60 degrees. (It will be more only if you are flying with a sadist!) Usually the duration of turn is a complete circle, 360 degrees, but two circles or just a half circle are often chosen. The airspeed used is usually below the published maneuvering speed, V_A, but not in all cases. Also, it is common to maintain the chosen speed throughout the turn by adding more power, but sometimes power is not changed and the airspeed is allowed to decrease during the turn.

When I ask my King Air and Duke students to practice steep turns, I usually specify the following parameters: 45-degree bank, 360 degree duration, and constant airspeed…usually 160 knots indicated in King Airs and 140 knots in Dukes. The parameters expected of a licensed and competent pilot are to maintain bank angle within 5 degrees, to maintain airspeed within 10 knots, and to roll out on the assigned heading within 10 degrees. A difficult maneuver, especially when using only instrument reference? Of course. So why do we instructors so often subject our students to this torture?

We do it because the maneuver improves our instrument scan skill and gets us familiar with the airplane in this non-routine attitude. When we feel good doing steep banks, regular banks become very easy. The easier and more relaxed we become in the *physical* aspects of flying the airplane, then the more time, energy, and attention we can give to the *mental* aspects of flying such as thinking ahead, staying oriented, listening to ATC instructions, etc. I will go out on a limb to state the following observation based on over 32 years as an instructor: If a pilot has trouble with steep turns, I will find that the pilot has trouble in other areas of flying as well. Conversely, if a pilot executes excellent steep turns, I can anticipate finding far fewer problems with the pilot's other flying skills. Maybe it comes down to an *attitude* thing, since the pilot who puts forth the effort to perfect his steep turn skill will probably put forth a similar level of effective effort in other areas as well.

"Enough philosophizing, Tom! Cut to the chase! Tell me the tricks for nailing the @#$%& maneuver! I am tired of working so hard and still not achieving the level I want. Help!"

Okay, here goes.

Basic Physical Laws

Don't worry; this won't take long. However, I need to remind you of three facts about turns that you may have forgotten.

First, during any level, constant airspeed turn, bank angle determines load factor. Airspeed plays no roll here. That is, whether you are flying your J-3 Cub, your airline's 747, or the Air National Guard's F-16, your body will feel the exact same G-force when doing 45-degree bank turns…about 1.4 Gs. A simulator cannot replicate this force all the way around the turn but if you are in the airplane, the knowledge that this "seat-of-the-pants" force will always be the same can be a helpful bit of information. If you start feeling lighter or heavier in the seat than you should, you are about to bust one of the parameters of the maneuver, either bank angle or altitude.

The second physical fact is this: For a constant bank angle, the rate of turn varies inversely with the airspeed. In laymen's terms, the faster you are going, the longer it will take to complete the turn. Although the G force you feel will be the same when doing 45-degree bank steep turns in either your J-3 or your F-16, the Cub at 60 knots is going to be done with the 360 turn long before the Fighting Falcon at 360 knots. One thing this means is that the faster we are going, the less rollout lead we will require. The old, standard, "Lead the rollout by a number of degrees equal to one-half of your bank angle" gets less useful the faster we fly.

Third, the *horizontal* component of lift, created by banking the wings, is the force that makes the airplane turn. Since the *vertical* component of lift must still be equal to the weight of the airplane – to hold level flight – then *total* lift must increase in the turn. With increased lift comes increased induced drag. This explains why power must be added in the turn, even though airspeed is not being increased.

Be Prepared

Don't start the steep turn until you are ready. When you have been assigned a starting altitude and heading, be right on them before you start! It is a lot easier to remain within altitude and airspeed parameters if you are starting out right on the targets. In other words, give yourself a plus-or-minus ten-knot margin, not a plus-four-minus-sixteen-knot margin because you began the turn while you were still six knots fast.

Getting stabilized in level flight at the target airspeed and altitude provides an excellent opportunity to learn the power setting that is working for you today to hold the assigned airspeed. You should know this reference number, either as a Manifold Pressure, Torque, Fan Speed, or perhaps Fuel Flow value. You will need to add additional power during the turn to maintain airspeed and you will need to return to the original value as you complete the turn, so learn it well.

If possible, set the miniature airplane symbol in the attitude indicator (AI) exactly on the horizon line. If visual, also take a mental snapshot of the nose's exact relationship with the horizon. These are your "zero pitch" references and are an important reference you will use during the turn.

For most four-inch or five-inch Attitude Director Indicators (ADIs) found installed with flight director systems, the airplane symbol's relationship to the horizon line cannot be adjusted by the pilot. You will need to carefully observe what the *indicated* zero pitch reference is – plus two degrees, perhaps – and use this as the *true* zero pitch reference.

Finally, don't forget to clear the airspace around you. Look over your shoulder. Anyone out there to hit? Got TCAS? What is it showing? Talking to ATC? Let them know what you are about to do. "It only takes one midair…" You know how that one goes.

Bank Index versus Sky Pointer

How many of you are familiar with the term, "Sky Pointer?" Hmmmmm. Just as I thought, not too many. Let me try to explain. Virtually without exception, the larger ADI instruments indicate the degree of bank in a totally different way than the smaller AIs most of us used when getting our initial IFR training.

The AI uses a "bank index" for the purpose of displaying the airplane's bank angle. In addition to the horizon line, the gyro display includes large reference marks that are 30 degrees and 60 degrees above the horizon line on both sides of the display, and one other mark 90 degrees above the horizon line…at the very top of the display. It also has smaller reference marks at the 80-degree and 70-degree points on both sides: making them 10 and 20 degrees away, respectively, from the top of the display. Fixed to the instrument installed in the airplane's panel are both the miniature airplane symbol and an indicator – the bank index – that is always perpendicular to it.

As the airplane enters a bank, the horizon line and its associated marks remain fixed in space, depicting the actual horizon's position. The bank index and the airplane symbol, however, move with the airplane and show the degree of bank. In a left bank, for example, the bank index is to the left of the display's "top" and the wings of the miniature airplane show the left one to be below the horizon and the right one above it. Pretty basic, right?

The ADI, on the other hand, does not contain marks that are 30, 60, 70, 80, and 90 degrees away from the *horizon*. Instead, they are away from the *airplane symbol*. Big difference! The bank indication now comes from observing the position of a "Sky Pointer" as it appears to move relative to these reference marks. The sky pointer is simply a symbol – usually an arrowhead – that remains fixed in space directly above the horizon, perpendicular to it.

Now, when we bank to the left, we carry the reference marks with us. As our left wing goes down, the bank angle is displayed by reading the sky pointer's position as it appears to move to the right. It's not really moving, however; it is staying straight up, pointing directly at the sky. (Sky Pointer. Get it?) The real airplane, the miniature airplane, and the bank reference marks are what are doing the moving. Nevertheless, the difference between what has moved and what has not moved allows the bank angle to be displayed easily.

Strangely but truly, most of our readers who fly with four-inch or five-inch ADI displays will discover that their panel has one of each: a Sky Pointer in the ADI and a Bank Index in the "artificial horizon" on the copilot's side. This is not the ideal situation. Why? Because it will likely lead to a moment of indecision and confusion when trying to ascertain the degree of bank. I have observed this time and again when watching students make adjustments to bank angle during steep turn practice. Invariably, it they are used to one type of bank display and are now using the other type, they will initially correct by turning the wrong way! Shortly thereafter, they will recognize their error and another input will be made, this time in the proper direction.

In the last few years, I have observed that Raytheon is now using a copilot's AI that also displays bank angle using a Sky Pointer; both sides of the cockpit now lend themselves to the same interpretive techniques. This is a really good improvement. I hope other manufacturers are following Raytheon's lead.

By the way, I do not have a strong preference for a Bank Index over a Sky Pointer, or vice versa. Either one works well when it is understood. However, I slightly lean toward the Sky Pointer as the preferable display. When one finds oneself in an unexpected and radical unusual attitude, the Sky Pointer always shows where Up is. Roll until your head is Up; then get out of the dive as necessary.

Entering the Turn

We are now ready. We have cleared the turn area, we are on altitude and airspeed, and we have carefully noted the power setting and pitch attitude. Now start a turn in the proper direction. Two keys should be paramount at this time: Maintain the same pitch attitude and add a touch of power. Allow the bank angle to increase to 45 degrees at a leisurely pace. I observe some pilots who seem to think that attaining the 45-degree bank very rapidly is important. Why make it harder than it already is? What I prefer is to start the turn as if it were going to be a shallower, standard-rate, maneuver, then simply let the bank angle continue to steepen until we are at the desired value.

The amount of power to be added will depend upon the airplane and its type of engines. Also, in airplanes with conventionally turning (clockwise, as viewed from behind) propellers, I am convinced it takes slightly more power to hold airspeed during a right turn than it does during a left turn. (Any aerodynamicists out there who can explain that phenomena? I have not seen it mentioned elsewhere, but I am certain it is true!) We are talking about power changes in the magnitude of two inches of Manifold Pressure, one hundred foot-pounds of torque, or a couple of percent in fan speed…not a whole lot, but definitely noticeable.

The G-force required to hold level, un-accelerated flight with a 30-degreee bank is about 1.15. It is difficult for most of us to feel that extra 15% weight on our bottoms. But as the turn progresses and the bank angle reaches 45 degrees, now the additional weight is over 40%…definitely easy to feel. Hence, to maintain pitch attitude, not much backpressure or pitch trim will be needed during the first 30 degrees of bank. But after that? Be ready to pull and/or trim considerably to maintain pitch attitude.

In the Turn

So far, so good. We have reached the target bank angle of 45 degrees, airspeed is fine, and altitude hasn't changed more than a few feet. Now what? Again, let me suggest two key thoughts: Keep the bank constant; adjust pitch within a 5-degree pitch window. Let me explain.

I know that many of my readers have been taught to steepen the bank if altitude is high and shallow the bank if altitude is low. Sure, there is some merit in this thinking. To get out of an uncontrollable spiral dive with a steep bank angle, level the wings, of course. But let me point out that a 45-degree bank is not in the least bit uncontrollable. Uncomfortable? For some, yes. Uncontrollable? Heck no.

If you allow the bank to change – either intentionally, as a misguided method of maintaining altitude, or unintentionally, due to inattention – you are making the maneuver much harder than it needs to be. Each change in bank angle requires a commensurate change in back pressure and G-force if altitude is to be maintained. By nailing the bank exactly at 45 degrees and keeping it there, we eliminate a huge variable. By eliminating this item from consideration, altitude control is reduced to one parameter, pitch control.

There is a proper range of pitch attitudes – I call it a Pitch Window – that will allow us to hold altitude during the turn and make necessary corrections. This window goes from a low value of 0 degrees (the previously-determined zero pitch reference point, and not necessarily an indicated pitch of 0 degrees) to a high value of +5 degrees. When you observe the altimeter starting to increase and you need to lose a little altitude, let the nose sag down to 0 degrees. Starting to go a little low? Then raise the nose to +5 degrees. Everything OK? Then hold the nose right where it is, +3 degrees perhaps.

These are small corrections, folks! In most AIs and ADIs, 5 degrees is the *first* little mark above the horizon. Easy does it! One of the most common errors I see while observing steep turns is that the pilot adds back pressure only by feel, not by pitch reference, and before we know it we have the nose 10-degrees or 15-degrees above the zero reference. Heard the golfing joke with the punch line that "Even God can't hit a one-iron?" Likewise, I am sure that even God could not hold altitude within 100 feet if the pitch attitude gets up to 10 or 15 degrees! Don't let it happen. Keep the nose within the pitch window and you will be amazed at how much easier the maneuver becomes.

As we keep our scan going, which instrument gives us the most immediate indication that we need to make a pitch correction? Is it the Altimeter or the Vertical Velocity Indicator? Yes, you're right.

"Wait, Tom! You didn't give an answer! Which is it? Altimeter or VVI?" It's whatever you prefer and whatever works better in your cockpit or simulator. For me, personally, I am an altimeter guy and have the opinion that the best of VVIs, even the "instantaneous" ones, are not very helpful. (Oh my! I'm gonna take heat on that one!) Buy, hey, if the VVI works better for you, then by all means use and enjoy it. My wife, Pam, prefers the VVI and her steep turns are excellent. Maybe someday I, too, will find one that beats the altimeter in showing quick and accurate responses. But so far, I am still looking.

What about using trim to help in pitch control? This, too, is a somewhat controversial topic, and I always leave it to the discretion of the pilot who is flying. If you prefer trimming out the pitch forces, do it. Of course, remember to "untrim" as you roll out of the turn. The only thing I would caution against is this: using the trim to *create* and *change* pitch attitudes. *Make* the pitch change with control wheel force, and then trim out the force to the level you prefer. If we actually try to adjust pitch attitude with trim, we usually get sadly behind the airplane and waste a lot of effort trying to catch up. (Can you read between the lines and find that I, personally, am a muscle guy here, not a trim guy? It's true. I am not saying it is better; it is just what I prefer.)

In summary, while in the steep turn, concentrate on keeping the bank exactly at 45 degrees and making timely pitch adjustments in the pitch window to keep altitude as close to the target as you can.

Departing the Turn

Whew! We are almost finished with this darn maneuver. Thank goodness!

As our scan shows us nearing the rollout point – in the two-place trainer at 80 knots perhaps 22 degrees before our target heading, in the faster machines, maybe as little as 10 degrees before – it is time to rollout. At about the same, slow, pace as the entry, roll the wings level, reduce power back to the original value, and return the nose to the zero pitch reference location. If you added nose-up trim during the maneuver, now's the time to take it out as you notice the significant push force required to hold the nose at the zero reference.

Keep the scan going! Due to precession in the ADI's Gyro and to other factors such as unstable air, there is no guarantee that the zero reference pitch attitude and the level flight power setting will be exactly the same as they were when you began the turn. Oh yes, they will be darn close to those values, but keep the scan going and make necessary corrections to pitch and power.

Summary

I hope these suggestions will help in your really impressing yourself and your instructor the next time you practice steep turns. These are great maneuvers to practice occasionally, either on your own or, better yet, with a safety pilot aboard to help scan for traffic. Skills you learn in doing this maneuver well – the discipline to make one-degree or two-degree pitch changes, the discipline to manage small power changes to control airspeed, the seat-of-the-pants G-force sense you develop – will help in making all of your flying more precise and enjoyable.

Let's all be careful out there!

USING THE FLIGHT DIRECTOR

Alright, class, it's pop quiz time: Define "Flight Director." No, wiseguy, it's not the person who arranged the *Top Gun* flying sequences. That's right, it has something to do with those autopilot mode buttons.

I, too, have struggled with a simple yet accurate definition of a flight director. This wonderful flying aid has become a common component of the avionics suite of virtually all newer twin and turbine aircraft, but it's an item whose precise definition proves to be a little slippery.

"A Flight Director is an electronic computer that provides guidance to the pilot so that flying the airplane by hand becomes an easier task." That definition satisfies my desire for conciseness. Short, sweet, simple. Now let me expand on some details.

In addition to the computer, the flight director system includes, at a minimum, mode selector buttons and a visual display of pitch and roll commands. The computer receives information from nearly all of the same sources as does the pilot: the Vertical Gyro (attitude information), the Compass System (heading information), the Air Data System (altitude, airspeed, and vertical speed), and Radio Navigation Systems (VOR, Localizer, Glideslope, GPS, etc.).

In days gone by, the flight director was independent of the autopilot. An airplane might have a flight director and no autopilot, it might have an autopilot and no flight director, or it might have both, yet the two would be totally separate from each other. Nearly 100% of the systems of recent vintage – since about 1975 or so – are integrated systems, in which many flight director and autopilot functions are combined and handled by a single computer. Flight Control System (FCS), Flight Guidance System (FGS), Autopilot/Flight Director – all of these terms refer to the same thing, an integrated system.

Here's another way to get a handle on what a flight director is: It is the brain, and the autopilot is the muscle. Like the human pilot, the flight director computer knows what's going on in the airplane. The attitude, altitude, heading, and location of the HSI's course deviation needle are always known. More sophisticated systems even know the airspeed and vertical speed. With that information, it is able to determine lots of additional information that is referred to as computed, or derived, data. Let's take a very simple example. You are flying an airplane by hand, trying to hold an exact heading of 090° and an exact altitude of 8,000 feet. Your instrument scan shows a heading of 085° and an altitude of 8,025 feet. It's obvious that a slight right bank and a small pitch reduction are in order, eh? But if some moderate turbulence and momentary inattention knocked you down to

The King Air Book

7,800 feet with a heading of 120°, it would be time for a much more aggressive pitch up and bank left adjustment, correct?

Your own brain processed some raw data – that the heading and altitude were not correct by certain amounts – and then the brain came up with some computed information – how much to adjust pitch and roll. That is what the flight director computer does for us. It looks at the raw data and decides what pitch and roll adjustments are needed to correct our flight path back to where it should be. It does a mighty fine job, too!

We interface with – "talk to" – the computer by means of mode selector buttons or, sometimes, knobs. It talks back to us by means of a visual display of what our pitch and roll attitude should be. The visual presentation is always overlaid on the face of the Attitude Indicator, or Artificial Horizon, and turns that instrument into an "Attitude Director Indicator," or ADI.

The most common visual display is a "V-bar," which takes the form of a wide, inverted, "V" symbol to which the pilot controls bank and pitch so that the airplane symbol on the ADI fits tightly into the V. Sometimes this display is referred to as "single cue," since both bank and pitch commands are given by the single V-bar. The next most common display requires two cues and hence is known as the double cue, or "Cross Pointer," display. The vertical pointer shows how much to bank; the horizontal pointer shows how much to pitch. By keeping the center of the airplane symbol at the intersection of the cross pointer, bank and pitch will be controlled properly. There are a couple of other, rather rare, display systems as well: "Bullseye" is one, and wingtip-orienting balls is another.

(For newcomers to flight director systems, the V-bar display is usually easier to use, being more intuitive in nature. However, the cross pointer system is excellent as well, and it can, perhaps, be followed with a bit more precision after some practice. At least one major airline, I believe, uses the cross pointer display exclusively.)

The pilot tells the flight director what to do by use of buttons on the mode selector panel. Since the display can only do two things at once – display a pitch command and a roll command – some of these buttons are devoted to pitch and others to roll.

Since pitch adjustments are made in the vertical axis, those modes go by the name of Vertical Modes. They include modes designed to hold a particular altitude (ALT), to hold a certain nose high or nose low pitch attitude (ATT), to track a certain Glideslope (GS), to hold a specific nose-up attitude appropriate for a missed approach maneuver (GA), and, in the fancier systems, to level off and capture a pre-selected altitude (ALTSEL), to maintain a certain airspeed (IAS), and to maintain a certain vertical speed (VS).

Since roll adjustments affect the airplane in the left and right or lateral direction, those modes usually go by the name of Lateral Modes. They include modes designed to hold a particular heading

(HDG), to track a certain radio signal (NAV), to track a certain radio signal with more precision and accuracy and to also pick up a glideslope, if available (APR), and to track a localizer in the back course direction (BC or REV).

Although every individual model of a flight director system may be a little different from the others, Heading, Altitude, Attitude, Nav, Approach, and Glideslope modes will virtually always be available.

I have been surprised through my years as an instructor in King Airs and Dukes to discover how many pilots don't ever really use the flight director. I have observed pilots who make excellent use of the autopilot – programming its modes perfectly and monitoring its performance well – yet who react with confusion when I ask to observe them fly an ILS approach using the flight director. "But we already did that, Tom. Do you want me to fly the approach with raw data?" When I reply, "No, with the flight director," usually the autopilot comes back on.

Remember: The autopilot is as dumb as a brick. On the ILS, for example, it doesn't have a clue as to how to track the localizer and glideslope. "But it must!" you say. "My autopilot does a wonderful job on a coupled ILS!" Yes, of course it does…but the dumb autopilot does it by following the flight director commands. The brain is required to tell the muscles what to do.

So when I ask to see a "Flight Director ILS," I am asking for you, not the autopilot, to supply the muscle to follow the displayed commands. The mode selector buttons are used identically as if the autopilot were flying, but now you take the wheel and "fly formation" with the V-bar or cross pointer. And you know what? ***It's easy and fun!***

There are three ways, in my opinion, to fly a sophisticated single, twin, or turbine airplane that contains a FD/AP system. First, leave the FD/AP off and fly raw data…the back-to-basics approach. Second, use the autopilot while you monitor the overall situation. And third, hand fly by following the flight director display.

Let me present an analogy. Each individual investor probably has, or should have, a plan as to what percentage of his investment capital goes into differing investments. For one person, 50% in stocks, 30% in bonds, and 20% in cash may be right. For another, it may be a 40-40-20 split. A third may vote for 70-20-10. Likewise, each pilot should decide how much of each type of flying he or she does. Is it 80% with the autopilot, 15% raw data, and 5% flight director? Or how about 50-20-30? Or 80-10-10?

Please realize this: That unless all *three* methods are practiced at least *some* of the time, no one can expect to stay proficient in their usage. I am certainly not advocating an even split by any means, and I think we are silly if we don't use our autopilots well over 50% of the time, but we mustn't let the autopilot become too much of a crutch.

Autopilots and flight directors can and do malfunction and fail, and that is why raw data flying may be needed at times. However, my experience tells me that, in the modern autopilot/flight director integrated systems, failure of a particular autopilot servo is a more-common malady than failure of the computer. Hence, it is very worthwhile to feel relaxed and comfortable in hand-flying with the flight director, since there is a good chance it will continue to work perfectly even though the autopilot muscle is broken.

"So how do I become a proficient flight director user?" you ask. Like most learning experiences, start with the basics and work from there. First of all, remember that your autopilot has been teaching you how to fly the flight director every time you've used it. See how it keeps the airplane symbol glued to the flight director V-bar or cross pointer? That's all that you need to do, along with programming the mode buttons exactly as if the autopilot were engaged.

Try this simple exercise the next time you fly. Select a heading and altitude to hold, and engage the HDG and ALT modes when your altitude and heading are exactly correct. Now, intentionally ignore the flight director display and turn off of the correct heading and change altitude a little. See how the FD display is no longer aligned with the airplane symbol? Now, go ahead and maneuver the airplane, using elevators and ailerons, so as to line them up together. Don't worry yet about being smooth, but aggressively bank and pitch as required to fly formation with the display as tight as you can. See what happened? If you didn't return to precisely the initial heading and altitude, then either you aren't following the display tight enough, or maybe your FD is malfunctioning.

Now fly an ILS, preferably in visual conditions, using the APR and GS modes. Follow the display as tightly as you can, even if you are initially being rougher than you'd like. See how easy it is to remain on the localizer and glideslope? Isn't it a lot easier than doing it with only raw data? Isn't it FUN?!

Once the light bulb of understanding illuminates about how easy flying can be when following the flight director, there is a danger of forgetting to include the raw data in our instrument scan, and to spend nearly all of our time intently staring at the V-bar or cross pointer. Even though flight directors are quite reliable, judicious suspicion tells us that sometimes the commands won't be correct. Perhaps the flight director is in error, or, more likely, we programmed an incorrect mode…for example, we still have the HDG mode selected when we thought we had APR. So remember to watch the altimeter, airspeed, course needle, etc., to verify that the flight path is proceeding as you want.

Another important comment: Turn the flight director off when you are not using it. When we are looking out the window while flying a traffic pattern, for example, the command bars are probably being ignored most of the time. Instead of forming a bad habit of having the command bars in view while intentionally *not* following them, I suggest that it is better to remove them from view and revert to raw data.

Many years ago I was instructing a pilot who was a novice both in the King Air and in the use of the fine flight director system which his new airplane contained. As we practiced with the unit, I kept encouraging him to follow the V-bars to correct slight flight path deviations. "Follow the bars," was a phrase I must have uttered fifty times that day. Each time he did so, we returned to our desired flight path properly. Near the end of the day, as he was following the V-bars nicely and hence executing a flawless hand-flown ILS approach, he turned to me with a big grin and announced, "Tom, I have finally figured this thing out! It's just like my mother-in-law!" "How's that?" I replied. "Well," he explained, "it's always telling me what to do...and it's almost always right!"

"The Flight Director is a mother-in-law." I like that! Maybe it's the best definition of all!

GIVE YOURSELF A CHECKRIDE

In the course of my work as a flight instructor for pilots of Beech Dukes and King Airs, I have had the great pleasure of watching hundreds of really superb pilots demonstrate their knowledge and skill as they successfully completed one of our Initial or Recurrent training programs. I often come away from these sessions feeling that I benefited as much as, or maybe more than, my student since I picked up some clever technique or tip or deeper understanding from him or her.

Yet other times, yuck! Now my feelings are often ones of inadequacy: Why couldn't I get the information across better? Why couldn't I find the source of the student's problem and solve it? Why couldn't I "click" with this person on a better level of communication? These feelings are spawned by the fact that the student and I, working together, could not manage to raise the student's level of performance up to that expected by me and the FAA's Practical Test Standards. When this occurs – and thank God it is not too often! – we both end up with frustration and anger.

How about you? Have you breezed through most of your checkrides and training sessions? Have they, in the main, been pleasurable experiences? Or has there been a time or two when it was just plain agony? And if you have experienced both situations, what accounted for the difference?

When it was a struggle, was it a cycle of bad biorhythms? A lack of recent experience and practice, perhaps? A lack of communication with the instructor or check pilot? A combination of a lot of things?

In order to get you better prepared for your next training or checkride session, let me provide some insight into common factors that distinguish the good pilot from the mediocre or poor pilot. The reasons for poor performance may be many, and oftentimes they are quite *subjective* in nature. But I think that the ability to distinguish the good from the bad can be based on quite *objective* standards, standards which each of us can use to give ourselves a checkride on any flight we make.

Radio Communications. Do you sound professional on the radio? That is, do you always use your full call sign during the initial contact, and then continue to use your abbreviated identification at the start or end of each transmission you make? Do you always tell the controller that you have the correct ATIS information during your initial contact? Do you always state your current altitude when first making contact with a new radar controller? (They must verify your Mode C is correct.) Do you always report when leaving an assigned altitude? Do you speak clearly, slowly, and with enough volume that the controller rarely asks for a repeat?

The King Air Book

If your answers to these questions about communications are usually "Yes," then you have earned good marks so far on your personal checkride.

Centerline Awareness. When taxiing, the good pilot is consistently on or near the taxiway centerline, or heading back toward it. Landings and takeoffs are always made with the main gear straddling the centerline, unless there is a good reason for not doing so. In crosswind situations, enough rudder and aileron control are used to put the airplane on the centerline, with the nose properly aligned with the runway direction and no touchdown sideways drift which puts undesired loads on the landing gear. Check yourself on this, the next time you fly.

Visual Airport Traffic Patterns. The sharp pilot always plans the descent so as to be at the proper VFR traffic pattern altitude (usually 1,000 feet HAA for piston and 1,500 feet for turbine airplanes) before he or she enters the pattern. The pilot considers the wind, and puts in wind correction angles appropriately on the various segments of the pattern. Bank angles are kept below 30° and speed is not excessive. The turn onto final is planned to avoid overshooting, and more often than not the VASI is showing Red over White when it comes into view. If the VASI is not correct when sighted, the good pilot immediately starts taking the appropriate action to get on the proper glidepath angle, and he/she follows the angle to the threshold. Touchdown usually occurs very near the fixed distance markers, about 1,000 feet from the threshold – on centerline, well-aligned, and without drift – unless there is a good reason for change. The CTAF (Common Traffic Advisory Frequency) has been monitored for a reasonable period of time before entering the pattern, the pilot's position, altitude and intention have been clearly communicated, and he/she has executed a pattern entry that causes no conflict with other existing pattern traffic. How are you doing on this part of your routine flying?

Instrument Approaches. The sharp pilot is well-prepared for the IFR approach before it starts, and is thoroughly briefed on both the approach and the missed approach procedures. No nav radio is tuned to a new frequency without the proper station Morse code also being identified. All available equipment is utilized in a thorough but simple manner to ensure maximum positional awareness. DAs (Decision Altitudes) and MDAs (Minimum Descent Altitudes) are treated with deserved respect. Unless a good reason exists for *not* doing so, the airplane is properly configured and the speed is near the target value from the FAF (Final Approach Fix) inbound. If the approach terminates with a circle-to-land maneuver, the good pilot has analyzed the airport diagram and made a plan of how best to maneuver the airplane to the proper runway, and does so without exceeding 30° bank angles.

Checklists. The sharp pilot can perform all normal, routine, tasks quite well without ever referring to a checklist. Bet you weren't expecting that, were you?! *But* – and it is a big *but* – the sharp pilot also has learned how vulnerable we all are to mistakes and lapses, and thus always does refer to the checklist to confirm that proper actions have been done. On the other hand, the sharp pilot does not try to "wing it" when faced with non-routine, abnormal procedures. Instead, he/she knows that the first priority is to always fly the airplane, and then, when time permits, the abnormal situation is addressed while referring to the appropriate checklist. Finally, the sharp pilot realizes that some events are true emergencies, and a certain few actions must be taken before a checklist can be consulted, and he/she has done the homework required in learning, practicing, and retaining these emergency Memory Items.

Working as a Crew. For those pilots who serve as members of a cockpit crew, much of the personal checkride can focus on grading the skills required to perform well in this important area. The good pilot has embraced the concept of CRM (Cockpit Resource Management) and strives for excellent communication with other crewmember(s) when he/she operates as a crew. Whenever a procedure or technique is out of the ordinary, the pilot clearly explains what is being done, and why. In that manner, both crewmembers are kept in the informational loop. Asking the right questions, frankly stating opinions, working out differences, criticizing constructively, making decisions, managing resources…the top-notch pilot knows these skills. By using them, the crew ensures that the flight runs more smoothly and safely.

I am sure there are lots of additional objective criteria that could be listed for analysis as you give yourself a checkride, but the list I have presented includes enough items that you will be able to form a reasonably accurate "grade" for yourself.

So how did you do? If you are happy with the result, great. I surmise that you are glad to be a pilot and take pride in being proficient and in doing a sharp, safe, job. If the results are not so pleasant, and you are concerned about them, that's OK too. It means that you and your instructor(s) will have to work a little harder in the future to get you back on track, but your attitude is good and your chances of success are great. However, for those of you – and there won't be many, since they won't have read this article to the end – who think the whole idea of a personal checkride is crazy, and who believe that the objective criteria that I have listed are capricious and untrue…I wish you lots of luck on your next checkride. You'll need it!

KING AIR PILOTING TIPS

As I have done a time or two in past articles, this one will not discuss a single system or technical topic but instead will address a compilation of numerous small things that have prompted more than passing interest from me during recent months of King Air flying and instructing. I hope you find the presentation worthwhile.

Setting the Pressurization Controller: A New Technique

In accordance with the Pilot's Operating Handbook (POH) procedures, most of you are probably doing exactly what you've been taught: First, before takeoff, you are likely setting the controller so that the inner index is pointed at an altitude about 500 to 1,000 feet higher than your planned cruise altitude. Second, as the descent begins, you are then resetting it so that the outer index is set for a cabin altitude about 500 feet higher than the destination airport's pressure altitude. Am I right?

Back in the days of yore when lots of passengers and even pilots smoked cigarettes while flying – I'm showing my age, aren't I? – it was very common for the pressurization system to be less than smooth whenever the differential pressure reached maximum, meaning that the outflow valve was now being regulated by the maximum ΔP relief function housed within it instead of by the controller itself. The theory – and probably the fact – was that the cigarettes' tar and nicotine residue was obstructing the relief valve's tiny opening making it difficult for it to operate properly.

It was for precisely this reason that the extra 500 – 1,000 foot cushion was dialed in…to prevent reaching maximum ΔP.

Well, let me cue you in on a secret: That's not necessary anymore. I fly lots and lots of different King Airs in the course of my work and I truly cannot remember the last time I have observed a fluctuating cabin vertical-velocity indicator when running at maximum ΔP. Without the tar and nicotine residue, it's a non-event…at least in the vast majority of King Airs.

This knowledge leads to two operational changes that I suggest you try on you next few flights and decide if you like. First, forget the 500 – 1,000 foot altitude cushion. If you're planning to cruise at FL220, set 22,000 feet right above the inner pointer. (Remember, all the controller "regulates," all it feels, is *Cabin* altitude, not *Airplane* altitude. The 22,000 feet mark is merely for your convenience in setting the controller. All the controller "knows" is that you have now dialed in a requested Cabin altitude of about 7,000 feet.)

By leaving out the cushion, you should be at maximum ΔP as you cruise at FL220, yielding the benefit of a marginally lower cabin. Given the slight inherent inaccuracies in the controller, the relief valve settings, and the combined Cabin Altitude/Differential Pressure gauge, you may or may not actually be at the true maximum ΔP at this time. How do you know? Easy: Reset the controller for a lower cabin altitude. If the cabin starts to descend, you weren't at the maximum attainable ΔP. On the other hand, if the cabin doesn't change a bit while you dial the controller's Altitude knob counter-clockwise, then you indeed are operating at maximum ΔP. Hey! It's just as smooth as before, isn't it?

The second operational change is this: Go ahead, while in cruise, to set the cabin altitude for your landing. In other words, don't wait until starting the descent to do it. Do it now.

Be honest: How many of us have gotten well into a descent before we got around to remembering to set the controller for landing? I bet nearly 100% of King Air pilots – especially those conducting single-pilot operations – have made that boo-boo a time or three. It's not dangerous, just uncomfortable, as the airplane altitude matches up with the cabin altitude and the whole rest of the descent is unpressurized, meaning that your ears are subjected to whatever descent rates the airplane is achieving.

Well, by setting the controller early, you cannot make that mistake!

"Certainly there must be some downside risks associated with this technique," you are thinking, right? Yes, there are, but they are so miniscule as to be insignificant. Allow me to explain three potential concerns.

First, if you decide to climb from FL220 to, say, FL260 to get above some higher clouds looming ahead – after you have already set the controller for landing – now the cabin's rate of climb is beyond your control…the relief vale is going to vent enough additional air out of the cabin so that maximum ΔP is retained as the airplane climbs.

As most of you have been taught, the airplane's rate-of-climb and the cabin's rate-of-climb at this time are not the same! In fact, the cabin will be going up at less than 60% of the airplane's climb rate. It's not magic, just a recognition that less height of the thicker air down at cabin altitude is needed to equal the pressure change caused by the height increase in the thinner air up at airplane altitude.

Let's be realistic. Your lovely C90B is not going to hop from 220 to 260 in a "spirited" manner, is it? Even if you can average 800 fpm – and I bet you cannot – then that means your ears are feeling less than 500 fpm. Not a problem.

The second potential concern with this new technique that I am advocating is that the initial descent rate of the cabin as you first begin your descent will not be controlled by the rate knob's setting and may be higher than desired. That rate control is a function of the controller and, by running on the maximum ΔP relief valve, the controller is momentarily out of the picture. This means that if you really "pull the plug" and push over immediately into a 1,500 fpm descent, then your cabin will start down at a rate about 60% of that…900 fpm. But quickly the controller "wakes up" and realizes that the rate knob is set for, say, 400 fpm. Since having the cabin descend at a considerably slower rate than the airplane means that ΔP is decreasing, soon the controller is back in action and it brings the rate-of-descent to the value you had previously set. If it's not what you want, you can use the rate knob to adjust it accordingly, just as in the past.

Even though this momentary cabin descent "spike" is not a big deal, of course it can be avoided by starting your initial descent a little less abruptly…as I am sure you already do most of the time.

The third and last potential downside risk – and actually this same "risk" exists using the traditional technique – comes into consideration when a descent is interrupted by one or more lengthy periods of level flight. How frustrating it is, and yet how common, to start down well before we'd prefer, then spend many miles bumping along at 16,000 feet, then 10,000 feet, then 6,000 feet! I know you've all "been there, done that" numerous times thanks to the way ATC treats us "little turboprops." Yuck!

I see some newer pilots, when the initial descent begins, set the controller not for the landing field's pressure altitude (plus a cushion) but instead they set it as if they were going to cruise at that slightly lower assigned altitude. Depending upon ATC's instructions, this could involve three or more settings before the landing setting is finally made.

What a waste of effort! As we have tried to present, the worst that can happen if you get a lengthy delay at an intermediate altitude with the controller already set for landing is that maximum ΔP will once again be attained and the controller will patiently wait – letting the relief valve do its thing – until the descent continues and the controller can once again take over.

If you are smoking onboard and if your cabin fluctuates when at maximum ΔP then ignore all I've said here. For the 99% in the other group…try it, you'll like it.

"Forced" Early Descents

Speaking of those all-to-common ATC requests to begin descent long before the "optimal" three-miles-per-thousand-feet point, try this: Give 'em 1,000 fpm, nothing more.

When traffic is not a big concern and ATC really can treat us as if we were the only one flying – hello, Wyoming! – what we observe is ATC also uses that "3 for 1" rule: about 3 miles for each 1,000 feet to lose. To make this work out, the rule-of-thumb is that your rate of descent should relate to your groundspeed in a ratio of 5:1. That is, if your groundspeed is 200 knots, come down at 1,000 fpm. For 260 kts, make it 1,300 fpm. In your Beechjet at 500 knots, use 2,500 fpm.

For these damned early descents, however, forget the groundspeed. I'll wager that if you descend at 1,000 fpm ATC won't ever come back and ask you to "Expedite your descent." On the other hand, you can almost guarantee hearing that phrase if you use 500 fpm.

The VSR Field

My educated guess is that most of my King Air owner/operator readers have some version of the Garmin 400 or 500-series GPS navigators installed in their King Airs. Aren't they marvelous pieces of equipment? Wow! What winners! Are you taking advantage of the VSR field? You should be.

VSR stand for "Vertical Speed Required." In the Garmin 400-series you access the VNAV page by going to the last page in the Nav chapter. For the 500-series, you access it through the VNAV button. Go to that page and set it up so that you will reach 1,500 feet Above Waypoint at 5.0 nm prior to the destination airport at 1,200 fpm. Don't stop there, however. Make sure that you hit the "Menu" button when your most common Nav page is displayed and then, if needed, select the "Change Fields" option and make sure you have VSR displayed on one of the normal fields of view. Man, you're set now!

That field will now show you what vertical speed is required to get to pattern altitude (for a turbine, 1,500 feet AGL), 5 miles prior to the airport. Remembering the 5:1 ratio, if you are doing 220 kts groundspeed, you should be starting down when VSR reads 1,100 fpm. At 280 kts, its 1,400 fpm. Easy, eh? As you descend, just keep matching your actual vertical speed to the VSR value. (The 1,200 fpm value you entered on the VNAV page is where you will get a message reminding you that you are nearing the Top of Descent point. Since very often your GS will be in the 240 knot vicinity, it is often exactly where you'll chose to start down.)

If you look at the VSR field and it doesn't make sense – much too steep! – then nine times out of ten it's because you had done some "Direct To" function and the waypoint got changed to that point instead of your destination. No problem; merely go to the VNAV page and select the Waypoint field. Start turning the small knob and find the proper destination waypoint…hit Enter; you're back in business.

For what it's worth, when ATC says something like "Descend at pilot's discretion so as to cross Swirl intersection at 11,000 feet," I suggest that you *not* take the time to reset the VNAV parameters for that point. Of course, you can do it if you prefer, but a faster – easier, in my mind – method of doing it is to check the FLTPLN page to determine the cumulative distance to that fix, then use the 3 miles per thousand feet ratio plus a little margin for error to determine when to start down. During the descent, passing thorough cardinal altitudes, make periodic "Howgozit" checks – i.e., 10,000 feet to go, I need a little over 30 miles; 6,000 feet to go, I need about 20 miles – to adjust the actual vertical speed to remain on the desired profile. Meanwhile, you can keep an eye on the VSR field to better estimate how easy or hard it will be to get to pattern altitude after that intermediate altitude restriction.

GPS Altitude vs. Barometric Altitude

Here's a little piece of trivia I picked up from the engineers/pilots at ACSS...the avionics manufacturer for whom I do some contract flying. If you have the capability of displaying an altitude derived totally from GPS info – all the Garmin units have that information available; most, but not all, of the other GPS manufacturers give access to it also – then check the difference between what it reads and what your barometric altimeter reads. Here's another secret: Guess which one is reading closer to your actual MSL height? No, not the altimeter. It's the GPS readout.

Here's the interesting fact: If the temperature at your altitude is right at ISA (International Standard Atmosphere), then you will find that there is excellent agreement between the two altitude information sources. When the temperature is more than standard (ISA + 12°C for example) then you can bet the GPS altitude will be higher than the barometric. The more the temperature deviation above standard, the more the altitude differential will be. Conversely, when it's colder than ISA, you can be sure the GPS altitude will read low.

Remember the old aviation adage "High to low, look out below?" When you fly into conditions where the OAT is lower than normal, realize that you will be flying lower than you think, lower that what your altimeter reads. If you ever lost your static source and its alternate back-up, such that the barometric altimeters were worthless, you could do a very good job of getting safely down through IMC by following the GPS altitudes! Not legal, but a heckuva sweet ace in the hole!

(Sitting on the ground at Rancher Rob's little private spread down in Texas after a couple of days of dove hunting and you forgot what he said the elevation was? Just set your altimeter to agree with the GPS altitude and you won't be far off.)

Remember the Particulars of the First Call-Up

According to the AIM, it's correct to (1) use your full, complete, call sign when making your first contact with any new controller, and (2) include in your first announcement to an Approach controller that you have the ATIS information. It irks me that both of these requirements are so often abused! Come on! Don't get lazy. Be professional! "Socal Approach, this is King Air 982 Gulf Bravo, leaving one-four-thousand-six-hundred for one-zero-(ten)-thousand, with information Lima."

(You do say *both* "One zero, Ten," and "One one, Eleven" when reporting 10,000 and 11,000 feet, don't you? It's what is recommended for those two, often confused, altitudes.)

It also irks me how many, many times ATC will then reply by saying "Advise when you have information Lima." Dang it! They listen as badly as we do! I suppose it is because so many pilots have become very sloppy about announcing the ATIS on the first contact that Approach facilities have fallen into this irritating habit pattern. My usual response is "*I say again,* I have information Lima."

High Idle for Normal Landings?

Since so many King Airs have now been modified or originally delivered with four-blade propellers and because these propellers give so much more drag when idle power is selected in the flare for landing as compared to the three-blade types, consider using the High Idle setting of the Condition Levers for Normal, not just Short Field, landings in the 90- and 100-series. I think you may find that the little extra power cushion makes for easier flares and smoother touchdowns. Try it; you'll probably like it.

Full Flaps and the Flare

The four-blade 90-series are especially apt to be difficult in getting the nose sufficiently high for a satisfying touchdown attitude. This is especially noticeable when flying with the CG rather forward, without a full load of passengers and baggage in the cabin.

If the runway is plenty long, experiment with landing using Approach flaps, not Full Flaps. Add about 5 knots to your over-the-fence speed and see what it feels like. You may find that this is a more-forgiving configuration.

Also – and a lot of readers will probably be mortified by this suggestion – if you have a copilot, it works quite well to use Full flaps as normal but then, either in the flare a few inches before touchdown or when the main tires first make contact, have the other pilot bring the flap handle to the Up position. It's pretty amazing how nicely this provides for holding the nose up. (You see, Full flaps tend to blank the airflow to the elevators and their lack of effectiveness makes the nose come "crashing" down.)

I surely wouldn't suggest diverting your attention to the flap handle at this critical time when operating single-pilot! When that cockpit helper is there, however, it's neat how well this works!

Icing Encounters

In the C90A, C90B, and C90GT-series, there are an even twelve items – a dozen – that must be activated for safe penetration of visible moisture with an OAT at or below 5°C: Two Engine Auto-

Ignition switches, two Engine Anti-Ice switches ("Ice Vanes"), two Windshield Anti-ice switches, two Pitot Heat, two Fuel Vent, and single Stall Warning Heat and Propeller Deice switches. As you climb out and the OAT goes below 5°, with clouds either in sight ahead or forecast to be there down the road, how many of these switches do you activate?

My suggestion is this: If icing encounters are likely, then turn on nine of the twelve and leave them on until you are assured of no further icing encounters on this particular flight. The three I am ignoring are the two Engine Anti-Ice switches and the Propeller Deice switch. The other nine, all on together, cause an insignificant change in generator load or aircraft performance. But the Ice Vanes slow you down by reducing engine power and the Propeller heat raises the generator load enough to cause a very small rise in ITT.

When it is obvious that you are about to penetrate clouds, switch on the remaining three and abide the loss of performance. As soon as clear skies reappear, kill the three until the next cloud encounter looms: Simple, safe, and effective. (And a whole lot easier than keeping track of twelve every time you are in and out of icing!)

Ice Vanes

Speaking of Ice Vanes – Engine Anti-Ice – realize that the amount of power loss they give is dependent upon indicated airspeed. If the speed is low enough such that the ram effect of the air is low, then the change caused by the Ice Vanes is correspondingly low.

My point is this: On the ground, the Ice Vanes have virtually zero effect. Even at takeoff speed, the effect is tiny compared to what is observed at 200 knots.

"When in doubt, get 'em out!" is the mantra I advocate. On 99% of my landings, I will extend the Ice Vanes before landing so there is less chance of FOD if I remain in Reverse too long after landing, trying to make that first turn-off perhaps. The only time I might not have them extended before touchdown would be in anticipation of a potential Go-Around from a high mountain airport on a hot summer day with a heavily-loaded airplane. That's very rare indeed.

It takes only one pebble or errant screw being ingested into your engine's compressor during ground operation to make you regret ever *not* having the Ice Vanes deployed!

Realize that the extension of Ice Vanes for ground operation is not a normal requirement for the older chin-style cowlings. We are talking here about pitot-cowl (F90-1, C90A and after) models, especially those equipped with four-blade propellers.

There you have it...my ramblings for this issue. I hope you will benefit from my suggestions. Fly well out there!

HANDLING CROSSWINDS

Instead of my usual discussion of some arcane King Air system, this article is going to deal with a more airplane-generic topic: Crosswind takeoffs and landings. I still intend to direct this presentation to King Air pilots but it will likely apply to almost any other twin-engine operator as well.

By this time in our growth as pilots, I am sure we can all handle minor crosswinds easily. However, when the wind really starts to whistle, when the gusts are gusting, and when the direction of the wind diverges a lot from the runway…well, now's the time we need to have sufficient skill and confidence to make safe operations assured.

We'll begin discussing the takeoff and departure. First, remember that no flight *has to* depart. Once an airplane flies, a landing must occur, of course. But when we are already on the ground, there's always the option of saying "Let's wait!" until the wind abates or gets more aligned with the runway. This may be difficult to do when the boss is chomping at the bit. However, it is a possibility that needs to be considered.

Is there a takeoff crosswind limitation? For that matter, is there a landing crosswind limitation? Let me count the raised hands out there in readership-land. How many say that these limitations exist in the POH (Pilot's Operating Handbook)? I see that about a third of the class has their hands up. Good. That means the rest of you, the majority, realize that there is no crosswind limitation whatsoever in the POH. Just like there is for almost all other FAA-certificated planes, there is a "Maximum Demonstrated Crosswind Component" listed: 25 knots for all King Air models. It is found in the Normal Procedures section of the POH, not in the Limitations section, because it is not a limit. It is just what it says: The highest value that the test pilots demonstrated they could handle in this aircraft.

To attempt a takeoff or a landing with a crosswind component greater than 25 knots means that you are on your own, exploring into a territory that the test pilots did not. Does that mean you are foolish or bad? Personally, I don't think so. After all, can the test pilots plan to encounter every single situation exactly as you will encounter those situations in your career? I strongly doubt it!

I am glad that the demonstrated crosswind value is not a limitation. Why? Well, if I ever showed up at my original destination, found the weather would not permit a landing, diverted to my alternate, and then found a crosswind stronger than the "demonstrated," I am very glad that I am not in violation of a published limit if I attempt this landing! Is that the reason the FAA chose to not make it limiting? I don't know for sure, but I'd surely guess that this reasoning played a large role in the decision to make it a Demonstrated number only, not a Limitation.

Here's my point: Since a takeoff is optional but a landing is mandatory, I would strongly encourage you to stay put and delay the departure if the crosswind component exceeds 25 knots. On the other hand, if you are low on fuel for landing and need to "Git 'r Done!" then you'd better have the skill and moxie to do it right, regardless of the wind you may have. I hope this article will be of help to you when you face that situation.

We'll start at the beginning: Taxiing out for departure with a gusty wind that borders on the 25 knot component. For goodness sake, position the control wheel properly!

Now I know that the chance of a King Air being tipped onto a wing by the wind is a lot less than the chance of this happening to a Jenny, Cub, or Husky. However, why take a chance? Instead, make sure that the wind will tend to press the wing down, not lift it up. That's why I want to see the wheel positioned away from the wind when taxing downwind and into the wind when moving upwind.

As for elevators? The main thing is to grasp the control wheel tightly so that the changing wind won't lift and bang the elevators against a stop. Although somewhat unlikely for this to happen in a conventional-tailed King Air, the T-tail models are very prone to having a tailwind lift the elevators up violently. This is due to the fact that, even when fully down, the elevators really are not down very much. (Have you ever noticed how hard you must push forward on the control wheel to insert the control lock on a T-tailed model? That's so you get the elevators as far down as they will go.) Make sure that you or your copilot keeps a firm grasp on the wheel, being especially careful to keep it fully forward when taxing with a tailwind.

Now we've managed to get to the runway and are ready to go, yet the wind is strong, gusty, and nearly 90 degrees to the only runway we have available. Now what?

If the wind truly is 90 degrees off of the runway – so that it's going to be 90 degrees no matter which end of the runway we choose to use – then make the choice to use the runway that provides you with a crosswind from the right, not the left. For all of the reasons you've learned – torque, P-factor, swirl-effect, etc. – we always need to use right rudder to combat a natural left-turning tendency when taking off with neutral wind. With a crosswind from the left, now we have one more factor – weathervaning, the tendency of the airplane to turn into the wind because there's more surface area behind the CG than in front of it – that contributes to the left-turning tendency. On the other hand, if we encounter a crosswind from the right, now the wind will help nullify at least some of the natural tendency to go left. Obviously, there are times when we may opt for the left instead of the right 90 degree crosswind due to other factors such as runway slope or obstacles in the departure path. Only opt for the right crosswind choice when the other factors are equivalent.

Suppose, due to the importance of these other factors such as slope and obstacles, that you make the decision to depart with a quartering tailwind. For purposes of simplification, let's say that this quartering tailwind gives you a crosswind component of 20 knots and a tailwind component of 5 knots. It's easy to fall into the trap of thinking that the 20 knot crosswind component will be experienced just the same if we have a 5 knot headwind instead of a 5 knot tailwind component. No way! You see, with the headwind component, as you accelerate down the runway your controls continually become more effective as they are subjected to more and more headwind component…air flowing directly over the controls. But with the tailwind, there comes a time, early in the takeoff roll, wherein your forward velocity exactly equals the tailwind component. Now there is absolutely zero fore or aft (longitudinal) airflow over the controls. Every bit of wind you feel is the crosswind component, with the ailerons totally ineffective because they are experiencing no airflow over them. Of course, as you continue accelerating beyond this stagnation point, all will feel normal again. Let me tell you from experience, however: Passing through that tailwind/headwind stagnation point, with a strong crosswind, isn't fun at all! If other factors force you to opt for the quartering tailwind, be prepared for some major use of brakes and/or differential power…you'll probably need them.

So let's put us on the runway, with a strong, gusty, quartering *headwind*, ready to takeoff. In this case, I suggest that it's best *not* to be on the centerline!

If we start the takeoff run from the extreme downwind side of the runway, aiming diagonally across the runway into the wind, two significant benefits are forthcoming: First, we slightly decrease the crosswind component by making our ground track more into the wind. On a very wide runway, this can be surprisingly significant. Second, if and when we need to straighten out and turn to more align with the runway – because we are getting uncomfortably close to the upwind runway edge – the turning forces on the tires tend to tip us over into the wind, aiding aileron effectiveness in preventing the upwind wing from lifting. So this is a time that an exception to "Stay on the Centerline!" is warranted…angle into the wind.

Next, use *full* aileron deflection into the wind as the takeoff begins. It amazes and disturbs me to observe so many pilots who will begin a crosswind takeoff with the ailerons still close to neutral. Why? Look, folks, I defy any of you to make the airplane rock over onto a wingtip because of full aileron deflection during a takeoff. There's just not enough aileron effectiveness to lift a wing significantly until at or after liftoff speed. Only when you truly see and feel some tendency for the upwind wing to lower and the downwind wing to rise – and this won't occur until close to rotation! – should you then slightly reduce aileron deflection as warranted. Is there anything to fear if the downwind main tire lifts off first? No! That's exactly what we want! And if we do have the upwind wing slightly down at liftoff, we can use that turning tendency to set up the crab angle that will align our ground track with the runway, before we neutralize the controls and achieve coordinated flight.

(A note here: If you put your GPS map on a small enough scale, it is really neat to be able to watch your progression down the runway after becoming airborne. It makes it simple to add or subtract wind correction angle so that you avoid drifting toward that parallel runway! Of course, another method of doing this is to adjust so your GPS-derived ground track is equal to the runway alignment.)

Another consideration on takeoff is to use split power levers, leading with more power on the upwind engine. I have found this technique to be generally unnecessary. Nevertheless, especially with that nasty quartering tailwind situation, realize that if the rudder pedals and brakes are not providing the control that you desire, one more method of keeping the nose where you want it to be is to use differential power. Since the airplane will want to weathervane into the wind, there will be a need for downwind rudder and/or brake. When you are having difficulty keeping control with rudder and brake, now is the time to lead with more power on the upwind engine. Typically, you may keep 500 ft-lbs (15% for the 300-series) more torque on the upwind engine until you reach 60 knots indicated airspeed or so and the rudders become sufficient. At that time, proper takeoff power can be set on *both* powerplants.

Well, we survived the takeoff, we quickly achieved coordinated flight, we are thankful that our yaw damper worked well while we climbed above the low level turbulence, and we've enjoyed smooth sailing at our cruise flight level. Now comes the landing and the only runway available has that dang nearly-25 knot crosswind.

Do we opt to use full flaps or select something less? Friends, I am not going to state with one hundred percent certainty that the selection of an intermediate flap setting for landing is not warranted in some cases, but I have never opted to do it because of a crosswind in over 14,000 hours of King Air time.

These airplanes have great aileron and rudder authority, they flare at about 100 knots (not the 50 – 60 knots of the little guys) and they have enough momentum to make them rather stable in the flare…so I find that they handle full flaps well even in a severe crosswind situation. Again, if you prefer something less, go ahead. After all, with the wind this strong, the landing roll won't be very lengthy no matter what technique we use!

Now's the time to push the propeller levers fully forward fairly early in the approach, definitely no later than 500 feet above touchdown. I always say that propellers should remain at their cruise setting until *after* touchdown for a *Normal* landing, but that whenever the landing becomes

HANDLING CROSSWINDS

Abnormal in the least amount, then don't worry about the increased noise level but push those propeller levers forward! With the propellers at maximum speed, (1) we can get full power whenever we need it by moving only one set of levers – the power levers – instead of two; (2) we have more gyroscopic stabilization; and (3) we are ready for immediate selection of Reverse after touchdown without any delay caused by moving the propeller levers at that time.

The old rule about adding half of the gust increment is, in my opinion, a good one. For example, if the ATIS says "Winds from 220 at 18, gusts to 32," then I would opt to add about [(32-18)/2] 7 knots to my "over the fence" (VREF) speed.

Do we fly down final coordinated, in a crab angle with the wind correction angle still applied, or do we fly it in a side slip, with the longitudinal axis aligned with the runway and the upwind wing down to prevent side slip?

I'm sorry, but those of you who voted for the side slip approach should now hand over your Commercial or ATP license and go back to being a pleasure pilot only. Harsh? You bet! But correct for the true professionals? Yes.

Why in the world do you want to subject your poor fretful passengers to 500 feet or more of uncoordinated flight? They are going to be nervous enough about the turbulence and winds without this extra worry. The other factor that explains why this is such a poor technique is that the wind near the runway will never be the same as what you experienced at 500, 400, 300, 200, or 100 feet on final.

Am I wrong? If so, then go out and show me that the aileron and rudder displacement you used at "X" feet on final is the same that you use to maintain alignment and to stop drift at touchdown. Ladies and gentlemen, it won't be the same! The effect of surface friction on the flow of air will always make the wind near the surface vary from what you experienced on final.

As you approach the runway and begin to flare, not until 50 to 100 feet height above touchdown, now is the time to start steering with your feet. Too many pilots haven't really learned to use rudder pedals effectively. One of the things that rudder input does is to provide coordination as we roll into and out of turns. We – or our yaw damper – do this hundreds of times on every flight. It becomes ingrained that a little left aileron is always aided by a little left rudder, right aileron by right rudder. During the flare for the crosswind landing, however, the rules of the ballgame do a complete 180-degree flip flop. Now we must learn to separate, to disassociate, rudder and aileron use. The rudders should now serve one purpose only: Keeping the nose, the longitudinal axis, aligned straight down the runway. The ailerons also serve one purpose only: Preventing drift. You need to steer with your feet, not with your hands.

As you stop conducting coordinated flight and use your feet to slew the nose into exact alignment with the runway, of course you will find that the airplane starts to deviate from the extended centerline that you had been so carefully tracking. That's the signal to put the wing down to slip the airplane back to the centerline. As the wing goes down, more rudder will be required to keep the nose straight. It's hard to do. It's unnatural. But, oh, it is so necessary!

I believe that far too many aviators tend to conduct their crosswind landings in a very mechanical method: If the wind is from the right, then they put in some predetermined amount of right aileron and left rudder and let the plane hit. Sometimes it works well but at other times the tires squeal and the plane darts one way or the other at contact...since the airplane wasn't aimed the way it was tracking. Let's face it: Tricycle gear airplanes are very forgiving of mismanagement at touchdown and they have a natural tendency to straighten themselves out, unlike the tail-draggers! Just because this mechanical method of landing usually works, please don't be satisfied in making crosswind landings in this haphazard manner. Landing straight – and thereby putting no side load on the gear struts and tires – pays dividends in being more gentle on the equipment. However, since that may be a dividend that is impossible to quantify, there is another important reason for making these nice landings: It is very ego-stroking to have the passengers rave about the sweet touchdown you gave them after that nasty ride they endured through the low-level wind and turbulence.

Don't misunderstand what I'm saying. In this context, a "Sweet" landing is not necessarily a greaser. In most cases of handling gusty, strong, crosswinds, you will be unlikely to squeak one on. To me, a sweet landing here is one that may be firm, yes, but one in which directional control is never in question: There's never that sudden swerve as the tires make contact, because you are properly steering with your feet and keeping the plane over the centerline with your hands.

I'll wager that many of you have never had an instructor or fellow pilot put you through a drill that can pay immense benefits in your development as a superior crosswind handler. Here's something fun to try and practice, either in your King Air or any other plane: Find a long, wide, runway that's not too busy and make some low passes, with gear down and flaps at Approach, over almost the entire length. Try to keep the plane within ten or twenty feet of the surface. Use enough power so that you'll fly level at a speed 10 knots or so above your normal over-the-fence target. Have the other pilot take the wheel while you take the rudder pedals. As he or she rolls in some aileron, practice using your feet to keep the nose pointed straight down the runway.

If you are doing this exercise on a day without a crosswind, it will become apparent very quickly that the banking of the airplane causes drift toward the low-wing side. Done properly, you will see the airplane slide left and right across the runway, even though the nose direction is not changing.

How do you know that you are keeping the nose straight? Do it this way: When you are taxiing out, put the seat of your pants right on a long taxiway centerline stripe and look as far down the stripe as you can while rolling straight. Now what reference mark, directly in front of you, lines up with the distant stripe? Is it the corner of the annunciator's fault warning flasher? Is it a rivet on the nose? Is it a smudge on the windshield? If there is nothing you can see that works, then take a crayon or grease pencil and make a mark of your own on the inside of the windshield. Unless you have a precise reference to use, any attempt at keeping the nose truly straight is a problem.

(As a side note, it is exceedingly common for new King Air pilots in the left seat to touchdown in a slight left crab angle, whereas when they fly from the right seat they invariably touch with a slight right crab angle. I think this is caused by a subconscious tendency to keep the airplane's nose in front of them. The problem is, they don't realize that the airplane is fairly wide and the airplane's nose – i.e., the airplane's centerline – is not the same as the pilot's personal centerline, since the pilot does not sit directly behind the nose. Make very certain, in any airplane that's new to you, you carefully locate your true personal longitudinal reference point before you ever leave the ground.)

Once you have that reference point located, now you know that you are using your feet correctly when you can make that low pass down the runway without ever having that reference point move very far, if at all, from the spot your eyes are seeing at the far end of the runway. I probably should have mentioned this comment earlier, but I'll insert it now: Look *far* down the runway! This is a basic bedrock rule for landings. Don't look at a point on the runway close to the airplane. Instead, keep your eyes aimed at the far end of the centerline. Doing so not only gives you a more precise aiming point on which to keep your reference spot, but it also helps avoid the sensation of speed caused by watching the nearby ground zip past the plane so rapidly.

After you've made a few passes down that long runway with your friend moving the ailerons, now do a few more in which you use all the flight controls. (Let your pal work the power.) Keep working to disassociate feet and hands. As you crank in a little bank angle, keep your reference point steady ahead. Slowly reverse the bank; keep the nose straight.

Now if you are really lucky, you will find another runway – maybe even at the same un-busy airport – that is experiencing a medium-strength crosswind. Make a couple of low passes to this runway and actually experience how much bank angle is required to create the drift that will exactly balance the crosswind component. Too much bank and you find yourself drifting to the upwind side of the runway. Too little, and you'll slide over to the downwind side. Neat, eh?

As a grand finale to this exercise, do it again, but this time with full flaps and slowly reducing the power so that the airplane actually lands. When the tires touch, don't stop flying! Keep on looking down the runway and using your feet to steer, to keep your reference point aligned. As the speed decays, keep rolling aileron into the wind until, as you approach taxi speed, you have full deflection. You are becoming a crosswind pilot! Doesn't that feel good? Congratulations!

As we near the end of this discussion, a few more points remain that I wish to cover. First, with a severe crosswind, you may opt to land diagonally across the runway, from downwind to upwind side, to achieve the same benefits we presented when discussing takeoffs. Once again, how wide the runway is will play a major role in this decision. If you opt to do this, realize that now maintaining proper alignment will no longer be achieved by looking far down the real runway centerline, but instead by using your feet to keep your reference point aimed at the imaginary end of your diagonal runway.

Second – and this can be a wonderful Ace-up-your-sleeve when forced to tackle a crosswind that may exceed the demonstrated maximum – use differential power to aid in longitudinal alignment. When you suspect that full rudder travel will not be enough to keep the nose straight while inputting the amount of aileron needed to prevent drift, now is the time to keep more power on the upwind engine. As the flare begins, instead of pulling both power levers back to idle, you may opt to reduce only the downwind engine, keeping the upwind engine right where it was on final. More correctly, perhaps I should say "where it was averaging out to be on final" since you were probably making some major power changes to combat the gusts! You certainly don't want to keep so much power applied that the airplane won't want to touch down and you prolong the agony of wrestling with the wind a few feet above the runway, but having the upwind engine at 300 – 500 ft-lbs (for the 300-series, 10 – 15%) of torque will cause enough of a yawing force that the rudder won't have to provide all the force alone in keeping the nose straight.

Third and last, as I said before, don't stop flying just because you've touched down. Keep those controls working! However, after touchdown, we King Air pilots have another arrow in the quiver to use: Reverse propeller thrust! Be careful and don't slam into Reverse as quickly as you may do normally!

Why? Two reasons. Remember that, if extra speed were carried during this nasty landing, it can be so high that the propellers are not yet off of the governors and onto the low pitch stops, meaning that the blade angle may not obediently follow our "request" to go into Reverse. (The fact that we pushed the propeller levers fully forward early in the approach is a good thing here and will help assure that we are ready for selection of Reverse, but it won't guarantee that reversing will occur if the speed when selecting Reverse is still too high.)

The second reason that we want to be careful, deliberate, and slow in our selection of Reverse after landing in this messy crosswind is that the airflow to the rudder will be greatly reduced as the blades start pushing the air forward, not back. All that neat rudder input you had been relying on to keep the nose straight is suddenly ineffective. What can we use instead? Nose wheel steering and differential thrust. Be absolutely sure that the nose tire is on the runway before cautiously easing into Reverse.

For the conventional-tailed King Airs, holding the nose off for any significant period of time after touchdown is almost impossible, since the elevators, like the rudder, lose effectiveness. The elevators on the T-tails, on the other hand, remain quite effective after touchdown since airflow to them is not being blanked by the props and wings. Relax any remaining back pressure on the wheel and keep that nose tire on solidly after touchdown.

As you slowly ease the power levers back, if your longitudinal reference point starts to move right of the aiming point at the far end of the runway, even though you've put in as much left rudder as you can, stop moving the right power lever back but keep easing the left one aft. If that's not enough, ease the right one forward until you're straight again. In other words, feel free to use differential Beta and Reverse to help steer.

Those that have flown and trained with me know that I am an advocate of having the SIC retract flaps at touchdown, even on a normal landing. Doing so anchors the plane on the runway much more solidly and helps to avoid scuffing or blowing a tire due to improper brake usage. Well, that procedure is definitely called for after touchdown in this horrid crosswind. As the lift provided by the flaps decreases, more weight is transferred to the tires and better directional control can be achieved.

In this article I have attempted to present some techniques and procedures for dealing with severe crosswinds. Some of what has been presented is very basic – sighting far down the runway, steering with your feet. Other parts are quite exotic – differential power, using the runway diagonally – and may be required only once in hundreds and hundreds of operations. I hope that this presentation gives you some meaty food for thought and adds some additional ammunition to the arsenal you have available to you when forced to deal with winds that are a true challenge even for the most prepared and competent pilot.

UTILIZING THE TRACK DISPLAY

So there we are, one dark and stormy night, sweating through another recurrent training session in the simulator. The instructor has just failed our slaved compass systems, causing the HSI and RMI cards to stop rotating, while he is having us execute a GPS approach to minimums. Geez! It's back to using the magnetic compass. Wow! In this turbulence, that sucker sure swings around a lot! Now let's try to remember: Is it Lags North, Leads South, or the other way around? Now what's this?! That *&^%$ has just failed the mag compass too! Give me a break! It's all over! I have no option but to *confess* that I have an emergency, *climb* safely away from the ground, and *communicate* with ATC, asking for a vector to VFR weather conditions. Hope I have enough fuel to get there!

Ah, but there *is* another option, and a relatively easy one at that!

For those pilots who have learned to take advantage of the Track display available on GPS (and other long range navigation) units, the lack of a compass card becomes almost a non-event. Hard to believe? Follow me through on this.

I remember back about six or seven years ago when I was conducting some training in a customer's King Air E90 that had recently been outfitted with a GPS navigator. It was one of the first GPS systems I had seen, and I was mesmerized by its capabilities. How fast it could update! It was much, much, better than the Loran units I had been using. This was really driven home during our practice of 45 degree bank steep turns: Our magnetic path over the ground – the Track feature that was being shown by the GPS – never lagged behind our heading buy more than 20 or 30 degrees, even during this quick-turning maneuver.

I recalled an incident years earlier when I complimented a pilot who flew for one of my Oregon-based customers on how quickly he was able to establish the proper wind correction angle (WCA) as we turned inbound heading south on a VOR approach, on a day when the wind was really howling from the west. "Thanks!" he said. "But you know it's really easy since we have a track readout on our new King KNS-660."

That incident gave me my first insight into the usefulness of a Track readout. However, the advent of GPS has made the Track display an even more useful tool due to the accuracy and stability of GPS signals and the more powerful computers contained in more-modern receivers.

All GPS navigators have the ability to display Track. It may not always be on the primary navigation page, but it often is. It is never more than a twist or two away with a control knob or with the push of a key. It is your exact direction of travel over the ground.

The King Air Book

Crosswind correction enroute. Let's suppose that we have just been cleared to some new waypoint. After calling up the waypoint and hitting "Direct" and "Enter" (or something similar), immediately we get a display of bearing and distance to that point. What do we do now?

For many if not most pilots, the answer is that we turn to that heading and watch what happens to the HSI's course needle deflection. If it drifts to the left after a few moments, we turn left to a new heading, perhaps 10 to 20 degrees less than the original heading. In a short time, as the needle re-centers, we take out half of the initial correction and watch the results. In other words, we begin to "bracket" headings until we find the one that works perfectly to keep the needle centered…at least for a while, until the wind shifts or our flight plan sequences to a new waypoint on a different course, requiring a different WCA.

Here is the other way to find the magic WCA, and to do it almost instantly. After Direct/Enter is keyed in, start turning toward the displayed bearing to the new waypoint. But, as you near that heading, start scanning the Track display. Make heading changes until the Track is equal to the Bearing. Bingo! You have nullified all wind effect and are proceeding directly to the new waypoint. Keep making minor heading changes so that Track and Bearing stay the same and you will be immediately making the proper corrections required due to wind, airspeed, or course changes. Simple, quick, easy.

If we always have the ability to know our exact path of travel over the ground, who needs a compass? Sure, I am being a bit facetious here. I very much like having that moving HSI card to follow ATC's vectors. I also need it to make an educated stab in the right direction whenever I first start heading to a new waypoint. And it is certainly wonderful to have a heading reference for myself or the autopilot to fly as I make small heading changes to stay on my desired Track. But I can do quite well, thank you very much, without the HSI, RMI, or magnetic compass so long as I have that quick, accurate, Track readout.

An autopilot trick. Speaking of autopilots, I know that you, like me, probably fly Heading mode quite rarely while navigating with a GPS. Instead, we take advantage of the stability of the course needle and couple to it using the Nav mode. When we hit the NAV button to track a newly-centered course needle, the autopilot/flight director computer always starts by turning to the heading to which the course needle is set. Then, like a human pilot, it begins turning toward the course needle as it drifts off center until it re-centers it, having found the proper WCA.

(Author's note: When Roll Command Steering and GNSS options became available, the need for the autopilot to begin by turning to the course needle's setting was eliminated. Hence, this discussion does not apply to those systems.)

If the setting of your HSI needle is done automatically – with a slewing needle such as that found on an EFIS display – then what I am about to say will be useless. However, if you must manually set the course needle to the proper desired track, here is another case in which awareness of the Track display can be mighty handy. Here's the situation: You have hit Direct/Enter, discovered that the new Desired Track (which is now also equal to the bearing, since you haven't drifted off this new course yet) is, say, 060 degrees. You manually set the course needle to that value and put the autopilot into Nav mode. As the autopilot rolls the wings level on 060 degrees, you note that the track is 080. Dang! We have a strong northwest wind today!

Instead of waiting patiently while the wind blows you southeast of course and the AP finally figures out the proper, wind-corrected, heading to fly, you can do this: Turn the course needle 20 degrees to the left, to 040. As the (dumber than a brick) AP turns to that new course datum, your track changes about 20 degrees left of what it had been, so now your track is very close to the desired 060 value. A couple of more tweaks to the course needle and you nail the 060 degree track perfectly.

But what about that mis-set course needle? Shouldn't it really be on the proper Desired Track, not 20 degrees less? Well, sure it should, and until it gets there, you won't see the proper WCA displayed as the difference between your heading and the course needle's position on the HSI. Does the AP care about the error? No. Does the GPS care? For some, the answer is Yes, because you will get a message asking you to set the proper value. For some other brands of GPS, no, they don't care what the HSI course value is.

So I suggest this: Over the next ten to twenty minutes, gradually move the course needle back to the correct Desired Track value a couple of degrees at a time, pausing after each movement until the AP has re-established the proper Track. Yes, it takes a little time, but the benefit is that you never have spent much time *not* flying smack dab toward your end-of-leg waypoint; you have never drifted very far off course.

What about when the flight plan involves a leg change? How does the AP handle this? Well, it continues to apply the old WCA to the new leg. In other words, let's say the AP has finally settled on a 045 degree heading to track the 060 degree course, using the strong NW wind of our example: a 15 degree left WCA. The next leg involves a right turn onto a 090 degree course. As waypoint passage occurs and the course needle moves to 090 – either automatically or by pilot action – the AP will initially turn to 075. Will this 15 degree WCA be proper for the new leg? No, probably not. However, it will certainly be a better initial "stab" at the correct heading than were the AP to turn all the way to 090!

Since typical on-route course changes are minor, the old WCA is usually quite close to the new WCA. During GPS approaches, on the other hand, it is common for the course to change by 90 degrees from one leg to the next. When the wind is strong, it is better to not fly coupled in Nav mode during these times of big heading changes. Instead, use Heading mode and turn until you see the Track and Bearing and Desired Track all coincide. Wind? What wind? You've immediately negated its tendency to blow you off course, no matter *what* it's doing!

Crosswind correction during approaches. Keeping Bearing, Desired Track, and actual Track all the same is the key to perfect lateral (not vertical!) navigating during an approach, be it a GPS, ILS, or any other type of approach. When the course needle centers, Bearing and Desired Track are the same. The trick, of course, is *keeping* them the same, keeping the needle centered.

If we fly headings that will keep our Track equal to the Bearing, with the needle centered, the needle can never drift off! By learning to include the Track readout in your instrument scan, the task of remaining on course – through wind shifts and such – is made ever so easy. If the Bearing and Desired Track are both 330 but the Track is 335, then we are on course right now, but won't be for long since we have a 5 degree right Track Angle Error (TAE) that is showing our drift off course to the right. Merely turn left 5 degrees to erase that error, to make Track equal to Bearing.

Some GPS navigators – the M3 Northstar unit comes to mind – include a Track Angle Error readout on the primary navigation display. Turning so that the error remains at 0 degrees, or darn close to it, is another way of achieving what we are advocating: Keeping Track and Bearing the same when you are on course will cause you to stay on course.

Even with "Turn Anticipation" enabled in the GPS unit, it has been my experience that few autopilots can fly accurately through the 90 degree turn that is often found in moving from an initial to an intermediate leg of a GPS approach. That's why I suggest, if flying with the AP engaged, to use the heading mode until established on the intermediate segment toward the Final Approach Fix (FAF).

Here's the method I use in deciding when to start the 90 degree turn: Look at the GPS's ground speed readout. Start the turn at 1% of that distance. (Yes. It is exactly the same method that I use for starting the turn onto a DME arc.) For example, if you are doing 150 knots ground speed, lead the turn by 1.5 nm. Zipping along at 200 knots? Lead by 2 nm. Slowed down to 120? 1.2 nm is the suggested lead amount.

Remember that there is no such thing as slant range error with GPS, unlike with DME. Regardless of your height above the ground, this rule-of-thumb always works well.

So when the GS shows 160 knots and you need to turn from a course of 270 degrees to a course of 180 degrees, start your left turn when the distance reads 1.6 nm. Watch the course needle and the Track value as the leg change occurs. Roll out of your turn a little early if you are left of course, but when the bearing starts hitting 180, make sure your Track also reads 180. You did it perfectly! You are on course, with the proper WCA already applied. Congratulations!

Arcs. One key to flying an immaculate DME arc is to get established close to the centerline initially. The key is to lead the turn by 1% of your current ground speed, as stated before. If arcing clockwise around the VORTAC, your initial heading will be about 90 degrees more than the radial you are on. Counterclockwise? Then 90 degrees less.

But again, who really cares about *heading*? To remain on the arc, the actual *track* over the ground must always be perpendicular to the radial: Either 90 degrees more or 90 degrees less than the radial you are on.

See how useful the Track display can be here? After making your initial stab at the proper heading, check Track. If it is about 90 degrees away from the radial, AOK. If not, turn until it is exactly perpendicular to your current radial. Are you now a little outside of the arc? At 11.4 perhaps, instead of the correct 11.0? Then make your track move in toward the center a little, by 20 or 30 degrees, perhaps. Sure enough, the DME counts back down to 11.0, and now you turn to again track 90 degrees away from the current radial. Where was this Track display when I was a novice instrument pilot?! It would surely have made this task a lot easier!

Wind awareness in the airport traffic pattern. If you are like me, there has been a time or two in our flying careers when we were landing at an uncontrolled airport without being able to get any weather report. It was nighttime, and the darn windsock couldn't be spotted. Are we choosing the correct, into-the-wind, runway?

Again, that nearly instantaneous and accurate Track display can be a great aid. On base leg, with your heading 90 degrees from the runway, where are you tracking? If you are angling toward the runway instead of perpendicular to it or angling away from it, then you are probably about to land downwind.

Compass rose visualization. Take this little quiz. You are on the 120 degree radial of a VOR, tracking 250 degrees. Will you cross the 180 degree radial of this VOR? (Answer: Yes.)

Here's another one: You are flying outbound from a VOR on the 290 degree radial from the station and need to turn onto an 8 DME arc and arc clockwise around the station. What should be the approximate initial heading when you complete your turn onto the arc? (Answer: 020 degrees.)

If these answers came quickly to you, my compliments: You enjoy good orientation skill and can visualize your position in two-dimensional space well.

However, if these questions left you a bit confused, you have some work left to do to become a first-rate instrument pilot. You *can* do it! A cocktail napkin, a ballpoint pen, and a fellow aviator can work together for some great practice and learning in this area of improving orientation skill. Let a dot on the napkin represent a VOR. Specify a radial, a track (or heading, if we're presuming no wind), and a new radial and ask if you will or will not intercept it. You can virtually pick these three numbers at random, between 001 and 360 degrees. Here's another skill that will pay benefits later on: Being able to quite accurately draw the proper position of radials. Draw a line away from your "dot" representing the 210 degree radial. Now take a compass rose and overlay it on the dot. How close were you? If you are not getting these within about 10 degrees, practice until you can.

Wait a minute? Where did *this* come from? Weren't we talking about utilizing the Track display?

Yes. We certainly were. But, friends, seeing a three-digit number representing your current path over the ground, and relating it to the correct path you wish to fly is a fruitless endeavor unless the numbers make sense, unless they can be visualized into a picture showing where you are and where you should be.

Moving maps are a great improvement! For those of you blessed with EFIS, Argus, KLN-90B, Garmin 430 or other moving map displays, another method of navigating properly is to fly so that the little airplane symbol stays on the proper course line. Easy? Well, not really, unless you have learned to watch the Track display and make it do what it should. Without that skill, you will meander your way toward the destination without any precision and always be lagging a bit behind. But when the two are combined – a moving map and a good utilization of the Track display – DYN-O-MITE! (You'd have to pry pretty hard to tear the KLN-90B's Super Nav display out of my clutching fingers!)

Summary. It is said that there are three essential skills required of the competent instrument pilot: Instrument scan, Instrument interpretation, and Aircraft control. When many of us attained our IFR ticket, there wasn't nearly as much to scan as there is now. Loran? GPS? RMI? Moving Map? Nah! We were lucky to have two VORs and an ADF. But as all of us move into newer and more sophisticated equipment, our scan and interpretation skill must evolve onto a higher level. If they do not, we fail to attain the level of competence and safety of which we are capable. It's my wish that this discussion of the Track display will encourage you to include it in your scan, interpret it correctly, and thereby make your flying more professional...and more fun, too!

FLYING ARCS

In a few more years, flying a DME arc will be as arcane and old-fashioned as tracking a low-frequency A-N range. According to the FAA plans for standalone GPS approaches, it will soon be *Good-bye* to arcs and *Hello* to 90° turns to final.

Until that day arrives, however, there are still numerous approaches – especially those in which radar coverage is somewhat spotty – in which a DME arc will be a desirable time-saving method of getting established on the final approach segment of an instrument approach procedure. Why go all the way to the VORTAC and execute a procedure turn away from the airport when a published arc can get us inbound in a hurry?

Most of us learned to do arcs when we were obtaining our instrument rating in a basic IFR training airplane that rarely included an RMI, Radio Magnetic Indicator. I presume that most readers fly airplanes with RMIs, or, if not, have the ability to digitally display either their radial from or bearing to a VORTAC. Of course, they also have DME, because without DME, arcs are out of the question altogether.

(Well, not really. If you haven't yet used an approach-approved GPS unit to fly an arc, you will be amazed at what a wonderful job it can do!)

The published minimum altitude on the arc should provide at least 1,000 feet of obstacle clearance if we remain within four nautical miles of the arc's centerline. Wow! That is a lot of airspace, just like a wide airway! However, to be professional as well as to be safer – and to satisfy the pilot examiner when we are going for an instrument rating practical test – we are expected to remain within one nautical mile of the centerline at all times. With an RMI and DME, this is a piece of cake!

The first item of concern is the question: How much distance is required so that we will roll out close to the arc centerline initially? In other words, what lead distance should be used?

Invariably, we will be approaching the arc by tracking a radial either to or from a VORTAC, and hence we will need to make about a 90° turn initially. The rule-of thumb is this: Lead the turn by 1% of the groundspeed. That is, if we are doing 200 knots over the ground, start the turn 2 miles before the arc. Doing 300 knots? Lead by 3 miles. Slowed down to 120? Then lead by 1.2 nm.

I have heard many pilots and instructors say they lead by 10% of the groundspeed. Get real, folks, and do the math! I don't think you are really turning 20 miles early at 200 knots, are you? No, it's 1%, not 10%.

The King Air Book

Let's visualize a simple example in which we are inbound to a VORTAC on the 270° radial, planning to arc clockwise around the station to intercept the 360° radial and track it inbound. Our present course, or desired track, is the reciprocal of 270°…090°. When we make our first turn, our new desired track will be about 360°, tangential to our present radial, correct?

Suppose the arc has a radius of 7 miles. If our ground speed is 180 knots, then at 8.8 miles we should make a nice standard rate turn to the left until we are heading about north.

The smallest radius for an arc which is to be used by fixed-wing aircraft is the example we have used: 7 nm. Remembering that the circumference of a circle is equal to pi (Π) times the circle's diameter, then the circumference of this smallest arc, if it were to be flown around the entire 360° circle, would be about 44 nm. Even if we flew the arc at a speedy 250 knots ground speed, it would take nearly 11 minutes to make a full circle. Who can establish and maintain a small enough bank so that 360° will require 11 minutes? Not I!

Hence, although arcs are drawn on instrument approach charts as segments of circles, they are not flown that way! Instead, they are flown as pentagons, or hexagons, or, octagons, or…well, you get the idea.

If we turned onto our 7 nm arc, with no wind whatsoever, and flew exactly north initially, until we were 0.5 nm away from the centerline, then turned about 50°, we would now be on a path that would gradually move us closer to the arc's centerline until we crossed it and moved about 0.5 nm closer to the arc's center. At that point, we would be moving exactly tangential to our passing radial, the DME distance would hold steady for a moment and then start to increase again. All told, we could complete the entire 360° of a full circle with no more than seven turns, each of about 50°. (If we allowed ourselves the full 1 nm of maneuvering room, instead of 0.5 nm, then we would only need to make five turns of about 70° duration.) Larger radius arcs will require more turns to stay on the arc properly.

Many of us were told, when first learning to fly arcs, to fly until we were 10° past our initial radial, then turn 20°. Is this wrong? No, but it sure isn't necessarily right, especially when flying on a windy day.

I suggest an easier approach. Namely, make your initial turn onto the arc so that the RMI needle is about 10° ahead of your wingtip. (In a no wind condition, this means that your initial turn will be about 80°, not 90°.) Maintain this heading until you are about 0.5 nm beyond the arc's radius. Now turn at least 30°. Watch the DME. What we hope to see is that it reaches a maximum value of about 0.6 or 0.7 more than the arc's radius during the time it takes us to reach our new heading, and then it starts decreasing. Ideally, it will decrease until it is a few tenths of a mile inside the arc, pause, then start increasing again. However, if it stagnates at a value that is either on or slightly outside of the arc, then turn another 30° and watch the results. When you are about 0.5 nm outside again, it's time for another turn of about 30° as the process repeats. Look at the figure below to get a mental image of the procedure.

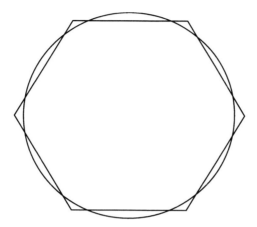

Remember this: In a no wind condition, if the station (RMI pointer) is *ahead* of our wingtip, even by 10° or less, the distance *should be* decreasing. That is, we *should be* moving closer to the station. Vice versa, if the station (RMI pointer) is behind the wingtip, the DME should be increasing. If these things are not happening, then we are experiencing the effects of wind.

As in a VFR, constant radius, turn about a point with wind, our wingtip will sometimes be ahead of the point and sometimes behind it. Likewise, the aircraft's nose will sometimes be inside of the ground track circle, sometimes outside.

Unless we really miscalculate the wind and turn too much initially, it is almost never necessary to turn *away* from the arc. A straight path over the ground, somewhat tangential to an arc, will always proceed away from the station if flown long enough, right? Unless you see the DME flirting with the 1 nm limit inside of the arc, just hold your present heading and be patient. Eventually, the DME will count up again until it is time for your next turn.

I was once observing a student take a type-rating checkride in a new Super King Air 300. The FAA examiner assigned an ILS approach, with the localizer to be intercepted from an arc that was based on a nearby VORTAC. We intercepted the arc on the VORTAC's 150° radial, and needed to track the arc in a counterclockwise direction to about the 080° radial before we turned to intercept the localizer.

What a great job the student did! He led the turn by 1% of the groundspeed, and made timely turns that kept us within 0.2 or 0.3 nm of the center at all times. It was a pretty thing to watch! We tracked beautifully from the 150° radial, past the 130°, the 110°, the 90°, the 70°, the 50°, etc.

The King Air Book

The examiner finally asked the student how much longer he was planning to "show off" his arc skills, since we had passed the localizer quite a long time ago!

This drove home to me a very valid and important point. Namely, the purpose of the arc is to intercept the *next* segment of the approach; it is not merely to fly large circles indefinitely!

One way to avoid this always embarrassing and sometimes dangerous overshoot is to have Nav 1 already tuned and identified to the localizer (or the VOR approach course) and to have the HSI course needle set on the inbound bearing. Then use Nav 2 and the RMI to track the arc. When the HSI course needle comes alive, forget the arc and intercept it.

Also, since most of us probably have a Flight Director/Autopilot system with Approach mode capability, we can hit the Approach button fairly early on the arc, use the heading bug to direct our turns around the arc, yet know that the intercept of the final approach course will occur at the appropriate time based on our approach to the Nav 1 course.

Here is an educational and fun training exercise for you to practice either in a simulator or in your airplane. Start over a VORTAC and track outbound on the 090° radial. Intercept the 10 DME arc and arc clockwise all the way around to the 270° radial. Intercept that radial and track it outbound, away from the station, and intercept a 15 DME arc. Track it counterclockwise to the 180° radial. Intercept that radial, but now turn inbound to the station on it. Intercept the 7 DME arc and turn left onto a clockwise arc that will take you all the way (270°) back to the starting radial, 090°. Intercept that radial and return to your starting point over the VORTAC. When doing that exercise – while always staying within 1 nm of the arc – becomes easy, then you have arrived at the point where arcs will never be troublesome for you again. Congratulations!

Short Field Techniques

(Author's note: Although most of this chapter applies to any *King Air model, the original article was written solely with the 90-series owner-pilot in mind. The V-speeds listed are those applicable to many of the 90-series but not necessarily correct for* all *King Air models.)*

Instead of "Short Field Techniques" perhaps I should title this "Showing Off the King Air to Your Pilot Buddies." You see, the King Air has such generally excellent takeoff and landing performance that the utilization of a truly maximum effort, short field, technique is hardly ever called for in the "real world" of flying in America. Of course, if you are flying missionaries in the jungles or supplying back-country strips in the wilderness, the story is different. The majority of the King Air 90-series owner-operators who are reading this are rarely faced with the need for such maximum performance. On the other hand, being able to execute a truly excellent short field takeoff and landing is a nice arrow to have in your quiver of ability…and it certainly does make your friends in their 421s or Barons mighty envious!

Let's begin with stop-on-a-dime landings: They are shorter and thereby more impressive than takeoffs in almost all cases.

Try to fly a relatively normal traffic pattern but take care not to be so close to the airport that the final approach segment is rushed. As soon as you begin thinking about the short-field landing, move the condition levers to the High Idle position. High Idle will keep N1 speed near 70% during flare and touchdown, making for quicker engine acceleration into Maximum Reverse as well as for quicker power response from idle if the landing must be rejected from close-in…as it well might when the water buffalo wanders onto that jungle strip. Additionally, ITT transients will be minimized when the engines are accelerated into Reverse since the 70% idle speed means that the engine has plenty of airflow through the compressor. Placing the condition levers to High Idle makes no change during the approach since your approach power settings will be higher than that. The only effect is experienced when power is reduced to idle in the flare.

Full flaps should be down during at least the last 500 feet above touchdown. Flaps provide quiet drag whereas maximum propeller speed provides noisy drag. On final, *after* selecting full flaps, smoothly advance the propeller levers fully forward. (This is unlike a *normal* landing in which the propeller levers are not moved forward until on the runway.) As you advance the propeller levers, let the drag of the flatter blade angle decrease your airspeed to 10 knots less than your normal landing speed. This will make your final speed at 50 feet AGL about 90 knots instead of the more normal 100.

Don't think of these speeds as touchdowns speeds. They are not. You won't be looking at the airspeed indicator as you touchdown but, done properly, it'll probably be 10 to 15 knots below the 50 foot speed.

High Idle will yield a comforting power cushion during the flare, so you must reduce the power levers fully to Idle when the landing is assured…the airplane will not fall out of the sky. Use the elevators to provide a *very slight, almost non-existent,* arresting of the sink rate prior to touchdown. Let it land! *Do not* attempt to land softly and hold the airplane off. To do so, with High Idle, will cause the airplane to float. It will consume lots of runway and blow the impression you are trying to make on your flying friends. Let the airplane land firmly on the centerline as close to the approach end as is safe to do so, considering obstacles and displaced thresholds. When the runway is truly short, the surface behind you at touchdown is of no value.

Immediately after touchdown release back pressure on the wheel so that the nose tire will contact the runway. In Reverse, the airflow to the rudder is so decreased that the rudder's aerodynamic effectiveness is nil. This is why it is important to have the nosewheel down before using Reverse. Also, if the nose is still up when the propeller blades flatten, it will come crashing down as the airflow to the elevators is decreased.

Once the nosewheel is down, immediately lift the power levers up and pull them rapidly *back* and *down* as far as they will go, to the Maximum Reverse position. Do not waste time moving your hand to the prop controls…they are already fully forward, remember?

It is worth reminding you that the drag of the propellers in Reverse depends on the forward velocity, squared. That means that the drag at 90 knots is *nine times* more than the drag at 30 knots! It's not realistic to think that Maximum Reverse will be achieved by 90 knots – there is some engine spool-up time to consider, even at High Idle, and touchdown speed should be lower than 90 – nor would one remain in Reverse at speeds below 40 knots except if it were the only way to keep from going off the runway end. Using more realistic speeds in the comparison: Drag at 80 knots is still *four times* more than that at 40 knots.

Since we want to achieve Maximum Reverse at as high a speed as we can, here's a time to forget about being smooth and gentle. Lift and slam those power levers all the way back…it doesn't hurt a thing. It's quite a common mistake to never reach the Maximum Reverse position of the power levers! Due to the arc in which the levers move, getting the power levers to their extreme aft limit involves more of a *push* downward instead of a *pull* back. Lot's of operators *think* they are using Maximum Reverse but they really aren't.

Keep in mind that you cannot practice this action – quickly moving the power levers fully aft – in your actual airplane in your hangar. To avoid stretching cables and getting the low pitch stops out of their proper position, the power levers should never be lifted and pulled back without the engines running and the propellers not feathered. Practice in a simulator if you can. Otherwise, you'll have to wait until you're doing the actual Maximum Performance landing to get that feel of the power levers being lifted up, pulled back, lifted up again (for C90Bs and after, ones that have the Ground Fine power lever stop), and then pushed *down* toward the floor.

Unless the flaps have been retracted by the copilot – or *very carefully identified and retracted* by you, something I *do not* recommend here – then reasonable care must be exercised to avoid locking up a wheel and scuffing or blowing a tire when heavy braking is used shortly after touchdown. By 60 knots, however, the weight of the airplane will be heavily on the tires even with the flaps still down and very heavy braking can be used with almost no fear of damage to the tires.

When the airspeed indicator shows 60 knots, begin moving the power levers forward out of Reverse at the same time you start getting very aggressive with the brakes. By the time the airspeed shows 40 knots, the power levers should be back at the Ground Fine stop (or near the top of the stripes at the flat blade angle position, for earlier models). Now reach over and pull back the condition levers for your normal idle setting.

Were your 414 or Navajo pilot owners shocked and envious? Did you make that taxiway turnoff a thousand feet from the arrival end of the runway? No? Then you need to practice some more on this procedure.

Now let's look at the takeoff situation. In all 90-series King Airs with the exception of the F90 and F90-1, the lift-off speed when using Approach flaps can be safely *above* stall and yet still be *below* VMC…and flying below VMC on takeoff is not safe flying. So, assuming that rotation will not occur until after VMC, flaps offer no benefit…they merely decrease climb performance by adding drag. That is why you will find no takeoff performance charts published in the POM or POH that show any use of flaps. If ever the field is short enough to require lift-off prior to VMC, use flaps. Better yet, *do not get in that situation!*

The F90-series – with their shorter wingspan, higher gross weight, and higher stall speed – can indeed safely utilize flaps for a shorter takeoff ground roll and hence their performance charts include the option for flaps. Use them here.

As you taxi into position for takeoff maneuver your King Air so as to get to the very last end of the surface: Use *all* of the available runway area. Line up with the nosewheel straight but with the whole airplane – its longitudinal axis – cocked slightly to the right, maybe 10 degrees. Torque effect will make the airplane want to veer left as brakes are released. Unless we are initially cocked somewhat to the right, we will have to drag the right brake to keep from swerving too far left and that, of course, will add to our takeoff distance.

The King Air Book

Full power prior to brake release will usually yield shorter distances. Based on the condition of the runway's lineup point and on the runway length available, decide how much power to apply before releasing the brakes. One must really stand on the brake pedals to hold the airplane against full power but it can be done using sufficient force.

Rotate at the published VR appropriate for the takeoff weight – usually between 85 and 95 knots – and pitch up to the standard +10° takeoff attitude. Holding this attitude will cause the airspeed to be about 130 – 140 knots passing through 400 – 500 feet AGL...well above VX and VY. If you have one *unbelievably* large obstacle ahead and you need to climb more steeply, 15° to 20° of pitch will be required to hold VX with two engines operating at full power. Is this steep climb fun? You bet! Is it frightening for most passengers? You bet! Is it challenging for the pilot if an engine quits during the maneuver? You bet! For these reasons, usually the old, "dull," +10° pitch attitude is still the best choice and will get you safely over all reasonable obstacles.

If the airport is high or hot enough, you may not be able to get maximum torque because ITT reaches its limit first. (In the earlier models with PT6A-20s or –20As, this is very common. Models with –21s or –135As rarely are temperature-limited on takeoff.) In that case, additional takeoff power can be achieved by leaving the bleed air valve switches in the Closed position and turning the Cabin Temp Mode selector off to eliminate the electrical load of the air conditioning compressor.

When safely airborne, above 500 feet AGL, turn the Cabin Temp Mode selector on and open the bleed air valves. To help avoid larger than necessary pressurization bumps, open them one at a time in the climb, with a 30 second or so delay between them.

As stated in our opening paragraph, King Airs enjoy such comforting takeoff and landing performance that these maximum performance maneuvers are rarely necessary. By being able to perform them confidently and consistently, however, not only will you be able to impress your friends but you'll also be a more competent and safe pilot. Plus, it's fun!

LEG MODE VS. OBS MODE

A critical concept that needs to be grasped before a pilot can successfully utilize most GPS navigation units is the difference between Leg and OBS modes of operation. Although good use of the GPS navigators can be made without this knowledge, it restricts the user to rather simple operations. Many, if not most, GPS approaches cannot be safely and correctly executed without this important knowledge. This article is an attempt to clarify the meaning of the two different modes, to discuss some unique characteristics or each, and to make it clear when each mode must be used. Although much of the information is applicable to most GPS units (as well as to other long-range navigation systems such as INS and Loran), I have the most operational familiarity with the AlliedSignal Avionics KLN-90B unit and hence details will be geared toward that unit.

Not all GPS manufacturers use the same terms, **Leg** and **OBS**. I was happy to see that the new Garmin 430 unit has an OBS key, but the terms also masquerade under various aliases such as Sequence and Non-Sequence, Sequence and Hold, Resume and Suspend, and probably a few more that I haven't heard or seen yet.

The shortest distance connecting two locations on the surface of the earth would be a straight tunnel from one to the other. However, since airplanes fly *over* the earth, not *through* it, the second shortest distance is the Great Circle route between the two points. Why is it called a Great Circle? Because the path of travel is on the circumference of a circle that is as large as the earth's diameter. In other words it is a circle as large as the equator. (I know, I know! The earth is a little pear-shaped and bigger at the bottom, but not by enough to be significant for this discussion.)

Visualize taking a model of the earth – a globe – and constructing a metal hoop exactly the size of the globe's equator. As we position this "equatorial hoop" at various locations around our globe – always being careful to position it so that there is no slop, so that exactly equal halves of the globe fall on either side of the hoop – then we are seeing the great circle routing between locations that the hoop touches. When we are traveling from the north pole to the south pole or between two locations on the equator, this is usually an easy idea to accept: That traveling on the equatorial hoop represents the shortest distance.

But how about when we are not going pole-to-pole or around the equator? Visualize a flight between two places in the northern hemisphere at nearly the same latitude: San Jose, California, and Norfolk, Virginia, perhaps, both of which lie at about 37 degrees north latitude. If we left San Jose and flew on the 37 degree latitude line exactly due east all the way to Norfolk, we would have flown on the edge of a hoop that is the size of the 37 degree latitude line. This "37 degree latitude hoop" is significantly smaller than the equatorial hoop, yet strangely enough the distance on this hoop between San Jose and Norfolk is longer than the distance on our equatorial hoop when we position it to touch both San Jose and Norfolk at the same time. Flying on the Great Circle, we would leave San Jose heading about 25° north of true east, and arrive in Norfolk heading about 25° south of true east. In other words, our true course would gradually change from about 065° to about 115°.

Let's now imagine that we leave San Jose and track the magnetic radial of the San Jose VOR that coincides with our initial desired course of 065° true. Because San Jose's magnetic variation is 16° east, this would be about the 049° radial. What would happen? Well, pretty soon, we would lose the San Jose VOR because we get too far away for good line-of-sight reception. But you know what? That is a good thing, because following that radial would not have gotten us to Norfolk! A little over 2,100 nautical miles from San Jose, to track our desired 115° true course inbound to Norfolk, and considering that the magnetic variation there is about 9° W, we would need to follow its 304° radial inbound, giving us a magnetic course of 124°, a whole lot different than 049°!

To summarize, the shortest distance between two points on the earth does not follow a constant magnetic course. If the points are very close together, the difference in the magnetic course is usually insignificant, and hence a particular VOR radial may be tracked from one point to another with very little difference between that path and the shortest path.

The increasing popularity and economical availability of long range navigators – GPS, for most of us – implies that we understand the nature of great circle routes. We must realize that the path we follow, the Desired Track (DTK), changes continually as we fly the shortest distance between the two locations (waypoints) that make up the starting and ending points of the leg.

For those of us who enjoy a Horizontal Situation Indicator (HSI) with a remote course-setting knob, or, better yet, an Electronic HSI (EHSI), the long range navigator will set the course needle to the proper desired track at all times and keep updating it as the DTK value changes. However, for the many of us who don't have that fancy capability, we must manually set the course needle to the DTK value, and check it every so often and update it as necessary.

By the way, an autopilot/flight director system usually can compensate quite well for a somewhat incorrectly set course needle if it is tracking a leg in "Nav" or "Approach" mode. For example, let's say that the desired track was 100°, but that we incorrectly set the course needle to 090°. As the airplane intercepts the proper leg and the Nav capture occurs, the autopilot computer will turn the airplane initially to a heading of 090°, the value it reads from the course needle's position. This is called the "Course Datum," and the autopilot thinks it is the heading to fly when no crosswind is present. However, when flying on the initial heading of 090°, yet trying to track a leg which is going 100° at this point, the airplane gradually drifts left (north) of course if the wind is calm. The AP "thinks" this is caused by a crosswind from the right (south) and so it turns right to return to the course centerline. Given enough time, the AP will return to the proper course and adjust the heading so that the airplane will properly track the leg. In due time, the HSI course needle, still incorrectly set on 090°, will be perfectly centered, yet the heading will be 100°. To the pilot it appears that the autopilot has achieved a 10° right wind correction angle, when actually no wind is present! There is a limit, however, to the Autopilot/Flight Director's ability to apply crosswind compensation, so a grossly mis-set course needle will result in poor tracking.

That is why it is important to keep the course needle set for the proper Desired Track. If your needle does not position itself, make sure that you know where to find the DTK value in your GPS display, refer to it regularly, and update your course needle appropriately. When on course, BRG (bearing) and DTK are identical; when off course, they are not.

The FAA/industry design team who decided what technical standards would exist for GPS approaches, realized that there was a benefit in requiring the unit to fly a leg between the Final Approach Fix (FAF) and the Missed Approach Point (MAP). This is a totally new concept to those who have mostly navigated by following VOR radials. On a typical VOR approach, we are either tracking a radial inbound to the VOR that often sits at or near the MAP, or else we are following a radial outbound from the VOR to the MAP, designated either by a DME value or by timing.

Be honest now. How many of us have ever mis-set our CDI's Omni Bearing Selector or HSI's course needle? I see…a nearly unanimous show of hands. Yeah, me too. Dang! For example, why did I put in 190 instead of 170? Because we all make mistakes, we are all prone to human error, an unfortunate but true fact. If this error is not caught during a VOR approach, especially one flown outbound from a VOR, our positional error increases as we get further from the VOR and we may miss the proper MAP by a large and dangerous amount.

But in leg mode? It is not a big deal! Set 190 instead of 170? Just fly so as to keep the needle centered and you will still hit the MAP perfectly! (But you'll wonder why the wind is howling out of the east when the surface wind was reported as calm, since it looks like you have a 20° left WCA!)

Now although not everyone will agree that this requirement to fly a leg between the FAF and MAP is the best idea, and many wish that they could select their own course to fly to the MAP, nonetheless it is the only way IFR approach approved GPS navigators work.

The following table lists and contrasts characteristics of the two different types of GPS navigation, Leg Mode and OBS Mode. Review the table, and then we will try to clarify a few additional points.

Leg Mode	OBS Mode
1. The course (Desired Track, DTK) is predefined as the shortest distance between the two waypoints that make up the leg.	1. The Omni Bearing Selector course is set by the pilot using the HSI course needle, and it may be any of the 360° radials originating at any waypoint.
2. Just like when using a localizer for navigation, the setting of the HSI's course needle has no effect on the left-right deflection of the needle. (However, to observe the proper picture on the display, the course needle should always be positioned to the Desired Track, just as it should always be positioned to the inbound bearing of an ILS.)	2. Just like when using a VOR for navigation, the radials may be flown either inbound or outbound and the To-From flag in the HSI will switch appropriately.
3. The Bearing and Distance displayed will always be from your present position to the active TO waypoint, the one that is at the end of the leg.	3. The Bearing and Distance displayed will always be from your present position to the active waypoint, the one through which the OBS course passes.
4. If multiple waypoints are in the active flight plan, *leg changes will automatically occur and cannot be avoided.* When you reach the TO waypoint at the end of one leg, it will become the FROM waypoint at the start of the next leg. The To-From flag in the HSI will always show TO, pointing toward the head of the HSI course needle at all times. Hence, this has been termed "To-To" navigation.	4. Even if multiple waypoints are in the active flight plan, *waypoint changes never occur* unless initiated by pilot action. The synonyms for OBS Mode such as Hold, Suspend, and Non-Sequence all refer to this fact: that waypoint changes never occur. The active waypoint is **held**, leg changes are **suspended**, and we will not **sequence** through the legs of our flight plan. Because we can cross over a waypoint and fly away from it, this has been termed "To-From" navigation.

5. This mode *must* be used from at least 2 nm outside of the FAF until passing the MAP.	5. This mode must be used for Procedure Turns (PTs), Holding Patterns (HPs), and Radar Vectors. In the case of radar vectors for an approach, the active waypoint should be the FAF and the OBS course should be the published course *inbound* to that fix.
6. The GPS can only achieve the Approach level of course needle sensitivity (0.3 nm) when in Leg mode. Only if Approach sensitivity is achieved is descent after the FAF authorized.	6. The GPS will never leave the Enroute (5.0 nm) or Terminal (1.0 nm) level of course needle sensitivity when in OBS mode. Hence, we can never execute a final approach descent to minimums in OBS Mode.
7. The KLN-90B navigator must be in the Leg mode to be initialized.	7. The KLN-90B navigator will not initialize if in the OBS mode.

Now let's elaborate on a few points made by this table. Concerning Number 4 in the table, there are two exceptions in which leg changes do not occur automatically:

A. A leg change will not occur automatically when the active waypoint is the last one in the flight plan. In this case, the inbound desired track is extended past the waypoint, the To-From flag switches to show FROM, and the airplane can keep navigating indefinitely beyond the waypoint on this course as the Distance counts upward and the Bearing shows the direction back to the waypoint.

B. A leg change will not occur automatically when the active waypoint is the MAP of a published approach. When reaching this waypoint, again the To-From flag switches to FROM, the Distance counts up, etc., just as discussed above. To make the leg change to the Missed Approach waypoint(s), the pilot must take some simple one-step or two-step action. (In the KLN-90B, it is hitting "Direct" followed by "Enter." In the GNS 430, it is merely pressing the OBS button under the "Susp" annunciator. "Susp" stands for Suspend, meaning that the unit has temporarily stopped or suspended making leg changes. It is tenaciously holding on to the MAP waypoint and won't make a leg change until you put it back to leg mode by tapping the OBS button.)

Concerning Number 5, it is rather obvious that if the plan is to cross a fix more than once, then a leg change should not be made. It is easy to fly a leg from A to B, but how does one fly a leg from A to A? The answer is, one doesn't! Instead, one uses OBS mode to treat that fix "like a VOR."

Concerning radar vectors, however, it may not be apparent that it is necessary to be in OBS mode. For example, why could we not select the leg from the Initial or Intermediate fix that precedes the FAF, wait for the vector that intercepts that leg, track to the FAF, and then follow the next leg to the MAP? In fact, this sometimes does work, but it is best not to do it this way.

The King Air Book

Here's why. You never truly know exactly where the radar vectors will take you. If – due to your arrival location in the terminal area, traffic, weather, or just the controller's way of doing things – he or she directs you to maneuver your airplane so that it is closer to the MAP than to the FAF, then there is nearly a 100% chance that an unwanted leg change will occur. Suddenly you will be looking at the bearing and distance to the MAP and you hadn't flown over the FAF yet! You have thus lost any opportunity to achieve Approach needle sensitivity; you cannot do the approach.

By selecting OBS mode, making the FAF fix the active waypoint, and setting the course needle on the published inbound course to the FAF, you are assured of no unexpected leg changes. Merely wait until you hear something like "Fly 300° until intercepting the approach course; Maintain 2,000 feet until established; Cleared for the Approach" and then switch back to Leg mode.

I have a worry concerning IFR approach approved GPS navigators that I have used that are made by a couple of manufacturers. One touts the ease of use of its "Vectors to Final" feature and the other has a quick method of selecting the approach course when vectors are being received. When either of these choices is selected, the FAF is automatically selected as the active waypoint and the unit suspends making leg changes until passing the FAF inbound. So far, so good. But the course it inserts is the one between the FAF and the MAP. In other words, it uses the *outbound* course from the FAF, not the *inbound* course to the FAF. Well, most of the time, that is probably fine, because there is no dogleg turn at the FAF. But what if there is? I am quite concerned that the unit will misguide us such that we fly the wrong inbound course to the FAF and thus compromise our terrain separation.

When asked about this, one manufacturer's representative stated that this was not a problem. For the great majority of approaches in which there is no course turn at the FAF, I agree. But he went on to say – if I understood him correctly – that the touted feature was only for "Vectors to *Final*." By that, he meant that if the vector will intercept the approach *outside* of the FAF, then this feature should not be used.

Huh? Excuse me? How many of us can recall the last time we were vectored to intercept the final approach course *inside* of the FAF?! This is definitely *not* common practice and does not comply with the controllers' Manual. How would we plan our descent? We obviously couldn't descend until we were established on course, yet we would be inside the FAF and need to make a steep descent. I don't think that I would be so quick to sing the benefits of a "Vectors" feature that cannot be used for all vectors used to get in position for an approach.

For the life of me, I cannot see why the unit is not programmed to automatically input the *inbound* instead of the *outbound* course, like the GNS 430 model does. Unless a software change in programming is made, **I encourage you never to select the "Vectors to Final" mode if a dogleg**

exists at the FAF. Instead, use OBS mode and input the proper inbound course to the FAF manually. Remember to go back to Leg mode while still more than 2 nm outside of the FAF!

I hope it does not come to the point in which we pilots must hold "Type Ratings" for each IFR approach approved GPS model that we operate…but it has been suggested! Instead, I believe the manufacturers will keep making large and small improvements that make the units more user-friendly and less prone to aggravation. I am truly impressed with the ease of use of the new Garmin 430. I predict they will sell a *lot* of those beauties! *(Author's note: I was right, wasn't I?!)*

Meanwhile, be of faith. Keep practicing with your GPS unit until it becomes easy to use no matter which of the three methods you use to get oriented inbound to the FAF: (1) radar vectors; (2) a published terminal route from an Initial Approach Fix (IAF) that entails no course reversal; or (3) a published terminal route from an IAF with a procedure turn (or holding pattern) course reversal required. It is easy to become frustrated and say, "I'm gonna stick with VORs! They are so much easier!"

Easier? Probably. Better? No way! When the light bulb of understanding and confidence finally illuminates, you will not do another VOR or NDB approach ever again if a GPS approach also exists at the same location. Try it; you'll like it. I guarantee it!

THUNDERSTORM AVOIDANCE IN THE NEW AGE

Introduction

Summer is here again and with it comes an increased opportunity – Is "opportunity" the word, or is it "risk?" – to hone our thunderstorm avoidance techniques. With the heat of summer comes more thermal activity and more thermal activity means more thunderstorms. I guess maybe it's the price we pay for being able to again enjoy the outdoor swimming pool.

Lots of weather flying techniques change little whether we are in a C-172 or a G-IV, but as speed, altitude, anti-icing capabilities, and installed weather-detection equipment escalate the higher we move up the airplane ladder, the pilot's role is impacted. This article is an attempt to review and discuss weather flying as it now relates to well-equipped King Airs. What do I mean by "well-equipped?" I mean that, in addition to the standard onboard radar, the airplane has at least lightning detection capabilities and, probably, a type of weather downlink or uplink system. Let's see how we may utilize the equipment to our advantage.

The Go/No Go vs. The Continue/Modify Decision

It is difficult for me to remember the last time I made a No Go decision, due to weather conditions, when flying a King Air. Surprised? I don't believe that I am an unreasonable risk-taker nor do I have a death wish. There were lots of times, back when I was routinely flying Bonanzas all over the country, that I spent time on the ground wishing that I could be winging my way towards my next client, but the weather conditions said "No!" In my 1972 V35B, the only anti-icing system I had was a heated pitot tube. The only weather detection system I had on board were my ol' Mark 1 Eyeballs. With those meager aids, the plane and I couldn't tackle much hard weather. When I moved up to a 1984 A36, I added a WX-8 Stormscope. Now, even when flying in clouds, I could better determine where the storms were ahead and better plan detours around them. Yet still, some hours and days were spent being ground-bound, wishing it weren't so.

Things are different in a King Air. First, we fly higher. By getting above the lower stratus and haze layer into smoother air aloft, the eyeballs can work a whole lot better. The chances of inadvertently running into an embedded thunderstorm are greatly reduced because we spend so much less time being embedded in the clouds ourselves! Do you know how easy it is to spot a whopper of a storm when the visibility is 100 miles plus? It's a piece of cake.

Second, King Airs have a lot of range. Of course, like most airplanes, range is affected by how much payload we are carrying, but even an early model 90-series King Air can usually go for at least four hours when full of passengers. At a meager 200 knots ground speed, that means about 800 miles. The typical business flight is, what, 300 to 400 miles? With that extra range available, some major detours around weather can be made while still leaving plenty of fuel to make it to the destination…and the alternate, if need be.

I did some math to satisfy my curiosity about the effect of detours. Suppose that we are flying from Departure Point A to Destination Point C on an exact magnetic course of North, 000°. Due to storms in our way, however, we must make a 30° track correction for half of the flight, to Point B. In other words, we fly 330° until we are half-way there, then fly 030° the rest of the way. Are you with me on this? How much farther will we travel due to this deviation? Fifteen percent.

Take an even bigger deviation for another example. This time we fly 45° off course! We track 315° to point B and then make a 90° right turn and track 045° to our destination. Even this unrealistically huge deviation added 41 percent to the trip!

My point is this: With the typical range we have available to us, we can make an unusual amount of twists and turns around enroute weather and still likely complete the flight without a fuel problem.

Third, we have airborne radar with us, at a minimum. Archie Trammel, teacher of all things radar, hates to hear it called "weather radar" since it is more than that. It can be a great TAWS system and even a very useful navigational device. Leaving those attributes aside, however, it can help us a great deal in not only seeing storms when embedded in clouds but also in analyzing the storm's characteristics, allowing us to decide how much we want to avoid it.

Fourth, the King Air has a full complement of anti-icing and deicing equipment and hence is approved for flight in icing conditions.

Fifth, the King Air has a second engine. If the unthinkable happens – an engine failure while in the soup – we don't have a single choice like we had in the Bonanza: A power-off glide down to whatever lies below.

These five benefits of flying a King Air instead of a light single – higher altitude, more range, radar, icing flight approval, two engines – mean that making a No Go decision becomes more of a rarity than before. However, at times, No Go is still the preferred choice.

One of my colleagues recently made a No Go decision in a King Air 300. I respect his decision and likely would have done the same had I been planning the flight that day. The flight was canceled due to the conditions at the destination airport. These included ceilings and visibilities often below published minima as well as freezing drizzle and freezing rain. Even if the weather had lifted enough to allow a successful approach and landing, the airplane may have been forced to remain at this remote location after it iced up while sitting on the ramp. No other nearby airports were offering much different current and forecast conditions. The decision was made to delay the flight. It proceeded uneventfully a day later than originally planned.

In a King Air, instead of Go/No Go decisions, I am more often confronted with *Continue/Modify* decisions. Do I continue onward toward the destination as planned or do I decide to modify the original plan? The modification may be small, such as a minor, 10° turn around a cell. It may be a little bigger, such as climbing to a different altitude or asking for a new routing. Finally, it may be quite large, such as changing the destination to another location entirely or landing short and getting more fuel.

Modern Weather Dissemination

I wonder how many of my readers still use a phone conversation with a FSS briefer – a real live person! – as their primary means of preflight weather information? I hope not many! I am not saying that one *shouldn't* talk to the briefer at all, but I am saying that using that conversation as the *foremost* method of getting weather information is passé and weak. DUATs and so many other web-based weather sources now permit us to get an almost instantaneous, real-time, picture of precipitation, clouds, lightning, winds, what have you. No longer do we have to struggle to create a visualization of the weather reports that we receive from the briefer verbally. We can see it ourselves! The morning news shows on TV, the Weather Channel, the FBOs' briefing room displays…all can help us keep track of the overall weather picture for the day, and they shouldn't be under-utilized. A picture is truly worth a thousand words!

It's only been in the last few years that FSS-like weather information has been available in the cockpit in a visual format instead of in an aural format via a voice call to Flight Watch. If you haven't yet used or seen demonstrated some of the systems that exist today, don't delay. Get to that next NBAA convention or Oshkosh Airventure or wherever, and spend some learning time at the manufacturers' booths. You'll be impressed. Take a flight with your friend and see his airplane's new system. Great strides are being made and I am anxious to see what the next five or ten years will hold, but as of right now excellent products exist to allow your airborne radar and/or lightning detection systems to be augmented amazingly well.

Downlink/Uplink Weather

Almost all of the new cockpit weather display systems allow one to view Nexrad radar images and graphical Metars. Some also include Tafs, textual Metars, Pireps, lightning data, and winds aloft. No longer is our radar information restricted to that which comes from our airborne unit. The airborne unit is limited in its effectiveness by range – anything much over 100 miles away is rather suspect – by attenuation, by ice on the radome, etc. Nexrad, however, has none of these shortcomings.

Because the Nexrad images are based on the returns from large antennas on the ground, they have the ability to see storms in much greater clarity and detail than has been available before. This can be a two-edged sword. It's great to no longer be worried about attenuation: "Does this cell really end eight miles ahead of me or is that merely the maximum depth my radar beam can penetrate this gunk before all of its energy is used up?" But on the other hand, Nexrad tends to cry wolf a lot. It is so powerful, so all-seeing, that it can see many more shades of intensity than our own units can. When Nexrad shows a red-colored return, it invariably won't show on our own radar display as red, especially when we are still fairly far away from it. If you make a vow to never fly through a yellow or red Nexrad return, you won't be doing a lot of weather flying in the summer!

Enroute Avoidance

I have found the Nexrad image to be most useful as a longer range tool. Whereas both my eyes and my onboard radar cannot do much good viewing storms over 100 miles out, with Nexrad, heck, I can see all the way across the country! By planning a detour well ahead of time, the additional distance and flight time can be minimized.

We are lucky to fly in a country that has nearly 100 percent ATC radar coverage at the altitudes at which we typically operate. Since ATC can always see us, they are much more likely to approve off-course deviations than if all of their traffic separation had to be accomplished using position reports alone.

Similarly, I use a lightning detection device primarily as a longer range tool. Also, it can help in analyzing how big and bad a storm cell really is. Due to the nature of these detection devices, a stronger cell will appear closer than it truly is…and that's an error I don't mind!

As the range decreases, the use of onboard radar and our own vision – the ol' Mark 1 Eyeballs, remember? – become increasingly important. I have spent plenty of time in unpressurized airplanes down at eight or ten thousand feet, in and out of clouds, knowing thunderstorms were nearby, craving for a slight break in the clouds so that I could look ahead. You all recall the old saying about instrument flight training under a hood, don't you? "One peek is worth a thousand crosschecks!" Well, when flying in clouds, I think that one visual peek ahead is the best weather detection and avoidance tool ever invented! "How about at night?" you ask. Don't worry. The lightning flashes inside the big cells make them as easy to spot and avoid visually as in the daytime.

As I said before, thank goodness King Airs are so often above the lower clouds so we can see clearly in all directions. Sure, there'll be a time or two we'll still be yearning mightily for a peek but, believe me, more of our time will be spent in clear air, merely flying around the worse build-ups.

Enroute Non-Avoidance

What if, even with all the latest whiz-bang goodies, we find ourselves in truly nasty conditions? The precipitation is coming down so hard we can't tell if it's liquid rain or solid hail. The autopilot has tripped off, perhaps, and even if it's still engaged, it's doing a horrid job in the severe turbulence we are encountering. There's so much static on the Comms they're useless. What now?

It's obvious we shouldn't have allowed ourselves to be in these conditions. That's why we have the weather avoidance tools we do…to *Avoid* horrid weather. We should kick ourselves hard after this is over and get more instruction on how to properly utilize the tools we have, but what about the immediate situation we are suffering?

First, don't panic. The airplane can take a lot. Second, pull torque back to the number that provides a speed close to VA, Maneuvering speed. It's better to be a little slower than faster here, since we are below maximum gross weight. In turbulence as bad as this, the airspeed will be fluctuating like crazy. That's why we need to have the proper torque value committed to memory. (Guidelines? 800 ft-lbs for the 90-series and 100-series, 1,000 ft-lbs for the F90 and 200, and about 35% for the 300 and 350.) Third, if the autopilot is still working, disengage altitude hold and set the pitch attitude for roughly zero degrees. (If it's not working, set the nose attitude manually.) Hold the nose level and allow the airplane to ride with the updrafts and downdrafts. Who cares if our altitude gets off by more than 300 feet?! When we have a chance, request of ATC a block altitude from one thousand feet below to one thousand feet above our last assigned altitude. Since, with the radio static and noise we probably won't know if ATC approved that request or not, don't sweat it. There's unlikely to be another fool in the same area of the same storm!

We're lucky that severe turbulence is localized within and around a single convective storm cell. Sure, there may be multiple cells in the general vicinity, but this encounter with severe turbulence won't last forever. Maintain control and continue straight ahead or with minor turns. I think that rarely is a 180 degree turn the proper option now. Usually, that will just prolong the agony. In a very few miles, you'll pop out of that cell and can now make the requisite turn to avoid the next one better than you did the last one.

Turbulence this bad usually comes with a high probability of a lightning strike and/or hail damage. An airplane that is struck by lightning or pounded by hail generally won't fall out of the sky

The King Air Book

or hurt the people inside. However, shed a wing because we get going too fast and pull too many Gs and the game is over. Slow down and let the airplane ride the wind!

Should we lower flaps and gear in this situation? No! Flaps extension lowers the maximum G-loading the wing can take without sustaining damage. Although landing gear has no significant effect on the ability to handle turbulence, it is easy to reach the safe Maneuvering-or-slightly-below Speed we mentioned earlier without using the drag the extended gear provides.

On the other hand, extending the gear as we start a descent in heavy turbulence is a fine technique for keeping the speed low enough while still getting the desired descent rate. I remember once a few years ago I was coming into Reno from San Francisco on a VFR day with a lot of wind blowing over the Sierras. As I descended through about 15,000 feet, the rough bumps started that are so often prevalent in the summer afternoons near Lake Tahoe. My friend Leon accurately and cleverly describes it as, "Rougher than a stucco bathtub!" I put the gear down at that time – at 15,000 feet! – and kept it extended all the way down. I was able to make a fairly steep descent while keeping the airspeed low and yet while carrying enough power to keep the pressurization system working fine.

Approaches and Landings in the Crud

Before we start the decent from the relative safety of our enroute flight level, we already have a good idea of what we'll encounter during the approach. How? Well, (1) even before we listen to ATIS, we can see the last hour's METAR readout on our cockpit weather display when we have an uplink or downlink device. (2) We can look at onboard radar, Nexrad images, and lightning displays, and compare them to the location of the destination. (3) We will overhear airplanes ahead discussing the weather towards the airport and possible deviations that they are making.

If weather conditions at the desired destination seem too fierce, don't descend yet. Instead, now's the time to make a decision to modify the original plans. Maybe it's time to land at that nice airport in the clear 50 miles short of where we want to go and wait an hour on the ground before going the rest of the way. Instead, maybe we ask for a holding pattern to buy time, or maybe we ask for an approach to another runway at the destination airport, one that avoids the big, bad, cell. Remember, we are the PICs, not the helpful ATC controllers/coordinators. Don't be afraid to speak up and ask for what you want. ATC cannot read our minds and they don't have the view that we have out through our windshields. "Center, N12345 would like to turn left about 30 degrees toward XYZ VOR and see if it looks better coming into the airport from that direction. If it doesn't, we can hold out there for thirty minutes before going on to our alternate." A statement like that is okay to announce. Now ATC has an inkling of what we are thinking and planning.

98

THUNDERSTORM AVOIDANCE IN THE NEW AGE

At last we decide to go for it. The weather looks like there is enough of a break that we can execute a successful approach to landing. So we leave the holding pattern and now we are on the ILS, but we are in heavy rain, lightning flashing around us at times, occasional moderate turbulence. "What the heck have I gotten myself into?!" we ask ourselves. Unless you are fuel critical, it's never too late to keep modifying the plan. Go ahead and miss the approach. Don't like what the radar shows straight ahead? Then see if ATC will approve an early turn in the direction you want to go. Realize that if you are initiating the missed approach closer to the outer marker than the threshold, you've got a lot more ground clearance cushion, so the likelihood of being denied the turn is less than you may expect even if it's not in the same direction as the turn depicted on the published missed approach procedure.

What if the controller won't approve that immediate 45 degree right turn off of the localizer that you're requesting, and yet the turbulence, rain, lightening, and maybe even hail are getting worse? Do it anyway! Again, who is PIC?! In an emergency situation – and I think you're in one now! – the PIC can do whatever he or she deems appropriate for safety. When you've got to, you've got to. Ask for forgiveness later if you cannot receive permission now. And what, really, is to be forgiven? Not a thing. You made the best decision that you could in the situation.

A few lines back I wrote, "Unless you are fuel critical, it's never too late to keep modifying the plan." When you are indeed fuel critical, it's a whole different ballgame. In rotten weather, please, please, please don't allow yourself to become short on fuel! With fuel comes time and with time come options. Without fuel, our options become very, very limited.

A few years ago I had the pleasure of ferrying a new King Air 350 from Wichita to Japan, via Canada, Alaska, and Russian Siberia. *(See the story of that adventure beginning on page 355.)* I flew one of three such planes that were traveling together, on separate IFR flight plans some minutes apart. As you can imagine, with the long legs we were flying in such remote areas, our alternate airports were few and far between.

During our initial meeting in Wichita before heading out on this adventure, the most experienced, lead pilot in our group provided a thorough and careful briefing. I will never forget one of his comments: "We don't make Missed Approaches." Shocking? Not to me, it wasn't. To me, it reflected a true knowledge of the real world of long range flying. When fuel is scarce enough, the option of a missed approach shrinks to non-existence. That's why all three pilots in our group were quite practiced and proficient in making hand-flown, zero/zero landings out of an ILS approach. I am very happy that I was never forced to utilize that skill in a real do-or-die situation, on that ferry trip or at any other time. My friends, have enough fuel or good enough weather so that you, too, never run out of viable options.

The King Air Book

Summary

I've covered quite a bit of ground here concerning the preflight, departure, enroute, descent, and approach phases of a flight that must deal with some severe weather. Let me recap the big picture ideas. Get a good weather picture before you go…and I do mean "picture," not merely a verbal description. The best weather avoidance device you have are your eyes. The best cockpit aid you have for longer range planning is a Stormscope or a Strikefinder device and/or Nexrad radar images sent to your cockpit on a "close to real time" basis. The best cockpit aid you have for close-in avoidance is onboard radar. Learn a lot about your installed aids and practice using them regularly. Use them to avoid severe weather. Lastly, if somehow you blunder into something horrible, slow down and deal with it as we've discussed.

The new weather information equipment that we may now utilize in our cockpits are fantastic aids but they are useless unless properly utilized by skillful, knowledgeable, proficient pilots. My friend Steve says, as I stare at my golf club in disbelief after a particularly lousy shot, "Remember, it's not the arrow, it's the Indian." That's his not-so-subtle way of chiding me into admitting that it's not the club's fault, it's mine.

By having the latest marvelous weather goodies in our King Air cockpits, we have more and better arrows. Are we the Indians we need to be?

USING THE BC MODE CORRECTLY

Of the many modes of operation found in typical Flight Director/Autopilot (FD/AP) systems, the one that is the most difficult to understand and to use properly is the BC mode, sometimes designated REV mode. This is my attempt at explaining this mode, so that it can become a useful part of your available aids to safe flying.

Let's clarify once and for all a simple fact that is often overlooked: When *localizer* course deviation is displayed on an HSI (Horizontal Situation Indicator), there is never any wrong-way information as long as the course needle is always set on the front course bearing. You always fly toward the needle to return to the course centerline. This has nothing to do with whether the HSI is teamed with a Flight Director and/or Autopilot. The HSI itself makes this happen.

And while we are at it, let me remind you of two other related items. First, VOR course deviation is *always* displayed properly on an HSI – namely, fly *to* the needle to get on course – regardless of whether the course needle is set on the radial or on its reciprocal. How nice the HSI is compared to the old-fashioned CDI! Second, when the HSI course needle is displaying GPS, Loran, or other long range nav data, the picture will only be correct if we put the head of the course needle on the Desired Track (DTK, in most systems) value. Remember that this number changes as we progress toward a distant waypoint. If your course needle does not slew automatically, you need to keep checking and inputting the proper value every hundred miles or so.

So what does the BC button do? Well, it does *not* reverse the operation of the course needle on the HSI as many pilots believe. Instead, it makes the FD/AP fly the selected localizer in the direction of the tail of the course needle instead of its head. In avionics-speak, the tail becomes the course datum.

For example, consider the LOC (BACK CRS) Rwy 35 approach at Mesquite, Texas. The localizer has a front course bearing of 175°, that normally guides us during the ILS Rwy 17 approach. We tune and identify the localizer and set the HSI's course needle on 175°. Once we are close enough to the localizer's center to avoid any false signals, the HSI always shows us a proper picture. If we are east of the localizer course, the needle will tell us to fly west to intercept. If we are west of the course, the needle will tell us to fly in an easterly direction to intercept. This is true whether we are north of the airport on the ILS side, or south of the airport on the Back Course side. If we hit the NAV or APR button on our AP/FD control panel, and – if necessary, based upon the exact type of system we have – set up an appropriate intercept heading, then when course capture occurs and the FD/AP begins to track the localizer, it will initially turn to 175° before it begins to compensate for crosswinds. If we are north of the airport, we will track the localizer toward it. But if we are south of the airport when the interception occurs, then we will track the localizer away from the airport.

On the other hand, if we use the BC button in this situation, when course capture occurs and the FD/AP begins to track the localizer, it will initially turn to 355° before it starts crosswind compensation. If we are north of the airport, we will track the localizer away from the airport; if we are south of the airport when the interception occurs, we will track the localizer Back Course to the airport.

In summary:

> 1. Always set the HSI course needle on the front course bearing.
> 2. Ask yourself…Do I want to fly toward the *Head* or the *Tail* of the needle after I intercept?
> 3. If the answer is *Head,* use the APR or NAV mode. If the answer is *Tail,* use the BC mode.

Be especially careful when there are ILS or Localizer approaches to two different ends of the same runway! It is not a Back Course unless it says BACK CRS! There is another simple way of verifying that you are, in fact, on a back course…the localizer depiction shows a solid black left side instead of a feathered right side. Have you noticed this?

Some IFR departure or missed approach procedures involve tracking a localizer Back Course away from the airport…the missed approach at Aspen, Colorado, for example. How easy it is to set this up wrong! As always, set the course needle on the front course bearing. Now, which way do you want to go? Toward the head of the needle? Then use NAV. (NAV is preferred, not APR, so as to avoid unwanted attempts at capturing false glide slope signals.) Want to go toward the tail? Then use BC.

Using the Aspen example, we need to track away from the airport, 300° northwest bound on the Back Course of a Localizer Directional Aid, or LDA. (The front course of this LDA is only approved for use by special authorization, and the approach plate for it is not included in normal subscription services.) Since this is the Back Course, we know that the front course has a bearing of 300°, which is what we set on the HSI's course needle. Since we want to fly toward the head of the needle, we would use the NAV mode. If we had hit the BC button in error, the system would turn us to the tail of the needle and track 120° toward the airport…and toward the mountains beyond!

A special note concerns the popular Century IV FD/AP system. Its REV button not only does all the things that the BC button of other systems do, but it also works on VOR radials. This is a neat deal!

Suppose we want to track out the 060° radial from a VOR for a PT, then re-intercept that same radial on a course of 240° back to the VOR. We can set 240 on the course needle right away, never 060. (Remember how a VOR course on an HSI is never backwards?) Hit REV to fly toward the tail of the needle when outbound from the VOR, use HDG for the PT maneuvering, then hit APR to fly toward the head of the needle when flying back toward the VOR. (Some other systems also use the abbreviation REV instead of BC, but that does not necessarily mean that they have this unique feature.)

Many Collins systems – FD-108/109, AP-104/105 systems for example – do not contain a BC button, although they do have a "Back Loc" annunciator and can do a fine job of tracking a localizer in either direction…toward the head or tail of the course needle. How is this possible? The system looks at the intercept heading the pilot has established to the localizer. Knowing that front courses are more popular than back courses, if we are on a 90° intercept, it will stay in the front course mode. 30°, 45°, 60° intercept angles will all obviously result in typical "Approach" mode operation. But if we set up an intercept of 106° or so – less than a 75° intercept toward the tail of the localizer course needle – then the system will automatically realize that BC operation is the probable desired result. Thus, the "Back Loc" annunciator will illuminate when APR mode is selected, and the course capture will result in tracking toward the tail of the needle.

Finally, if the Attitude Director Indicator (ADI) contains a runway symbol within it – the expanded localizer display commonly found on big Collins, Honeywell/Sperry, or Bendix-King units – BC mode reverses *that* localizer display to avoid a wrong-way picture on the ADI that would conflict with the proper picture on the HSI.

Fewer and fewer Localizer Back Course approaches exist. They appear to be a dying breed, and their passing probably won't cause many tears of grief. Until they are gone, however, I hope this discussion has shed some light on making the job easier when you fly one.

Avionics Updating

Introduction

I've been asked to supply some comments dealing with panel upgrades and I am happy to do so. The Super King Air 300 that Pam and I manage for a couple of owners in Phoenix is just now getting ready to have some upgrades installed so the topic is quite timely. Also, with the TAWS mandate less than a year away, lots of King Airs and other airplanes will be heading to an avionics installer in the next few months to have a TAWS system installed. If you haven't yet decided what system you want and made plans to have it added, you need to get cracking!

The 1976 Super King Air 200 that we flew around the world in 2001 – see www.worldflight2001.com – underwent a *huge* panel change prior to our flight. All of the original King Gold Crown radios came out and a bunch of new, mostly Garmin equipment, went in: Dual GNS 530s, audio panel, transponders, CD player, along with an Avidyne Flight Max 850 and a Sandel SN3308 EHSI. About the only original equipment remaining was the autopilot/flight director (a King KFC-300 model) and the Bendix 1200 radar. The owner's desire to have the latest and greatest equipment prior to our worldwide adventure prompted this project, and I was the one to suggest most of the changes. The installation was accomplished by Autopilots Central in Tulsa and what a great job they did!

Be Careful About Putting Too Many Eggs in One Basket

Multifunction Displays, MFDs…Wow! They're great! To be able to have a moving map overlaid with traffic and weather and flight plan and terrain information is a marvelous addition to any cockpit. Positional awareness becomes many-times easier when we can see our position clearly on a moving map, rather than when we have to deduce our exact location based on a paper chart, a VOR radial, and a DME distance.

Unfortunately, however, when the display fails – as it certainly will, sometime! – we may find ourselves losing more than we expect. Take the case of the Worldflight2001 BE-200. When first installed, our Avidyne Flight Max 850 was the *only* location where we could control our radar, our Stormscope, our Skywatch traffic system, and our CD player. The Garmin 530s provided redundancy – so we thought! – for the display of Stormscope and Skywatch information.

But then one day the Avidyne unit gave us an ugly green screen of death and we had to send the unit back to the factory for repair. (By the way, the repair was done very quickly and we had the unit back in just a few days.) Without the Avidyne MFD we found that, even though the Stormscope and Skywatch were *able* to operate and display on the 530s, we could not activate them because the control had been provided *only* though the MFD! The next month, we returned the airplane to Tulsa where Autopilots Central – At their expense, conscientious shop that they are! – added switching relays so that the Stormscope and Skywatch could be controlled by *either* the Flight Max MFD *or* one of the 530s. Now, if the MFD failed again, we would lose its moving map and the radar information, but still have redundant ability to control and see lightning and traffic information.

As we started planning the panel upgrade to the BE-300 that we currently fly, we were told that Avidyne's new EX 500 unit requires a separate display of Stormscope data when installed in the 300. That's a good requirement, in my opinion, that contributes to increased safety by offering an extra level of redundancy.

I suggest that you give careful thought to how a failure of your new MFD may compromise the plane's ability to give you the information that you desire. If your old radar screen died, all you lost was radar. That's no longer the case when the radar screen becomes an MFD! Keeping or adding a separate screen for traffic and lightning is one idea.

Uplink/Downlink Weather

Just now, I am starting to see and fly more and more King Airs that have cockpit access to real-time weather data that is received either through a ground based uplink system or via a satellite-based downlink system. This is cool stuff!

So far – May 2004 – I'd give the gold medal to the Bendix/King / Honeywell / AlliedSignal (What do we call them this week?) uplink system. *(Author's note: Now, in 2009, the satellite system has won the battle and it's awesome!)* I hope and expect great strides to be made in this area in the next months and years by all of the providers but already many products exist that allow Nexrad images, Metars, TAFs, etc. to get into the cockpit in a timely manner.

Being able, from the pilot's seat, to see radar maps just like you'd see in your living room at home on The Weather Channel is exciting and fascinating. Looking at the current Metar for your foggy destination and seeing how it changes each hour is also wonderful.

On the other hand, isn't that what Flight Watch is for? Can't you key the mic and get updates from FSS? Of course you can! But the amount of accurate information transmitted, received, understood, and visualized via a verbal description of the weather provided by the voice of the FSS specialist cannot begin to compete in the depth and breadth of understanding that comes from seeing the weather map in person. "A picture is worth a thousand words" is the trite adage that really does apply to this discussion.

I, personally, have always felt that lightning detection/Stormscope data was better utilized for longer-range planning – Should I go over Kansas City or up over Omaha to get around that group of storms? – whereas onboard radar and the good old Mark I Eyeball were better when it came to picking our way around the actual cells when we got to them. Having Nexrad radar images provides another option.

I still think that the view my eyes provide through the windshield, along with the onboard radar returns, will be what I relay upon most when near the storms. On the other hand, I think Nexrad will become my method-of-choice for the longer-range planning. Only if the Uplink/Downlink weather is unavailable would the Stormscope be very necessary.

My conclusion is this: If the airplane already contains a lightning detection system, keep it. If it does not, however, and if you are adding a weather data link of some type, then a lightning detection system may not be a very worthwhile addition.

Traffic Collision Avoidance Systems

TCAS II, TCAS I, Skywatch HP, Skywatch…there are lots of good choices available. Once you have flown with one of these systems it is almost frightening to go flying without one! I cannot recommend a plan for avionics upgrading in this class of airplane that does not include the installation of a traffic information system of some type.

Many years ago an airline pilot friend was presenting his views on TCAS II after his first few flights with it in the jetliner. He made a couple of observations that were good then and they are still sound advice today. First, he noted how easy it was to get mesmerized by the traffic display and spend far too much head-down cockpit time looking at it. He suggested that the unit not really be included routinely in one's instrument scan until a Traffic Advisory (TA, "Traffic! Traffic!") was received. His second observation had to do with the best response to the TA. When a TA is received, he believed that the display should be examined only long enough to decide the approximate location of the traffic threat. Then the important thing is to start visually scanning *outside* in that direction in an attempt to see the traffic and be ready to take the appropriate evasive action required, if any.

I wonder if there will be many last words on Cockpit Voice Recorders that go something like this, "Gee, I've been watching the TCAS and that traffic right at our altitude has been getting closer and closer! I wonder if ATC…(end of recording)."

Is the RMI a Thing of the Past?

Second only to a moving map, I believe that the combination of an RMI (Radio Magnetic Indicator) pointer and a DME readout to the selected VORTAC station is the best thing ever made for maintaining correct positional awareness. However, I think those of us who use and love the RMI may be a dying breed. Although I prefer to have an RMI in any airplane that I fly regularly on instruments, I think that they may well be going the way of readily-accessible payphones and cheap fuel…fading from the scene, becoming faint memories of things long gone.

If your plane has redundant GPS navigators with at least one good moving map, and if you've never quite seen the beauty of or need for an RMI anyway, then maybe it's time to use that chunk of panel real estate for something more useful to you. Go ahead. Be my guest.

In fact, Sandel makes their TAWS product with the thought that it will most probably be installed in an old RMI panel position.

Paperwork, Paperwork, Paperwork

Any avionics installation shop that is good at what they do will be ahead of the game in making certain that your new whiz bang installation is fully legal and FAA-approved. I have been surprised and disappointed often in the past, however, to find that a King Air I have been asked to fly and evaluate or conduct training in does not appear to have an approved installation.

An FAA 337 form, a Weight and Balance change, an Airplane Flight Manual (AFM) Supplement are all necessary, at the least. It is not at all uncommon for the installation of a new GPS navigator to be restricted to "VFR Operations Only" until a test flight and receipt of the FAA-paperwork is completed. Be sure that you don't fly away home from the installation shop without either having all the i's dotted and the t's crossed before you leave, or having been informed exactly what remains to be done and when it will be done to make the installation 100% legal and approved.

By the way, whomever does the flight test should verify that the three levels of GPS course needle sensitivity are working correctly. An easy way to do this is to intentionally fly away from a course centerline while monitoring both the HSI (or CDI) course needle as well as the Cross-Track (XTK) readout you'll find on one page of the new GPS. In Approach sensitivity, the course needle needs to hit the peg when you are 0.3 nm from center. In Terminal, you need to see 1.0 nm just as the needle pegs, and in Enroute, the value is 5.0 nm.

I have stumbled across at least three installations – all of which were utilizing an Electronic HSI, EFIS system – that were displaying very incorrect needle movement that could lead the pilot to believe he or she was much closer to the proper course than in fact he/she was. In at least one case, the solution was quite an expensive upgrade to the EHSI's Display Processor.

Speaking of paperwork, I suggest that you have a discussion with your avionics installer about the issues involved in replacing, say, your MFD with a loaner unit. Suppose your Comm 1 unit broke and Collins sent you a loaner to install while they repaired yours. Plug it in the rack and off you go, right?

But that loaner Multifunction Display is another game entirely! You see, it needs to be programmed – usually while it sits right in your airplane's avionics panel – to recognize and be compatible with your particular type of radar, particular type of TAWS, particular type of traffic system, etc. Just plugging it in the panel and expecting it to play properly with all of the other goodies is wishful thinking.

One of the shops I worked with in the past prepared a very nice, neat, and tremendously useful binder that explained in detail how to access the programming functions of the MFD and then showed precisely what options were selected and how to select them, so that this MFD was configured right for our airplane. On the other hand, I know of another shop that balked totally at this idea and adamantly insisted that only *they* could install and program the replacement unit. That's fine if they are nearby, but what happens when the problem strikes when you are far from home and far from that shop?

Remember: Loaner units of some of these sophisticated avionics items will be useless until *someone* – whomever that may be – programs them correctly for your airplane.

TAWS – Terrain Awareness Warning Systems

As mentioned earlier, our airplanes must have one of these systems installed by March 2005. King Airs can get by with the less-expensive Class B TAWS, not the Class A types required by the airlines. Having been privileged to be a crewmember during a lot of the certification flight testing for ACSS's Class A product (T^2CAS), I can vouch for the extra level of safety these systems will bring to the cockpit.

No TAWS alerts or warnings *should* ever be issued! If the crew is following charted procedures at the proper altitudes, no CFIT (Controlled Flight Into Terrain) accidents will occur. However, we all know that CFIT accidents do indeed occur with depressing regularity and with an horrific loss of life. Pilots are human; humans make mistakes. TAWS should catch these types of mistakes before they lead to loss of life.

"Paint the cockpit windows black. Send me in any direction at any altitude. I won't hit a thing!" That's the line I used often when talking to prospective buyers of the ACSS TAWS system after it had been perfected and had received FAA approval. TAWS is a marvelous system!

On the other hand, the alerts and warnings that TAWS provides are useless unless the pilots have been taught how to react and then make the proper reactions in a timely fashion. Proper training on this new system is necessary. As a minimum, the AFM Supplement should be read and studied carefully. Then, I strongly suggest going out in your plane on a lovely VFR day for a little TAWS practice. This should include making a few low altitude runs at hills or mountainsides, making one or two "mistakes" where (1) you set up to land in Farmer Brown's pasture instead of at the nearby airport, or (2) you intentionally duck well below the glideslope near the Outer Marker, or (3) you delay landing gear extension for too long, or (4) you stop climbing and start sinking soon after takeoff. By doing some of these maneuvers – in a safe, controlled, planned environment – you will learn exactly how your system's alerts and warnings are presented and you will have opportunities to practice the proper recovery maneuver as presented in the AFM Supplement.

Know Thy Stuff

I have mentioned the need for proper documentation and AFM Supplements that cover the new equipment you have had installed. With rare exception, the AFM Supplement will make reference to the Operating Manual for the particular item of interest – the MFD, or the TAWS, or the Skywatch, etc. – and likely require that the Manual be available to the crew in the cockpit.

The information contained both in the AFM Supplements and in these Operating Manuals is so very, very, important! Spend sufficient time so that you know well what the manuals and the supplements contain. If you need help in understanding what you read, get it. Call the manufacturer, or talk to a more experienced friend, or call your King Air training provider. Heck, go ahead and e-mail me if you'd like! (twcaz@msn.com)

It is saddening to me when I fly with pilots and find that they have so little accurate and worthwhile knowledge about the great equipment that their airplanes contain. It is rarely ever easy obtaining that knowledge, but obtain it you must if the thousands and thousands of dollars you have spent on the upgrade is going to truly buy you convenience and safety, not just window dressing.

Cabin Options

As you are making plans for your panel upgrades in the cockpit, don't overlook the consideration of changes in the cabin as well. On the BE-200 we flew around-the-world, we had a handheld Garmin 295 in the cabin with a power plug and a fitting to an external antenna that had been added on top of the fuselage. (With proper FAA-approval, too!) The owner and his wife absolutely *loved* being able to have their own moving map, always able to see exactly where we were, how fast we were going, when we'd get to the destination, etc. What a cheap "Air Show" system this proved to be! Of course, it also made for a great back-up navigation system if we ever lost the good stuff in front.

Likewise, how about power plugs for laptop computers, DVD players, etc.? Do you want to use just cigar lighter plugs or actually have the shop install an inverter with 110 volt, 60 Hz output, just like at home? How about a satellite phone antenna with a jack?

All of these things and many more are available that you may want to consider as you upgrade your plane.

Conclusion

In the last few years, the pace of avionics development seems to have picked up a great deal of speed and we are now faced with a myriad of desirable upgrade options, many of which did not exist a short time back. Do your planning carefully, ask questions, do research, select a good installation shop, be patient, then enjoy the fruits of your labors. And oh, I almost forgot....bring lots of money!

PART 2

TECHNICAL TOPICS

STARTING PT6-POWERED KING AIRS

For pilots who are new to turbine-powered aircraft, starting the engines is one of the most difficult of the new tasks to be learned. However, in a relatively short time, the procedure becomes quite simple. In fact, most experienced pilots actually prefer the turbine start to the piston-engine start, finding it easier and more consistent. Is there any pilot who hasn't faced major embarrassment starting a hot, fuel injected, Continental or Lycoming on a summer afternoon? But the turbine start, whether the engine is cold or hot, and whether the OAT is –10°C or +50°C, is virtually always successful with exactly the same procedure.

All newer King Airs with the "Five-Bus" electrical system – C90A, C90B, F90-series, 300-series – have provisions that allow the starting procedure to be slightly simplified. Even in the 200-series, the 1993 and later serials incorporate a change that leads to the same result. Namely, the operating engine's generator may be left on while initiating the start of the second engine.

Let us presume that the Before Starting procedure has been completed...the parking brake is set, the power quadrant levers are positioned properly, the battery switch is on, the voltage has been checked, etc. Now we are ready to activate an Ignition and Engine Start switch, often called the "Starter switch."

Which engine to start first? In 90, A90, and B90 King Air models, the right engine, without the pressurization supercharger, spools up more easily than then left and so it is the better choice. However, in other King Airs, the difference is immaterial. Yes, the battery is closer to the right engine, but the difference in line resistance is hard to objectively measure.

When using the airplane's own battery to provide starting power – instead of using an External Power Unit (EPU) – the first engine that is started always starts with a hotter ITT (Interstage Turbine Temperature). This is because the battery alone cannot spin the engine as fast as the combination of battery and generator that will start the second engine. With less rotational speed, the compressor delivers less cooling air to the combustion chamber and hence the engine starts hotter.

Also, because the generator of the first engine that is started will help provide power for the second start, its brushes, bearings, and drive shaft splines all receive more wear and tear than the opposite side's generator. So, to better equalize generator wear and engine hot section deterioration, the technique we advocate, for King Airs without superchargers, is to alternate which engine is started first.

> Whenever an EPU is *conveniently available,* the crew should use it for starting. Doing so allows both left and right engines to benefit from a faster, cooler, start. It eliminates starting wear and tear on either generator.
>
> The airplane's battery needs to be exercised regularly to remain strong, and hence using an EPU for *every* start can be detrimental to the battery. However, since EPUs are *not* "conveniently available" at many locations King Airs frequent, plenty of *internal* starts – those using the airplane's own battery and generator – are accomplished during routine aircraft operation. For that reason, conducting an EPU start when you can makes a lot of sense.

We suggest that your right hand be placed on the Condition Lever of the engine to be started while your left hand is used to move the Ignition and Engine Start switch up from the center, off, position. After the switch is activated, take your left hand away from it…it will remain activated until you turn it off later. Especially for pilots new to turbines, a beneficial procedure is to now use the left hand to point to the annunciator lights and gauges of interest as the start progresses.

There is a potential danger of keeping your left hand on the starter switch. A PT6 engine does not become self-sustaining until past 40% compressor speed (also known as gas generator speed or N1 speed). This means that the exhaust gases driving the compressor's turbine (the Compressor Turbine, or CT) are not yet strong enough to overcome the drag of the compressor itself and its associated bearings and accessories. If a pilot were to inadvertently turn off the starter switch too early, the engine will begin to slow down. With the reduction of cooling airflow, ITT will rocket toward the starting redline. Unless the pilot is quick in cutting off the fuel by moving the Condition Lever to Fuel Cutoff, a hot start will result, with a high probability of major and expensive hot section damage being incurred. By using your left hand to help direct your eyes to the proper locations during the start, there is zero chance that you would cause a possible hot start by turning off the starter too soon.

The first item at which to point is the "Ignition" annunciator for the appropriate engine. As the name says, the Ignition and Engine Start switch activates the ignition system as well as the starter motor, so now the engine's glow plugs or spark plugs should be energized. If the Ignition light is not on, perhaps the ignition relay is faulty or the Ignitor circuit breaker is tripped. In either case, it is pointless to proceed with the start unless the light is verified illuminated.

By the way, the relay and annunciator could work properly, and yet the ignitors themselves could both be bad. If the engine does not start at the proper time, the most likely cause is inoperative ignition, even though the annunciator had been on. King Airs manufactured after about 1980 contain spark plug instead of glow plug ignitors, and a kit allows earlier airplanes to be modified to this latest configuration. Often it is possible to actually hear the snapping sound of the sparks to verify that this system is working. But with glow plugs? There is no real way to know. If the start is successful, then the glow plugs must have been okay!

Point at the Fuel Pressure annunciator next and verify it is now extinguished. For the 90, A90, B90, C90-series, and the straight 100 – the models that have no engine-driven boost pump but merely the electric boost pump – it is common practice to have the boost pump on prior to start so the annunciator would have extinguished at that earlier time. For the others, now is the time that the engine-driven boost pump should be turning at sufficient speed to create enough fuel pressure to turn out the light.

Next, point at the N1 gauge. By now, the big hand will be past 10% heading toward 20%. Once you have noted this, direct attention to the little hand. It makes one complete revolution, from 0 through 9 and back to 0, each time the big hand increases by 10%. So if the big hand has moved past 10 and the little hand is moving upward between 5 and 6, you are seeing 15 – 16%. The minimum speed for proceeding with the start is 12%. Below that, so little airflow has been provided that the likelihood of a hot start is too risky. But with a good strong battery and starter, you will usually see between 16 and 20% speed when the little hand stops increasing. (If we were using an EPU, we would see about 4% additional speed.)

That is what we are waiting for…full stabilization of N1 speed. By letting the starter spin the engine as fast as it can, we are establishing the best amount of cooling airflow before we introduce the fuel and start the fire. Also, a "blanket" of cooling air should now be ready to support the soon-to-be-created fireball in the center of the combustion chamber liner, or burner can. Yes, the engine will start just fine, so it seems, if fuel is introduced earlier. Some misguided pilots bring the fuel in right at 12%. Perhaps they think they are saving the starter motor by this technique. Although universal agreement that one method is better than another is probably impossible to achieve, we are very strongly of the opinion that attaining maximum stabilized N1 is very important before fuel is introduced.

N1 gauges – prior to the change to digital gauges – are notoriously "sticky." Use a finger of your left hand to lightly tap on the gauge bezel – not the glass! – to be sure that the N1 displayed is correct and has not hung up due to gauge friction.

The King Air Book

If your airplane has spark ignitors, now is the time to bring in the fuel. But with glow plugs, start a five second count before doing anything else. This delay allows the glow plugs to reach maximum operating temperature to better guarantee that lightoff will occur as soon as fuel is present.

One of the horror stories we have heard regarding King Air starts involves a crew picking up the airplane after some maintenance had been performed. The shop had pulled the Ignitor CBs, a practice they had adopted to ensure that no engine would ever be started by accident while the airplane was in the shop's hangar…as had happened once before.

Sure enough, someone forgot to reset the breakers and the crew failed to notice. The crew also failed to observe the lack of the Ignition annunciator when the starter switch was activated. The Condition Lever was advanced to introduce fuel and, of course, nothing happened…no N1 increase, no ITT rise, no sound change. Instead of pulling the Condition Lever back to Fuel Cutoff, turning the starter switch off, and analyzing the problem in a methodical manner, one of the pilots suddenly recalled that this particular shop often pulled the CBs. Sure enough! He found them tripped and – are we ready for this? – he reset them.

In a few moments, as the glow plugs became warm enough to ignite the fuel, what a spectacular sight! Flames shot out of the exhaust stacks and traveled nearly the entire length of the airplane!

Exterior paint was scorched, deice boots were damaged, and the engine had to endure a premature hot section inspection. The lesson is obvious: Ignition needs to be on before fuel accumulates in the engine!

So let's see where we stand now. We have verified that the Ignition annunciator is on and the Fuel Pressure annunciator is not on, we have waited for N1 to totally stabilize, and – when equipped with glow plugs, not spark plugs – we have counted up to five. Now move the Condition Lever fully forward, to the High Idle position with your right hand, and start counting…1, 2, 3, etc.

Moving straight to High Idle does not cause the engine to start with more fuel than if we had moved only as far as the Low Idle position. The starting ITT will be the same. Many pilots start at Low Idle, then move to High Idle later, which is perfectly fine. By going straight to High Idle initially, however, the procedure is simplified, there is no chance of forgetting to go there later, and the engine experiences only one acceleration cycle and ITT peak instead of two. The 300-series' Fuel Control Unit is made by Woodward, not Bendix as in the other models, and it does appear that the starting ITT peak is a smidgen higher when one goes straight-away to High Idle. For that reason the preferred method for the 300 and 350 is to move the condition lever to Low Idle first, then advance to High Idle just as the ITT peaks and starts to fall. In fact, this method works fine for all, if you prefer it.

As is usually the case, an argument exists for *not* going to High Idle straight away…it takes a little longer to pull the lever to Cutoff when a start must be aborted. Yep, that's true, but we believe that the advantages outweigh the disadvantages.

Lightoff must occur within ten seconds. If your count hits ten and nothing has happened, pull the Condition Lever to Fuel Cutoff, turn off the starter switch, and wait at least sixty seconds to allow the starter to cool. (You Super King Air 300-series pilots need to wait *five minutes;* your starting time limits are *much* more restrictive than those that apply to other King Air models!) This delay period also permits residual fuel to be vented out from the engine case drains if, in fact, the engine had received any fuel.

How often does this situation – this no lightoff scenario, sometimes known as a "wet start" – actually occur? Hardly ever. In the author's 14,000+ hours of King Air flying, the number of ground starts that have been unsuccessful or abnormal in any way probably number fewer than ten. Surprised? Certainly the potential for a very expensive problem exists during every turbine start, and constant vigilance must be exercised during the start process. But, having said that, don't worry excessively. When the procedure is performed correctly, the dreaded hot start, or wet start, or hung start is just not going to happen. There might be a higher probability of winning a million dollar jackpot at Las Vegas than having a PT6 starting problem!

After the Condition Lever has been pushed forward, the lightoff is usually almost immediate, typically less than three seconds. How is lightoff observed? In three ways. First, you will hear a sound change as the exhaust gases start to flow. Second, you will observe that the little hand on the N1 gauge leaves its stabilized location and starts to increase again. (Remember that your left hand should still be pointing at this gauge.) Third and final, the ITT needle will start rising.

Once you have observed the N1 gauge start to increase, move your finger from that instrument to the ITT gauge. Place your finger on the bezel at the 900°C mark. If the ITT needle gets to your finger – if it reaches 900° – pull the Condition Lever back to Fuel Cutoff. And remember, the chance of this happening is almost nonexistent.

The ITT gauge contains two redlines. The first represents the limit for Takeoff and Maximum Continuous power. The second, much higher, redline is the starting limit. Because about 75% of the air that enters the engine during normal operation is used for cooling, not combustion, and because very little mass airflow occurs at 20% N1, the internal engine temperature rushes upward quite rapidly when lightoff occurs, even though the engine is receiving minimum fuel flow at this time. But the exhaust gases that are causing the ITT to rise are also helping the compressor to turn faster and therefore to bring in more cooling air.

The King Air Book

The result is that ITT rushes up quickly, slows down, and then hits a peak reading before dropping lower as the N1 keeps increasing. If the peak ever exceeds the starting redline for more than a few seconds, the engine must be overhauled due to the overtemperature condition.

Except for starts with very, very, little airflow – either starts conducted in flight at high altitude, or starts conducted on the ground with a very weak battery that barely creates a stabilized N1 of 12% – the chance of going past 900° as a peak starting temperature is minuscule. Basically, something is very wrong if the temperature passes 900°. That is why we suggest that you use this easy-to-read, conservative, value as the point at which you will abort the start.

Once the ITT needle has peaked and fallen – with the peak well, well, below 900° – now it is time to reposition your left hand back to the N1 gauge to verify that it stabilizes at about 70%, the High Idle setting. A "runaway" engine is another potential problem – very, very, remote – associated with a turbine start. If the engine keeps going up to 75% – 80%, again it is time to chop off the fuel with the Condition Lever.

So let's review. Starter switch on, the left hand moves away from the switch and points at the Ignition annunciator to verify that it has illuminated and the Fuel Pressure annunciator to verify that it is not, it then points at the N1 gauge and we wait for fully stabilized speed, above 12%. Next – after a five second count if equipped with glow plugs – the right hand moves the Condition Lever forward and we start another count. By the time the count hits about three – and definitely by the time it gets to ten – a sound change is heard and the N1 gauge begins to increase again. Now the left hand points at the 900° mark on the ITT gauge. After ITT has peaked, the left hand returns to the N1 gauge to verify it stabilizes near 70%.

The first engine is started. Congratulations! Turn the Ignition and Engine Starter switch off.

In virtually all turbine engines, the starter motor and the electrical generator are the same unit. It is usually listed as a Starter/Generator, abbreviated S/G. In the King Air, the starter circuit has priority over the generator circuit, so that the generator will not operate until the starter switch is turned off. Unlike the starter motor on a piston engine, the turbine has no clutch or gearing to engage/disengage the starter. If the engine's compressor is turning, so is the S/G.

Nothing harmful happens to the starter motor if the starter switch is left on after starting! Since the exhaust gases are now driving the compressor, the starter is no longer working hard and getting hot. It is merely "going along for the ride."

We would hesitate to estimate how many times a pilot thought his generator was broken, only to discover that the reason it was not operating was that he had forgotten to turn the starter switch off. It has happened thousands and thousands of times. You, too, will join the ranks of pilots who have made this minor, embarrassing, error if you haven't done so already. Don't worry; just try to remember better next time.

You have already learned that turning the starter switch off too early, before the engine is self-sustaining, is a sure-fire way to create a hot start situation. Now you have also been told that leaving the starter switch on indefinitely is not really a problem…it just won't let the generator operate. That is why we advocate leaving the starter switch on until the engine is totally stabilized at high idle speed, then turning it off. Yes, it is perfectly acceptable to turn off the switch any time the engine is past 50% N1. But, to keep things simple and consistent, we teach waiting until the stabilized speed is reached.

A typical King Air battery has a lot of capacity – 34 amp-hours or more – when fully charged. This is enough to make about six starts in succession without ever recharging. How important is battery recharging between starts? If it could be eliminated, we could get on with the second engine start more quickly. It would allow us to operate the air conditioner or heater and be ready to taxi a little bit sooner. The passengers might appreciate these things!

Our belief is that the battery recharge between starts is not important at all, **as long as the battery is well-charged initially.** It is included only because "it's always been done that way." It probably generates more battery heating than if the step were eliminated.

Wait a minute! How do we know if the battery *is* "well-charged initially?" If it is weak, then we *should* take the time to charge between starts, right? Right. There is a very simple way to tell.

What was the stabilized N1 of the first engine? Did you barely eke out 12%? If so, then your battery was puny; it needs to be recharged before it's ready to help with the second start. On the other hand, if your stabilized N1 zipped right up to the speed you were expecting – 16% to 20% – then you are wasting time charging your battery.

Because battery charging between starts is so traditional, and because sometime you *will* have a weak battery initially, our discussion will now proceed with the steps involved in the use of the first engine's generator for charging. **We will never say that a pilot is using incorrect procedures when he/she does the charging.**

On the other hand, the author, as well as hundreds of other pilots, will always shorten the starting procedure by eliminating the charging step…as long as the first engine's stabilized N1 met our expectations.

After the Ignition and Start switch is off, turn on the generator *if* you are going to charge the battery between starts. For earlier King Airs manufactured before 1976, the generator switch has two positions: Off at the bottom and On at the top. For later models, the switch has three positions: Off at the bottom, On in the center, and Reset at the top. Furthermore, the switch must be held up to Reset against spring tension; it will spring back from Reset to On of its own accord. If you have the three position switch, be certain to deliberately hold the switch up to the Reset position for at least one second, preferably two, before releasing it to On. This ensures that the GCU (Generator Control Unit) has time to set proper voltage before the line contactor relay closes and connects the generator to the electrical distribution system.

An interesting note: If one generator is already operating when the second generator is turned on, and if the pilot mistakenly taps the switch to Reset too quickly instead of deliberately holding it there for a second or so, invariably a very strange result occurs. Namely, the generator being activated comes on as expected, but the opposite generator trips off! We have observed frustrated pilots play "ping pong" with the generators…the left one comes on and the right one mysteriously shuts off, so they reset the right one and now the left shuts off, they reset the left and now the right shuts off, etc., etc. You get the idea. They can avoid this frustration by pausing a moment longer in the Reset position.

About this time, typically, it gets noticeable louder. What happened? The propeller of the engine you just started has finally received enough oil to come fully out of feather and is now resting on the Low Pitch Stop, at a rather flat blade angle. At high idle, in feather, the propeller has so much rotational drag that it will turn only about 400 RPM. When at the low pitch stop, however, its rotational resistance is much less and the RPM rises to about 1,300 – 1,600, depending upon the model type. That is the noise you are hearing.

Numerous pilots start PT6 powerplants with the propeller levers in feather. Many Beech checklists advocate this technique when doing an EPU start. By so doing, you are being nice to the ground crewman who must eventually unplug the External Power Unit by minimizing wind and noise. This technique has much merit. There is no question that the technique is quieter and results in less prop wash that may harm the flight control surfaces on that Bonanza whose tail is facing your King Air only one row away. On an icy, wintry, ramp, starting in feather may become mandatory if you want to avoid a scary, brakes-locked, slide on the ice into the hapless lineperson in front of you. A lot of taxi thrust exists at high idle when the props are out of feather!

Because of the free turbine nature of the PT6, what the prop is doing during the start plays virtually no role in how the engine starts. The N1s and ITTs observed will be nearly identical. Have you heard that a person can actually hold the propeller and keep it from turning while a PT6 is started? It's true!

So why not start in feather all of the time? A few reasons come to mind. First, earlier King Airs contain oil pressure gauges that are inoperative during the start because they rely on Alternating Current (AC), but AC is not yet available because an inverter is not normally on at this time. Hence, observing the propeller come out of feather is the only initial verification that the engine has enough oil pressure to get the oil from the engine's integral tank up to the propeller governor and its pump. Second, by moving oil from the governor pump into the propeller, more lubrication is being received at the propeller shaft's oil transfer location inside the engine. Third, the quicker that the propeller unfeathers, the quicker we start using prop wash (A) to promote better airflow across the oil cooler, (B) to promote better airflow across the battery box and its vents, (C) to promote better dissipation of exhaust gases so that the potential for heat damage to the airplane from stagnant, hot, exhaust is eliminated, and (D) to blow the exhaust fumes aft so that they are not sucked back into the engine and, possibly, brought into the cabin through the bleed air system.

Concerning items A through C just presented, a significant amount of time must transpire before any of these reasons becomes critical. Problems due to excessive exterior temperature near the engine are not going to happen immediately. Consequently, as stated before, we have no complaints with those who wish to make a feathered start their normal routine. However, unless the extra wind or noise created when the prop unfeathers will be a big problem, and presuming we are not starting on a slippery ramp, then our preference is to start with the propeller levers fully forward, and allow the propeller to unfeather right away.

So where were we? At high idle, with the starter switch off and the generator switch on. Now we wait for the generator load to decrease to a specified value...50% or 30%, depending upon whether your airplane has a NiCad or a Lead-Acid battery. NiCads permit higher charging rates than Lead-Acids, and thus the generator load may initially go as high as 100% when battery charging begins. The initial Lead-Acid charging rate rarely exceeds 60% load.

When the load decreases to the desired 50% or 30% value, turn off the generator switch. Activate the Ignition and Engine Start switch for the other engine, pause a couple of seconds, now re-activate the operating engine's generator just as you did before.

What we have just accomplished is the *initiation* of the start using battery power only, then the *continuation* of the start using both battery and generator power. This is known as a *generator-assisted start*. The generator's additional power is a great aid for starting the second engine. Instead of observing 16% – 20% stabilized N1 as we did on the first start, now, with the generator helping, we may see 20% – 24% speed. The extra speed and additional airflow will permit the second engine to start with an ITT peak that may be 100° cooler than that of the first start...similar to the ITT peak that occurs on *both* engines when starting with an EPU!

Beech procedures for the Super King Air 200/B200 models (prior to BB-1444) *mandate* the generator-assisted technique we have just introduced. However, for other models, the manufacturer

The King Air Book

permits the second start to be an actual *generator cross-start,* wherein the first engine's generator remains on at all times, even during second start initiation.

We firmly believe that enough benefits accrue from the generator off-then-on procedure – the generator-assisted procedure – that it is the best method to use for all models…except those with the "five bus" electrical system and the latest B200s. The greatest starter motor demand, the greatest starter workload, occurs when initiating compressor rotation. That is when the starter's current demand is the highest…perhaps 800 amps or more. Can the operating generator sustain this much current for a very short duration? Yes. However, by doing so, the generator certainly experiences more wear and tear. The generator adds additional load to its engine causing the Fuel Control Unit to introduce more fuel in an attempt to keep the engine from slowing down, resulting in a large ITT rise. Also, the generator sends a huge amount of current across one of the infamous *isolation limiters* and increases the potential for overheating and melting the limiter. These big 325 amp current limiters – fuses – are installed to prevent the entire electrical system from being wiped out by a major electrical problem and our electrical system's integrity is dramatically compromised if we blow one during engine start.

As engine speed increases, electrical demand decreases to 200 – 300 amps by the time N1 reaches about 20%. By initiating the start using the battery only and waiting a couple of seconds before turning the generator on, the demands placed on the generator and isolation limiters are greatly reduced.

Once the starter switch is activated and the first engine's generator is re-activated, the procedure becomes exactly the same as for the first start, with one exception. That is, when introducing fuel, there is no need for, nor benefit derived from, moving the condition lever all the way forward to High Idle. Instead, simply place it at the desired idle location.

Let's review this "desired idle location." If it is warm enough to be running the air conditioner or cold enough to require the use of Ground Maximum electric heat, then we do not want to operate the engines near 50% N1, the minimum low idle speed for those with three-blade propellers. Instead, 57 – 62% is better, since it is in compliance with generator load versus N1 speed limitations and also reduces ITT due to the extra engine airflow. Therefore, when we introduce fuel during the start of the second engine, we need to "guesstimate" where to position the Condition Lever between Low and High Idle, then set the position more accurately after the start is completed.

(All models equipped with four-blade propellers have their low idle speeds set high enough so that an even *higher* idle speed, following the second engine start, is virtually never required.)

Okay, let's catch up to where we stand. The first engine has been started and is running at High Idle speed. Using the generator-assisted start technique, now the second engine has also been started and is running at the idle speed we have chosen. Since the second start is now finished, turn off the second Ignition and Engine Start switch.

Now, for all models with the older style electrical system – *not* the five-bus version – find the buttons on the lower left corner of the loadmeters and push them both in together to inspect left and right main bus voltage.

Remember that only the first engine's generator is operating now. However, with proper electrical system integrity, *either* generator will supply its voltage to *both* main buses. That is what we need to carefully observe at this time…that both voltmeters are reading normal generator voltage, about 28 volts.

If we had experienced the unfortunate event of blowing one of the 325 amp current limiters – it seems to happen once out of a few thousand starts even when we do everything correctly – the voltage on the side we started second would be slightly low, about 24V, battery voltage only. In that case, it is time to shutdown and replace the limiter.

After we have verified that 28V exists on both sides, our next-to-last starting step is to activate the second engine's generator using the same technique we mentioned before. That is, if equipped with three position generator switches, hold to Reset, pause, then release to On.

Lastly, since two generators are on line together, sharing the workload, there is no reason to retain the High Idle setting on the first engine. Now is the time to adjust both condition levers to attain the exact idle speed you desire for the existing conditions.

Wow! We are finally done starting both PT6s! And we said it was *easy*?! Well, it really is, but enough expensive pitfalls exist during the procedure that it must never be done in a too casual or careless manner. Let's all be careful out there!

ENGINE STARTING...AGAIN

Class, it's time to revisit the topic of how to start the King Air's PT6 engines. Yes, I know we've plowed this ground before, but lately I have been observing enough incorrect procedures that I think it's time for a review.

I am going to presume that you are all ready for the start. In other words, you've completed the interior and exterior preflight checks and the Before Starting procedure. You've got the parking brake set, the power quadrant levers positioned where you want them, the lighting switches set appropriately, and you've verified the fuel quantity is to your liking. In the case of the 90, A90, B90, C90, or straight-100 variants, you've also either turned on the boost pump or are poised to do it as soon as you hit the start switch...my preferred technique. So let's move the start switch up to the Ignition and Engine Start position and take it from there.

While the starter spins and you wait for N1 to come up, you have time to check a couple of annunciators and it's important to do so. You are looking for the presence of one light and the absence of the other. The Fuel Pressure (red) annunciator should have extinguished and the Ignition light (yellow or green, depending on your model) should have illuminated.

If the Fuel Pressure light hasn't gone out, it could simply be due to a slow-to-respond pressure switch and the light will go out shortly. On the other hand, it may mean that the boost pump isn't working. Go ahead and finish the start and keep an eye on the light. If it is still on, try using the other side's electric boost pump via the crossfeed system to see if you can extinguish the light. If you are successful, it indicates that the pressure switch is operating properly so you must have a bad boost pump on the side you just started. Since it is illegal to takeoff with a known failure of the boost pump (the electric pump on the 90, A90, B90, or C90 variants, plus the straight 100, and the engine-driven boost pump on the others), shut down and seek professional help.

If, on the other hand, even crossfeed doesn't extinguish the Fuel Pressure annunciator, then you probably have a defective pressure switch. This is another no-go item, so, sadly, again it's time to abort the flight. Thank goodness that boost pumps and pressure switches are very reliable!

As for the Ignition annunciator, if you don't see it illuminated then you likely don't have the ignitors operating...either an ignition relay that didn't work or a tripped Ignitor circuit breaker. If you remember where the CB is and can locate it without a lot of fumbling around, go ahead and make a quick check and do a reset of the breaker if it's popped, while waiting to introduce fuel. If you are not sure where the CB is, abort the start and take time to find and check it.

What you absolutely, positively, *don't* want to do is move the condition lever forward to introduce fuel and *then* reset the CB as you belatedly discover that the lightoff didn't occur as you expected! It is definitely not a good idea to accumulate fuel first and then throw in the match!

To summarize, check for the two annunciators – one off, one on – while waiting for N1 to stabilize.

The next thing I want to remind you of is the desirability to let N1 totally stabilize at maximum speed before introducing fuel. The 12% N1 value quoted in the POH is a *minimum* value for ground starting. By allowing the starter to spin the compressor as fast as it can, more air is brought in which leads to cooler starts and a better guarantee that the fireball will be suspended in the middle of the burner can and not get so close to the liner as to cause heating and distortion problems. Also, by allowing N1 to stabilize, you can get a feel for battery condition. Seeing barely 14% for a final value tells you that the battery is quite depleted and you'll need to use the generator to charge it before the start of the second engine. Seeing 18% or more tells you that the battery is strong and that the charging step is unnecessary.

When the compressor speed has reached its peak, now is the time to slide the condition lever forward. Where to, Low Idle or High Idle?

Although I believe that taking that first engine's condition lever straight to High Idle is the better way to do it (except for the 300-series) – giving only one ITT peak instead of two – I guess it makes quite a few pilots feel uncomfortable. "Oh golly, what if I have to abort and I get caught by the hook when pulling the condition lever back?!" (Well, pull the lever out and around to miss the hook, just like you do at the end of the flight!) I am going to stop asking you to go straight to High Idle if it bothers you. However, I am now going to beg and plead that you don't leave the first condition lever at Low Idle very long.

Here's the thing: For those of you with three-blade propellers and hence have the Low Idle N1 set closer to 50% than 60%, you cannot turn on the first generator at Low Idle without violating at least one and possibly two limitations! The first limit – the one I will guarantee is being exceeded – is the one dealing with maximum allowable generator load as a function of N1 speed. In a nutshell, if you exceed 50% load at 50% Low Idle, you've blown it! The generator is getting hotter than it should because of the high workload without sufficient airflow. There is a fan attached to the generator shaft sucking air across the armature and windings. The more speed the generator has, the better it can cool itself.

The second limitation – the one that *may* be exceeded – is the Low Idle ITT limit. Remember that this important number is not marked on the gauge or placarded in the cockpit at all…dumb! It's in the POH of course. Here's a summary of the limit: For the PT6A-20, -20A, -135, and –135A: 685°C. For the –21, -28, and –41: 660°. For the –42 and –60A: 750°.

You know that the generator will be subjected to a reasonably high workload as soon as it is turned on, since it begins recharging the battery. If the engine is still at Low Idle, as the FCU (Fuel Control Unit, merely a governor of N1 speed) adds more fuel to give the engine sufficient power to drive the generator without a decrease in idle speed, up goes ITT. On a hot day at a higher elevation airport, it is easy to drive it past the Low Idle limit.

So the thing to realize about all of this is to never, ever, ever, turn on the first engine's generator while you are still at Low Idle. On the other hand, when the engine is at High Idle, now it is virtually impossible to exceed generator or ITT limits, no matter how hard the generator is working at the time. That's one of the reasons I like to go straightaway to High Idle, not hesitating first at Low Idle, when I move that first engine's condition lever forward.

Now for you folks with your Low Idles set closer to 60% than 50% – you with four-blade propellers – the chance than you will exceed generator cooling or ITT limits if you were to switch on the generator at Low Idle is almost impossible. Notice I didn't say "impossible," but "almost impossible." It'd take one hellishly hot day and a very depleted NiCad battery – NiCads receive more charge current initially than do lead-acid batteries when partially depleted – to cause the ITT limit to be busted, but it could happen. And since it "could happen," that's why I suggest that all of you, regardless of where your engines' Low Idle speeds are set, go to High Idle before you turn on the first engine's generator! Another consideration is that someday you may be asked to fly someone's older three-blade model, and if you have developed the incorrect procedure of turning on the generator at Low Idle – and haven't seen any problems with the four-blade model you usually fly – well, you are going to see problems now!

The next time you have your POH available, go to the Normal Procedures section and read, again, the manufacturer's own checklist for doing a battery start. Do you all see that the first generator switch doesn't get turned on until *after* the condition lever is at High Idle? I get disappointed seeing so many pilots do this backwards!

Many readers are already aware of my belief that charging the battery between the start of the first and second engine is usually unnecessary, wasteful of time, and, perhaps, detrimental to the battery's longevity. The only time that charging is important is when the battery showed itself to be weak during the first start, by not giving you the high stabilized N1 that you were anticipating.

I am going to concede that there is one – only one – situation in which I would feel comfortable seeing someone switch on that first generator at Low Idle. It would involve all of the following facts: (1) you are choosing to charge the battery between starts; (2) your airplane is

The King Air Book

equipped with a lead-acid type of battery, not a NiCad; (3) your airplane has four-blade propellers and hence has its Low Idle setting near 60%; (4) there is a reason for keeping noise and wind down…such as being near an open hangar with people working inside. In this unique case, I think it would show great judgment to charge the battery at Low Idle until the loadmeter dropped to 30%. At that time, however, if you are to avoid exceeding generator load limits, it is critical that now you move the condition lever to High Idle before hitting the second engine's start switch.

If your battery caused the first engine to spool up to the stabilized speed you were expecting, now you have the option of initiating the second start without battery charging. I suggest you do this: When the first engine reaches Hi Idle speed, turn off the first start switch, turn on the second start switch (and boost pump switch, if applicable), pause about two seconds, then turn on the first engine's generator. This technique – namely, doing a *generator-assisted* start of the second engine instead of a true *generator cross-start* – is mandatory per the POH procedure for the 200-series prior to BB-1444. Although the other models allow a cross-start, I see no advantage of doing it that way when you are not taking the time to do between-start battery charging. Waiting to turn on the first generator until the second engine has accelerated past 12% or so reduces the chance of overloading and failing a current limiter and reduces the shock-load that the first generator experiences. That reduced generator load, in turn, means less wear on the generator's drive splines and brushes and less rise in ITT.

The second engine, being assisted by the first engine's generator, will stabilize at a higher N1 speed than did the first one. This extra speed will bring in more air and make for a significantly cooler start. To allow both engines to share the benefits of cooler starts and to better-equalize generator workload…those are the two main reasons that I prefer alternating which engine I start first. For the older 90-series King Airs that have a supercharger on the left engine for their pressurization air source instead of using bleed air, starting the right engine first makes sense. Although some pilots argue that the battery's proximity to the right engine is a factor, it is such a tiny one as to be insignificant. If you have a King Air with bleed air, consider alternating your starts.

The next item I want to shed light on in this starting discussion is the turning on of the second generator, after you've finished your normal current limiter integrity check, of course. The second generator will not be subjected to the same high loads as the first, since it's not assisting in a start. Therefore, the emphasis I've tried to convey about the importance of being at High Idle *before* activating the first engine's generator does not apply.

I observe a lot of pilots who appear to believe that the engines should be close to the same speed before turning on the second generator. Where this comes from, I don't know, but it's bogus. There is no limitation whatsoever on having one generator operate at a faster speed than the other.

ENGINE STARTING...AGAIN

What this misguided belief leads to is the pulling back of the first engine to Low Idle before switching on the second generator. Again, read the manufacturer's checklist: You should get the second generator on *before* coming off of the first engine's High Idle condition. If the battery is still being charged significantly by the first generator after the second engine has finished being started, then we again stand the rare chance – I might say "almost impossible," remember? – of exceeding generator load limits and Low Idle ITT limits if we return to Low Idle with only one generator doing all the work. Instead, it is correct to get the second generator on while the first one is still spinning merrily away at about 70% speed. Only now, with both generators sharing the workload between them, is it 100% safe to pull that first condition lever back from its High Idle setting.

For you 60% Low-Idlers in the crowd, there is rarely ever a situation in which you cannot come to Low Idle on both condition levers now and be fine. But for you 50% Low-Idlers, you will almost certainly again exceed generator load limits if you operate either the air conditioning system or the electric heater while at Low Idle. Consequently, when it's time to leave High Idle, give careful consideration to where you want your idles to be. If you will have the AC or heater on, I strongly suggest that you set a mid-way idle condition of about 60%, snug up the friction knob for the condition levers, and don't move them back further until shutdown. It'll make your engines very happy!

Even the 60% Low-Idlers may need to tweak their condition levers forward a little bit at times. Why? To elevate the propeller speed above the minimum value limitation that all four-blade props have and that three-blade props don't have. There is a harmonic vibration that can negatively affect four-blade propellers if they idle too slowly on the ground. If you don't know what your minimum idle propeller speed limitation is, run get the POH – it'll be in the AFM Supplements section if the four-blade was not factory-installed – and find it now! Depending on your model, the number varies from 1050 RPM to 1250 RPM. Especially on cold mornings or with large electrical loads operating, you may need to adjust the condition levers slightly forward to ensure that the propellers do not fall below this important limitation.

One last comment: You'll notice that I have not mentioned whether the propeller levers were full forward or in feather prior to the start. It doesn't matter! When you desire to minimize prop wash and noise, feel free to start in feather. It should affect the start procedure in no way whatsoever. However, if one leaves the propellers in feather for a long time on the ground, then the risk of problems caused by the heat of the engine exhaust that is not being blown away by prop wash becomes a concern. Starting in feather is fine, but leaving the propellers in feather after starting is not fine. Shortly after you've turned on the second generator and have set the desired idle N1 with the condition levers, push those propeller levers full forward!

THE PT6 FUEL SYSTEM

This article will discuss the flow of fuel from the nacelle fuel tank to the engine's combustion chamber. How the fuel gets into the nacelle fuel tank varies widely among different King Air models and is fodder for another presentation. Once the fuel leaves the nacelle tank, however, whether the model is a straight 90 or a 350, there are more similarities than differences. By the time this presentation is completed, you should know more about such things as the High Pressure Pump, the Boost or Low Pressure Pump, the Fuel Heater, the Fuel Flow Transmitter, the Purge Valve, the "EPA Kit," and the Fuel Control Unit...the components in the engine compartment.

The High-Pressure Pump

Jet Fuel, basically kerosene, doesn't burn as easily as one may think. Some gutsy firemen demonstrate this by throwing a lighted match into a bucket of the stuff. Nothing happens, no big flash and boom! The match is merely extinguished by the liquid.

For Jet fuel to combust easily, it needs to be atomized into tiny vapor particles. The PT6's fourteen fuel nozzles exist for the purpose of properly atomizing the fuel. Their continued ability to do this is ensured by regular fuel nozzle maintenance. Allow a nozzle or two to clog such that the fuel squirts out in a nasty stream instead of in the desired, even, circular pattern, and expensive combustion chamber liner (i.e., "burner can") damage will eventually result.

Although the nozzle provides the passageway or shape that can create the desired atomization, the desired result cannot occur unless the fuel flows rapidly through the passage. If the flow is weak and slow, liquid fuel dribbles out of the nozzle; no atomization occurs. The flow of any fluid depends primarily on two factors. One is resistance. The other is differential pressure. If the pressure drop – differential pressure, usually abbreviated ΔP – across the resistance is low, then there isn't much "shove" to motivate the fluid to move. Even with a relatively high ΔP, little flow results if the hole is small.

The passage through the fuel nozzles is very small, making their resistance very high. Hence, there needs to be a very high differential pressure across the nozzles to achieve the fuel flow required to create the power desired. The pressure that exists downstream of the fuel nozzle is beyond our control. It depends upon the combustion process occurring in the burner can. The upstream pressure is determined by a pump that is capable of creating very high pressures.

This pump goes by various names: "Engine Fuel Pump," "High-Pressure Pump," "Engine-driven Pump" have all been used. The earlier King Air models – 90 through C90 as well as the straight 100 – have only one engine-driven pump per side, per engine. In the early days, referring to the "Engine-driven pump" always directed our attention to the high-pressure pump. Later King Air models, however, introduced another engine-driven pump, a low-pressure boost pump. For these models, reference to an engine-driven pump results in confusion. Do we mean the high-pressure pump or the boost pump?

That is why I always try to include "high-pressure" whenever I refer to this pump, the only one that is strong enough to atomize the fuel. Without the high-pressure pump, a PT6 cannot run. There is no backup for it. When we contemplate the relatively low number of complete PT6 power failures, we conclude that the high-pressure pump is very reliable and dependable. But when they fail – and they do, rarely! – Goodbye engine.

A pump that is designed to produce very high discharge pressures must have little if any "slippage." The moving and stationary parts of the pump must fit tightly together. Each revolution of the pump delivers the same amount of fuel. For this reason, these pumps are characterized as "Positive Displacement" pumps, since each turn of the pump displaces or moves the same amount of liquid. A positive displacement pump not only is capable of producing very high discharge pressures but also it is capable of creating very low inlet pressures. In the truest sense of the word, it really sucks!

If the sucking – the reduction of pressure at the pump inlet – gets strong enough, vapor bubbles begin to form in the incoming liquid. Dissolved gases can come out of solution, as they do when a soda pop bottle is uncapped allowing the pressure to suddenly decrease. In the soda bottle, the bubbles are expected and harmless. In the pump, they can be quite destructive.

Bubbles destructive? How can that be? First, as the vapor bubble displaces liquid in the pump, pump lubrication suffers. The moving parts no longer contain a protective coating of liquid, so cooling and cushioning of the parts are reduced. Second, as the fluid mixture of liquid and vapor move through the pump, pressure rises as the pump "does its thing." Soon, the vapor bubble finds itself surrounded by higher and higher-pressure liquid until it cannot remain a bubble any longer. Like the bursting of a balloon, but in reverse, the bubble "implodes" back to liquid. The inrush of liquid into the bubble void may smack the pump walls and gears or vanes with a force similar to that a diver feels when he or she belly flops from the three-meter platform. Ouch! Given enough time, these mini-implosions will destroy the pump.

There is a word that describes the events we are discussing…Cavitation. Cavitation can be defined as the formation and subsequent collapse of vapor bubbles in a liquid caused by the liquid pressure getting too low. All King Air models contain a limitation that restricts accumulated time of operation in a cavitating-likely environment to ten hours. After that, the high-pressure pump must be replaced, since the guarantee of its continued safe operation has been compromised. How do we know that cavitation may be taking place? Because the "Fuel Pressure" warning annunciator is illuminated, indicating that the inlet pressure to the high-pressure pump has dropped low enough that vapor bubbles may be forming. (The 90, A90, and B90 models contain left and right fuel pressure gauges by which boost pump pressure can be monitored. Cavitation is presumed to be occurring when the gauge reads zero with the engine running.)

The Boost Pump or Pumps

Since only the high-pressure pump can provide the fuel pressure necessary to run the engine, the boost pump's purpose is *not* to act as a backup unit for the high-pressure pump but instead it is to protect the high-pressure pump from cavitation. It does this by supplying a nominal value of about 30 psi to the inlet or suction side of the high-pressure pump.

The straight 90 and straight 100 King Air models contain two electrically-driven boost pumps, referred to as the Primary and Secondary Boost Pumps. Either pump may be operated to prevent cavitation. If one fails, the other is readily available. (In fact, in the straight 90, the Secondary Boost Pump's switch has an "Auto" position that enables the pump to start up automatically whenever the Primary Boost Pump quits.) The A90, B90, and all versions of the C90 contain a single electrically-driven boost pump and an automatic crossfeed system. In the event of a boost pump failure, the crossfeed valve automatically opens to permit the remaining boost pump to supply fuel to, and prevent cavitation of, both left and right high-pressure pumps.

(Before we continue to talk about the later models – the ones with an engine-driven boost pump – let me remind you of the downside to the A90, B90, and C90 automatic crossfeed system…because it can be a major headache! To prevent cavitation is an admirable goal, sure, but to prevent fuel starvation is a better one! When a boost pump fails and the crossfeed system automatically begins to supply fuel from the remaining boost pump to both left and right high-pressure pumps, the airplane's fuel supply has been cut in half. The fuel on only one side of the airplane is supplying both engines.

What if that is not enough? If we need the fuel on the bad pump's side, how do we get it? The answer is simple…we move the crossfeed switch to the Closed position. The "Fuel Pressure" light illuminates as the high-pressure pump begins to "suction lift" the fuel without the boost pump's assistance. Cavitation is now likely to be occurring, so the clock starts running, accumulating time toward the ten-hour limit. Ten hours is a long time! We surely won't reach it before we land from *this* flight!

Unfortunately, a few pilots appear to have made the avoidance of cavitation their number one priority, placing it above the importance of not inducing an engine failure! Here's how it goes: To make things easier to follow, let's presume the boost pump on the left side was the one that quit. The right fuel is supplying both engines. Being reluctant to close the crossfeed switch, and thereby requiring cavitation time keeping, the pilot continues until the right side fuel is nearly consumed. Seeing that he now *must* use the left side fuel – maybe the headwinds were stronger than forecast – he reluctantly stops crossfeeding, by moving the switch, closing the valve. In a short time, the right fuel supply is exhausted. Can you see what is coming? You got it! The right engine quits.

All that lovely fuel on the left side is useless to the right engine, without a good left boost pump to push it across! The right high-pressure pump much prefers to suck vapor (air) out of its own empty tank than to suck liquid (fuel) all the way from the other side.

For goodness sake, people, don't allow a boost pump failure on one side to lead to an engine failure on the other side just because you were reluctant to close the crossfeed valve! If there is *any* doubt that you may need more than half the existing fuel, move that switch to the Closed position!)

(*Author's note: In the summer of 2009 the latest instance of C90 fuel mismanagement was described in the media. Following the illumination of the Crossfeed annunciator – indicative of boost pump failure – it seems the crew continued on without performing the proper checklist procedure and, so it seems, without examining the fuel quantity gauges at all! Now when the side feeding both engines went empty, of course both engines quit simultaneously since they both sucked air from the empty nacelle. Had they at least noticed that the feeding side was getting low and had closed the crossfeed switch in response, only one engine would have quit, not both.*)

Where were we? Oh yeah, we were discussing the different boost pump arrangements in PT6-powered King Airs. E90s and F90s, A100s, 200s and B200s, 300s and 350s…all have an engine-driven boost pump as well as the engine-driven high-pressure pump. What a great improvement!

Now, the electrically-driven boost pump becomes primarily a backup, to be used in the exceedingly rare situation of engine-driven boost pump failure. Hence, its name: Standby Pump. Yes, it is still needed for crossfeed and may be required when using volatile gasoline at very high altitudes, but most of the time the electrically-driven pump is not used at all.

All boost pumps in King Airs are non-positive displacement pumps, with loose clearances and plenty of slippage. Even if the engine-driven boost pump should lock up and not be able to turn, the electrically-driven pump can still easily move fuel through the dead pump on its way toward the high-pressure pump.

Since the boost pump does not contain the tight clearances that make for high discharge pressures, it cannot push too hard and it cannot suck too hard. That helps explain why it is the *first* component that the fuel goes to after it leaves the nacelle tank and passes through the open firewall shutoff valve…we don't want it to have to suck through too long of a pipe! It is upstream of all other components forward of the firewall.

The Firewall Fuel Filter

Fuel flows from the boost pump through a filter that is located near the bottom center of the engine firewall…the firewall fuel filter. All King Air models contain a drain at this point. A few models – F90s, F90-1s, 300s, and 350s – contain a red-colored button that, when popped up, signifies that the filter element is being bypassed. The cowling of these models is not typically opened during a normal preflight inspection – except for the F90, that requires opening the cowling to check engine oil quantity and to pull the ring that drains the firewall fuel filter – hence the bypass button is inspected more often by maintenance instead of flight crew personnel. Don't sweat it too much. Remember that most models don't even contain a bypass indicator.

The Fuel Flow Transducer

One of the engine instruments of importance to the flight crew is, obviously, the fuel flow indicator. This is an electric gauge powered by 26 volts AC from the inverter on earlier models and by 28 volt DC on the later ones, after about 1977. The fuel flow transducer is the device that measures fuel flow (by use of spinning vanes in the fuel stream), converts the measurement to an electric output, and sends it to the indicator for display. For the great majority of King Airs – and we will cover the exception later – this transducer is located on the firewall, just downstream of the firewall fuel filter. At that position, it is measuring the fuel flowing between the boost pump and the high-pressure pump.

It is understandable that many King Air pilots and mechanics are surprised by this location. In their minds, the Fuel Control Unit (FCU) – as it does its job of metering fuel to the engine – sends excess fuel through a return line back to the nacelle tank…kind of like many fuel-injection systems in piston engine-powered airplanes. If this concept were true, then the fuel flow reading would not be correct; it would be too high, since it would include the return fuel as well as the fuel received by the engine.

In truth, however, the FCU doesn't work like they assume it does. Think of it this way: The high-pressure pump supplies the FCU with an over-abundance of fuel, but the FCU only uses what it needs. Instead of a return path, the unnecessary fuel merely "backs up" at the FCU inlet and prevents additional flow. This is not a very scientific description, but it works for me and I hope it helps for you.

"But wait, there is a return line from the FCU back to the nacelle tank! I can see it in the POH's Fuel System Schematic! It has a valve in it labeled "Purge Valve." What's it all about?" Good question! Read on!

The Purge Valve

Bubbles in the high pressure fuel stream to the nozzles are not a good thing. In fact, they can be quite harmful to the life of the hot section. When the bubble passes through the nozzle, the atomized spray is momentarily interrupted and the fire in that localized area of the burner can goes out. In the next moment, new liquid fuel returns and the fire begins again. This stopping and starting of the fire, extinguishing and relighting, wreaks havoc on the poor combustion chamber, leading to cracking, distortion, and premature replacement.

Where do the bubbles originate? First, whenever this part of the fuel system is opened up for maintenance – replacing a fuel filter, repairing a leaky firewall shutoff valve, etc. – air will enter the lines and displace the fuel that was there. During the next start, the air must get purged from the system before the liquid fuel is allowed to flow to the nozzles. Second, high temperatures in the nacelle have the potential for boiling fuel in the system after shutdown. Once again, these bubbles must be eliminated before fuel reaches the nozzles.

The activation of the purge valve in earlier King Air models – all 90s except the F90, F90-1, C90A and C90B, plus the 100 and A100 – is triggered by the Ignition and Engine Start switch. Whenever that switch is in the up (Ignition and Engine Start) or down (Starter Only) position, electric power is applied to the normally-closed purge valve to power it to the open position. In the later models – all 200s, B200s, C90As, C90Bs, F90s and F90-1s – not only was the purge valve triggered by the Ignition and Engine Start switch but also by the Auto-Ignition switch, in combination with low torque. In other words, the act of merely *arming* auto-ignition does not activate the purge valve, but when auto-ignition actually *operates*, then the purge valve opens. It is my opinion that this inclusion of the auto-ignition trigger is a good improvement, since there is no purging of vapor bubbles in the earlier models during a windmilling airstart procedure.

It is quite easy to verify that the purge valve is operating properly by observing a drop in fuel flow reading when the starter switch is turned off. Also, for the later models, seeing a slight (10 to 20 pph) increase in fuel flow when Auto-Ignition switch is armed at idle power checks the second triggering mechanism. Remember that many earlier models have AC-powered fuel flow gauges that will not typically be operative during the start. Turn on the inverter to activate the fuel flow gauges when you want to conduct this starting check.

Purge Valve Exceptions, and the 300-series

If your airplane has been modified with a digital fuel flow sensing system, or if it contains the Foxboro fuel measuring system option, then the fuel flow transducers are likely located downstream of the FCU where the returning purge fuel cannot be measured. There is no cockpit check that can be made to verify purge system operation.

The FCU is manufactured by Woodward, not Bendix, in the 300-series of King Airs, which includes 300s and 350s. In these models, Raytheon places the fuel flow transducer downstream of the FCU in the line to the nozzles, in such a location that the additional purge fuel flow will never be seen. Due to this change, there is no longer a need for an electrically-operated purge valve. That is, since the fuel returning through the purge line will not lead to an inaccurate fuel flow indication, the purge line can remain open at all times. Hence, there is always a slight trickle of fuel returning back the nacelle tank, clearing out any vapor bubbles.

The most recent B200s and C90Bs also have their fuel flow transducers in the downstream location, making purge valve checks impossible from the cockpit.

The Oil-to-Fuel Heat Exchanger

Before the fuel enters the high-pressure pump, it is heated, using the energy contained in warm engine oil. A thermostatic valve senses fuel temperature and adjusts the oil flow in an attempt to maintain a desired fuel temperature of about 90 degrees Fahrenheit. On hot days, with the fuel already having been warmed by the sun on the ramp, oil may bypass the heat exchanger totally. Since the temperature of the heated fuel will prevent the formation of ice crystals that may clog the FCU's metering passages, "Prist" is very rarely needed as an additional anti-icing fuel additive.

The Pilot's Operating Manual for earlier models contains a graph that allows a "Minimum Oil Temperature" to be determined, based upon altitude and OAT. So long as the oil temperature is above this minimum value, then Prist need not be used. Unless the oil cooler's vernatherm valve is malfunctioning, giving a much cooler-than-typical oil temperature, it is a rare situation indeed in which the anti-icing additive must be used. (It is always okay to use it, if you want!)

In all of the Pilot's Operating Handbooks for 300s and 350s as well as some later B200s and all C90Bs, Raytheon took a more conservative approach. They removed the Minimum Oil Temperature graph and replaced it with a blanket requirement to use Prist whenever operation is conducted with an OAT below minus 40 degrees.

Fuel density changes as fuel temperature changes. By heating the fuel to a constant temperature before it is metered, the FCU has an easier task to perform. Without the temperature control, there would be situations in which the FCU has to work with warmer, thinner, fuel and others in which it must cope with colder, thicker, fuel. This would lead to variations in metering that would show up most predominately as differing acceleration rates when power is increased. If your left and right engines are not accelerating together, and if rigging adjustments fail to cure the problems, fuel temperature at the FCU is an important item for maintenance personnel to check.

The Fuel Control Unit

What a complex device! We could spend pages and pages describing the detailed operation of the FCU, but we won't. (See *Pneumatic Fuel Management,* starting on page 153.)

Instead, let me boil it down to the essentials: ***The FCU is a pneumatically-controlled governor of N1 speed.*** When we move the power lever to a certain position, we are telling the FCU what compressor speed we desire. The FCU then adjusts fuel flow to give us that desired speed. When we leave the power lever in one position, all significant engine parameters except N1 can change considerably. Torque? Watch it decrease as ice vanes are extended. ITT? Watch it increase when bleed air is turned on. Fuel Flow? Watch it drop as you climb into thinner air. But N1? No, it is as solid as a rock, never changing until we reposition the power lever.

In a similar, more familiar, example, it can be said that the propeller governor is a hydraulically-controlled governor of propeller speed. If the hydraulic pressure (oil pressure) is lost, the King Air's blade angle is designed to fail into the feathered position, adding to safety by cleaning up drag. Likewise, if the FCU's pneumatic pressure (P3) is lost, the FCU's fuel flow decreases to the minimum value, preventing harm to the engine. Depending on the engine's power rating, minimum fuel flow values are usually between 80 and 100 pph.

One should suspect problems with the FCU if N1 fluctuates or if acceleration or deceleration rates are improper. However, a malfunctioning FCU cannot cause changing ITT, N1, and Fuel Flow trends as determined by Engine Condition Trend Monitoring, ECTM. What the engine does with the fuel it receives from the FCU is determined by the engine, not by the FCU.

The FCU also contains the fuel shutoff valve that is closed by pulling the Condition Lever into the Fuel Cutoff position (except for the E90 and F90, as discussed below).

The Flow Divider/Dump Valve

The metered fuel from the FCU goes directly to the single fuel nozzle manifold on PT6A–6, –20, and –20A engines, and that manifold, in turn, supplies all fourteen fuel nozzles. All other PT6 models contain two fuel manifolds, primary and secondary. The FCU sends fuel to a device located at the bottom of the two fuel manifolds: the *Flow Divider/Dump Valve.* This device, as the name implies, divides the flow such that it feeds only the primary manifold first, causing the combustion process to begin more gradually and cooler since all fuel is not received immediately. As the engine accelerates, as fuel pressure rises, a spring-loaded transfer valve within the Flow Divider opens to allow fuel to fill the secondary manifold, and the remaining nozzles join in. A slight hesitation in N1 acceleration and ITT rise as the secondary nozzles join in is the typical indication of the "two-stage" start caused by the Flow Divider.

Once the condition lever is pulled back into the Fuel Cutoff position, fuel pressure in the manifold(s) drops immediately. No longer can the fuel be atomized into a fine mist by the nozzles. Unless an alternate "path of least resistance" were provided, the residual fuel would seep through the nozzles into the hot combustion chamber, be converted into vapor, and exit the engine in the form of white smoke. Seeing this fuel "steam" at shutdown indicates a problem. "Coking" of the fuel nozzles – leaving carbon that will interfere with proper spray pattern creation – will likely result if the residual fuel must exit through the nozzles. A Dump Valve – part of the Flow Divider/Dump Valve on the later engines and a separate device on the single-manifold engines – is provided to eliminate the coking problem. As soon as fuel pressure in the manifold decreases, the dump valve springs to the open position and allows residual fuel to find a path of least resistance away from the nozzles. Where does this path lead?

Up until about 1975, the dump valve merely dumped the fuel onto the ramp. At every engine shutdown, a few tablespoons of fuel would be vented onto the tarmac. By the way, since this fuel used the oil breather outlet – just behind the oil cooler and in front of the wheel well – as its drain tube, it was found that the propeller's idling air flow could blow this fuel aft onto the main landing gear tires. Over a period of time, the Jet fuel tended to deteriorate the rubber of the tires. To eliminate the "prop wash," the Beech checklist for earlier King Air models directed the pilot to feather the propeller before cutting off the fuel...Propeller Levers *before* Condition Levers. Since no King Airs in the United States still exist that dump fuel onto the ramp at shutdown, Raytheon's current thinking calls for Propeller Levers *after* Condition Levers.

An Environmental Protection Agency directive led to elimination of the fuel dumping onto the ramp at shutdown. Two methods have been employed to comply with the directive...a Fuel Drain Collector or a Purge Accumulator. The Fuel Drain Collector system – often referred to as the "EPA Kit" – is provided so that the fuel leaving the Dump Valve will be directed into a small tank instead of being allowed to dump onto the ramp. The system is surprisingly complex, yet quite reliable. It includes a float switch in the tank to sense the fuel being received there, an electric pump, a return line to the nacelle fuel tank, a checkvalve, and an overboard vent just in case something fails to work properly.

The Beech engineers needed to find a power source for the left and right fuel drain collector pumps. Before two dedicated circuit breakers – located on the right side panel – were installed in the

The King Air Book

later models with this system, the engineers used the existing "Fuel Control Heat" circuit breakers…which are the Fuel Control Heat switches themselves. Some King Air instructors believe that it is best to leave the Fuel Control Heat switches on until after shutdown, so that the pump can operate at that time. Although I see nothing wrong with this procedure, I don't teach it to my students nor follow it myself. I see nothing wrong in allowing the fuel to sit in the collector tank until after the next start, and then get pumped into the nacelle tank after the Fuel Control heat switches are reactivated. After all, each shutdown only fills the tank to about one-third of its total capacity.

It is not an unheard of condition to find a steady drip of fuel finding its way onto the ramp or hangar floor, with the fuel coming from the Fuel Drain Collector tank, via the vent into the oil breather tube. Maintenance personnel should inspect the checkvalve in the return line between the collector tank and the nacelle fuel tank. If it allows backwards flow, the nacelle tank will drain back into the collector tank. Since one cannot fit a gallon into a pint container, overboard it goes!

Starting in about 1980, a simplified system replaced the Fuel Drain Collector. Pressurized air from the engine's compressor – P3 air – is fed through a checkvalve into a hollow cylindrical tank or accumulator bottle. The other end of the tank contains a line with another checkvalve, and this line terminates at the Dump Valve. In normal operation, fuel pressure is greater than air pressure but the checkvalve prevents the flow of fuel into the accumulator. After the condition lever is moved into the Cutoff position, causing fuel pressure to decrease, the trapped high-pressure air now automatically flows into the fuel manifold. This air charge allows the nozzles to continue to atomize the fuel properly until nothing remains but air…a simple, elegant, solution to help prevent environmental contamination.

A couple of comments are in order about the accumulator system. First, if kerosene odor is experienced in the cockpit and cabin, especially during power application for takeoff, a likely source is the accumulator. If the checkvalves leak, fuel can find its way into the bleed air system and be fed into the airplane's interior. Second, smoking at shutdown indicates that the accumulator is not performing well and it should be checked for malfunction. I have never seen a comment from Raytheon advising that high power be applied, at least once, prior to engine shutdown. However, common sense and some empirical evidence suggests that the accumulator won't be properly charged with air if the engine is started, allowed only to idle, and then shutdown…such as may occur during some maintenance checks. In my opinion, achieving at least 85 – 90% N1, followed by at least a minute of idling cool down, is a good idea.

E90 and F90 Differences

The PT6A-28 or –135 engine models, as used on E90s and F90s, have a slightly different engine fuel system. On those two models, the Flow Divider/Dump Valve is replaced by the Start Control. Two fuel lines, not one, leave the FCU and arrive at the Start Control. This unit contains the shutoff valve operated by the condition lever and the mechanisms that allow it to act as a flow divider and dump valve. Two lines also leave the Start Control…one feeding the primary nozzles and the other feeding the secondary nozzles. It is exceedingly common for later E90s and F90s (LW-334 and after, LA-57 and after) to smoke slightly at shutdown. I think I know why.

These models use the same accumulator tank as their later King Air brethren (C90s, 200s, etc.) but they have twice as much fuel to purge since two lines, not one, flow to the nozzles! I believe that all of the air charge is used up before the last bit of fuel gets blown forcefully through the nozzles. Someone devised a surprising but effective way of eliminating the fuel vapor smoke…they burn it by turning on the Auto-Ignition Switches prior to shutdown! This has been done for years with no apparent detrimental side effects. If you haven't learned this technique, and if you have a smoker, give it a try.

Summary

So there it is, more than you ever wanted to know about the fuel components in the engine compartment! Isn't it amazing that they all work so well, so much of the time?

THE CONDITION LEVER

(AN OFTEN OVERLOOKED TOOL)

Introduction

While teaching courses to pilots who are new to the PT6-powered King Air, one of the many new and challenging items that is presented is the Condition Lever, that mixture-like device that sits on the right side of the power quadrant. I often find that the newcomer finishes his or her training knowing that the Condition Lever is the normal method by which fuel is introduced and terminated during starts and shutdowns, but with little further knowledge about this very important engine control. The intent of this article is to educate King Air pilots about the entire gamut of worthwhile uses of the Condition Lever. I firmly believe that this control, when used correctly, has a direct bearing on overall engine health.

Starting and Shutdown

After the engine's compressor speed (N1 or Ng) has stabilized at its maximum value as driven by the starter, fuel is allowed to flow into the combustion chamber by pushing the Condition Lever forward out of the Fuel Cut-Off position. This action does two things: It opens a manually-controlled fuel cut-off valve and it sets the Fuel Control Unit (FCU) to govern N1 at a particular speed, based on how far the Condition Lever is moved forward.

Going about halfway forward to the Low Idle position – in which the Condition Lever is either inside of or abeam the hook in the gate that prevents inadvertent fuel cut-off – selects the lowest of the idle-range N1 speeds. Depending upon the type of King Air, this can be a value between about 50% and 60%. Going all the way forward to the High Idle position selects about 70% N1 for all models. Positioning the Condition Lever between the Low and High Idle positions will select a corresponding idle speed between 50/60% and 70%.

How the engine gets from starter-stabilized speed to final idle speed usually depends on the FCU exclusively…the only role the Condition Lever plays is in telling the (Bendix) FCU the value of the desired final idle speed. In other words, placing the Condition Lever further forward will not cause more fuel to be initially introduced and hence it will have no affect on starting temperature or starting acceleration characteristics. The only thing that the Condition Lever can affect is where the acceleration stops.

The King Air Book

That explains why I suggest that most King Air pilots go straight to High Idle when moving the Condition Lever forward when starting their first engine. It is very important that this engine is at High Idle speed before using its generator to help start the second engine, and by going to that position straight away there is no chance that we may forget to move the lever forward later.

There are at least two exceptions to this "straight to High Idle on the first start" suggestion: First, while starting an extremely cold engine, cold-soaked at below freezing temperatures, I would feel better running at Low Idle for a minute or two, allowing the propeller to unfeather and for oil pressure to stabilize, before going on to High Idle. Second, the Woodward FCUs used on the 300-series of King Airs, contain a 3-D cam that does indeed seem to make the engine start a few degrees hotter if the Condition Lever is pushed up to High Idle initially. For those models, I suggest leaving Low for High Idle just as the ITT reaches the starting peak. This eliminates a second, much smaller, spike that occurs if the engine is allowed to stabilize at Low Idle before going the rest of the way forward to High Idle.

At shutdown, make certain that you move the Condition Lever fully and firmly all the way to the far aft, Fuel Cut-off, position. The goal is to stop the fuel flow entirely, and have no potential for residual fuel seeping through the nozzles, dribbling into the combustion chamber, and yielding clogged-up, coked-up, nozzles and localized combustion chamber liner cold spots where the liquid fuel impacted.

Milking the Condition Lever...a No-No!

The first versions of the PT6 series of engines – the –6 and –20 models – had a single fuel manifold feeding all fourteen nozzles, unlike the more modern versions that have two manifolds and hence introduce fuel during start in a two-stage manner. With all nozzles spraying together initially, while so little air exists in the combustion chamber, the early versions tend to start with a noticeably higher ITT peak than do the later ones. Because of this, a couple of methods were devised by misguided, inventive, pilots that enabled the engine to start cooler, even when operating with a very weak battery that failed to generate much more than the minimum required 12% speed. I have heard both of these techniques referred to as "milking" the Condition Lever.

Where did the term "milking" come from? My guess is that it relates to the Webster's definition that says one meaning of milking is "...compelling or persuading to yield profit or advantage illicitly or to an unreasonable degree." For example, "Yeah, he milked all the sympathy he could get out of that sprained ankle!" Although I bet there is some old-timer who could enlighten us on the true story behind these milking techniques, here is my understanding of the two versions.

In the first milking method, the inverter was turned on before starting so that the old AC-powered fuel flow gauges would be operative. Then, when moving the condition lever forward, it was done very slowly and carefully, and forward motion was stopped just when the slightest fuel flow indication was observed. By not opening the manual fuel cut-off valve all the way, added resistance was introduced, flow was decreased, and the engine usually started cooler. Sounds good, eh? Sounds good, but is bad! The added resistance lowers the pressure of the fuel at the nozzles and leads to weak and improper spray patterns that are detrimental to the hot section's health due to the localized hot spots that result.

The second milking method involves a series of On-Off actions with the condition lever. The pilot using this technique starts with a self-imposed starting ITT limit. For example, suppose the chosen value is the normal redline for PT6A-20-powered models (750 degrees), instead of the actual starting redline (1090 degrees). After moving the condition lever forward, as the rising ITT approached 750, the pilot would immediately snatch the condition lever back to Cut-Off. Instantaneously, ITT would fall as the combustion process ceased, but the compressor's momentum would cause the reduction in N1 speed to lag a bit. Before the N1 dropped too much, fuel was again introduced. This time, however, due to the slight gain in compressor speed that was achieved before the first cut, there is now slightly more cooling air available so the ITT peak would tend to be lower. Still, if it approached the self-imposed limit, another cut was made. This series continued until finally the engine started, with the ITT staying below the target value.

Again, sounds like a rather clever way of minimizing ITT, doesn't it? But, like before, the disadvantages tend to outweigh the advantages. The igniting and then sudden quenching of the flame in the combustion chamber leads to thermal stress that in the long run is likely to be more harmful than the stress caused by one ITT starting peak, even though the peak is higher.

So file away the milking techniques for times when you are stranded in Podunkville with a very weak battery and no help around. Maybe, just maybe, these weird techniques could get you started and on your way home, whereas a standard technique would yield an unsuccessful, hot-start, situation. Better yet, don't leave something on and run the battery down! The Condition Lever was never meant to be a milking tool!

Adjusting Low Idle Speed

I mentioned previously that Low Idle speeds were in the 50% to 60% range, approximately. To determine exactly what your minimum N1 should be at idle, do the following. Turn to the "Engine Limitations" table in your Pilot's Operating Manual or Pilot's Operating Handbook (POM or POH) and find what is listed for the limiting Low Idle speed. Now, if your King Air has been modified by changing to a four-blade Hartzell or McCauley propeller, go to the POM/POH supplement that covers the installation and review what the new limitations are. At the end of a flight, when all is warm and stabilized (and with the power levers slightly behind the Idle position, slightly into Beta, so that you are certain you are truly seeing the lowest idle speed), what do you see as the idling N1 when the Condition Levers are set at Low Idle?

Is it okay? Great! Is it below the limit or more than 3% above the limit? If so, then record this as a squawk that you will have maintenance personnel address during your next Phase inspection. Meanwhile, if the N1 is too low, use your Condition Lever for tweaking the idle speed up to the proper value. It is touchy! Take your time, set it carefully, then tighten down the friction knob and don't move the condition lever again until shutting down.

Also, for all of you with four-blade propeller installations, notice that the Engine Limitations – either in the POM/POH or in the propeller supplement – state a minimum idle propeller speed. This value ranges from 1050 to 1250 RPM, depending upon the model and the propeller.

Again, at the end of a flight, and preferably on a day with calm winds, determine if your idling propeller speed is above the limit. It is? Good! No? Then, until your maintenance shop has a chance to work its magic, tweak the condition lever until your gas generator is generating enough gas that it forces the propeller to idle fast enough. It is amazing how that little Condition Lever, adjusted properly by the pilot, can compensate for some careless, incorrect, maintenance adjustments!

Even if both left and right propeller idling speeds are acceptable, it is a minor nuisance if they are operating at slightly different speeds. Again, tweaking the slower side's condition lever to increase idle compressor speed will also increase idle propeller speed until both sides are identical. Isn't that nicer? Doesn't it sound better? Doesn't it tend to taxi straighter?

Complying with Generator Limitations

While you've got your POM/POH open, checking the idle limits, check something else. Review the table that shows the minimum N1 speed as a function of generator load. Find that one? See what it says? Typically, for many King Air 90 and 100 models, when carrying more than 50% generator load, the minimum N1 speed has to be above 57%. Well, with the electrically driven air-conditioning system on and while charging the battery after starting, it is almost a certainty that generator load will exceed 50%. Were you aware of this? Have you been inadvertently violating a generator cooling limitation by operating your air conditioner at Low Idle? Again, here is where proper condition lever usage is so important! On hot days with air conditioning on, make sure you tweak the condition levers forward enough to comply with the generator load limit. Want to make it simple? I would always suggest operating at about 60% N1 speed, minimum, if the OAT is above 25 to 30 degrees Celsius. For all you four-blade guys and gals with properly adjusted Low Idles, you are already set in this vicinity. Nice!

By the way, I have observed many pilots move the condition levers away from their nicely tweaked proper Low Idle-corrected settings and slip them back to the Low Idle hooks when taking the runway for departure. Why? Don't do this! If it's okay for pre-takeoff taxiing, then it is okay for post-landing taxiing. Leave them alone!

In a similar fashion, don't hesitate in shutting the engine down by moving the condition lever from its elevated idle position right back to cut-off in one motion. Do you, like many other pilots, always pull back to Low Idle and let things stabilize before shutting down? Don't! If it is hot enough to operate the air conditioner, then it is hot enough to do all in our power to minimize ITT for at least the last minute prior to shutdown. How do we do this? By turning off the bleed air and the air conditioning as we leave the runway (while leaving the vent blower on for comfort), leaving the condition levers set for about 60%, avoiding power applications while taxiing in, and then shutting down in one smooth motion to cut-off with the condition levers. Your engines are going to have warm fuzzy feelings for you when you treat them like this!

Maximum Reverse Utilization

Let's face it: Few King Airs really need to demonstrate maximum-effort short field landing practice, since the takeoff roll is usually longer than the landing roll, even when no special short field technique is used. But for those times you really want to show off and stop on a dime, what technique works best? Here again, condition lever position plays a big role.

The classic recommendation for a maximum effort short field landing is to push the condition levers fully forward to the High Idle position before beginning the short field approach. In so doing, the N1 speeds should never decrease below about 70%. Since a typical traffic pattern is flown with N1 speeds well above 70%, the condition levers' position makes no noticeable change until the flare. Now, the airplane tends to float more due to the increased idle power. If this floating tendency is not anticipated and combated using proper airspeed, power reduction, and flare techniques, any short field benefit to be realized is nullified by the excessive distance consumed by the float prior to touchdown.

However, when properly learned and executed, I believe that the selection of High Idle for short field landings really does lessen the total landing distance. By keeping the engines spooled up to 70% while the power levers are transitioning between the Idle and Maximum Reverse positions, maximum reverse N1 speed (about 85%) can be obtained more quickly, without unnecessary spool-up time. Does High Idle yield *more* reverse power? No! Not at all! But it allows full reverse power to be achieved more rapidly. Furthermore, if the short field is a real one in the backcountry or jungle, very often it lies in a rather precarious location without easy approaches to it. If we really blow it as we wend our way up the canyon to the strip, and find ourselves with the power levers at idle as we dive for the strip, high idle will guarantee quicker response when we wisely decide to abort the attempt and take the airplane around for another try.

For the optimum short field practice, I select High Idle no later than on the downwind leg. (If there *is* a downwind leg!) On final, after full flaps are extended, I slowly place the propeller levers fully forward and strive for VREF minus 10 knots at 50 feet. Then, with the power levers at idle, I do the very slightest of flares, let the airplane land firmly, and immediately slam the power levers all the way back and down into the Maximum Reverse position. As the airspeed approaches 60 knots, I slip the condition levers back to the "guesstimated" desired idle speed setting (as determined by OAT, altitude, and air conditioning load) and then move the power levers forward so that they are out of reverse and back at the "flat" blade angle position at the bottom of the Beta range by 40 knots. Try it. You will see that it really works well!

Finding Flat Propeller Pitch

This next use for the Condition Lever is one not too many people know about. It can help you and your maintenance people decide how correctly your Beta range is rigged.

Let's review. What is Beta? Beta refers to the range of power lever travel between Idle and the start of the Reverse range. In this range, propeller blade angle should decrease from the highest setting of the low pitch stop to "flat" while there is no change in compressor speed. Even though flat pitch would imply zero degrees of blade angle, that is rarely the exact case. After all, blade angle is measured at one station only, yet the propeller has quite a twist to it, making the angle different at different stations. The effect of the whole propeller being as flat as it can be is that it has the least amount of rotational resistance. It slices through the air easily and turns quite freely.

If Beta range rigging is correct, both propellers should reach flat pitch as their respective power levers near the top of the stripes designating the Reverse range, and they should do it together. That is, I don't have much concern if flat pitch is found to occur when the power lever is a half-inch or so above or below the top of the stripes. Either will be okay. However, if the left is a half inch above and the right is a half inch below, then a full inch of power lever stagger is needed to maintain directional control while minimizing taxi thrust…this isn't so nice.

On a day when there is little if any wind, go to a clean run-up area and set the parking brake securely. Move both condition levers to High Idle and verify that the N1 speeds are where they should be: 70% to 73%.

Now take one power lever at a time and pull it back slowly behind idle as you watch propeller RPM and N1. What you hope to see is a steady rise in propeller speed until it reaches a peak and starts to decrease while seeing no change in N1. The power lever position when peak RPM occurs designates your actual flat pitch position, your actual bottom of the Beta range. Is it near the stripes? Are both sides fairly close together? Yes? Great! Give your maintenance shop a compliment.

But many of you will find that no peak RPM occurs. Instead, N1 will begin to increase and the resultant increase in gas generation will drive the propeller to a higher speed. What is happening here is that the power lever is already well into the Reverse range. In Reverse, unlike in Beta, the FCU is told to select higher and higher N1 speeds, finally stopping near 85% as Maximum Reverse is attained. In theory, Reverse is entered when the power levers start into the striped region. In practice? Wow! Sometimes things are very badly messed up!

By having the condition levers at High Idle during this little exercise, we have widened Beta's N1 deadband a lot. Instead of extending (correctly!) from Idle to the top of the Reverse range stripes, now it should extend from a half-inch or so above Idle well back into the stripes. If we cannot find flat pitch while working with this huge deadband, then our powerplant controls need some major rigging adjustments!

(Author's note: This was written before the advent of the "hard" power lever stop between Beta and Reverse: Ground Fine. That is where flat pitch should occur. It is an even more difficult challenge for the maintenance personnel to rig perfectly to this precise spot.)

By the way, here is an unsolicited, honest pitch for a company that can definitely solve your engine rigging problems if your local maintenance provider cannot. Give Paul Jones a call at Specialty Turbine Service: 724-776-3925. His team, in my opinion, really are the experts in rigging and overall knowledge about PT6 engines! They are independent, they tell it like it is, they do an efficient and correct job the first time. I feel very strongly that you will not be disappointed with them. They can also act as your agent when negotiating and conducting your next Hot Section Inspection or Overhaul. I used them when I did HSIs on my C90 a year or so ago, and I am convinced that they not only saved me money but I also came out with better post-HSI engine performance than if I had gone it alone. Paul will send one of his well-trained technicians to your location or you can go to them near Pittsburgh.

Conclusion

I hope this discussion has shed some light on the variety of good benefits that can be realized with proper condition lever usage. As always, I enjoy hearing your input and suggestions. Let's be safe out there!

PNEUMATIC FUEL MANAGEMENT

A King Air instructor – not I! – had just completed his detailed explanation of the PT6's Fuel Control Unit (FCU) to a class taking Initial C90 training. With the students' eyes showing the glazed-over TMI (Too Much Information) stare, he lightened the mood by saying, "Well, it's really just PFM." The student who chuckled the loudest at this well-known acronym was targeted by the instructor and asked, "What's so funny?"

"Oh, you know. PFM. That's a good one!" replied the student. "What do you mean?" countered the clever classroom leader. "I merely used the abbreviation for Pneumatic Fuel Management…that's what the FCU is all about!"

And so it is. Keep in mind, folks, that the PT6's FCU is very basic, having been designed back in the early 1960s. This is no FADEC, push-the-power-levers-to-a-detent, fancy-shmancy electronic control like those installed in the latest jets. No, this is a rather simple, straightforward, mechanical governor.

This short discussion is my attempt to make the FCU easily understandable. I have used this method of presenting the FCU quite successfully for a long time and many students have been kind enough to let me know that it really lit the light bulb of understanding for them. Here goes.

The FCU is a gas generator (Ng or N1) speed governor. If you remember nothing else in this article, retain that sentence.

Nearly every pilot who moves to a King Air for the first time has already had experience in operating a better-known governor: the Propeller governor. The pilot has learned that the prop governor is going to maintain the speed that is selected by the position of the propeller lever or knob, to the best of its ability.

For example, when we push the prop knob or lever all the way forward in our shiny A36 Bonanza, we are asking the governor to maintain 2,700 RPM. After start, we don't get that speed; more like 1,000 RPM. Why the governor cannot give us the requested speed is simple: We don't yet have enough power to spin the propeller that fast. But on the takeoff roll, as power is added and airspeed builds, now enough forces exist to send the propeller to 2,700 RPM. If this were a fixed pitch propeller, the faster we flew the higher the propeller speed would rise, right on up to 3,000 RPM and even more! What allows the governor to keep the speed at 2,700 is the ability of the governor to change the blade angle. As the propeller attempts to overspeed, the governor adjusts the blade angle to a higher number – greater pitch, coarser setting, take your pick of terms – and the consequent increase in rotational load prevents the propeller from going to the higher speeds. You knew that, right?

In the Bonanza, as in most single-engine airplanes, it takes oil pressure to make the blade angle increase. In a Baron or a King Air, as in most multi-engine airplanes, the opposite is true: It takes oil pressure to make the blade angle decrease. Why the difference? Safety. In a twin, we would prefer that the malfunctioning governor's propeller defaults to feather, the highest angle, minimum drag configuration, since we can use the other engine to get to a safe landing. In a single, we want the bad governor's propeller to default to the low pitch, minimum angle, maximum speed, maximum potential power setting, so we can use our only engine to get to an airport…presuming the engine does not seize due to lack of lubrication. If the propeller exceeds speed limits when the blade angle remains at the default low pitch position, we merely have to reduce power or airspeed to slow it down. You also knew that, right?

Let's write a paragraph that describes the operation of a typical multi-engine propeller governor. It goes like this: *The propeller governor maintains a constant propeller speed by adjusting blade angle to meet changing conditions. When the pilot moves the propeller lever to a certain position in the cockpit, he is asking for a certain speed by setting a speeder spring tension. Based upon that tension and also upon the current speed of the propeller, the governor adjusts blade angle appropriately. Oil pressure supplies the force that makes blade angle decrease whereas springs and counterweights supply the forces that make blade angle increase. If the oil pressure is lost for any reason, the blade angle defaults to feather.*

Now I am going to rewrite that same paragraph to make it apply to the FCU: *The Fuel Control Unit maintains a constant gas generator speed by adjusting fuel flow to meet changing conditions. When the pilot moves the power lever to a certain position in the cockpit, he is asking for a certain speed by setting a speeder spring tension. Based upon that tension and also upon the current speed of the gas generator, the FCU adjusts fuel flow appropriately. Air pressure supplies the force that makes fuel flow increase whereas springs supply the force that makes fuel flow decrease. If the air pressure is lost for any reason, the fuel flow defaults to minimum flow.*

Now isn't that fairly straightforward? Just as it's not important for a pilot to know exactly what pressures in the propeller dome cause certain blade angles, likewise it is not important to know exactly how the FCU works with its bleed air-derived (P3) pneumatics. The big picture is as we have said: We need more air pressure to get more fuel flow just as we need more oil pressure to get flatter blade angles.

Although P3 air tends to be at high temperatures, due to compression, the line that brings the air from the engine's P3 tap-off to the FCU passes by the compressor's screen-covered inlet and thus is surrounded by lots of potentially very cold air. Given just the right (wrong?) combination of compressor speed, OAT, and humidity, it was found that sometimes the air line could be blocked due to ice formation. That is why most PT6s have an electrically-heated jacket around this line. In the earlier King Air models, there were Fuel Control Heat switches on the subpanel that were required to be activated for every flight, hot or cold, high or low. These switches activated the P3 air line heaters to make certain that ice blockage could not occur.

Recognizing that it was a little silly to force the pilot to activate these switches every single time that the engines were operated, the later King Air models have the switches relocated to a position inside the power quadrant such that they are activated whenever the respective Condition Lever is moved from Cut-Off to Low Idle. That is a nice improvement.

By the way, for you who *do* have the switches on the subpanel: Do not leave them on all the time, even at shutdown. Why? Because if the heaters are operated while the engines are not running, with no air moving through the tubes, then the heating elements may get so hot as to melt the insulation and create an electrical short. This would most likely occur when ground power were being used for a lengthy period of time.

I have mentioned a time in which the propeller governor cannot give us the requested speed: When low power and low airspeed cause the governor to flatten the blade as far as it can, to the Low Pitch Stop setting. Similarly, the FCU cannot always give us the requested Ng speed. The thinner the air, the easier it is for the compressor to rotate at a given speed since less air is being pumped, less drag is being experienced. Consequently, less fuel flow is required to maintain the speed. The thin air at higher altitudes, combined with a request for minimum gas generator speed – Low Idle, in other words – leads to a situation in which the FCU hits the limit of decreasing fuel flow: The Minimum Flow Stop. When this happens, the FCU can no longer deliver the expected idle speed. Instead, the Low Idle speed increases as we go to higher altitudes because the fuel flow has reached the minimum value.

In the older, three-bladed, King Airs that had a Low Idle Ng setting near 50%, one could observe the elevated idle speed at any density altitude above about 3,000 feet. At 4,000, 5,000, 6,000 feet, etc., one would see the fuel flow stuck at about 80 pounds per hour – closer to 100 pph for the model 200 – but the Ng would increase the higher one went. In the later King Airs and those that have been modified with four-bladed propellers, the Low Idle speed is in the 60% range and observing the increase in Low Idle speed is rarely seen on the ground because it doesn't happen until around 10,000 feet. However, in any model, watch what the Ng values are as you practice an emergency descent at 20,000 feet. (Power Idle, Props full forward, flaps Approach, gear Down, and nose over about 15 degrees to hold the gear extended speed limit.) Pretty high Low Idle N1 speeds are seen, aren't they?

The King Air Book

The FCU cannot decrease fuel flow as much as is required to maintain the normal Low Idle setting. The air is too thin to slow the gas generator sufficiently.

When one grasps the fact that the FCU is merely a gas generator (compressor) speed governor, so many other things fall into place!

For example, why does torque decrease as we climb when we don't move the power levers? As the air gets less dense, it is easier for the compressor to spin because it has less drag. Since we have not moved the power levers, the FCU will do what is needed to maintain the same Ng speed. If fuel flow were not changed, Ng would speed up with the less drag of the thinner air. Consequently, the FCU decreases the fuel flow to maintain the speed. Less air, less fuel…there has to be less power so torque has to go down. (Power = Torque X Propeller Speed, remember.)

And what about ITT during this "locked power lever" climb? As you have observed, it doesn't change much at all, merely creeping up a tiny bit. The thinner air yields less cooling, making ITT want to rise. The reduction in fuel flow, however, makes ITT want to decrease. The two opposing tendencies almost nullify each other perfectly, don't they?

What happens when we turn on Engine Anti-Ice, extend the Ice Vanes? We all know that we lose power. Torque goes down. But what about fuel flow? What about ITT? Have you looked closely at what happens to them? My friends, the engine cannot tell any difference between extending the ice vanes and climbing to a slightly higher altitude. In both cases, due to the reduction in air density, Ng wants to speed up but the FCU prevents it from doing so by reducing fuel flow. With thinner air and less fuel, power (torque) must decrease but ITT remains nearly constant as the two factors oppose each other. (Less air: ITT increases; Less fuel: ITT decreases.)

(As a side note, how do you think your fuel efficiency changes with the deployment of Engine Anti-Ice? It must get worse, right? No, in almost all cases – except with an extremely severe headwind – the specific range is actually higher with the ice vanes out. Yes, you lose speed, but you lose proportionally more fuel flow. Amazing!)

I have never heard nor read of a case in which a PT6's propeller governor sent too much oil to the propeller, causing the blade to flatten more than desired and elevating the propeller speed. Nonetheless, that is why we have an Overspeed Governor, a separate device that will start to relieve oil pressure and cause the blade angle to adjust so as to maintain a safe – albeit above normal redline – speed value. On the other hand, there have definitely been cases in which an FCU has sent excess fuel to an engine, causing Ng, torque, and ITT all to exceed redlines. What has been the predominant cause of this?

The answer is that the coupling that transmits the gas generator speed to the flyweights inside the FCU breaks. This coupling – between the high pressure fuel pump and the FCU – is made of plastic and is encased in a lubricated cavity. If a seal fails, allowing fuel to enter the cavity, the lubricant can be displaced, the coupling starts to wear excessively, and if it breaks…runaway fuel flow. You see, without the flyweights being driven, they start to slow down. The FCU interprets this as the engine slowing down and responds by providing more fuel. Even though the engine now starts to accelerate, the flyweights continue to slow down and so the FCU keeps putting in more and more fuel in a futile attempt to make the flyweights increase speed. Although the gas generator is now spinning much faster than it should – with lots of air, lots of fuel, lots of torque and excessive ITT – the FCU is oblivious to all of this because it still "thinks" that the engine is turning too slowly.

The lubricant in the cavity contains a blue dye. If fuel begins to wash out the lubricant, blue stains may possibly be noted coming from the "universal drain" tube in front of the wheel well. If you ever observe blue drips on the hangar floor, get it checked before further flight. Also, during routine engine inspections, a cotton swab should be inserted into the cavity to check for color and condition.

(Note: Only the 200-series, both the straight 200 and the B200, contain a torque limiter that causes the FCU to reduce fuel flow when torque exceeds the redline by a significant margin. In these models, the runaway fuel flow caused by a broken drive coupling will be limited before torque gets so high as to be damaging. Depending on density altitude, ITT and Ng limits may or may not be exceeded. At cruise altitude, they almost assuredly would be exceeded by a large margin.)

The FCU on all King Airs except the 300-series was designed and manufactured, for many years, by Bendix. It's designated the DP-F2 controller. Honeywell now owns the manufacturing rights for the unit. On the PT6A-60A engines on the 300-series, the FCU is made my Woodward. Although the Bendix and Woodward units have many internal differences, the pilot-level understanding of their operation and function remains the same as we have discussed

The table on the next page summarizes the Propeller Governor to FCU analogy.

	Propeller Governor	Fuel Control Unit
What speed is attempting to be governed or maintained?	Propeller Speed, Np	Gas Generator Speed, Ng or N1
Where is the device located?	Front of engine, sensing Np rotation	Back of engine, sensing Ng rotation
How does the pilot make inputs to the device?	Propeller Lever	Power Lever
The lever adjusts...	Speeder Spring tension	Speeder Spring tension
If the lever disconnects...	Defaults to takeoff RPM	Defaults to Idle speed
What is being adjusted or changed?	Blade Angle	Fuel Flow
What is the low limit of adjustment?	Low Pitch Stop	Minimum Fuel Flow
What is the high limit of adjustment?	Feather	As much fuel as can be forced through the lines and nozzles
What force makes the adjustment?	Oil Pressure (Hydraulics)	Air Pressure (Pneumatics)
Where does the force originate?	An oil pump inside the propeller governor	A tap-off from the compressor outlet of the engine (P3 air)
What happens if the force is lost?	Blade Angle goes to Feather	Fuel Flow goes to Minimum

I hope this improves your level of understanding of the FCU...a simple governor of gas generator speed.

As for PFM? In addition to Pneumatic Fuel Management, I am told it stands for Pure Fantastic Magic, or something like that.

SETTING CRUISE POWER CORRECTLY

So you've leveled off at your requested cruise altitude, allowed time for the airspeed to stabilize, and are about to bring the propeller levers back from climb to cruise and then adjust your power levers for the desired cruise power. How?

Wow, there are lots of different methods that I've observed!

Pilot A: "Well, I just match the ITTs at 680°C." Pilot B: "I'll run the hotter engine at 760° and then match the torques." Pilot C: "For me, I like to match fuel flows and run the hotter engine at 720°." Pilot D: "I'll match the torques at the value shown on the Normal Cruise Power graph out of the POH." Which of these pilots is most in line with what you've been doing? Although the ITT values that I've used in these examples will vary, depending on the engine model you are operating, most of us can probably relate to one method more than the others.

Is there a best way to do it? Indeed there is! The purpose of this article is to convince you that Pilot D has the best idea. Let's proceed.

From your initial King Air training, you probably recall that the power required to rotate any shaft is the product of torque and speed: Power = Torque x Speed. When we assign typical units of measurement – torque in ft-lbs, speed in RPM, and Power in Horsepower – then a conversion factor needs to be introduced to make it all work out: Shaft Horsepower = Torque x Speed x K, where K is 0.0001903.

Beech and Pratt & Whitney have put their heads together and decided that there is a maximum realistic power that the engine can produce at any particular density altitude, considering the engine itself, the cowling that houses it, and the magnitude of the power losses – generator load, bleed air deduction – that the engine must endure. To present this "Maximum Realistic Power" to the pilot, torque is the parameter that must be presented since the cruise RPM is specified by Beech. That explains why the Pilot's Operating Manual (POM) or Pilot's Operating Handbook (POH) – the name depends on the King Air model – contains both tables and graphs that show, among other things, the maximum torque to set for any particular pressure altitude and indicated OAT.

Notice that it is *indicated* OAT not *actual* OAT. Beech presumes that the speed of the airplane in cruise and the location and design of the OAT probe lead to a predictable difference (ΔT) between the Indicated and the True OAT. Since we pilots read Indicated on the OAT gauge, they've simplified it for us by converting the True OATs to the Indicated OATs that we'd actually observe. Effort has been wasted in the past by pilots who carefully calculated True OAT and used that number as the temperature parameter in the charts. No! Use *Indicated*, just as you read it from the gauge. Beech has done the conversion work for you.

Please take a moment and review the Engine Limitations table in your POM or POH. There you will find a listing of various conditions of flight – Takeoff, Maximum Continuous, Maximum Cruise, Low Idle, High idle, for example – and the limits that apply under those various conditions. Go to the line for "Maximum Cruise." Look at the ITT limit presented. It may be as low as 635°C for early PT6A-21-powered C90s and as high as 820°C for the 300-series. For Beech to consider an engine to be acceptable during the factory test flight, it must be able to achieve the charted Maximum Cruise Power torque without exceeding the ITT value that you've just discovered. In fact, the factory always desired a margin for the deterioration that will inevitably occur as the engine ages, so typically they would reject an engine that didn't exhibit ITTs at least 5° cooler than the limit. Beech ran their engine acceptance checks at 16,000 feet pressure altitude for the 90 and 100 series and at 26,000 feet for the 200 and 300 series although any reasonable altitude could have been used since the charts present different cruise torque values for each altitude and OAT combination.

Since the single parameter that most affects engine deterioration is excessive ITT, it is understandable why many pilots simply set power so as to achieve a reasonable and conservative ITT. It's simple. It's easy. It's wrong.

Stay with me here as I present a rather far-fetched but surprisingly apropos analogy. Imagine that you were going to hire a couple of guys to do manual labor for you. Perhaps you have a slew of post holes to dig for a new fence or maybe you need a winter's supply of firewood to be cut. Would it make sense to pay these workers based on the actual rate of work they produce – the number of holes dug per day or the number of cords of wood delivered – or to pay them based on the number of shirts they drenched in sweat?

It's obvious that you'd be throwing money away if you chose to base your compensation on sweat production instead of on post holes dug/cords of wood delivered. Suppose one of the workers was older, out-of-shape, and overweight. It's likely he'd work up a heckuva sweat even though his production efficiency was quite low. Now consider a robust, athletic, trim, college athlete doing a part-time summer job. Why, he may never even break a sweat while chopping lots of wood or digging lots of holes!

Setting power by setting ITT is a lot like paying for sweat, not for work production. You see, no two engines are identical, and if you have a weak engine – equivalent to the older, out-of-shape, and overweight worker – then when you set a reasonable ITT, this poor powerplant may be loafing on the job and not delivering anywhere near the power it should. Likewise, an engine that is equivalent to the robust, athletic, trim, college athlete would be working too hard and perhaps heading for a brief stay in the hospital emergency room if you were to work him so hard that his sweat production was equal to what you'd come to expect from the average worker.

If all engines were identical, then every power choice would result in a uniquely identical, predictable, fuel flow and ITT. But engines are not identical. Some are weaker, some are stronger. We cannot expect them to produce identical power by running them at an identical ITT or fuel flow. Only torque and propeller speed determine the power we are actually producing.

Expressed another way, setting power by setting ITT is like calculating a person's weight by measuring his height…there's some relationship between height and weight, of course, but it varies for each individual.

I presume you would not be satisfied paying your workers based on sweat production instead of work efficiency. If this is the case, then why be content to accept an engine that is lacking in its ability to provide the power it should? Well wait, I know your answer. You're accepting it because you don't want to spend money to have it fixed. That's a cheapskate answer but an understandable one. But what if you or your boss just received a bill for a bucketful of money for a hot section inspection or an overhaul but the engine still won't make power? This situation happens more often than it should! You have a solid leg to stand on to say loud and clear that you're not going to pay the final bill until the engine *does* make specified power!

Let's get specific with a couple of examples, beginning with the PT6A-21 powerplant on the later C90s. Here's an engine that is one of the very best PT6s from the standpoint of being able to achieve the Beech/Raytheon specified power without exceeding its 695°C ITT redline nor the 101.5% N1 redline. To run this engine all day long at a power that pushes the ITT near the redline is unlikely to increase hot section inspection/overhaul costs in any appreciable way.

On the other hand, consider the E90. Here's a model in which the Maximum Cruise Power settings were influenced too much by Marketing, not by Engineering. The cruise power settings published (for flight above 10,000 feet) are selected such that the nominal engine will exhibit its ITT at or below the PT6A-28's redline of 750°C. Running a –28 this hard is a poor choice, leading to a disappointing rate of hot section deterioration. Instead, most E90 pilots back off power ten to fifteen percent below the POM's Maximum Cruise torque values and observe ITTs slightly below 700°. A similar situation exists in the –41-powered 200s. Recommended cruise powers are designed to keep nominal ITT below 725° but many pilots prefer pulling off 10% torque and seeing temperatures near 680°, since there have been too many expensive hot sections for those operators who run close to 725°.

The King Air Book

For the F90, F90-1, and C90GT, it turns out that the 101.5% N1 limit is often encountered before cruise power can be set and thus becomes the limiting factor that explains why target cruise power is lacking. Again, this is not right.

How we set power and what ITT, N1, and fuel flow values result becomes an exercise in futility if the gauges are telling us lies. At least at every hot section inspection – and more often, if you observe unexplainable shifts in readings – be certain you have a competent mechanic do an engine instrument calibration, commonly known as a "Jet-Cal." If ITT or Torque is indicating higher than it should, it will lead to the engine's running at less power than it should. Even a gauge as simple as the OAT indicator will cause the power you set to be off if it is reading incorrectly: Reading high, you'll set less power than you should; reading low, more.

I am sure that one of the main reasons that many pilots do not look up the recommended torque setting for their particular pressure altitude and OAT is because the information is not as readily available as they'd like. Although some of the manufacturer's cockpit checklist binders include copies of the appropriate pages out of the POH, some do not. Obviously, the pages are available in the POH itself, but spreading out that bulky binder in the cockpit is a bit messy.

I suggest you do this: Make good quality copies of two pages from your POH. These should be the "Normal Cruise Power" graph ("Recommended Cruise Power" was what it was titled for the straight 200s) and the commensurate Fuel Flow graph. These pages are usually consecutive in the POH and it's a good idea to print them back-to-back on a single sheet. If you have the Jeppesen binder-sized POH, now's a good time to use your copy machine to blow these two pages up to a more easily readable size. For some models you may find only "Maximum Cruise Power" graphs, not Normal Cruise Power. If that's the case, go ahead and make copies of them, even though some of you may be modifying the values later on, as we'll discuss.

There is another very important graph in the POH that deserves some comments. It is the "Minimum Takeoff Power" chart that appears in the POH before the takeoff distance charts begin. This chart presents the takeoff power that a barely-acceptable-with-no-margin-for-error engine should produce at a specified pressure altitude, outside air temperature, and airspeed. If your engine falls short of this torque – either because it hits ITT or N1 limits first, or the power lever hits the stop – then your engine is not meeting the minimum required specification and is considered unacceptable for continued use.

But here's an interesting point: Some engines can meet the Minimum Takeoff Power target and yet fall short of meeting the Cruise Power target. Why? Well, it is assumed that each engine will exhibit a predicable loss in power as air density decreases. This loss of power with altitude is often referred to as the engine *lapse rate* – similar to a temperature lapse rate with altitude – and the sad fact is that some engines have a significantly higher lapse rate than the norm. This means that they cannot meet target power at altitude even though they were meeting the requirements satisfactorily on the ground. Since an engine spends a lot more of its life in cruise than in takeoff, meeting cruise target power is every bit as important as meeting takeoff target power. In fact, in my opinion, it is more important, since I don't desire to buy or operate an airplane that isn't delivering the cords of wood – i.e., the actual power – that it promised.

Let's discuss the details of how to use the power graph that you've copied from your POH. First, give plenty of time for the cruise airspeed to stabilize while you maintain climb power and propeller speed. During this time – while the autopilot flies the plane – use the graph to determine the target cruise torque. Three things to mention: (1) Indicated OAT will rise as the airplane accelerates, so recheck the value occasionally and make sure that it is truly correct. (2) Use Pressure Altitude, not indicated altitude. In the U.S., above FL180, that's a done deal. Down at 16,500 feet, however, either do the math in your head (for each 0.1 inHg higher than standard, subtract 100 feet from indicated altitude, and vice versa for lower altimeter settings) or merely reset the altimeter's Kollsman window to 29.92 momentarily and read the pressure altitude directly. (3) I have found that it is much better to start on the graph at the sloping line equivalent to your altitude and then line it up on top of the indicated OAT vertical line. If you do it the other way, starting with OAT, invariably your right hand now gets in the way of the altitude line labels making them difficult to read. Once you've got the exact point where altitude and OAT intersect, then go horizontally left to find the target torque value.

Notice that this graph also has ISA (International Standard Atmosphere) reference lines sloping from lower left to upper right. Ignore them. Engineers like to compare atmospheric conditions to the international standard but the lines unnecessarily clutter the graph and play no role in our determining the target cruise torque value.

Let's use the C90B's graph as an example. (Page 5-38 in its POH.) At 22,000 feet PA and –20°C IOAT, the torque we find is 1,000 ft-lbs. Also, checking the Fuel Flow graph (Page 5-39, the other one that you copied) in exactly the same manner, it shows a fuel flow of 241 pph per engine. These numbers presume that Engine Anti-Ice is off, that the Ice Vanes are not extended. If they are, wait until you are free of the clouds before the charts can apply.

We pull the propeller levers back to set 1,900 RPM, as specified on the graphs, and look at torque. Often times, we will find them already very, very, close to our target. Let's say that the left side is now reading 1,030 and the right side shows 1,020. What I do is loosen the friction knob for one power lever at a time, then use two hands – for more accurate control – to slowly set the torque as close to the target as possible, retighten the friction knob and proceed to do the same on the other lever.

The King Air Book

Now sit back, refresh your cup of coffee, complete the Cruise checklist. In other words, wait a while, at least ten minutes, to allow all engine parameters to totally stabilize. After this time has elapsed, recheck OAT and torque one more time. If OAT has changed a degree or so or torque 20 ft-lbs or so, so be it. If the change is larger than that, start all over and reset torque to the new proper value as best you can and wait another ten minutes. (This is fairly uncommon and probably indicates that you weren't patient enough the first time in letting OAT stabilize.) If you are taking Engine Condition Trend Monitoring (ECTM) readings – and I hope you are! – now's the time to fill in the form.

Since this article is about setting cruise power, not about ECTM, how do we know if our engine(s) is more like the typical normal model, like the overweight out-of-shape worker, or like the robust athlete?

ITT, N1, and Fuel Flow tell the story…which is why they are the parameters ECTM plots and follows.

If ITT is at or slightly below the limit for Maximum Cruise per the engine limitations table – 695°C for the C90B – that's good, and that's the first step in accessing engine health. The margin we see – how much our ITT is below the limit – is a telling factor. Although a 0° margin is officially acceptable, seeing a 5° to 10° margin is desirable and quite typical. What if you see a 20° margin or more? Don't celebrate just yet, because what you are seeing is, quite literally, too good to be true. Recheck your target torque number. Did you make an error in reading the graph? Maybe ITT is reading lower than it should or torque is reading higher, meaning that you are not really pulling the power you think you are.

There are some checks we can make, right here in the cockpit, to help us decide where the problem lies. First, look at the N1 value. There seems to be a common misconception that lower is better for all engine parameters. When it comes to ITT, that's right. As for N1, if the compressor turns slowly it means that not enough airflow is entering the engine. Since 75% or more of the air is used for cooling, not for combustion, less air leads to higher ITTs. Seeing N1s close to 100% is not bad at all, contrary to popular opinion. It is much less desirable to see them below 95%. Hardly any engine is so efficient that its compressor can turn this slowly and yet still deliver the proper amount of airflow.

The second item in our list of things to check in the cockpit is to look at fuel flow and compare it to the value you looked up on the fuel flow graph. The fuel flow values presented by Raytheon are based on the concept of a "Minimum Acceptable Engine," one with no extra margin for deterioration. This is the same concept used in determining the Minimum Takeoff Power target torque, you'll recall. So, pulling the target torque, your actual observed fuel flow should not exceed the book values. Having a fuel flow exactly the same as the charted value or perhaps 5 pph low is great. Again, seeing a 20 pph low figure is too good to be true.

Third, check airspeed. You may find this hard to believe – I surely did, at first – but the cruise values presented in the POH are actually based on readings taken from a real airplane, with deice boots, antennas, and all. There is no reason why your airplane's airspeed shouldn't perform equal to or better than the book if you are in fact pulling the same power as the test airplane and if you don't have a gear door drooping open or flaps badly out of rig.

How do you determine book airspeed? There are two ways. One method is to get out the E6B – or the equivalent page on your GPS – and calculate TAS. In the POH, right next to the two pages I've suggested you copy, is a third page that shows Cruise Speeds at Maximum Cruise Power. (In the C90B, it's Page 5-37.) Since weight affects TAS, notice that this chart specifies a middle weight of 8,500 pounds. You will be about five knots slower if you're still close to 10,000 pounds.

The second method is to go to the POH and look at the many pages of tables that precede the graphs we've mentioned. (In the C90B, these tables run from Page 5-29 through 5-36.) The challenge with these tables is that some interpolation is almost always required. The beauty of the pages, on the other hand, is that they present not only target torque, but also target fuel flow and target airspeed – presented both as CAS and TAS – all in one location. Since IAS and CAS are so close as to be indistinguishable – unless your airspeed indicator has a huge error – all you need to do to see if your airplane is flying as fast as it should is to compare your actual IAS to the tabulated CAS value.

Let's consider some examples of what might be seen, using our previous C90B at 22,000 feet and –20°C IOAT numbers.

Example 1: Torque could not reach the target setting of 1,000 ft-lbs because the ITT limit was reached first. These readings are observed, at 1,900 RPM: 695°C ITT, 930 ft-lbs of torque, 95.6% N1, 250 pph fuel flow, and IAS is 4 knots below the book value. In all likelihood, this is an unacceptable engine that needs work immediately. Since the lower-than-target torque accounts for the lower-than-target airspeed, the torque gauge is probably reading fairly accurately. With such a low N1 and yet with fuel flow above the target value, it is certainly reasonable for the engine to run as hot as it does. It's very likely that a hot section inspection will find significant problems, such as a burned compressor turbine guide vane ring and/or excessive clearance between the compressor turbine blades and the surrounding shroud. Sorry. It's probably going to be costly.

Example 2: Torque could be set at the target setting of 1,000 ft-lbs and these readings are observed: 660°C ITT, 1,000 ft-lbs of torque, 96.7% N1, 225 pph fuel flow, and IAS is 8 knots below the book value. My educated guess is that the torque gauge is reading higher than it should. Instead of pulling the 1,000 ft-lbs like we think we are, we are probably pulling something significantly less.

The King Air Book

Less power will explain the slow airspeed, the low fuel flow, and the low N1 speed. (Yes, 96.7% is still rather low.)

Example 3: Torque could be set at the target setting of 1,000 ft-lbs and these readings are observed: 685°C ITT, 1,000 ft-lbs of torque, 98.8% N1, 240 pph fuel flow, and IAS is 1 knot above the book value. Hey! We have a winner! Everything looks fine and dandy.

I could go on and on and on with examples like these, but I hope now you have some idea of what makes sense and what doesn't. Keep in mind that torque correlates quite closely with airspeed so if your airspeed is close to what it should be when you set the target torque, then it is likely your torque gauge is good. Also, keep in mind the old truism that only *one* parameter out-of-line must indicate a gauge error. In other words, ITT cannot be high without either fuel flow being high or compressor speed being low, or a combination of both. Likewise, N1 cannot be low without torque and fuel flow being low also and/or ITT being high.

I alluded earlier to the opinion that some of the King Air models have Maximum Cruise Power targets set unrealistically high, due to pressure from the Marketing department. Although running the engine at these high power settings briefly – for the purpose of deciding if the engine is meeting specifications or not – has merit and should be done at times, doing it routinely will, I am sure, lead to premature and costly hot section inspections. As a rule-of-thumb, I recommend taking 10% off of their target torque values. That is, if the book target is 1,000 ft-lbs, set 900 ft-lbs instead. Of course, you will go slower than book and burn less fuel. The models that fall into this category are the 90, A90, B90, PT6A-20 and –20A-powered C90s, E90, F90, F90-1, and straight PT6A-41-powered 200s. Using the previous 22,000 feet, -20°C parameters, the E90 target torque is 1,077 ft-lbs, but you'd be better off setting 969 (1,077 – 107.7).

The King Air 100 and A100 models are unique in that they have targets given for both normal cruise (based on keeping ITT at or below 695°) and maximum cruise (based on 750°). Stick with the normal numbers and you'll be fine. (As for the TPE331-powered B100? This discussion does *not* apply!)

Now listen up, folks! Do you think I'm asking you to do this laborious method of looking up a target torque *every single time* you push up the power levers? No! Once you've learned what typical ITTs are in your airplane when you set the torque, merely set that ITT when you're in a hurry. When ATC descends you from FL220 to 16,000 feet, and you're going to be there a while, simply push the power levers up to whatever torque at 16,000 feet yields similar ITTs to what you had when you carefully set torque to the target at FL220. Also, when down below 10,000 feet, in most cases you will be well-advised to limit power based on fuel flow. I stop at 250 pph on the –20-powered planes, 300 pph on the –21 and –28-powered ones, and 400 pph on the –41, -42, and –60A-powered ones.

More fuel flow than these values gets rather wasted because of the extra drag it produces when the indicated airspeed is so high.

Realize that we have been discussing how to set *cruise* power, not *climb* power. It would be pointless to calculate climb torque for an altitude and temperature because, by the time we had found the value, we'd be at a higher altitude with a different OAT. Consequently, we are forced to eventually use ITT as the primary power-setting instrument when we climb high enough that full torque can no longer be maintained. Given the fact that ITT is a less reliable/accurate gauge than torque, it is wise to use a comfortable margin below redline when forced to use ITT as the primary power-setting instrument. In fact, that explains why the E90's climb limit is 710°C even though its (misguided) cruise power is based on an ITT limit of 750°. The only PT6 model that I would feel comfortable climbing at the ITT redline is the highly flat-rated –21.

While teaching a King Air ground school class years ago, I was discussing the various power ratings and their limits: Takeoff, Maximum Continuous, Climb, Maximum Cruise, Normal Cruise, Best Range. At the end of the discussion a student voiced the opinion that I had forgotten an important engine power rating...Radar Power. "Radar Power?" I asked. "What's that?" "It's when you try to push the power levers through the %&*#@ radar screen!"

We all got a good laugh from this comment even though his humor presented a very correct philosophy! If it comes down to a choice between observing all engine limits or *not* hitting that bridge that's looming above us, it's time for Radar Power. Although some, not all, PT6 models would exhibit ITTs and torques well past the redlines if we were to push the power levers to the stops, it would be highly unlikely for the engine to experience any catastrophic failure. Increased rate of engine deterioration? Yes. An engine explosion? No. In a true emergency, use redlines as limits. If that's not enough – and it usually will be plenty – it's time for Radar Power!

In summary, then, it's important to realize that setting cruise power can only be done accurately by setting torque, according to altitude and temperature. By doing this on most of your flights you will develop a feel for typical values of ITT and N1 and may use these guidelines as a quick method of setting power. However, if one never compares available torque to book values, then there's no way of knowing whether you are paying the fat man or the athlete for the sweat produced.

RECORDING ENGINE CYCLES

Since 1972, the year I first began flying King Airs, I have had the pleasure of flying hundreds if not thousands of these fine airplanes. I have reviewed lots of log books and seen a multitude of different "Flight Record Sheets" in use by various operators. During all of that time, I believe that I have seen exactly one – One! – airplane that had a properly kept record of engine cycles! My hat is off to IASCO, the company in Napa, California, that trained Japan Airline Pilots for many years. It was one of their C90As, as it changed hands after being retired by IASCO, that had the perfect cycle records.

What gives? Why is this such a misunderstood area? Is it hard to do correctly? No! There are only two things – Flights and Starts – that need to be carefully tracked. Yet, there is widespread confusion over what a "Flight" and a "Start" truly mean, as defined by Pratt & Whitney Canada (PWC).

Take this two-question quiz:

An A & P mechanic has installed a new Fuel Control Unit on your PT6 and starts/stops the engine a total of six times while adjusting the power control rigging. Twice, he takes the engine to takeoff power but the other four times he merely runs it at idle. How many "Starts" and how many Cycles – per the PWC rules – should be recorded? Answer: Zero!

A brand new PT6 is installed on one side of a King Air, where it remains for 3,600 hours before it is removed for overhaul. No engine parts were changed in the 3,600 hours. True or False: Every part inside the engine will have the same cycle count at this time. Answer: False!

Totally confused now? Let me try to clarify the confusion.

For each model in the PT6 family of engines, a set of Service Information Letters exists, and usually the second one in the series of these SILs addresses the issues of overhaul times, hot section inspection intervals, and life-limited parts. Parts are limited based on time-in-service and on Cycles. The exact definition of a Cycle is presented in this SIL, and I will try to paraphrase that definition here.

Engine parts tend to deteriorate as they are heated and cooled. It would be very simple if every time the engines on a King Air were started, a single flight would occur. This "Ideal Flight Model," furthermore, would be made up of only one application of takeoff power, one climb segment, one cruise segment, one descent segment, and one landing and shutdown. Almost everyone would

The King Air Book

likely agree that one Cycle had occurred during this Ideal Flight Model. However, flights in the real world are rarely as cut-and-dried as the model.

Does the engine deteriorate more than this model suggests if a go-around is made before the final landing occurs? Most would say "Yes." Does the engine deteriorate less if we stay below 10,000 feet and hence see lower ITTs than if we go up high and run near the ITT limit? Again, most would say "Yes."

The point is this: There are so many variables in the real-world operation of the engine that comparing actual Cycles to the Ideal Flight Model becomes virtually impossible. However, if everyone agrees to track Cycles in the same manner, then deterioration of various parts may be categorized and compared, even though these Cycles are not exactly the same as those represented by the Ideal Flight Model.

First of all, PWC has decided that a *Start* will occur every time the engine is started *and* a takeoff and landing takes place. Doesn't matter if it's a hot day or cold, doesn't matter if you made a twenty minute flight at 6,500 feet or a five hour flight at FL270, doesn't matter if you missed the approach before you made the landing…one *Start* has occurred.

Second, PWC has decided that "maintenance starts" – starts on the ground that are not followed by flights – won't count. Amazing? Sure! Something of a loophole? You bet! But true, nevertheless! Remember, so long as everyone does it the same way, it all washes out in the end. You and I both know that it cannot be "good" for the engines to be started up again as you taxi over to a new parking spot, due to the fact that the FBO's tug that you thought was going to reposition you is broken today. Officially, however, this extra start is immaterial; no Start, Cycle, nor even a partial Cycle has been logged.

Third, PWC agrees that every landing and takeoff involves enough of a heat change in the engine that they should be considered in the officially-approved Cycle count, but they aren't as "bad" as those that involve an engine shutdown and restart. In fact, they conclude that some parts in the engine are affected more than others by these types of "partial cycles." So here's what PWC says to do: Keep track of every *Flight* (every combination of one takeoff and one landing) as well as every *Start* (every start that is followed by at least one flight). Now, when overhaul time comes around, a formula is applied that goes something like this:

Cycles = Number of Starts + (Number of Flights – Number of Starts)/ACF

ACF stands for "Abbreviated Cycle Factor" and it depends on the exact engine part being considered. A typical ACF is three, but it may be higher or lower.

For example, let's say that during a training flight the engines were started only once but that seven landings were made. (Doesn't matter if they were full stop, or touch and go, or stop and go.) Applying the formula, and using an ACF of 3:

Cycles = 1 + (7 − 1)/3 = 1 + 6/3 = 1 + 2 = 3

Hence, three Cycles were added by this training flight.

On the other hand, if this flight had been a typical passenger-carrying one from the classic Point A to Point B, then the formula would be:

Cycles = 1 + (1 − 1)/3 = 1 + 0/3 = 1 + 0 = 1

Okay, here's the bottom line, here's the importance of this article: The records that you are keeping on your airplane need to have a column tracking Flights and another column tracking Starts. I have a simple Excel spreadsheet that I use as my Flight Record Sheet for the King Airs that I operate, and I will be happy to email you a copy. Just request it from me at twcaz@msn.com.

Don't even try to track Cycles! It is impossible for you as a pilot to do so! Unless you have access to the PWC SB that lists the ACFs for each and every cycle-limited part, you don't know what the cycle count is. Remember, it can be and often is different for different parts! So remember, log every takeoff and landing as a *Flight*, and record every *Start* that was followed by at least one takeoff and landing.

Lastly, I recommend that common sense be applied as you record your Flights. Recently, my wife, Pam, and I have been doing contract flight test work with ACSS, LLC, as they certify and develop their new T^2CAS TAWS and TCAS system. (Try it! You'll like it!) This involved many low approaches at runways and mountain sides, followed by full power go-arounds and pull-ups. Sometimes landing gear and flaps were extended. Sometimes they weren't. Were these *Flights* by the PWC definition? No. However, I decided to list a few extra *Flights* in the records, going with about one recorded *Flight* for every two actual pull-ups. Similarly, if you go up one afternoon and practice a whole bunch of idle-power, dirty, stalls, wouldn't it make sense to throw in a few extra *Flights* in the records? I think so, but that's just my opinion. Officially, if the airplane didn't touch down, no *Flight* occurred.

C90B FUEL MANAGEMENT

(Author's note: The following article, although directed specifically to the C90B model, applies almost verbatim to the A90, B90, C90, C90-1, and C90A fuel systems as well. However, the Transfer Pump switches on earlier models have only two positions (On and Off) not the three positions (Override, Auto, and Off) of the C90A and C90B. Any reference herein to the Transfer Pump switch's "Auto" position means the same as the "On" position in the earlier models. There is no "Override" equivalent for the earlier models.

If you are operating an E90 or F90 or a member of the 100, 200, or 300-series of King Airs, then this article is not for you.)

At first glance, there isn't very much to fuel management in the C90B: (1) Turn the boost pumps on before starting and leave them on until engine speed decays to about 10% N1 at shutdown; (2) After starting, position both transfer pump switches and the crossfeed switch to their respective, center, Auto, positions. Either leave them there until shutdown or turn off the transfer pumps after the respective *No Fuel Xfer* annunciator illuminates; (3) When weird things happen – like the crossfeed opening itself in flight – get out the appropriate Abnormal checklist and do what it says.

Yes, that's about it and that will get you by, but I'm here to offer a few more suggestions and thoughts, some of which might be quite thought-provoking. Read on.

First of all, I hope you already know the quick and easy method of converting pounds to gallons. This works with uncanny accuracy for Jet-A fuel, not for gasoline. Just in case you haven't yet been taught the trick, here's the rule: Take the pounds you want to convert, drop the last zero, add half to itself. That's it.

Some examples will help you grasp the technique. How many gallons is 100 pounds? "Take the pounds you want to convert (100), drop the last zero (10), add half to itself (10 + 5, or 15)." So, 100 pounds is 15 gallons.

Try 1,400 pounds. Dropping the zero, we get 140. Half of 140 is 70. 140 plus 70 is 210. 1,400 pounds is equal to 210 gallons.

Now do 2,200 pounds. Dropping the zero we get 220. Half of that is 110. 220 plus 110 is 330; 330 gallons. (Want to convert 1,330 pounds? Round it to 1,300. It'll be close enough!)

This is so dang important when we are carrying lots of passengers and therefore we need to bring the fuel up to a specific amount due to weight limitations. Let's say that we landed with 300 pounds per side remaining and we can only carry 2,000 pounds total for the next flight, or 1,000 pounds per side. To get from 300 to 1,000, we need for the fueler to pump in 700 pounds in each wing. How many gallons do we request? Did you get 105 gallons per side? (70 + 35 = 105). Good for you!

Also, this method allows you to make a "reasonableness" check on the credit card receipt when you top off all the tanks. Suppose you landed with 600 pounds on the left and 500 pounds on the right, 1,100 pounds total, when you told the lineperson to "Fill all four." Knowing that full fuel is real close to 2,600 pounds (2,573 to be exact), about how many gallons should the FBO have on your bill? The answer is 225 gallons, isn't it? (2,600 – 1,100 = 1,500. 150 + 75 = 225.)

By the way, most countries in the world use liters, not gallons, as their volume measurement for fuel. Get the calculator out. Multiply the gallons you figured by 3.8 and you'll get the liters, at least "close enough for government work."

Here's a second fuel thought: Be on the ground within one hour after the first *No Fuel Xfer* annunciator has illuminated near the end of the flight.

The illumination of the *No Fuel Xfer* annunciator normally means that the wing tanks are empty and only nacelle fuel remains, somewhere between about 50 and 60 gallons (330 and 400 pounds) on that side. You have a guarantee – At least as good of a guarantee as any aircraft fuel system ever has! – of over one hour of flight time remaining before you're going to run dry, since it is extremely unlikely that you're burning more than 300 pph per side. (You're probably closer to 200 pph up at FL230, so conceivably you might even have two hours left. You will almost certainly have that long when you have the power levers pulled back to 500 ft-lbs of torque in a holding pattern.)

By being on the ground no later than sixty minutes after the wing has gone empty, you will never have an accident caused by fuel exhaustion!

(By the way, if the *No Fuel Xfer* annunciator illuminates before the wing tanks are empty it is then notifying us of a transfer pump failure. Remember that now 28 gallons – about 190 pounds – are unusable on that side, since they sit too low in the wing to gravity flow to the nacelle. Also, be aware that the nacelle quantity will drop to a much lower value than we are used to seeing before the fuel will flow naturally from the wing to the nacelle.)

Here's a third thought, related to the second: Move the crossfeed switch from Auto to Closed when both *No Fuel Xfer* lights have illuminated near the end of a flight.

When you are down to the last portion of the flight, with the fuel level safe but definitely low, do you really want to cut that meager fuel supply in half? If you lose a boost pump and have the crossfeed switch in Auto, that's exactly what's going to happen! To prevent cavitation, crossfeed will open automatically when it senses the loss of boost pump pressure and the remaining boost pump will feed both engines using the fuel from its own side. But friends, think! What's the cavitation time limit? Ten hours! How long are we talking about before we are on the ground? Maybe an hour? Two hours maximum? It's just not a big deal. You'll need to be the unluckiest King Air pilot on the face of the earth to ever reach that 10 hour limitation before engine overhaul.

Yet, if crossfeed is allowed to open and you don't close it afterwards, then you'd better be on the ground within 30 minutes, since you're now using the fuel from one side at twice the rate.

"Wait a minute, Tom! Why the worry? If I see that I'm getting low on one side, *then* I'll close the crossfeed and start the cavitation timer. I'll still be able to use all the fuel that remains in both sides, won't I?"

Yes, you'll be able to use all the fuel. That's the good news. You'll also get some single-engine practice while doing it! That's the bad news.

To make the scenario easier to follow, let's say that you lost the *left* boost pump when you had 300 pounds remaining on both sides. The good right boost pump now feeds both engines and sooner than you think you are down to an uncomfortably low level on that side, say 100 pounds. You move the crossfeed switch down to Closed. The left *Fuel Pressure* annunciator comes on, cavitation begins. Now those 300 pounds on the left side are being "suction lifted" and are back in use, while those 100 pounds on the right side return to feeding just the right engine normally...until all of the 100 pounds gets consumed. Then...bye, bye, right engine! You see, without the shove provided by the left boost pump – the failure of which started this whole thing! – there is no way that any of the 300 pounds on the left side can get over to the right engine.

In summary, the failure of the boost pump on one side led to fuel starvation on the opposite side after a large fuel imbalance was allowed to develop due to the crossfeed switch being in its normal Auto position. This event *can* happen and it *has* happened in the past, more than once.

So when your fuel level is already rather low, don't allow it to go lower still due to automatic crossfeed. Remember our third thought: Move the crossfeed switch from Auto to Closed when both *No Fuel Xfer* lights have illuminated near the end of a flight.

Here's the fourth suggestion: When you are really sweating bullets and very concerned that you may indeed run out of fuel, move the crossfeed switch up to the Open position.

I know this will never happen to *you*. You will always plan the flight with plenty of fuel reserve and never eat into it. It's the *other* pilot we're talking about, of course. But just in case you talk to this other pilot, tell him or her this fourth suggestion.

Now don't confuse the third fuel thought with the fourth. This *other pilot* is having a bad enough day already...missing the approach, having un-forecast headwinds on the way to the alternate, etc., etc. It is highly unlikely that he or she is also going to lose a boost pump, so I am presuming that the only problem is very low fuel, nothing more.

When this hapless pilot had the second *No Fuel Xfer* light come on, he or she may have closed the crossfeed switch as I suggested. Now, unfortunately, the airplane is still not on the ground and those darn fuel gauge needles are bouncing on empty! By opening the crossfeed, a "common manifold" is being created. This manifold – the crossfeed line – feeds both engines and in turn is being fed by both boost pumps. If one pump begins pumping air, no problem. The other pump will keep the line filled and a check valve will prevent backwards flow out of the manifold into the empty tank on one side. In fact, if sloshing fuel causes first one side, then the other to momentarily pump vapor, nothing will occur so long as the other side keeps pumping liquid. Only when every last pound of usable fuel is burned – from either side to either engine – will both engines finally expire together. It's glider time!

A fifth idea: For partial fuel loads, add only to the wings, not the nacelles.

Yes, I know what the placard says: "The nacelle tank must be full before putting fuel into the wing tank." However, what it fails to say but what it really means is: "If you want to guarantee getting *all* of the 384 gallons of usable fuel onboard, fill the nacelle tanks and then fill the wing tanks."

If you taxi in and shutdown with very low fuel and then want to top all of the tanks, you may not quite have full tanks if the lineperson fills the wings first. Because fuel gravity flows from the wing to the nacelle, fueling the wing also fuels the nacelle, but usually at a much slower pace. As the fueler sees the fuel reaching the level of the wing filler cap, he probably replaces the cap and moves on to the nacelle, the cap of which is higher than the wing cap. What he fails to see is that the wing level is slowly going down as the fuel flows to the nacelle. However, the reverse is not true. That is, because of a check valve, fuel from the nacelle won't gravity flow back into the wing. After topping off the nacelle, if the fueler returned to the wing he will likely be able to fit in a few more gallons.

By topping the nacelle first, however, now there is no way for fuel to flow from the wing to the nacelle, so when the wing cap shows full, it really is.

When you are carrying lots of passengers or cargo, filling all four caps isn't an option. You'll exceed weight limitations. Thus, quite often we are asking for only a partial fuel load. "Add 90 gallons per side," or "Give me 60 in each wing," something like that. After starting, when we position the transfer pump switches to Auto, the wing fuel will begin being pumped into the nacelle. So, no matter where the nacelle level happens to be initially, it will probably be within 10 gallons of full by the time we are airborne.

By adding fuel only to the wing, the fueling job is simplified and the nacelle paint doesn't get scratched by the hose!

One more thing: By not topping off the nacelle, a common annoyance is avoided. It is not at all uncommon to watch some poor new lineman work to fill a nacelle for fifteen minutes or longer, until we finally stroll out and tell him "That's enough! Go on to the wing!" You see, there is a plate about two inches below the level of the nacelle filler cap. This plate contains a line that vents air and fuel from the nacelle to the wing tanks and vice versa. As the nacelle fuel level drops, this is where air comes into the tank. If a transfer pump is positioned to Override and keeps pumping fuel into the nacelle continuously, this is where the excess returns back from whence it came. When we say "Top the nacelle" we really mean "Bring the fuel up to the level of the plate," because any fuel above that is slowly going to drain back into the wings. (A very, very, patient, conscientious – and half crazy! – person could fill one entire side by just filling the nacelle if that person took enough time.) The potential for this embarrassment to the fueler is eliminated when he or she only fills the wing cap. So remember the fifth idea: For partial fuel loads, add only to the wings, not the nacelles.

My sixth fuel management thought concerns crossfeed or, more correctly, the lack of being able to do it legally in the C90B when we desire. The POH says that we can only crossfeed in the event of (1) Boost pump failure, or (2) Engine failure. It also says that the maximum allowable fuel imbalance is 200 pounds. What rubbish!

There have always been two traditional, logical times, that crossfeed capability is desirable in a twin-engine airplane.

The first is engine failure. If the right engine fails and is shutdown and secured, for example, only the left fuel quantity feeds the left engine. If, however, we cannot get on the ground quickly enough – Maybe we're coming back from Europe over the north Atlantic – the right side's fuel quantity is available via crossfeeding. Simple. Easy. Forthright.

The second time that crossfeed capability is desirable in a twin is for fuel balancing. If an imbalance occurs – due to an error in fueling, due to a leak on one side, due to single-engine operation – crossfeed could be used to balance out the load.

Until the C90A appeared (1984), there was no limitation about crossfeeding whenever we desired. Suppose the fuel truck broke down after the left side had been filled but the right side had only 500 pounds in it. No problem. Crank in a little right-wing-down aileron trim, takeoff, level in cruise and balance out the fuel. How? Move the crossfeed switch to Open and turn off the right boost pump, allowing the left pump to feed both engines. When the left quantity comes down to the same level as the right, turn the right boost pump back on, position crossfeed back to Auto and we are back in a balanced state. *The system was designed to do this, and it does it well!*

Then, "product liability" reared its ugly little head. Beech was judged negligent in a jury trial back in the 1970s in which a Beech twin – not a King Air, but rather a model 95 Travel Air – crashed, killing all occupants, and the crash was "caused" by fuel starvation to both engines. Why did this happen? Because both engines were being fed, using crossfeed, from one side only. When that side went empty and the engines quit, the pilot both failed to maintain control and failed to ever utilize the quantity of fuel that remained on the other side.

"Pilot error!" we all cried. "The pilot screwed up, big time!" The jury, however, thought differently. Beech was found at fault for not cautioning this pilot that feeding two independent powerplants from one common fuel supply, and then running that fuel supply empty, was a stupid thing to do. Ever since this sad, tragic, and oh-so-avoidable, event, the Beech legal team has responded by saying that crossfeed is for one reason only…to make all fuel usable when one engine is shutdown. Most King Air POHs now list Engine Failure as the *only* permissible reason for using crossfeed. The truly ironic thing is that, here in the domestic USA with all of its thousands of airports, the airplane will probably have already made a successful single-engine landing long before crossfeed would ever need to be utilized!

All *other* King Air models do not have the automatic crossfeed system that the A/B/C90-series contains. So, although the limitation on crossfeeding – only to be done when single engine – is a royal annoyance, preventing fuel balancing, we at least can somewhat see the thinking behind it and give the lawyers the benefit of the doubt. In other words, if we decide to crossfeed for fuel balancing with two engine operating – Yes, in direct violation of the POH limitation – we can accept the responsibility that we'd better monitor fuel quantities carefully, and stop crossfeeding long before the feeding side goes empty.

But that darn C90B POH! On the one hand it tells us not to crossfeed except with an engine out while on the other hand it says, "Oh, go ahead and do it if a boost pump quits." They're telling us it's okay for their system to automatically crossfeed but it's not okay for us to do it ourselves.

As we have discussed, a boost pump failure is automatically followed by crossfeed operation, presuming we have the crossfeed switch in the Auto position. Yes, I admit that I do not always leave the switch there during flight – see thoughts Three and Four above – but that still leaves about 95% of flight time with the crossfeed switch in Auto. The benefit of this position is the absence of cavitation following a boost pump failure, but at the expense of a fuel supply usually reduced by 50%. Raytheon has designed the C90B fuel system to crossfeed following a boost pump failure, so they "had" to approve this as another time we must be permitted to crossfeed.

The C90 was first manufactured in 1971, and it had essentially an identical fuel system to the B90 and A90 models that preceded it, dating back to 1966. The C90-1 (1982), C90A (1984) and

C90B (1992) have all continued with the same basic fuel system design. With the exception of the C90B, *every single one of these previous models contains no fuel imbalance limitation.* If we had the improbable but possible situation of having, say, 1200 pounds on one side and 300 pounds on the other, we were still legal to go. In other words, the airplane had been flight tested and the FAA and Beech were satisfied that enough aileron authority and aileron trim existed that the imbalance would not lead to any unmanageable roll control problems. It is interesting to realize, also, that the A90's ailerons were smaller and much less effective than those on the B90 and later models.

I have been told that the only reason the C90B has this very, very, stupid and unsafe imbalance limitation is because it made the certification of the autopilot easier to accomplish, since the autopilot would always be operating with a fairly well-balanced airplane. I sincerely wish they had merely added a limitation telling us not to engage the autopilot if the fuel imbalance exceeds 200 pounds! That would have been a lot smarter way to go.

Why am I so incensed about this? Why do I think it is stupid and unsafe?

Here's why. What are we going to do when a boost pump fails, automatic crossfeed begins, and the fuel imbalance now being created reaches 200 pounds? I guess Beechcraft expects us to pull off at the side of the road and stop, eh? We obviously can't keep going, or we'll be in violation of the imbalance limitation. Maybe they want us to move the crossfeed switch to Closed, let suction lift and cavitation begin on the left side and keep our imbalance right at 200 pounds. The imbalance is not getting better or worse, but now we are recording cavitation time too. Darn! Is this *really* what they want?

Or, maybe they expect us to balance the fuel. Well, let's think this through: How will we balance the fuel following a boost pump failure? If, say, the left boost pump was the one that quit, the right boost pump would have been supplying both engines, leading to the 200 pound imbalance – usually in less than thirty minutes, by the way. Now how can we get the left quantity down? We cannot crossfeed it to the other engine because we lack the necessary shove of the failed boost pump.

Wait! I've got it! I know how to recreate balance: Close the crossfeed *and* shut down the right engine! That will get us back into balance!

I hope you realize that I am being facetious here! Rather than shut down the engine, I am going to either (1) close the crossfeed immediately and start cavitating, the preferred choice if I really need to utilize all of the remaining fuel, or (2) let the imbalance exceed 200 pounds, if I have plenty of fuel on the right side (the side of the good boost pump) to see me safely on the ground at a suitable airport. If (2) is my choice – As it probably would be in most reasonable situations – then I'll also turn the autopilot off periodically, do a little hand flying to see what aileron trim is needed, then turn the AP back on. Friends, I *know* the AP can fly well with a lot more than a 200 pound imbalance!

The King Air Book

Combining the fuel imbalance limitation and the crossfeed limitation in the C90B really places us pilots in a bind. First, if the fuel truck breaks down and leaves us with more than a 200 pound imbalance, we are grounded. Second, if a boost pump fails we can only utilize automatic crossfeed until a 200 pound imbalance is reached, usually less than thirty minutes. Makes us wonder why we are still told to use the Auto position of the crossfeed switch, doesn't it?! Third, if a fuel leak develops in flight on one side, we are neither permitted to crossfeed that fuel to both engines before it all leaks out nor are we permitted to crossfeed from the other side to supply both engines when the leaking side is empty. If a fuel leak ever drains one side totally, strict adherence to the POH limitations will cause us to lose an engine!

To summarize, thought six is this: The crossfeed and fuel imbalance limitations did not exist for many, many, previous years, and they shouldn't be in the C90B POH either.

The seventh fuel management suggestion I will make is this: The Override position of the transfer pump switches can sometimes be used to speed the fueling process.

If you want to depart on the next flight or next leg with full fuel and you had not yet depleted the wing fuel before landing, now is the time – probably as the descent begins – to position the transfer pump switches up to Override. Doing so means that the pumps will pump continually, even after the nacelles reach the top. (Remember, the excess fuel merely returns to the wing through the vent line.) By the time the descent, landing, and taxi-in are completed, you can be sure the nacelles are as full as they'll ever be. Turn off the pumps at shutdown, tell the fueler to "Fill the wings," and you'll have the airplane totally full of fuel. Using this technique, there's no need to fiddle with the nacelle filler caps at all.

(Remember that prior to the C90A the transfer pump switches had no Override position, just On and Off. The On position wasn't really On but instead acted like the Auto position on the C90A and C90B. Namely, the transfer pump cycled on when the nacelle level decreased by about 10 gallons and cycled off when the nacelle got within a couple of gallons of full. Whenever the transfer pump is *not* operating while the switch is in On or Auto – because the nacelle hasn't dropped 10 gallons yet – it immediately begins pumping when the transfer test switch is momentarily moved to the appropriate side *and it doesn't shut off until the nacelle gets nearly full.* Hence, although not as guaranteed as use of the Override position on the C90A and C90B, the pilots of earlier models can achieve nearly the same thing – almost full nacelles – but tapping the transfer test switch left and right a few times during the descent, landing, and taxi-in phases of the flight.)

Suggestion eight is this: Turn on the boost pump *after* you activate the start switch, rather than before.

C90B FUEL MANAGEMENT

Years and years ago – in Oshkosh, interestingly enough – I was doing some refresher training with a client who had moved into a B100 King Air (the one with the Garrett TPE331 engines instead of PT6s) from a B90. We talked about many subjects, including their many years of experience in the old B90. He fascinated me with the following story:

They bought their 1969 B90 new, picked it up at the factory, and began flying it using the procedures they had been taught at the Beechcraft Training Center. Within a couple of years, they had replaced both boost pumps. Thinking they should be getting more life than this from the pumps, the old chief pilot, a WWII veteran, decided that they'd make a change in their standard operating procedures. He theorized that the worst time the boost pump ever experienced was when a start switch was activated. This mammoth electrical load causes a major decrease in aircraft voltage that is felt by the boost pump and any other electrical components operating at that time. Perhaps this was causing the pump to fail prematurely.

They decided to reverse the normal order of events: Instead of turning on the boost pump (actually, pumps, plural, for most pilots) and *then* hitting the start switch, they'd try it in the opposite order. Any cavitation that might occur when engine speed was less than 10 – 15% must be infinitesimal, they thought. (After all, it's okay to turn the boost pumps off at 10% at shutdown.)

From that day onward, they would always activate a starter and then immediately turn on that side's boost pump. Lo and behold, they never replaced a boost pump again in the years they operated this B90!

When I operated my own 1972 C90, I followed this program and never had a boost pump failure during my nine years of ownership. Does it really work? Heck, who knows? Maybe we were just lucky.

Nevertheless, knowing that we are not hurting anything with cavitation in these minor moments, it is a technique that I use and advocate. By the way, the other King Air models have engine-driven boost pumps and their electric pumps are not on during start. It is interesting to observe that the *Fuel Pressure* warning light does not extinguish on these models until a few moments after the starter begins to spin the engine…just like it does if we turn on the boost pump right *after* activating the start switch.

At long last, we come to my last suggestion, number nine: Except for the times you are using Override, as discussed, turn off the transfer pumps and the crossfeed before you get to the ramp.

This is nothing more than a minor time-saving maneuver. Rather than reach the ramp, set the parking brake, and then go through the entire shutdown procedure, you can plan ahead and flip off a few switches while taxiing in. I usually turn off six: The crossfeed switch (which may have been closed already), both transfer pump switches (unless I am still trying to keep the nacelles totally full

The King Air Book

using Override), both EFIS Power and EFIS Aux Power switches, if so equipped, and the Cabin Temp Mode selector, to reduce the electrical load of the air conditioner or electric heater. (I leave the Vent Blower switch in Low or High, not Auto, so that it keeps circulating air for comfort.) Now, once stopped on the ramp, all I really have left is the Avionics Master, the Inverter, the Cabin Sign, and Vent Blower before the condition levers are pulled to Fuel Cutoff. (Never turn off the Avionics or Inverter while the airplane is still turning. Might be bad for the gyros.)

Since this has been so lengthy, I will close by re-listing all nine of my fuel management ideas.

1. To convert pounds of Jet-A fuel to gallons: Take the pounds you want to convert, drop the last zero, add half to itself.

2. Be on the ground within one hour after the first *No Fuel Xfer* annunciator has illuminated near the end of a flight.

3. Move the crossfeed switch from Auto to Closed when both *No Fuel Xfer* lights have illuminated near the end of a flight.

4. When you are really sweating bullets and very concerned that you may indeed run out of fuel, move the crossfeed switch up to the Open position.

5. For partial fuel loads, add only to the wings, not the nacelles.

6. The crossfeed and fuel imbalance limitations did not exist for many, many, previous years, and they shouldn't be in the C90B POH either.

7. The Override position of the transfer pump switches can sometimes be used to speed the fueling process.

8. Turn on the boost pump *after* you activate the start switch rather than before.

9. Turn off the transfer pumps and the crossfeed before you get to the ramp.

I know that some of what has been presented here may be items that you had not previously considered and some of it may be worrisome since it appears to conflict with the POH. Stay within your own personal comfort zone and only utilize the ideas and suggestions that seem right to you.

The addition of engine-driven boost pumps, the elimination of automatic crossfeed, the replacement of the electric transfer pumps with simple jet pumps…all of these changes make the fuel systems of *other* King Air models a lot easier to manage and more reliable than the one we still have on the C90B. However, operated properly, it is still a very fine system that has proven itself in service for over forty years.

BLEED AIR USAGE TIPS

I believe that a lot of King Air pilots haven't been taught thoroughly enough nor correctly enough about the subtleties of bleed air usage. My observation is that a great many pilots of these fine airplanes rarely if ever touch the Bleed Air Valve switches. They leave them open at all times. In so doing, they may be inadvertently contributing to increased maintenance costs on these units as well as running their cabin temperature control system at less-than-optimum performance. Let's see if I can shed some illumination on this topic.

Quite a few years ago, Beechcraft decided that one of the contributing factors to Bleed Air Flow Control Unit ("Flow Pak") malfunction was contamination with trace amounts of engine oil. Someone then recalled that the PT6's labyrinth seals – the devices that prevent oil from entering the engine's gas flow path – require positive P3 pressure to operate. That is, they do not seal until the engine is running. With that realization in mind, the thought became, "I wonder if most of this oil contamination occurs during engine start and shutdown, before and after P3 has risen to a reasonable value? Maybe if we kept the Flow Pak turned off until after starting, we'd have fewer Flow Pak problems."

That technique was tried and the outcome appeared to support the theory. Hence, for some time now, the King Air model 350 Pilot's Operating Handbooks have had their checklists revised so that Bleed Air Valve switches are never turned on until after starting and they are turned to the "Envir Off" position prior to shutdown. Slowly but surely, the change is making its way into the other King Air POHs and is gaining acceptance in the King Air pilot community. Unfortunately, in my opinion, the change has not been publicized enough. Maybe this article will help.

My company, *Flight Review, Inc.,* owned and operated a 1972 C90 for nine years, from 1991 to 2000. The other pilots and myself who flew this airplane were conscientious about following our company procedures and we always started and shut down with the Bleed Air switches off, in the Closed position. I admit that perhaps it could have been just a wonderful stroke of good luck, but we had absolutely no Flow Pak problems in nine years! Furthermore, these were the older-style pneumatic Flow Paks, not the newer Electronic Flow Paks as used on 300s, 350s, and newer B200s. In fact, they are identical to the ones used on the present-day C90B. It is my firm belief that Flow Pak health is very, very, well-served by this technique, regardless of the style your particular King Air contains.

Hence, here is my first Tip: Move the Bleed Air Valve switches to the Closed position (or to the center, Envir Off position, if you have three-position switches) before you position the Condition Levers to Fuel Cutoff and don't reposition them to Open until after the engines are started.

Here's the second Tip: After you've started the engines, if you want cabin heating, turn the bleed air on. If you don't, leave it off.

Now that summer is here – Of course in Arizona, where I live, it's always summer! – it demonstrates a lack of understanding to turn the bleed air switches on right after starting. If the cabin is hot, the last thing we want to do is pump in more warm air! Yet that is precisely what we are doing if the bleed air is on!

Just like our cars have a "Max AC" mode that circulates and cools inside air without bringing in outside air, so too we achieve this maximum cooling in the King Airs by excluding outside, warm, air. However, unlike our cars, the benefit may be even *more* pronounced in the airplane. Why? Because the air we are bringing in is not just the *same* hot temperature as the outside air. No, it is even *warmer*, since it has been compressed by the engine.

When it is warm enough to operate the air conditioner, I trust that you pilots of 90-series and 100-series King Airs with three-blade propellers aren't leaving the condition levers at Low Idle, are you? You are always exceeding generator load limits if you do that, if you run the electric air conditioning compressor motor while Ng is near 50%! You need to have those condition levers set closer to 57 – 62% Ng to get the job done properly. (The engine-driven compressor on the 200- and 300-series won't even operate if Ng is less than about 60%, since it is too much for the engine to handle at idle, without raising ITT dangerously.) Most four-blade propeller systems, when rigged properly, require a Low Idle Ng setting near 60% anyway, so this is not the same concern as with the three-blade systems.

Although the compression of the air in the engine – and the consequent temperature increase – is not nearly as great at idle power settings as it is at in-flight power settings, nonetheless it is a significant factor since the idle speed is usually near 60% at this time. The hot bleed air being introduced into the cabin will really degrade the effectiveness of our air conditioning system if it is not eliminated...but it can be, by merely leaving the bleed air off after starting on hot days.

The third Tip: When taking off on hot days, unless you need to, don't use both bleed airs.

Two facts about all King Airs: One, they should be able to achieve maximum differential pressure using one Flow Pak only. Second, one engine runs hotter than the other, almost always. With these two facts in mind, if we takeoff with only one bleed air switch on – the one on the side of the engine that normally runs cooler – then we achieve a couple of nice benefits...not earth-shaking, but nice. First, we introduce less hot air into the cabin so the air conditioning remains more effective as we takeoff and get away from the warm air down at low altitudes. Second, the engine parameters tend to match up more evenly. Furthermore, for a great many King Airs out there, they will have no difficultly whatsoever in fully pressurizing even though they are using only one Pak.

Let me repeat the third Tip: When taking off on hot days, unless you need to, don't use both bleed airs. Let me clarify what I mean by "…unless you need to…"

Excessive cabin leak rate is probably the most universal discrepancy in the entire King Air fleet! Sadly but truly, there are a lot of airplanes in the fleet that will not pressurize fully on one Pak alone. If your airplane is one of these, then at some point you need to have both bleed airs turned on. Should it be at takeoff? Maybe. But also, maybe it could come at 10,000 feet or FL180. Just monitor what the cabin is doing as you climb. If it starts climbing more rapidly than desired or goes higher than the selected cabin altitude, then you need to get that other bleed air switch turned on.

Another situation that makes you "need" to use both bleed airs is lack of cabin heat. Depending on your cruise altitude, OAT, how much time you have been up there, and the strength of a single Flow Pak, it may well develop that the passengers start complaining of being cold, even after you've cranked the temperature knob up a lot. Well, friends, one Flow Pak can often be enough for full pressurization but still not be enough for sufficient heating. In that case, go ahead and turn on the remaining bleed air switch. The passengers will be happy and you'll just have to accept that the engines won't be as nicely matched in ITT as before. Oh well.

Finally, as you well know, as power is reduced significantly (as Ng decreases) the Flow Pak delivers less air. Often, especially when trying to get down rapidly and yet while keeping the airspeed down – Descending through summertime bumps! – one sees the cabin start to climb, signifying insufficient inflow, not enough air supply to overcome the cabin leaks. Here is another time the need of the second Flow Pak certainly justifies its use.

When the second Flow Pak is turned on in flight, its supply of air will momentarily overwhelm the outflow control system and you'll get a pressurization "bump," a momentary cabin dive that may be felt in one's ears. It's not really a big deal and sometimes is barely noticed by passengers. However, there is a technique that can often lessen the bump: After turning on the second Bleed Air switch, grasp the controller's Cabin Altitude knob and start watching the cabin's vertical velocity (or rate of climb) indicator. As soon as you see it start to descend, twist the knob clockwise rapidly, asking for a higher cabin. It's surprising how easy it can be to tone down the bump. After things have stabilized, slowly dial the knob back to the cabin altitude setting you want.

Let's face it, there is definitely a downside or two to operating on a single Flow Pak. One problem is lack of redundancy. If the single Flow Pak that we're using suddenly decides to shoot craps, then we'll have the cabin starting to climb at the cabin leak rate until we remember to turn on the other Bleed Air switch. Or, if the engine fails on the side of the bleed air that we are using, then in addition to handling the engine failure scenario we also need to switch on the other side's bleed air if we want to remain pressurized.

Since the 90, A90, and most of the B90 King Air models had a single pressurization air source – the supercharger driven by the left engine – the lack of redundancy is not really a dangerous thing, more of a nuisance. On the other hand, having redundancy certainly is advantageous and – especially for the B200s, 300s, and 350s that can easily operate above FL290 – the second pressurization source is quite nice to have.

Another possible problem with single Flow Pak operation is that we are never exercising the unused Pak. It may have developed a malfunction and no longer operates, but we'll never know it until we try it. I have no scientific evidence to support this, but my gut feeling is that each Flow Pak should be exercised and used somewhat regularly, at least once per month.

With these thoughts in mind – thoughts about the disadvantages of single Flow Pak operation – I suggest that, if you haven't turned it on before, that you go ahead and turn on that second Pak when you pass FL180, where a loss of pressurization would be more critical than at lower altitude. Now we have redundancy, we exercise both Paks, and we have all the heating potential that we should ever need.

There's another quite important advantage of turning on the second Pak before we level off in cruise at higher altitudes. Namely, our Engine Condition Trend Monitoring (ECTM) readings are now more equalized and realistic. We are more closely comparing "apples to apples" when we follow engine trends, and more likely to pick up on a Flow Pak shift that shows up as a change in engine parameters.

In summary, on hot days there's no need nor advantage of taking off with both Bleed Air switches on but by the time you climb above FL180, why not go ahead and turn the other side on, too?

If it is hot enough and/or high enough that you are ITT-limited, not torque-limited, on takeoff, remember that more power can be developed by turning off unnecessary engine accessory loads. There is certainly a time when leaving *both* Bleed Airs switches off for takeoff makes a lot of sense, combined with turning off the air conditioning at this time. Go ahead and leave the Vent Blower switch in Low or High. It's not that much of an electrical load and it surely improves comfort for pilots and passengers alike. When you are safely airborne, over all of the close-in obstacles and climbing well, that's the time to turn on at least one side's bleed air and the air conditioning.

Finally, before I leave our present topic of Bleed Air, let me remind you of a method that allows you to compare one Flow Pak's air supply to the others. On a test flight or a deadhead leg, while fully pressurized, turn off one Bleed Air switch while watching the cabin vertical velocity indicator. It should quickly show a cabin climb, but one that lasts only momentarily. Your job is to carefully look for and record the peak climb that occurs. Turn that switch back on, watch for the momentary cabin dive as the air enters, and wait long enough to get fully stabilized back at the original conditions. Now repeat the check using the other side's bleed air switch.

What you hope to see are similar and sizeable numbers. For example, 1,500 fpm peak on the left and 1,700 fpm on the right, or vice versa, make me happy. They tell me that the Paks are quite similar in the amount of air they are supplying and that they are supplying a goodly amount, as indicated by the magnitude of the climb when the supply was terminated.

On the other hand, let's say that the peak climb was only 300 fpm when the left side was turned off, but 1,400 fpm when the right side was killed. Can you agree that the left side is in need of repair? You are not alone if this goes against your initial way of thinking.

Think of it this way, however: If the cabin climbs a very small amount when one side's inflow is stopped, then that side isn't doing enough. Also, realize that if a Flow Pak is totally dead, supplying zero air, then you'd see zero change when it is shut off!

Get it now? To summarize, when a bleed air switch is turned off: Big climb, good; little climb bad.

Try to incorporate these bleed air usage tips into the day-to-day operation of your King Air and enjoy the benefits that you'll find. Be careful up there!

OLD MYTHS THAT REFUSE TO DIE

Introduction

Many of the procedures and techniques used when operating King Airs are out of date. This excellent airplane has been produced since 1964. In just a few years, the earliest model 90s will be fifty…it is hard to believe!

During this long production run, a multitude of product improvements have been made, keeping the King Air a competitive and desirable airplane long after most of its competition has seen production cease. However, it seems to me that there are still lots of procedures in use that date from the early days of King Airs, even though better procedures have been developed. The intent of this article is to discuss a few of these and to encourage pilots to amend their techniques for the betterment of the fleet.

Starting

Those of you who have read my previous discussions about starting procedures will find nothing new here, but let's re-visit the argument about which engine is started first. The right engine became the default first-started because, in the original 65-90 model, it provided bleed air to pressurize the reservoir of the hydraulically-driven supercharger of the left engine, thus helping to prevent cavitation of the hydraulic pump. The A90 and B90 models did away with the hydraulic pump/motor drive combination, opting for a simpler mechanical drive system, and the *requirement* to start the right first went away. However, the drag of the supercharger and its drive mechanism – which was always connected to the engine's accessory case and always turning when the gas generator rotated – resulted in a very slight loss of stabilized spool-up starter speed, causing the left engine to, usually, start a few degrees higher than the right. This was a good reason for continuing the tradition of right side first.

With the advent of bleed air pressurization sources provided equally by both engines the choice of first-started became inconsequential. Those who choose to alternate starts – other factors being equal – will tend to equalize starter/generator wear as well as starting temperature cycles. Is this a big deal? Probably not. Although some hot-section and overhaul folks maintain that they can tell which of two engines was started first, others report they cannot.

"But wait, Tom! You are overlooking the battery's right wing location. Since there is less resistance in the shorter wire between the battery and the right engine, there will be more voltage available at the starter so the right side spool-up will be greater." In theory, you are absolutely correct.

The King Air Book

In practice, the difference cannot be seen because it is so small. In fact, any difference is canceled out in the 200-series and 300-series because the right engine has the additional accessory drag caused by the air conditioner's mechanical drive. (Of course the clutch is not engaged during start and the air conditioning compressor is not turning, but its drive assembly certainly is!)

Another argument for right-side-always-first is that the habit patterns will remain the same, since the left-right switches and levers are always activated in the same sequence. Yes, true, but the counter-argument is that the procedure may become so automatic that the pilot stops thinking and observing, merely going through the motions by rote, and hence may not be as alert as if he were forced to think about which lever and switch is to be moved.

Anyway, like we said, it is no big deal. There are still pilots out there who somehow have been led to believe that starting the right engine first is critical, even in later models. Nope, far from it. Take your choice; do what you prefer.

Bleed Air Switches – Turn 'em Off!

When the pressurization air source changed from a single supercharger to identical left and right bleed air flow control units ("Flow Paks"), new trails were being blazed. The air from the supercharger (on 65-90s, A90, and B90s) was always being vented overboard while the airplane was on the ground, not starting to be supplied to the cabin until the landing gear squat switch sensed that the airplane had lifted off. (The air could also be introduced into the cabin while still on the ground – a rare event – by activation of the "Supercharger Vent / Pressure Test" switch, either up or down.)

This may explain why the early checklists were written such that the bleed air switches remained in the "Open" or "On" positions virtually all of the time except when a "Bleed Air Failure" annunciator illuminated. If we were to read the fine print in the Normal Operations section of the Pilot's Operating Manual, we would also find that it was recommended to turn the bleed air switches to the "Closed" or "Off" position to maximize the effectiveness of the air conditioning while on the ground. Why introduce warm air to the cabin when we are trying to cool it?

Little by little, more and more pilots became accustomed to turning the bleed air switches off on hotter days, for better air conditioning operation. However, when the weather is cool, I still find that the majority of pilots with whom I fly tend to leave the switches on all of the time. **I highly recommend that, regardless of outside air temperature, the bleed air switches should be off for every start and every shutdown.** Why?

Maybe a better question is, "Why not?" Factory checklists for later B200s as well as 300 and 350s are now being written to reflect this operational change. I will try to shed some light on why this is a better procedure.

190

The Flow Paks are delicate and complicated mechanisms. Although for years their internal valves were positioned by regulated bleed air pressure – the "pneumatic-style" – more recent B200s and all of the 300s and 350s use a model in which most of the valves are positioned by electric motors – the "electronic-style." In both styles, however, when the engine is shutdown and bleed air pressure drops to ambient value, the main shutoff valve springs to its closed position. Thus, regardless of switch position in the cockpit, all flow paks are "off" before engine start.

A study that Beech conducted a few years ago tried to ascertain why so many flow paks were being replaced prematurely. This component was developing a bad reputation as a device that was none too trustworthy. A conclusion reached by the study was that the flow paks were being contaminated with engine oil residue. Researching further, it was felt that most of the contamination was occurring during engine start and shutdown. A PT6 obtains its oil seals through differential air pressure. Remember hearing in your training about "labyrinth seals" and how they require P3 air to operate? The theory developed, as I understand it, was basically this: If the bleed air switches are on during starting, there comes a time when the flow pak has enough pressure to begin opening up and yet the engine does not yet have enough pressure to provide perfect seals. The result? Oil contamination and early flow pak malfunctions.

Does anyone really know if the theory is sound? I don't, but it does seem to make sense. Let me tell you this: My company owned a 1972 C90 for about ten years. We always shut the bleed air switches off before shutdown and never turned them on until after starting. In the ten years, we never had one ounce of trouble from either flow pak! Maybe we were just lucky, sure, but maybe the operational change really is a good technique to follow.

Have I convinced you? Are you always going to switch the flow paks off when taxiing in and leave them off until after start? Great! When are you going to turn them on?

If you want heat, then turn them on right after starting as you reach over to activate the Cabin Temp Mode selector and/or the Vent Blower switch. On the other hand, if you are cooling the cabin, leave them off. When taking the runway, I always conduct a right-to-left flow pattern that starts at the environmental controls. Now is the time to turn on at least one bleed air switch.

One? Why not both? Most of the time, you will probably *will* do both, sure. But suppose you are in Arizona – where I live – in the summer. You know from experience that even the best of air conditioning systems don't really bring the sweltering cabin temperature down to a comfortable level until you get up fairly high in cool air. Why pump in more hot air that necessary? At climb power settings, your airplane will pressurize just fine using only one flow pak, even if you have a somewhat leaky pressure vessel. So turn on just one side when taking the runway – I suggest choosing the side that has the lower ITT, so that the engine temps will tend to match better, not worse, during initial

The King Air Book

climb – and then get the other one on at 10,000 or 18,000 feet. In fact, if your flight is short and you have a good tight cabin, you may decide to operate on only one pak for the entire flight duration.

Auto-Ignition

That right-to-left flow pattern I use when taking the runway ends up on the pilot's left subpanel where two items are given attention: Engine Anti-Ice ("Ice Vanes") and Engine Auto-Ignition. If you are operating a four-bladed King Air model with the newer style cowling design (the "Pitot Cowl") then I am sure that you are extending ice vanes for *all* ground operation, right? Good! Unless the runway is slushy or unless we will be entering cold clouds early in the departure climb, then the Ice Vanes should get retracted as the next-to-last step of the right-to-left pattern.

And Auto-Ignition then gets armed as the last step, correct? Not really. Think of it this way: If you need Ice Vanes (slush on the runway, low cold clouds), you need Auto-Ignition; if you don't need Vanes, you don't need Ignition.

"Blasphemy! Let's lynch this guy! We *always* use Ignition! The checklist says to arm it! Where is he getting this information from?" Now take a few deep breaths and relax. Hear me out before heating up the tar bucket and collecting the feathers.

First of all, the great majority of the checklists found in the Pilot's Operating Manuals or Pilot's Operating Handbooks, do *not* say to arm the Auto-Ignition switches on takeoff. Go ahead. Read the POH. I'll wait.

In fact, about the only POHs that *do* direct us to arm the switches for every takeoff are the ones for the "straight" 200 and the ones for the F90-series. A100? No. B90? No. 350? No. Oh yes, those manuals do indeed direct us to arm the switches *if we are taking off into icing conditions* and hence need to activate all of our ice-protection items, but with the exception of the early 200s and the F90 and F90-1, it just is not supported by factory checklist procedures.

I can tell you why you don't need to arm them and I can also tell you why the step is there in the 200/F90 manuals. Read on.

Why do virtually all jet airplanes turn on their igniters when landing and taking off? Birds. Ol' "B-1-R-Ds." That's all. If a bird gets sucked in, then the engine should relight and keep operating even if the bird ingestion causes a flameout.

Can a bird have the same effect on a King Air's PT6? Absolutely, positively, not! Sure, we may hit a bird and that little (wood)pecker might even enter the cowling intake. But then what? No way can it turn the corner and get past the first screen. Even if it could, how will it get past the second screen, the one that surrounds the compressor's intake?

There is only one thing entering the cowling of a King Air that can cause an engine to flameout…"Visible moisture when the OAT is 5 degrees Celsius or below." That is why the Auto-Ignition switches – just like Prop Heat, Fuel Vent Heat, etc. – were only discussed in association with flight in icing conditions until 1974.

That is the year when the first 200s started being delivered and when the newly developed checklist for that model started advocating full-time use of Auto-Ignition. Why was the procedure changed? Because Champion did too good of a sales job.

You see, the 200 was the first model to use spark plug type, instead of glow plug type, igniters, and a sales representative of the Champion Sparkplug Company went a little overboard when selling Beech on the merits of the spark igniters. "Why, they'll last forever! Not like those old easily-burned out glow plugs!" "Well," thinks the Beech engine engineers, "if they're gonna last forever, why not use them all the time? It's not really necessary, but, hey, why not?" In fact, the procedure was to turn them on after start, leave them on all during taxi and runup, and not to turn them off until shutdown. That is, to the best of my knowledge, an accurate description of what transpired.

Yet there was a downside that showed up before too long. Namely, the "infinite-life" plugs weren't lasting too much longer than the old ones! Analysis of the problem showed Beech that using the plugs so much – as would happen when torque was low with Auto-Ignition armed – was causing more rapid deterioration that they had hoped. I actually attended a meeting that discussed the situation. Although I proposed merely going back to what we'd been doing in the C90s, E90s, and A100s that were being concurrently manufactured – namely, use them in icing, what they are designed for! – the consensus disagreed, being swayed perhaps by the emerging worry of product liability. A compromise was worked out and this is the procedure still in print in the 200 and F90/F90-1 manuals: Arm them for every flight, but make it the *last* thing on the Runway Lineup list and the dis-arming of them the *first* thing on the After Landing list.

It took about ten years before Beech realized that they were over-reacting to a non-event. I say again, you only need to relight an engine that suffers a flameout and, barring fuel starvation or fuel pump failure, the only thing that can flameout a PT6 is ice ingestion. In 1984, when the model 300 was introduced, Auto-Ignition was relegated back to its proper position as an ice-protection device. See where it is mentioned in the BE-300's Runway Lineup procedure? It is not a blanket directive to arm it; instead, it is grouped with all of the other ice protection items in an "As Required" status.

Again, similar to when you decide to turn on your bleed air switches, whether or not you use Auto-Ignition for every takeoff and during every flight is not going to make a ripple's worth of difference in overall operating costs or safety. If you want to use them all the time, be my guest. Just don't look at me like I've forgotten something when I choose to leave them off!

One last comment about Auto-Ignition is this: I faithfully use every single one of all the ice-protection items whenever the plane is in "visible moisture when the OAT is 5 degrees Celsius or below." However, I have recently had a worrisome realization. If the engine were to ingest ice at, say, FL250 and flameout, the automatic relight attempt that follows, due to Auto-Ignition being armed, will be above the 20,000 foot limit of the windmilling airstart envelop. Dang! I bet it will be impossible to keep the starting ITT peak below the upper redline in this thin air! Since I always have the ice vanes extended in icing flight, I will never have to contend with this relight scenario. Still, it makes me question whether keeping Auto-Ignition armed above FL200 is a wise idea. Any thoughts, readers?

Autofeather

Here is another system that, in my opinion, is not being used in the best manner by many King Air pilots. Based upon the perspective that I gained as a factory instructor in the '70s, as well as upon my thirty years of King Air experience, I think I can talk intelligently about some of the history behind the truly marvelous autofeather system.

Autofeather was certified and became a factory option on the later B90 models. My hat is off to the team or individual who came up with this design. Not only is it highly reliable and malfunctions of any type are very rare, but also it is absolutely failsafe. That means that any failure mode will never result in feathering a propeller that shouldn't be feathered. Of course, the system may *not* operate due to a rare malfunction, causing the pilot to need to feather manually, but it has never sent a power-producing propeller into feather.

This fact was not yet established in the early days of the system and some pilots had experienced incorrect feathering of other such systems installed on some older recip transports. Hence, a lot of pilots – including Beech factory test and transportation pilots – didn't really like to use the system and, when they did, they couldn't turn it off fast enough after leaving the critical takeoff phase. I think there was a macho philosophy that "Real pilots feather their own props! They don't need no sissy automatic system to do it for them!" That probably explains why the checklist procedures got written in such a way that the autofeather switch was only moved to the Arm position for takeoffs and landings.

As stated above, time has proven this system to be bullet proof. I suggest that there is really no problem with leaving it armed all of the time and I encourage any pilot who may want a little helping hand during engine-out work to leave it on. Speaking for myself, I prefer to turn the switch off in cruise. Why? To extinguish the lights! That is my main reason, and it is inconsequential. As soon as I start the descent, the switch goes back up to the armed position. In fact, for a short hop, less than an hour or so, I usually leave it on continuously.

Remember that just because the autofeather switch is in the "Arm" position doesn't mean that autofeather is ready to work. The system remains unarmed until *both* power levers are positioned far enough forward to hit switches that are hidden inside the pedestal. The exact value depends upon the model, but usually these switches complete the arming process when the power levers near the 90% Ng position. It is very important to advance *both* power levers, not just one, when a power loss is suspected.

Furthermore, why does Beech/Raytheon persist in including the "Autofeather – Off" step in their shutdown checklists?! It is ridiculous! The system is already "off" due to power lever position, isn't it? If it makes sense to turn this switch off, then let's also turn off the Rudder Boost switch, the Electric Trim switch, and, while we are at it, let's not rely on the Avionics Master switch, but rather let's turn off each individual radio! Come on, Raytheon, what are you trying to achieve here? Leave the switch in the Arm position! That way, there will be less risk of forgetting to re-arm it for the next takeoff. (Don't give me the line about "You'll have to move the switch anyway, for the Before Takeoff check of the autofeather system." Yeah, right. *Every* time? I don't think so!)

Perhaps this article will give the checklist writers at Raytheon a gentle nudge to revise the older checklists and bring them more into compliance with newer, better-thought-out procedures, but I am not going to hold my breath. Meanwhile, I hope that I have given you some food for thought and that many of you may change some old diehard habit patterns for the better.

PROPELLERS – WHAT PILOTS CAN CHECK

Introduction

King Air pilots have endured many hours of Initial and Recurrent ground training courses during which the topic of interest was propeller operation. For some lucky souls, the light bulb of understanding and clarity has illuminated and they have attained a good grasp of understanding about this surprisingly complex system. For others – the majority, perhaps? – propeller operation remains an enigma that keeps its mysteries tightly hidden.

One can be an excellent King Air pilot without enjoying a deep knowledge of propeller system operational details. After all, this system is notable for its reliability. Few flight delays are due to propeller problems and few Abnormal nor Emergency procedures dealing with the propeller must ever be performed. Thank goodness!

As I fly with my customers in their aircraft, I find that many of these King Airs have propellers that are quite badly out of proper adjustment. I believe this is due, in part, to the fact that we instructors often spend too much time discussing theory and not enough time presenting practical, easy, steps that pilots can take to decide if their propellers are rigged properly. That is what I want to do here…provide some simple procedures that will allow you to decide if the propellers on your King Air have been set up correctly.

Primary Propeller Governor (PPG)

Every time propeller speed stabilizes at normal maximum RPM during takeoff, and every time we set climb or cruise RPM values and find that the propeller speed remains constant at the number we selected, we are "testing" the PPG. It is a marvelously trustworthy unit that rarely if ever fails.

What should we be looking for when we examine this unit for proper rigging? Two things.

First, make sure that both propellers really do stabilize at the proper maximum value when propeller levers are fully forward and sufficient power and airspeed exist to stabilize the propeller speed on the governing value. When the propeller lever is fully forward, the governor's speed selecting arm should also be fully forward, with its travel being restricted by an adjustable screw on the governor. It is an easy task for the A & P technician to adjust this screw in or out to decrease or increase the takeoff RPM value. Set both sides as accurately as possible. Who wants to hear the annoying *Whaa-Whaa* out-of-sync beat on takeoff?

Verifying that your propeller speed indicators – Np gauges – are accurate is a simple matter with the neat little handheld "Proptach" unit made by Cardinal Electronics, Inc., of Lansing,

The King Air Book

Michigan. Just turn it on, point it at the rotating propeller, and – Voila! – you can read the speed right down to one RPM accuracy.

Second, make sure that the propeller lever's minimum speed setting, the detent where stiffness is felt before the lever moves into the feather range, is set properly. The minimum governor speed should be about 400 RPM less than takeoff RPM. Thus, for a standard C90, the PPG should be capable of governing at 1,800 RPM. However, since this low speed is rarely if ever used, whether the minimum governing speed is 1,750 or 1,850 is not very important. But what *is* important is that the propeller lever will never be pulled into the feather position by mistake when setting cruise RPM...Hello, overtorque! So make sure that the stiffness is encountered before the RPM starts to rapidly drop off as the propeller starts to feather. The stiffness is an artificial feel generated by the mechanism within the power quadrant. It can get out of adjustment, and it can get so weak that it is virtually nonexistent, but it can be fixed relatively easily...if we know that it is bad.

Overspeed Governor (OSG)

The Overspeed Governor (OSG) is designed to "kick in" if the propeller speed ever gets about 4% faster than takeoff RPM, which implies that the Primary Propeller Governor (PPG) is not functioning properly. All King Air models contain a switch – usually labeled "Prop Gov Test," and sometimes there are two switches, one for each propeller – which allows the speed of the OSG to be electrically/hydraulically lowered to a value that can be reached without intentionally failing the PPG. The following table shows the proper normal and testing speeds for the OSG, depending on model.

Model	Normal Speed (RPM)	Test Speed (RPM)
90 (non-reversing)	2,266	< 2,075
A90, B90, C90, C90-1, E90	2,288	2,000 ± 100
C90A, C90B, C90SE	2,288	2,020 ± 40
4-blade Raisbeck A90, B90, C90	2,288	2,000 ± 100
4-blade Raisbeck E90	1,976	1,750 ± 100
F90 and F90-1	1,976	1,760 ± 40
100 and A100	2,288	2,000 ± 100
4-blade Raisbeck 100 & A100	2,080	1,800 ± 100
200 and B200	2,080	1,870 ± 40
300 and 350	1,768	1,565 ± 45

Most King Air pilots are quite familiar with conducting the OSG test…hold the brakes tight, make certain the propeller levers are fully forward, then add power and observe that the RPM stabilizes below the normal takeoff value. I want to emphasize the importance of observing the correct test value. If it is not within the test range specified in the table, and if the accuracy of your propeller tachometer has been verified, then the OSG probably needs to be overhauled. (By the way, it is interesting to note that the above listing of test speeds – derived from the Pilot's Operating Handbooks or Manuals – does not always jive with the data presenting in the Maintenance Manuals. In truth, the value for all PT6A-21–powered airplanes, including the C90 and C90-1, should probably be the same as that shown for the C90A: 2,020 ± 40.)

When the OSG moves from its normal setting to its test setting, it does so very rapidly. Hence, it can be quite a shock to the system to start with the RPM high and to knock it back when you activate the test switch. Always ease up to the test RPM slowly by adding power. On the other hand, when the test switch is released, the RPM rises rather slowly because it takes time for oil to bleed out of the OSG test chamber.

Also, have you ever considered what would happen if you accidentally activated the Prop Gov Test switch during cruise flight? Since normal cruise RPM is below the typical test setting – except for some Raisbeck E90 and 100 series – nothing noticeable will occur. Yes, the OSG is now ready to operate at a lower-than-normal value, but the PPG is still regulating the actual propeller speed at an even *lower* value. Want to actually go ahead and finish the OSG test in flight? Easy. While holding the Prop Gov Test switch(es) up, merely advance both propeller levers fully forward. As the PPG is "told" to give takeoff RPM, the propeller speed rises until it hits the test value of the OSG and stabilizes there. Done? OK, now smoothly bring your propeller levers back to establish normal cruise RPM and release the test switch(es).

Low Pitch Stop (LPS)

Review the terminology shown on the following drawing. The numbers apply to three-blade propellers on most 90-series airplanes, but the basic concepts apply to all.

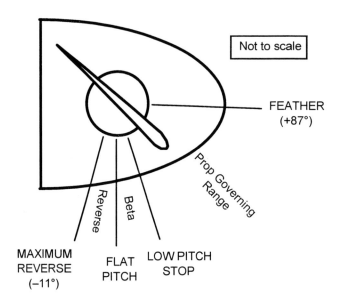

FEATHER
(+87°)

Not to scale

Prop Governing Range

Reverse

Beta

MAXIMUM
REVERSE
(−11°)

FLAT
PITCH

LOW PITCH
STOP

Whenever propeller speed is being held constant by the Primary or Overspeed governor, then the blade angle must be somewhere within the section marked "Prop Governing Range." Higher power settings and higher airspeeds – factors that cause a *fixed-pitch propeller* to increase speed – cause the governor of a *constant speed propeller* to increase blade angle instead. ("Increase blade angle," remember, means to move the angle to a greater value, to move it more toward Feather and further away from Maximum Reverse. "Increase *Pitch*" is another method of saying "Increase blade angle.") Vice versa, lower power settings and lower airspeeds will eventually result in the governor decreasing the blade angle *so much* that it encounters the Low Pitch Stop (LPS). The LPS prevents the governor from decreasing the angle any further. As pilots, we know that the Low Pitch Stop has been reached when the propeller speed drops below the selected value, when we see and hear the propellers come "off of the governors," and when propeller speed follows airspeed and power changes.

It is very important that the LPS blade angles on both left and right propellers be set properly. If one side is set at a noticeably different angle than the other side, the airplane will want to yaw toward the flatter side every time we land. We will have a built-in crosswind, or so it may seem.

So what is the easy method to determine if the LPS is set correctly on both propellers? I'll give you a "quick and dirty" method first, then I'll give some details.

First, the quick and dirty: Sitting in the runup area, aimed squarely into any wind so that both left and right propellers experience the same effect from it, with the propeller levers fully forward, add power until both propellers are exactly in sync at 200 RPM less than takeoff value. For example, if takeoff value is 2,000 RPM, set 1,800. Read left and right torque gauges accurately. Are they nearly the same? Good, then your LPSs are set about the same.

Think how much harder it would be to spin a feathered propeller at 1,800 RPM than to spin a flat one to that same speed. Does it make sense that each different LPS setting would require a different torque to reach the same speed? That is the basic principal behind this check. Air density affects the required torque, too. The thinner air found at a higher field elevation or on a hotter day will allow the propeller to spin more freely and hence require less torque to achieve the specified RPM.

The following table lists the test speeds and Sea Level, 15°C (Standard), torque values for various models. (Values for other elevations and temperatures are found in the "Engine Controls" chapter, Chapter 76, of the appropriate King Air Maintenance Manual.)

Model	Test Speed (RPM)	Torque Value (ft-lbs)
All 3-blade 90-series	2,000	600 ± 40
C90B (4-blade)	2,000	605 ± 40
4-blade McCauley 90-series	2,000	580 ± 40
4-blade Raisbeck 90 & 100-series	1,800	505 ± 40
4-blade Raisbeck 90 & 100-series with Magicam	1,800	805 ± 40
F90 and F90-1	1,800	360 ± 40
100	2,000	600 ± 40
A100	2,000	440 ± 40
3-blade Hartzell 200 and B200	1,800	800 ± 40
3-blade McCauley 200 and B200	1,800	750 ± 40
4-blade McCauley 200 and B200	1,800	660 ± 40
4-blade Hartzell-Raytheon B200	1,800	520 ± 20
4-blade Hartzell-Raisbeck 200 and B200	1,800	635 ± 40
300 (1)	1,500	42 ± 2%
350 (1)	1,500	36 ± 2%

Note 1 in the above table is to indicate that the test is to be conducted on the *Flight* LPS, not the *Ground* LPS, for the 300 and 350.

Once you have verified that the LPS blade angle is proper – or have had it adjusted to make it so – those of you operating King Airs with four-blade propellers need to do another simple check.

What is your propeller speed with the power levers at idle and the condition levers at Low Idle? One more table, this one to show the minimum allowable speed:

Model	Minimum Propeller Idle Speed
300 and 350	1,050
C90B (4-blade)	1,100
4-blade McCauley 90-series	
4-blade Raisbeck 90 & 100-series	
4-blade McCauley 200 and B200	
4-blade Hartzell-Raisbeck 200 and B200	1,150
4-blade Hartzell-Raytheon B200	1,180
F90 and F90-1	1,200
A100	1,250

When idling below these values, the propeller is subject to the onset of the "reactionless mode" of vibration which, in extreme cases, can be quite destructive.

Two factors make the propeller idle too slowly. One is the LPS blade angle…the bigger it is the slower the propeller will turn. That is why we must set it correctly first. The other factor is Low idle N1 speed. By adjusting the Fuel Control Unit to increase idle N1, the extra gas generation that occurs will obviously drive the propeller faster.

(Some King Air models contain two Low Pitch Stops…a *Primary* and a *Secondary* for those A, B, and C90s powered by PT6A-20s, or a *Ground* and a *Flight* for some 4-blade systems such as those on the A100, F90, 300 and 350. The simple checks being discussed here apply only to the *Primary* LPS or *Ground* LPS, with the exception of the 300 and 350 as noted previously.)

Beta Range Rigging

On a level taxi way with no significant wind, it should be possible to bring a King Air nearly to a stop by lifting the Power Levers and moving them back far enough into the Beta range so that the blade angle is flat and all residual propeller thrust has been eliminated. Furthermore, the Low Idle N1 speed should not have changed while this is being done. If it requires leaving Beta and going into Reverse – as evidenced by N1 starting to increase – to achieve flat pitch, your Beta range rigging needs attention.

PROPELLERS – WHAT PILOTS CAN CHECK

The latest King Airs – 300, 350, C90B, and 1993 and later B200s – incorporate a "hard stop" in the power levers to differentiate between Beta and Reverse. Beta ends at this *Ground Fine* position, and a second lift of the levers is required to enter into Reverse.

Once again, what is a relatively simple method of determining how we stand?

Select a day when there is little if any wind. With brakes set in a clean runup area, move both condition levers to High Idle. You should see 70% N1, or a little more. If needed, adjust the Condition Levers so that both N1s indicate exactly the same. Now lift up one power lever and move it slowly back as you watch both propeller speed (Np) and gas generator speed (N1).

By selecting High Idle, you have widened the Beta range *deadband* so that no N1 increase should be experienced until the blade angle is on the negative side, the reverse side, of flat pitch. As the blade angle flattens, but with no change in gas generation, the propeller should spin faster until it becomes flat. At that time, a peak Np value should be reached. As the Power Lever is moved back even farther, the negative bite of the propeller will cause it to slow down. If N1 starts to increase before you reach peak RPM – a very common misadjustment! – stop the test and tell your A & P that the Beta range deadband is too small…your N1 is picking up much too early.

Do this two or three times – you will probably find some slop in the linkage and some inconsistencies in the results – until you have a good feel for what Power Lever position yields the flattest blade angle on average. Note the position mentally or mark it with a pencil. Repeat the same procedure using the other Power Lever.

If the left and right "flat" positions that you have now found are more than a half-knob width or so different from each other, your airplane will tend to pull toward the side that goes flatter first while using Beta during the landing rollout and even while taxiing. (Or, alternately, you will have to split the power levers in the Beta range to achieve symmetrical drag. Dangerous? No. It's an easy thing to live with, just a little annoying.)

Now for the test that truly makes a difference. With High idle still selected, position both Power Levers to their respective flat blade angle positions – side by side, we hope – and pull the Condition Levers back to Low Idle. Observe the stabilized N1s. They *should* return to your normal Low Idle settings, the same as you would see if the Power Levers were a bit over the gate into Beta. Do they? Great! Then you can achieve the elimination of all residual propeller thrust without adding power. Your propeller blade surfaces and your brakes are going to last a long time.

When Low Idle is supposed to be near 50% N1, suppose that the left N1 decreases only to 63% while the right side goes to 58% after you select Low Idle with the Power Levers in the flat blade angle position. See the problem? Before you can kill residual blade thrust, you are already starting to increase power above Low Idle. As you use Beta to try to slow taxi speed, it is not going to

203

be very effective. You will be adding power while the blade angle is still taking a positive bite of air…you'll start to go faster when you are trying to go slower!

If you pull further back, and get the blade angle flat at the expense of spooling up a lot of N1, you will be sand-blasting the heck out of the blades. (Remember that the POH says we are not supposed to be in Reverse at speeds below 40 knots.) Alternately, you can stop pulling back before N1 increases, find that the airplane is taxiing like a barn-sour horse, and ride the brakes to slow down. Either choice is bad.

Maximum Reverse

The last check to mention is the Maximum Reverse one. Do this check when decelerating after landing before the speed reaches 40 knots.

Namely, with propeller levers fully forward, lift and pull both power levers back and down as far as they will go and hold them there in the Maximum Reverse position until Np and N1 stabilize. What do you see? What do you feel? If both propeller speeds are nearly equal, if the airplane tracks straight, and if the deceleration force is strong, this is good. Pulling to one side? Nps and N1s significantly different? Not much slowing-down action felt? These are bad. Typically, N1 should reach about 85% in maximum reverse and the propeller speeds should be within 50 RPM of each other.

An amateurish attempt to correct one propeller item can lead to "tweakitis" that only makes the overall situation worse. Finding the technician who can rig our propellers well may require a lengthy search. But knowing what to strive for is important for both the technician and the pilot.

Propeller rigging rarely gets out of whack so badly that safety is badly compromised, but it certainly makes flying easier and more pleasant when our King Air's propellers are set up like the designers intended.

AUTOFEATHER – WHAT A GREAT SYSTEM!

For the last many years, all new King Airs have left the factory with the Autofeather system installed and that is a very good thing indeed! When an engine quits, the battle to control the airplane while it tries to turn toward the mammoth drag of a windmilling propeller is a difficult experience that multi-engine pilot applicants must face and master before receiving their ratings. However, if the propeller never had the chance to windmill, if some magic invisible hand would instantaneously identify and feather the dead engine's propeller with 100% accuracy…well, gee whiz, multi-engine training would lose most of its challenge! Autofeather is that magic invisible hand, and it's worth its weight in gold!

Before discussing how the system works and how to best utilize it, let me provide some of the history behind this great system.

For the first five years of King Air production – 1964 through 1968 – the autofeather system that is now so common on King Airs had not yet been invented. It wasn't until 1969, when the B90 and the straight 100 comprised the King Air production line, that autofeather was made available as a factory-installed option, after its design, testing, and certification had been successfully completed. Back then, few multi-engine airplanes had any type of automatic propeller feathering system. Unfortunately, the autofeather system installed in those few applicable twins back in those days of yore had – justifiably or not – created a negative impression on their pilots. The rumors were (1) that either the system would not work correctly and reliably when needed, and (2) that it would malfunction in such a way as to feather the propeller on a perfectly good engine! Those rumors, combined with the basic machismo of the many pilots who would – Thank you very much! – prefer to do their own feathering, led to a general lack of acceptance of the need for nor desirability of this new option. Throughout much of the 1970s, the majority of King Airs were ordered and delivered without autofeather.

Why order a system that wasn't truly needed? VMCA – Air Minimum Control Speed – was determined with a windmilling propeller, after all. If the crews of those days survived in Apaches, Twin Beech 18s, Queen Airs and other twins that had so much less relative performance than the turbine-powered King Air, and all of which had no autofeather, then why waste the boss's money on something that was never needed nor available up until now?

It was that line of reasoning that caused autofeather to get off to a slow start. Even in those airplanes that were built with the system, pilots tended to use it only for takeoff and landing. Once the plane was a few feet above the ground, most pilots were glad to turn off the autofeather switch, afraid that something bad might happen if they left it on! Even the Beech-written checklists of that era – some of which are still current today! – tended to support this line of thinking since the procedure directed the pilot to turn off autofeather relatively early in the Climb (After Takeoff) checklist.

Times change.

Raisbeck Engineering tested the first four-blade propeller system on a King Air 200 in the early 1980s. A combination of the fourth blade and a flatter low pitch stop setting led to a propeller that had a significant increase in its windmilling coefficient of drag. Doing the VMCA testing as in the past – with the critical engine's propeller windmilling – yielded a new VMCA more than ten knots above the old one! Yuck! That meant that, if nothing were done, takeoff V-speeds would need to be increased, yielding longer required takeoff distances. Although the new prop shined in providing lower noise and smoother operation, few if any pilots would ever recommend a modification that led to worse takeoff performance!

Back to the drawing boards. The FAA rules allow for VMCA to be based on a feathered propeller if there is a system that feathers it appropriately without pilot action. The elegantly simple solution for the Raisbeck Engineering team was to mandate that the optional autofeather system be required – be a No-Go item if inoperative, in other words – whenever a King Air had their propeller modification installed.

I am a big fan of the Raisbeck propellers and I must not be alone, based on the number of Raisbeck-Hartzell propeller kits that have been sold! As years passed and more and more autofeather-equipped airplanes entered the fleet, it pleased a lot of us when the data supported our contention that instances of autofeather-caused problems were non-existent.

Interestingly enough, the Raisbeck four-blade system on the 200-series was not the first four-blade propeller on a King Air. That distinction goes to the King Air A100 model that appeared in 1972. However, the characteristics of this propeller – aided by the incorporation of separate low pitch stop settings for flight and ground operation – allowed Beech to still base VMCA on a windmilling propeller and still keep autofeather as an optional, not a required, system. The same is true for the F90-series that appeared in 1979 and the C90B that appeared in 1992. Both of these models have standard four-blade propellers yet autofeather is an option only. (To the best of my knowledge, there has been no C90B delivered without the option. However, I have seen a few F90s *sans* autofeather.)

In the case of the 300-series – both the original model 300 and its replacement, the version that the FAA recognizes as the B300 but the one that the Beechcraft marketing department tags the 350 – autofeather is a required system for certification and therefore is standard equipment. The same is true for the latest B200s, the ones delivered in 1993 and after, those manufactured with Raytheon-

AUTOFEATHER – WHAT A GREAT SYSTEM!

Hartzell, four-blade propellers. In all of these models, just as with the Raisbeck-converted 200s that we've discussed, VMCA is now predicated on a feathered propeller. (Surprisingly, the four-blade McCauley "Black Mac" on the 200s got approved without autofeather.)

I should also briefly mention Raisbeck's "Magicam" system before we leave this historical review. Although the Raisbeck propeller was only for the 200-series originally, his team quickly designed models for the 90- and 100-series so that they, too, could enjoy the quiet and smoothness of the conversion. Unfortunately, many of these models were not suitable candidates for the conversion because they were not built with the autofeather option and since it was quite an expensive one to retrofit. Jim Raisbeck, ever the brilliant engineer, devised a new Beta Cam Box that would allow windmilling drag to be reduced so much that VMCA would not be increased even when his propellers were installed. He achieved this by making the low pitch stop move to a higher blade angle when the power lever was advanced forward. You can quickly recognize an airplane with his Magicam system since there is a cockpit placard on the power quadrant warning the pilot not to retard the power lever until feathering has been manually completed.

(As a side note, it is my experience that rigging the Magicam system properly must be a maintenance nightmare, because few of the planes that I have flown with the system act as they should.)

I hope by now – if you did not know before – that you know exactly whether the autofeather system on your particular King Air is a required or merely nice-to-have item. Now let's talk about how the system works.

We want autofeather to be able to differentiate between a power loss caused by us, the pilot, versus a power loss caused by an engine malfunction. How do we do this? Power lever position, of course!

If the power levers are advanced, then it is expected that engine power will also be "advanced"…relatively high. Conversely, when a power lever is retarded, we expect engine power to be low. Our autofeather system, consequently, must be able to sense both power lever position – The Power we *want* to have – as well as the engine's true power output – The power we *actually* have.

Determining power lever position is relatively simple. It is done by installing switches inside the power quadrant console that are activated when the power levers are pushed forward past a predetermined location. These switches are very similar to the ones that trigger the landing gear warning horn when the levers are pulled back past a predetermined location.

Measuring actual engine power output is also relatively easy, especially in a turboprop. You will recall that the horsepower at the propeller shaft is the product of propeller speed and torque.

The King Air Book

Since propeller speed is usually governed so that it varies little, that means that usually torque and horsepower are directly proportional: Increase torque by 25%, power increases by 25%.

The autofeather system does not truly get ready to operate – to be "Armed," in other words – until three things happen. First, the Autofeather switch must be in the up, or "Arm," position. Second, both power levers must be advanced far enough to trigger the switches inside the console. Third, both engines' torque must be above 400 ft-lbs (or about 17%, for the 300-series, which equates to the same thing). When these three conditions are met, the green Autofeather Armed annunciators should illuminate, telling us that the system is ready to feather a propeller if a real engine failure occurs.

Notice that if we see the autofeather lights illuminate during the takeoff roll but then we must abort the takeoff prior to rotation speed for some reason, our action of pulling the power levers to idle – and then to Ground Fine or Reverse – as we abort will nullify two of the three conditions that caused autofeather to be armed. Namely, no longer will we have the console switches activated and no longer will both engines' torque be above 400 ft-lbs. The result is that no automatic feathering will occur during the aborted takeoff. Thank goodness this is the outcome, since a feathered propeller – or two – would decrease the overall drag significantly and increase our stopping distance a whale of a lot!

Remember that the Fuel Control Unit (FCU) is nothing more than a governor that regulates fuel flow for the purpose of maintaining the N1 speed selected by the power lever. In other words, the power lever is merely a selector of desired N1. Hence, each position of the power lever corresponds to a unique N1 speed and the power lever location switches that we have mentioned are referenced to that speed. Depending on your King Air model, the autofeather power lever switches should be activated when the power lever position exceeds 86% to 90% N1.

N1 speed and engine power are not directly proportional. If other parameters such as altitude and outside air temperature are held constant, it is of course true that a higher N1 means a higher power level....but not in a direct or linear relationship. For example, at 50% N1, power is less than 5%! To achieve 50% power, N1 must be near 90%.

So avoid making the mistake of thinking that the autofeather switches don't activate until *power* is near 90%. Wrong! Typically, slightly more than 50% power will cause autofeather to arm, meaning that the 86 – 90% N1 switches have been activated.

What power do you use for an ILS or visual final approach? If you are approaching on the normal 3 degree glide path, power will be well below 50% and thus autofeather won't be armed, even though the autofeather switch is in the Arm position. It arms when both power levers are moved forward to begin a go-around or balked landing procedure.

AUTOFEATHER – WHAT A GREAT SYSTEM!

Consider an engine failure that occurs inside of the outer marker when you are descending on the glidepath. Will autofeather help us now? Yes, but not unless we do our part. And what is "our part?" Our part is to react to the suspected loss of power by taking *both* power levers forward so that we double the torque on the remaining engine. Now – Voila! – the dead engine's propeller feathers because we activated the power lever switches.

If we add power on only the "good" engine's side we have made a gross mistake typical of a neophyte multiengine pilot, not of a competent professional. The old "Mixtures – Props – Throttles – Flaps – Gear – Identify – Verify - Feather" mantra of the Engine Failure procedure that was drilled into us by our ME flight instructors has been disregarded and ignored, since when we advanced only one power lever we put the "Identify" step ahead of all the others. Don't do that! It's stupid and dangerous!

Instead, we should be doing the King Air version of the "Suspected Power Loss" mantra: Power – Props – Flaps – Gear – Identify – Verify – Feather. Notice that I didn't call this the "Engine Failure" procedure but rather the "Suspected Power Loss" procedure. How do you know that you have a real engine failure until you shove both power levers forward? Wouldn't you feel silly manually feathering the propeller of an engine whose only problem was a loose friction control that allowed the power lever to migrate back toward idle?

To review, realize that the position of the power levers during a normal approach will not cause autofeather to yet be armed. If ever you suspect that something is not quite right with an engine now, start by advancing *both* power levers and see what happens. If both engines, surprisingly, respond together, then I guess you were needlessly worried about nothing: Pull the levers back and continue the approach. On the other hand, if only one torque gauge responds as both power levers are advanced well then – Wonder of wonders! – looks like you really do have an engine failure on your hands.

Since torque and power go hand-in-hand, and since you've just lost half of your torque, the airplane will continue performing almost identically if you regain that torque by doubling the torque on the good side. For example, if you had 500 ft-lbs, stop shoving both power levers up when the responsive side hits 1,000 ft-lbs. Next, continue by pushing both propeller levers smoothly forward to their stops. Flaps and Gear come next; you'd probably leave them alone if you are on the ILS or visual approach, right?

Now comes the hard part (chuckle, chuckle): Identify – Verify – Feather. Let me tell you, folks, it is darn easy to Identify and Verify the dead engine when it's propeller is already feathered! That's the beauty of using Autofeather correctly!

Now let's review how the system actually goes about feathering the correct propeller when a real engine failure takes place.

As the engine stops producing power and torque decreases below approximately 400 ft-lbs, the first thing that occurs is that the opposite side's system is disarmed. Reflecting that change, the annunciator extinguishes on the good engine's side. Autofeather is designed to never be able to feather the *wrong* propeller or *both* propellers. It does this by disarming the good side before *any* feathering takes place.

Now, as torque continues to fall – getting below about 200 or 260 ft-lbs (or about 10% torque in the 300-series) – feathering of the dead engine's propeller occurs.

Manual feathering is achieved – when the pilot pulls the propeller lever fully aft into the feather detent – by opening a passage in the Primary governor that allows oil in the propeller dome to freely release into the engine's nose case. This release of oil permits the feathering springs and counterweights to drive the blades to feather.

Automatic feathering is achieved by sending electric power to a normally-closed solenoid valve attached to the Overspeed governor. When this valve is energized open, oil in the propeller dome again is freely released into the nose case and feathering takes place. Notice that even if the propeller cable between the propeller lever in the cockpit and the connection to the Primary governor were to come disconnected or break, automatic feathering would not be affected in the least. Neat!

What criteria did Beech use in selecting the two torque values we have presented, 400 and 200 (approximately) ft-lbs? I am not 100% certain, but can offer educated speculation. First, the 400 ft-lb switch already existed, since it was the trigger value for the engine Auto-Ignition system. By merely modifying the switch to include another set of electrical contacts, the switch was made to perform double duty. Second, the 200 ft-lb value was selected because it is very close to a Zero Thrust power setting. If the engine somehow had a fuel flow restriction that brought power back to, say, 300 ft-lbs, we would find that the engine – although certainly not developing the amount of power that we'd like to have – is still producing more thrust than drag. It is helping propel the airplane more than hurting the propulsion, in other words. What good would there be in feathering a propeller that was more helpful than harmful? None.

When torque gets below 200 ft-lbs, however, now the thrust has turned negative and the windmilling propeller is hurting more than helping…it's time to feather it.

Let me present a weird problem: Can you envision a situation wherein both power levers are well-advanced, one engine's power is above 400 ft-lbs, the other engine's torque is below 200 ft-lbs, and yet the lower-powered engine has not failed? Seems impossible, no?

AUTOFEATHER – WHAT A GREAT SYSTEM!

I hope you never experience this – and with proper training and technique you won't – but the scenario I've presented can and has happened, leading to a perfectly good propeller starting to automatically feather. How? By moving the power levers forward from idle much too fast.

The PT6 powerplant, like most jet engines, exhibits considerable lag or spool-up time when accelerating from idle. Although a lot of King Airs are set to idle close to 60% N1 many three-blade models still have a Low Idle setting close to 50% N1. If both power levers are rammed forward starting from a 50% idle setting, there is a definite probability that one engine will accelerate so much faster than its companion that its torque will rise above 400 ft-lbs before the other engine has reached 200 ft-lbs…setting up a situation of undesirable automatic feathering. This occurred during a training flight on a Navy T-44A (a cross between a C90 and an E90 that Beech called the H90) at Corpus Christi Naval Air Station during a touch-and-go, and resulted in an overrun into the sand.

I always have taught that when adding power rapidly from idle – such as for a rejected landing or a power-off stall recovery – that you need to "bump" the power levers forward very rapidly but only about a third of the way. Pause about three seconds, for the engines to catch up with you, and then complete the application of the desired power. By only going that one-third amount of travel initially, the autofeather switches have not yet been activated. Engines that don't spool up together after the one-third power lever position is reached are rare to find and in need of some serious attention!

Got some questions for you. When you land, do you move the Cabin Pressure Control switch to the Dump position? After you turn the Avionics Master switch off, do you also turn each individual radio off? Do you make sure that the electric trim switch is off before leaving the cockpit at the end of a flight? I take it that your answer is "No!" to all of these? Good for you. I agree. So here's another question: Why in the world are you turning the Autofeather switch off before shutdown?!

The only answer is "Because the Raytheon checklist tells me to." I hate to break the news to you, but even aircraft manufacturers blow it occasionally and this is one of those cases. It makes no logical sense whatsoever to move the autofeather switch from Arm to Off between legs or at the end of the day. All that action achieves is increasing the chance that you'll forget to arm it for the next departure. With both power levers retarded, with both torques below 400 ft-lbs, without either autofeather annunciator light illuminated, what is the system "doing" just because it's switch is still Armed? Nothing! Just like the radios aren't working, even though their switches are on, after the Avionics Master is off. Leave the autofeather switch in the Arm position on the ground between flights…please!

Yes, I know that sometimes you'll be moving the switch to Test and then will need to re-arm it. Fine. But if you do the autofeather test before *every* flight…well, we need to talk!

The King Air Book

What about that Test position of the Autofeather switch? What is it really doing? The answer is very simple: The Test position bypasses the power lever switches and allows autofeather to function even when both power levers are not pushed forward.

Were it not for "Test," we'd never be able to see autofeather function unless we truly shut an engine down with the Condition Lever. You see, the only way that the power lever can be forward and yet have low torque on that side is with an inoperative engine.

While holding the Autofeather switch in Test – negating the need for advanced power levers – the autofeather annunciators should illuminate soon after both torques exceed 400 ft-lbs (or 17%, for you 300-series people). Now we can retard one power lever and check to see that what we expect to happen actually does happen: At about 400-ft-lbs the annunciator on the other side extinguishes, indicating that it has disarmed. At about 200 ft-lbs, the annunciator on this side extinguishes and the propeller RPM starts dropping rapidly, indicating that the prop is starting to feather.

During the test the engine is never shut down. It is always operating at idle power or more. Hence, as the propeller starts to feather, torque increases. (Remember: Power = Torque x RPM. If power is constant, as RPM goes down torque must go up.)

As torque increases due to the feathering that is taking place, it rises above 200 ft-lbs and now the autofeather system stops operating. As the autofeather valve on the Overspeed Governor closes and oil stops dumping from the prop to the engine, the blade angle begins to flatten, RPM begins to rise, and torque begins to decrease again. As torque drops below 200 ft-lb, the whole cycle repeats again.

The outcome is that, during Test, you will not see the propeller actually feather all the way. It will merely cycle into and out of a partially-feathered condition, with RPM and torque fluctuating.

After one side is tested, its power lever is advanced until both annunciators re-illuminate and now the other side is tested. After the second side is tested, the test procedure concludes by making sure that no feathering occurs when both power levers are at Idle together.

As the Autofeather system has become more prevalent and has proven itself to be trouble-free, more and more pilots are realizing that this is a system that virtually cannot be over-used. I understand that a number of pilots are flying with the autofeather switch armed at all times. In my view, that is totally fine.

However, my personal preference is to turn autofeather off in cruise when I am at an altitude that gives me plenty of time to analyze and troubleshoot any engine malfunction that may occur. On 90% or more of my flights, I leave the Autofeather switch Armed on the ground, during takeoff and climb, and during descent and landing. But during cruise, I usually turn the switch off for two very flimsy reasons. First, I like having a blank annunciator panel at this time. No big deal, I know, to have

212

two green lights glowing, but I prefer the panel to be dark. Second, I know that I have lots and lots of time, at this high altitude, to think through a suspected loss of engine power and to make my own decision about whether I think immediate feathering is the best course of action. Just in case I decide to allow the propeller to windmill – perhaps to try for a windmilling airstart after I get down in thicker air below FL200 – I now have that option.

Compared to Apaches, Twin Beech 18s, Queen Airs, Aerostars, 421s, Seminoles, etc., etc., etc., the King Air *needs* autofeather like it needs a tailwheel...it doesn't. But, since autofeather is available on the King Air and not on those other twins, it is one of the very best components that your airplane may contain!

300-Series Low Pitch Stops

Breathe a big sigh of relief if the King Air you fly has only one propeller low pitch stop per side. You lucky devil! For those of us who fly King Airs with two different low pitch stops...Golly, it gets mighty confusing very quickly!

This article will attempt to shed some light on the topic of the two low pitch stops that are found on 300s and 350s (350s are, officially, B300s)...why they are needed, how they may malfunction, how they may be checked and tested. I hope that I can make this complex topic somewhat understandable. For simplicity, I'll often use the abbreviation LPS to mean Low Pitch Stop.

What is a Low Pitch Stop?

It is the device that prevents the propeller blades from reaching too flat of a blade angle, an angle that would yield too much drag. When a constant speed propeller is on the governor, maintaining a constant rotational speed, the blade angle of the propeller is being controlled by the governor and no low (or high) pitch stop is required. When power and airspeed are both reduced until the RPM begins to decrease, the drop off in speed is because the blade angle has flattened as much as it can. The propeller is now off of the governor and the angle of the blades is being determined by the setting of the LPS.

On non-reversing propellers, the LPS is simply the mechanical limit of blade angle travel in the flatter position. On reversing propellers, however, that same mechanical limit is past flat pitch into the area where the blade angle is negative, causing air to be pushed forward instead of propelled backwards. Thus, on the reversing propeller, the LPS must be a removable or flexible device such that it provides the necessary protection against excessive drag when needed but one that may be removed or repositioned when reverse thrust is desired...for quicker stopping after landing, of course. In many turboprops, including lots of King Airs, a single LPS per side is all that is needed. However, some turboprops have two low pitch stops. Why?

There are two reasons for having two low pitch stops. The first reason is that the second stop acts as a back-up to the first stop. In these models, if the first stop were to fail, nothing would prevent the propeller from eventually – when airspeed and power are both sufficiently reduced – going to an un-commanded full reverse blade angle if it weren't for the second stop. The second reason – the one that applies to the 300-series – is that the extra low pitch stop provides a propeller blade angle limit in flight that is different than the blade angle limit while on the ground. (*Flight* low pitch stop vs. *Ground* low pitch stop.) Let me elaborate on that.

Avoidance of Ground Vibration

On the ground, the problem of too much drag when a propeller goes too flat is not the dangerous concern that it is in flight. On the ground, who cares if the excessive drag would raise VMCA? If the blade went too flat while parked on the ramp, so what? Well, for one, it might be hard to get the plane rolling! Unless some positive bite of air exists, adding power would merely cause lots of RPM rise – lots of sound and fury! – but little tendency to roll forward! In fact, if the blades were sitting at a negative angle on the ground, adding power would make us tend to back up instead of move forward, eh? So, for practical purposes, we need some positive blade angle on the ground but it can be very slight.

So why have such a flat ground low pitch stop? What is the problem with having a bigger positive bite, one that makes it easier for the airplane to start rolling when brakes are released?

If engine power is not changed, sitting on the ramp, an increase in propeller blade angle will always yield a decrease in propeller speed, and vice versa. When the first King Air model with a four-blade propeller appeared – the A100, in 1972 – the engineers recognized that they now had to contend with a potential problem that never existed before with the three-blade propellers that had been used up until then. Namely, these new propellers exhibited a "reactionless vibration" mode in which two opposing blades could bend their tips forward while the two other opposing blades were bending backwards. Since the forward and backward movement of the blades canceled each other out, the engine felt no net positive nor negative thrust. But the propeller? Wow! Both the hub and the blades were experiencing lots of stress as the blades flexed so much.

It was found that this potentially destructive phenomenon only appeared at lower propeller speeds. (Even then, it wasn't likely unless the propeller encountered a sudden changing load, such as that caused by gusting winds.) So, to lessen the possibility that the vibration would ever begin, a limitation was established stating that the propeller must not be allowed to idle at too low of a speed. For the 300-series, this minimum speed limit is 1,050 RPM.

If a 300 or 350 had only one LPS at the "optimum" position, the propeller idle speed would probably be around 900 RPM, much too slow for safely avoiding reactionless vibration. One way to increase the speed up to the 1,050 minimum would be to simply increase the Low Idle N1 speed…say, to 70% or even more. Doing that, however, would make the airplane want to taxi much too fast. The other way to increase the idle propeller RPM would be to move the LPS flatter. In fact, it might need to be nearly at flat pitch to achieve the target speed, meaning the airplane would have little tendency to roll forward when the brakes were released. The final solution was a little of both: Increase Low Idle to about 62% and flatten the blade angle quite significantly also.

The negative aspect of these changes is that the airplane is noisier on the ramp and the potential for propeller FOD is increased. The positive aspect – in addition to ensuring that the minimum propeller speed limitation in assured – is that, due to the extra airflow through the engine caused by the elevated idle N1 speed, the ITT is lower and the generator is capable of sustaining up to 75% load at Low Idle.

On the ground, all would be fine having only the single, relatively flat, LPS. During an aborted takeoff, the flatter blade angle that the blades found when power was suddenly reduced, would make the stopping action more intense.

But in flight, oops…two negatives arise. First, VMCA – measured in the traditional way with a windmilling propeller – would be higher because of increased drag on the windmilling propeller, since it is at such a flat angle. Second, the flare for landing characteristics would not be as benign as desired. As the propellers came off of the governors and found the low pitch stops, their flatter aspect would yield extra drag and more rapid deceleration. In other words, the airplane would tend to fall out of the sky on landing.

The solution? Don't allow the blade angle to go so flat until on the ground. In other words, provide for a second, less drag-inducing, low pitch stop that would operate only in flight, not on the ground. Thus, we have both a *Flight* and a *Ground* low pitch stop.

Now, just between you and me…

I wonder if any of the flight test pilots and engineers at Beechcraft who thought that the landing characteristics were unsatisfactory with the LPS set for the Ground position, not the Flight position, ever flew the TPE331-powered B100 or MU-2? I cannot help but think they did not. If they did, they'd think the landing characteristics of the A100 or F90 or 300/350 were pretty darn good when the blade went to the ground LPS! Oh sure, it decelerates more rapidly and you dare not reduce power to idle too early, but it's something any pilot could learn to handle…just like pilots learn to handle B100s and MU-2s. Well, no matter that, in my opinion, the Flight LPS is rather unnecessary, the designers made the decision to require it, and so it is.

As for the lower VMCA argument, yes, that is important on the other four-bladed King Air models (A100 and F90-series), since their VMCA is based on a windmilling propeller. As for the 300 and 350, however, it becomes a moot point since their VMCA is predicated on a feathered propeller, which is why Autofeather is a required piece of equipment on these models.

Ground and Flight Low Pitch Stops – How They Work

Let me review how the ground and flight LPSs are created, how they can malfunction, and how you can test them on the 300 and 350 models. We are going to come at this from the standpoint of intelligent pilots but not as engineers. I am choosing to leave out most of the nuts and bolts details and instead concentrate on the big picture.

As we know, oil flowing into the propeller dome sends the blades to a flatter or finer pitch, a lower blade angle. As the dome receives this oil, it moves forward and a mechanical connection to it causes a valve – the Beta valve – to start to close. When the dome has moved enough that the Beta valve goes fully closed, it stops the flow of oil into the dome. Without the oil, the blades cannot continue to flatten. That is what we mean by the term "mechanically activated hydraulic stop." Namely, physical linkage causes the propeller oil inflow to be terminated. Without receiving new oil – oil is a liquid, and that's what "hydraulic" refers to here – the possibility of reaching flatter angles is stopped.

When the pilot moves the power lever aft – by lifting over the Idle gate, then the Ground Fine gate, and pulling backwards, of course – he or she is using physical cable linkage to re-open the Beta valve and allow additional oil to flow to the propeller, sending the blades even flatter. As they flatten, however, again the Beta valve closes until the hydraulic stop is again created, preventing further travel to flatter or even reverse blade angles. In other words, the mechanically activated hydraulic LPS is *movable*, based on where the pilot positions the power lever in the Beta and Reverse ranges.

Now try to visualize in your mind's eye the cable that connects the power lever to the Beta valve: the Reversing cable. Just think of a wire rope with the power lever on one end and the Beta valve on the other. Pulling back on the power lever pulls back on the Beta valve, opening it up and permitting more oil to get to the prop. Now let's add one more piece to our mental picture. Suppose that we cut off the end of our reversing cable and insert an equal-length, two-position, electric device (*solenoid* is the fancy word here) between the end of our cut cable and the Beta valve. When this device is *not* powered – receiving no electricity – it is in the *long* position such that the overall length between the power lever and the Beta valve is unchanged. In other words, there's no way to even know that this device is now installed. All works just like it did before.

However, when the device *is* powered – receiving electricity – is moves to its *shorter* position. This re-opens the Beta valve and allows the LPS to move to a flatter position. The Beta valve would feel exactly the same effect as if the pilot had picked up the power lever and pulled it back enough to move the Beta valve the same amount as that caused by the shortened solenoid.

This, folks, is how we achieve our two different LPSs, Flight and Ground. When the solenoid is *not powered*, meaning that the LPS is at a larger blade angle, we have the *Flight* LPS. When the solenoid is *powered* and shortens up, we have the *Ground* LPS. I guess that's why the name given to this device is the Ground Low Pitch Stop solenoid. You think? Duh!

The source of power for both left and right GLPS solenoids comes through a single circuit breaker on the cockpit's right side panel labeled "Prop Gov Test." Darn! I wish they had labeled that sucker "GLPS!" Why is it called what it is? Because this circuit also provides the power for testing the left and right Overspeed Governors (OSGs). Every PT6-powered King Air ever built has always needed a source of power for making the Overspeed Governor's operating speed move from the normal, above redline value, down to a lower value that can be achieved during the test. So, this "Prop Gov Test" label has existed from Day One. When models were developed that needed electric power for certain LPS functions, the designers merely piggy-backed onto this existing CB. It makes sense, sure, but I firmly believe that it is much more important that the pilot realizes this CB controls the GLPS – something that is needed on every flight – instead of knowing that it allows the OSG test to occur – something that is somewhat rarely done.

In the 300-series, either one of two different actions will cause the GLPS solenoid to receive power and shorten the cable: Lifting either power lever or landing (putting weight on the landing gear, compressing the strut and activating the squat switch). A memory jogger that I use is "L or L." *Lift* or *Land*…either action moves the LPS from Flight to Ground.

The old A100 and F90-series have a very small difference in blade angle between the two distinct LPS settings, about 3 degrees. The 300-series have a huge difference: about 12 degrees. Want to land hard enough to damage your shiny 300 or 350? It's very easy to do: Merely lift up either or both power levers when you are still about 10 feet up in the flare! (It's been done, and it's ugly!)

To allow the pilots to easily determine that the blade angle has flattened to the GLPS setting, left and right Prop Pitch annunciators are provided. In the 300, they are yellow and hence they trigger the Master Caution Flashers when they illuminate…which they do on every landing. What a bummer! You do nothing wrong and yet the darn flasher must be acknowledged and canceled on every touchdown. In the 350, Beech learned from their "mistake" on the 300 and made the light white: a Status instead of a Caution annunciator. No flashers are triggered upon touchdown in the 350.

Malfunctions

Let's now examine a few malfunction scenarios. First, if we lose the ability to send power to the GLPS solenoid, then our landing flare will be totally normal but we won't experience that sudden extra drag after touchdown as the landing gear struts compress. Nor will we feel the drag when we lift up the power levers as we are rolling on the runway after touchdown. However, as we pull back from Idle to Ground Fine, now we would feel some extra deceleration. There is a good chance that one or both of our "Prop Pitch" annunciators will not illuminate as they should. If we lift up the second time and pull aft over the Ground Idle gate back into Reverse, now we have – depending on our exact power lever rigging – an excellent chance that we will start to pick up forward speed! What's happening here is that the power lever linkage starts telling the engine we want more power but, because the blade angle is about 12 degrees larger than it should be, the propeller is still providing *positive* rather than *negative* thrust!

So, in this first malfunction scenario – landing without GLPS power – it is important to select a longer-than-normal runway, expect little if any reversing action, and use only Ground Fine and brakes, not Reverse.

Suppose we were forced to make a No Flap landing at the same time that we had no GLPS. Not a very happy thought, is it? Now we'd better select a *really* long runway, maybe twice as much as we usually need. You may be thinking this situation would occur only during a landing that followed a *total* electrical failure…a once-in-a-lifetime chance. Not quite. Sadly, the first 300s – FA-2 through FA-110, over 100 airplanes – will leave us in exactly this situation if ever we have an electrical short that wipes out our Left Generator Bus. Both the Flaps and the GLPSs are powered from this bus! Starting with FA-111, and for all the FL-series (350s), this oversight was corrected and the GLPS power source became the Right Generator Bus while the Flaps remained on the Left.

Remember, however, if you ever do lose both generators, *Automatic Load Shedding* causes all equipment on *both* Generator Buses to be lost. Unless you can restore the buses by use of the Manual Close position of the Bus Tie switch –You wouldn't want to do that, of course, except with the landing assured and with enough energy remaining in the battery – then I hope you have been able to select a double-normal-length runway.

The second malfunction scenario I will present is much more common than the first we've just presented and can be easily fixed. It is the situation on the ground wherein, almost always after conducting a battery start, that we observe one or both propellers sitting on the Flight LPS, not on the Ground LPS. How do we know this? Because the Prop Pitch annunciator is not illuminated and the propeller speed is well below the 1,050 minimum ground limit. To explain what is causing this, we need to present a little more technical "nuts and bolts."

When the designers decided that the big 12 degree shift from Flight to Ground is what they desired, the solenoid they needed to accomplish this was larger and more heavy-duty than one they'd utilized in the later F90 King Air models. In use, the heat generated when this big solenoid was powered was found to cause a high number of premature solenoid failures. As most of you know from experience, it takes a harder shove to *start* something rolling than it does to *keep* it rolling. In a like fashion, it takes more electricity to make the solenoid initially pull to shorten the cable than it does to hold it in the shortened position. Hence, the designers reduced the heat in the solenoid by making the *holding* power less than the initial *pulling* power. They did this by cutting the input voltage in half two seconds after the solenoid initially receives power.

Just in case that the designed power reduction fails to occur – increasing the chance of damage to the solenoid – I make it a habit to pull the Prop Gov Test CB whenever ground power is to be applied for a lengthy time. Sitting in the hangar updating the GPS database or on the ramp running the electric heat in the winter, with the engines not running, there is no advantage gained by the GLPS solenoids remaining powered.

Follow me through on the explanation of why the propeller is not on the GLPS after starting. Since weight was on the gear, the GLPS solenoids activated when the Generator Buses first were powered and, within two seconds, went to their holding voltage. So far, so good. But during the battery start, when voltage took a momentary nosedive due to the starter demand, there is an excellent chance that the solenoid experienced enough loss of power that it could no longer hold the shortened position. The spring won the tug-of-war and the solenoid returned to the Flight (long) position.

So now the engine starts are over, aircraft voltage is normal, yet one or both GLPS solenoids do not have the strength to make that initial pull to the shortened position. How do we fix it? Easy: Take power away from the GLPS solenoid, reapply it, and let the extra initial pulling power have a chance to work again.

The most obvious way of "taking power away…and reapplying it" is to cycle (pull and reset) the Prop Gov Test CB. That works just fine, but it involves a stretch across the cockpit – if you are flying alone – and a search for the correct CB. The easier method is different for the 300 than for the 350. In the 300, merely hold up and then release the Ground Idle Stop test switch on the bottom row of the pilot's left subpanel. (This is the switch I call the Turbo Boost switch. I'll explain why I call it that a bit later in this article.) In the 350, it is easier still: Bump the power levers forward about an inch and then back to Idle as quickly as you can. We will review the details why this bumping of the power levers works before our article is concluded. Stay tuned a little while longer.

The King Air Book

The third and last malfunction scenario I will discuss is one that "can't happen" but sometimes, it does! Namely, it is the case in which the LPS moves to the Ground position without either of the "Ls" having occurred: No Landing nor Lifting. What I think is happening – and it is more of a theory that a fact – is that that GLPS never truly stopped operating when the liftoff occurred. Once the propeller is governing, the position of the LPS is immaterial and cannot be determined. Suppose, at liftoff, even though power was removed from the GLPS solenoid as the strut extended, the reversing cable remained stuck in the shortened position. Unless you were to conduct slow flight and stall practice during this flight, there would be no way of realizing that the LPS were stuck in the Ground position until the flare for landing. But then, as the reduction of both power and airspeed caused the blade angle to flatten, the "missing" FLPS would become obvious as the blade angle continued flattening to the GLPS setting. Since this is unlikely to happen on both sides simultaneously, the outcome is massive yaw to one side and the illumination of the Prop Pitch annunciator light on that side, right before touchdown. In both my personal experience and the experience of others who have ridden through this event, the airplane was not bent nor hurt but the landing was not a good one and the event was certainly an attention getter!

Speaking with my best PT6 A & P experts, it seems that the most common causes of this somewhat scary scenario is that the reversing linkage has been adjusted too tight or the solenoid is not properly aligned with the cable and is binding.

350s with serial numbers after FL-114 have an extra caution annunciator, *Prop Grd Sol,* that illuminates whenever either left or right GLPS solenoids are receiving power when the airplane is airborne. (The squat switch disables the light on the ground, since at that time the solenoids *should* be powered.) Of course in flight, having neither Lifted nor Landed, neither the left nor right GLPS should ever be powered. If one is receiving power for some strange, unexplainable, reason, then we are set up for the excessive drag on that side in the flare. If the light comes on in flight – in time for us to see it and read the checklist before landing – we will be directed to pull the *Prop Gov Test* circuit breaker to disable the GLPS solenoid and to expect a longer landing since we will not have normal reversing. If pulling the CB does not turn off the annunciator – highly unlikely! – then we are told to fly a somewhat faster, power-on, approach with the propeller speed set at the lowest possible governing value, about 1,450 RPM. By keeping extra power and airspeed, with the governing speed set low, what we achieve is remaining on the governors as long as possible, so that we may not experience the lack of the FLPS until at or very close to touchdown.

Test Switches and Power Lever Switches

On the pilot's left subpanel sit a couple of switches used for testing the propeller system. The one on the left, "Prop Gov Test," is the simple one that all PT6-powered King Airs contain. When held up against the spring tension, it causes both the left and right Overspeed Governor (OSG) to change their speed settings to a value that can be achieved without disabling the Primary Governor. In the case of the 300-series, the test moves the OSG from about 1,768 RPM down to 1,565 +/- 45 RPM.

The other test switch, the right one of the two, is the one we need to discuss here since it serves for testing the Low Pitch Stops. The switch is labeled "Ground Idle Stop Test." That's a poor choice of words! Why? Because in fact the switch allows testing of the *Flight* Low Pitch Stop while on the ground, not the other way around.

GLPS Test on the 300

In the straight 300, what the switch does is exceedingly simple: It removes power from the left and right GLPS solenoids. With no power, remember, the cable lengthens and the LPS moves to the Flight position.

The actual test procedure is to add sufficient power to spin the propellers at 1,500 RPM without holding any switch. Since the blade angle is so relatively flat while on the GLPS, it takes little power to achieve this 1,500 RPM speed. Now the switch is held up and two responses need to be observed: First, the Prop Pitch annunciators extinguish as the blade angle increases to the FLPS setting. Second, the decrease in RPM needs to fall within a fairly narrow range as the blades take their larger bite of air. The POH specifies that the new stabilized speed be between 1,100 and 1,200 RPM. Expressed another way, the drop must be 350 +/- 50 RPM.

I haven't come across an A & P yet who is willing to get his protractor out and measure blade angles while the propeller is spinning! Instead of actually measuring blade angles, your maintenance people determine if the angle is correct by measuring how much torque is required to spin the propeller at a specified speed: 1,500 RPM in this case. If the change in angles is correct going from the GLPS to the FLPS – about 12 degrees, you will recall – then that extra rotational drag should slow the propeller by about 350 RPM. If you see only a 200 RPM drop, the two LPSs are too close together. A 600 RPM drop, on the other hand, means there is too much separation.

By the way, if you want to check your FLPS blade angle like the mechanics, the Sea Level, standard day torque values at 1,500 RPM are 42% for the 300 and 38% for the 350. Charts exist in the Maintenance Manuals to show the proper value for any reasonable field elevation and OAT combination. The thinner the air, the less torque required.

The King Air Book

I know of an event in which the propellers on a 300 were reinstalled after overhaul and both the maintenance and the pilot folks did a poor job of conducting this test correctly. They did not notice that the RPM drop was hugely excessive...meaning the blades were nearly going to the feathered position when the FLPS activated. Right at rotation, as the squat switch removed power from the GLPS solenoids, both propellers instantly lost about 500 RPM and the torque rocketed well past redline! Fortunately, the plane was light and could fly successfully even when the pilot pulled the torque back to get within limits. As the airspeed increased during the climb to pattern altitude, the RPM also increased until it reached governing speed. At that point, all appeared normal. However, as the plane came around for the landing, the crew observed the propeller speed going slow – falling off the governors – much earlier than normal and the flare for landing was weird: Hardly any drag was felt, since the blade angle was so large.

If ever there is a plane "designed" to give a surprise right at rotation, right at V1, it's the straight 300! Unless the LPS test is conducted before takeoff, one would never be able to determine that the FLPS was set to a bite so excessive that it will drag down the RPM. Now don't get me wrong. I am not advocating that you need to conduct the FLPS test prior to *every* takeoff. However, you surely need to do it on some regular basis and especially whenever the propellers have been adjusted in any way!

As I have mentioned, the extra thrust provided at idle when the blade bite moves from the GLPS to the FLPS is very satisfying and useful. Need to start the plane rolling from a standing start? Need to expedite across that runway? Need to keep the speed up to the end of a long runway? In all of these cases, reach down with your left hand and hold up the *Turbo Boost* switch. Yep, that's what I often call the *Ground Idle Stop Test* switch, since it yields such a nice boost to taxi power when it's held.

Many, if not most, 300-pilots – and I am one of them – have adopted the technique of holding the Turbo Boost switch up on nearly every takeoff, especially rolling takeoffs, until they observe that the propeller speed stabilizes on the governor at 1,700 RPM. What's the purpose of this technique?

The first benefit this procedure gives is making the application of power much smoother and easier. Because the blade angle is so flat on the GLPS, the addition of just a little power has a huge effect on prop RPM. Unless the pilot is very good at watching the RPM gauges and being v-e-r-y slow and smooth on the power until the props stabilize at 1,700 RPM, invariably a lot of propeller/power surging will occur as the governors are reached at too fast of a rate. On the other hand, with the blades biting at the FLPS setting, now the power response and acceleration rate of propeller speed is nice, just what one expects in a typical propeller-driven airplane.

The second benefit of this procedure – one that few pilots recognize they are achieving – is that it prevents the potential for the rotation surprise if ever the FLPSs are set at too large of an angle. The story I related about the big RPM drop at rotation would not have happened had the Turbo Boost switch been held. Instead, the pilot would have – I hope! –observed that the RPM never reached 1,700 even with full power going through 60 or 80 knots! An abort would have, should have, been conducted and no rotation surprise would have occurred.

GLPS Test on the 350

The manufacturer became aware early in the history of 300s that pilots did not like the standard takeoff power application characteristics. Unless they used the Turbo Boost switch technique, smooth takeoff power applications were the exception, not the rule. Yet, some pilots were reluctant to use that technique, either because they didn't want their left hand off the wheel for the first few moments of the takeoff roll or because they worried about the implications of the propeller speed dropping below the 1,050 RPM minimum limitation for a few nanoseconds.

Beechcraft addressed this complaint – the complaint that smooth power application was nearly impossible using no special technique – by adding two additional switches into the system. These switches – one left, one right – are hidden inside the power pedestal and one activates whenever the appropriate power lever is moved slightly forward from Idle: At about the 69% N1 position, or about a half-inch forward of Idle. When the switch is hit, power is removed from the GLPS solenoid on that side. As you now know, the result is that the reversing cable lengthens and the LPS moves to the Flight position.

In effect, when power starts to be added on a 350 model, it acts as if an invisible hand reaches down and holds up the ol' Turbo Boost switch. Neat! This desirable change, however, causes a couple of changed operational considerations.

First, the GLPS Test switch is now rewired and no longer functions as it does on a straight 300. Instead, it is essentially "backwards." Rather than *removing power* from the GLPS solenoids, now the switch *keeps power applied* regardless of power lever position. Holding the switch up now, at idle, causes nothing to occur. However, as power is added and the power levers pass the 69% switches, still nothing happens. In other words, holding up the GLPS test switch *prevents* the power lever switches from *removing* the GLPSs.

The LPS test procedure changes also. To make the LPS move from the Ground to the Flight position while at 1,500 RPM – so as to observe the proper RPM drop and the extinguishing of the Prop Pitch annunciators – the pilot must now hold the test switch up while power is set for 1,500 RPM. This keeps the GLPSs activated even though the power levers will be above the 69% N1 switch position. To make the blade angle increase to the FLPS setting, the switch is released. That's when the annunciators going off and the RPM dropping the correct amount may be checked. By the way, now the POH states that the drop must be 300 +/- 50 instead of 350 +/- 50 like the straight 300. Do they do this just to confuse us?!

The second operational consideration that arises due to the changed 350 system is that we can no longer reach down and get that satisfying burst of taxi power by holding up the Turbo Boost switch. I suppose now I need to stop calling it by that slang name. There are two ways to get the boost in blade angle/thrust: Bump the power lever up a little, so that the 69% switch is activated, or have the SIC pull the *Prop GovTest* CB. I must admit that this is one situation in which I prefer the 300 over the 350. By using the test switch on the 300, I can determine exactly whether the GLPS stays activated or not on the ground. In the 350, I am forced to change power a little to achieve the same result. I cannot have idle power and maintain the FLPS setting in a 350…unless I resort to the CB.

Modified 300s

Both the Beechcraft factory as well as Stevens Aviation (of Nashville) have offered modifications that change the straight 300 LPS operation and make it like the 350. In the case of Beechcraft, their Aircraft Kit Part Number 130-9600, referenced in the POH, exactly mimics the 350 design. With the Stevens' STC, there are subtle differences. Namely, the Ground Low Pitch Stop Test switch is changed such that it is no longer a spring-loaded switch but rather is a two-position toggle. When in the down position, the system is unchanged and continues operating exactly like a straight 300 but without the Turbo Boost function. In the up position, now it is almost like a 350. Why "almost?" Because, instead of left and right 69% N1 switches, it has only one that happens to be on the *left* power lever even though it removes power from *both* left and right GLPS solenoids. When the switch is up – where it routinely remains – one would be hard-pressed to notice any difference between the operation of a 350 and of this modified airplane. However, what the modification does not allow is making only one side take the bigger bite. It's either both or nothing. Only the 350 can boost bite up on a single side by adding power on just that side…helpful for making a tight turn.

The test for the Stevens-modification involves moving the toggle down, running power up to 1,500 RPM, then moving the switch up and observing the proper Annunciator Off / RPM Decrease indications. (And, yes, it's the 350 +/- 50 value we are seeking here.)

Summary

Wow! Quite an intricate system, isn't it? Nevertheless, the result is that we avoid propeller vibration on the ground and yet have an airplane that is a delight during the flare for landing…just like a big ol' Cub! Y'all be careful out there!

KING AIR RAMBLINGS

The article will cover a smattering of topics that have arisen lately. I hope you find my thoughts interesting and enlightening.

***

A few weeks ago I rode in the right seat of a King Air 200 model while I did an evaluation of the airplane for a prospective buyer. Although usually I do the flying on these evaluations myself, the owner's professional pilot flew from the left seat. He didn't know me from Adam and was clear in expressing his opinion that his insurance policy requirements specified no one fly except himself.

Before we flew, I'd done an extensive interior and exterior check of the airplane as part of the pre-purchase evaluation. I always run the flaps down for these checks so that I can inspect the flap actuators, bonding straps, and the general condition of the flap wells. Much to my amazement, I found that the split flap protection mechanism on the right side had been surgically removed! There were the stubs where the mechanism once attached, but the attachment arms were gone!

I pointed this out to the owner's mechanic and expected that the flight would be delayed a day or so while that squawk got repaired. Surprise! The parts were found and within a couple of hours it was reinstalled correctly! How do these things happen? Weird!

Even in the hot summertime of the southern city we were in, I found the cockpit bleed air switches in the Open position as I did my cockpit checks. I moved them down to the center, Environmental Off, position, where they should be. As the pilot settled in the left seat, his first comment was that he'd get the air conditioning on quickly so that we'd get some cooling. "Good plan!" I said.

He started the right engine and went to High Idle. So far, so good. I was now expecting him to start the left engine then get the AC going. Nope. Instead, he turned on the right generator, turned on the air conditioning and immediately moved the right bleed air switch up to Open. Huh?

"Let's leave that switch off until takeoff, so the air conditioning doesn't have to fight against that hot bleed air coming in," I suggested. "No, we need that for cooling," was the reply. I bit my tongue and said nothing.

Now he switched on the avionics master and picked up ATIS and our clearance for the IFR test flight. The cabin was starting to cool…but not as quickly as it would have without the hot bleed air coming in. He next reached for the left starter switch.

"Uh, I think we should probably kill the radios first, don't you think?" I opined. "Oh yeah. I guess so," he said.

With the radios now off, with the right generator selected off, but with the air conditioning still on, he initiated the start of the left engine. As it accelerated past 12% N1, I expected the right generator to be turned on again so as to enjoy the benefits of a generator-assisted start of the second engine. Again, I was wrong. The pilot proceeded with a battery-only start of the left engine. Without the generator boost, of course, the N1 speed barely got to 16% and the starting peak ITT – while still far below limits – was probably 100° hotter than it would have been with the generator assist.

With the left start completed and with both engines selected to High Idle, the pilot turned on both generators. I donned my Bose headset and heard the whine of the air conditioner's compressor blower. "It's still working, thank goodness!" I thought to myself. Shortly after this I noticed the pilot hitting the squelch button on a Comm radio in an attempt to find why he wasn't hearing anything. I took off my headset so we could talk more easily – since the intercom system was not yet being powered – and pointed out that the Avionics Master switch was off. I also suggested that the inverters be checked and one of them selected on before the avionics master was re-activated. He followed those "suggestions," we could now use the headsets and radios, and the gyros came up to speed. My suspicion was that he was in the habit of leaving the avionics master switch on during the second start, so my having him kill it had thrown off his normal habit patterns. Or, maybe he was just a little nervous with another pilot up front with him.

What's my point to this story? Did the pilot actually hurt any equipment in doing what he did? No, it didn't seem so. Not this time. Before I remind you of the potential problems with his procedures, let me tell you of another experience I had last week. I think they are quite closely related.

In this second situation, I was giving a flight check in a King Air E90 to a young pilot with a rather low level of experience, especially in King Airs. I began by asking him if he had any questions about a system or procedure that were unclear to him, so that we might discuss those topics and clarify the confusion as best we could. His first two queries involved flying in icing conditions and engine starting. As a preface to my reply to him, I asked him "What does the POH say?" His knowledge of the Pilot's Operating Handbook – the Bible of airplane operation – was weaker than I would have liked.

I am the first to state that sometimes procedures in the POH are out-of-date, not in line with the latest, improved procedures that have been published in a more recent POH, and often written more based on legal liability concerns than on what's best in flying the airplane. ***However, it is still the bedrock starting point! Without that foundation, there's nothing to build upon!*** I will go so far as to emphatically state this: Unless someone – someone who's opinion you respect – can convince you that a modification of some procedure or technique has merit and will be beneficial, then stick with the book! Don't go off on your own into uncharted territory!

The pilot with whom I flew in the 200 seemed very prone to penetrate into these uncharted territories with disconcerting frequency. There is no starting procedure whatsoever in the POH – even when an External Power Unit is utilized – that directs one to have the AC or avionics on while starting! With the AC operating, the Condenser Blower is pulling current and increasing the chance that a current limiter will be blown during the second start. And why even *have* an avionics master switch if you are going to zap the radios with a big starting voltage transient anyway?

The 200's POH also clearly states that Environmental Bleed Air should be off for more efficient ground cooling.

Are you familiar with the acronym RTFM? It stands for "Read the Full Manual" or something very close to that. Dear readers, unless you have spent the time and effort to RTFM, you shouldn't be flying the airplane as PIC. As I told my young E90 pilot, "Always start by reviewing what the POH says." Once that bedrock is established, only then should one consider making modifications to improve upon it.

Come along with me and return to the 200 pre-purchase evaluation, after we got airborne. I truly believe that this highly-experienced pilot had very little understanding about both his own airborne radar and the Nexrad radar downloads that he was receiving on his Garmin GNS 530. With nothing but ground returns showing on our radar, with the Nexrad images showing all green ahead, and with visibility that showed we wouldn't be IMC for at least another five thousand feet of climb and probably thirty miles of forward travel, this pilot began demanding weather deviations from Departure Control and then from Center. I was shocked and wondered what he did when there really was enough crud around that avoidance was prudent.

This airplane was equipped with the King KFC-300 autopilot/flight director system. Although perhaps not my all-time favorite King Air automatic flight control system, it is a fine unit, does an excellent job when working properly, and has some unique features that few other systems contain. One of these is Speed Profile, abbreviated SPD PRF on the selection button. This is a pitch mode that causes the indicated airspeed that existed when the button was pressed to be maintained but, unlike a simple IAS hold mode, it decreases this speed by 1.75 knots per thousand feet of climb. Doing this makes the cruise climb speed fairly well match the cruise climb speed profile shown in – Guess where? – the POH!

The 200 pilot I was with selected this mode, called it "Speed Performance," and when I asked what it did, he didn't answer. He'd been told by someone to use it while climbing, so he did. Also, since the climb speed when he engaged it was about 25 knots faster than what it should have been for that altitude, our climb speed continued to be unnecessarily fast and by the time we got to FL230, we were climbing at less than 500 fpm. (You're supposed to advise ATC whenever that happens, remember?) I asked if it would be OK to climb steeper and slower to expedite our arrival at the filed FL260. He was very reluctant to decrease climb speed below 140 knots IAS, even though the POH shows the speed going to 130 between 20,000 and 25,000 feet and then to 120 above 25,000 feet. (We were in clear air, too.) That's just one example, folks, of how easy it is to pay an unnecessary penalty – in this case, a very low rate of climb – when one doesn't have the knowledge contained within the POH.

The last observation about this pilot that I will pass along before I finally get off my rant – and off of his fanny! – concerns his landing. I watched him cross the threshold on the VASI but about 10 knots fast. Not bad, so far. But then the power was never reduced to idle and no flare was begun. Rather, he flew right down into strong ground effect with no power reduction at all. He forced the nose down to get it on the runway and we finally touched down in a nearly flat attitude about 3,000 feet past the fixed distance marker, with a good bump, and having allowed a minor crosswind to move us well left of the centerline. We had over 7,000 feet of runway to use, so I won't say that the landing was unsafe. However, it certainly made me wonder if this was his normal technique. If so, I wondered how he handled short runways. Without the ongoing practice of touching down near one's aiming point, it's harder to pull that act out of the hat when it's required. By the way, our parking spot was near the approach end of the runway...there was no benefit in landing long this time.

***

I entitled this article "King Air Ramblings" so I am now going to ramble on about a few topics that all deal with King Airs but which aren't closely related. First, let's review the use of the Engine Auto-Ignition switches.

As I mentioned earlier in this article, there are many instances in which improved techniques or procedures make their appearance in the POHs of models that were certificated more recently – improvements based on later knowledge and clearer thinking – and yet these same procedures appear in a revised version of the POHs of earlier models either much later or not at all. The adage, "Out of sight, out of mind" seems to have become, for Beechcraft, "Out of production, out of mind." How one is directed to use Auto-Ignition is a case in point.

The first King Air models did not have Auto-Ignition switches. They had Ignition switches that energized the ignitors – glow plugs, then – whenever they were activated, but there was no tie-in to torque. If selected on, the Ignitors ran continuously until selected off. But then, due to an oversight in the cowling design that was quickly identified and rectified by Beech at their expense, it became obvious that King Airs were experiencing some flame-outs in icing conditions. The examination of this phenomenon led Beech to recognize that the initial cowling design was in error, make the necessary changes, and include in the solution to the problem an Automatic re-light system installed on all new King Airs as well as retrofitted to the small existing fleet. That was way back in the mid-60s…ancient history.

When Auto-Ignition made its appearance, the POMs – they were Pilot Operating Manuals back then, not yet POHs – directed the pilots to activate the auto-ignition switches whenever there was a chance of ice ingestion. The manual writers expressed this by saying "Whenever in visible moisture with an OAT below 5°C and at night above 14,000 feet."

The model 200 was the first King Air to have spark ignitors instead of glow plugs. Thinking that these new ignitors would offer nearly infinite life – a false assumption, as it turned out – led Beech to take an overly-conservative approach and direct that pilots should arm Auto-Ignition for *all* flight operations, regardless of the likelihood of icing being encountered. When the Army, Air Force, Navy, and Marine Corps began operating their various C-12 models – the military version of the BE-200 – they decided to copy Beech's procedures and use Auto-Ignition all the time. Hence, an awful lot of pilots learned that turning on Auto-Ignition upon Runway Lineup was the normal thing to do.

Yet now reports starting arriving at Beech telling of frustration with the limited ignitor life being experienced. In some cases, the 200s spark ignitors were being replaced just as often as the old glow plugs in B90s! Not good!

To correct this "problem," the writers of the 300-series POHs realized that Auto-Ignition was unnecessary in non-icing environments and wrote the checklists accordingly, such that Auto-Ignition only needed to be armed "Before visible moisture is encountered at +5°C and below, or at night when freedom from visible moisture is not assured at +5°C and below."

That's the best way to utilize Auto-Ignition. Namely, if it's cold outside and you can't see the cloud you may be penetrating, then arm Auto-Ignition. On the other hand, when it is severe clear, why use 'em?

In my 35 years of King Air flying and teaching experience, I have found that there is but one event that can cause a flame-out in a King Air's PT6 and hence lead to the desirability of Auto-Ignition being armed…and that is failure to extend the engine's inertial separators, or ice vanes. Let's talk about their usage a bit.

***

"When in doubt, get 'em out!" That trite memory-jogger was the method by which one of my old Beechcraft Training Center colleagues tried to instill into his students the importance of ice vane usage. It's darn good advice.

The King Air Book

Clouds are such fickle things! One day you can go through a lot of seemingly wet, icy, clouds, and never get the least bit of frost on the wings. Yet, on other days in what appears to be identical conditions, Geez, you turn into an icicle within the first moments of cloud penetration! In the words of Clint Eastward playing the role of Dirty Harry, "Are you feeling lucky, punk?"

Those who don't always extend the ice vanes – or those who don't turn on the Engine Anti-Ice switches, for you pitot-cowl-equipped models – are playing a game of Russian roulette. You must be feeling mighty lucky, punk! If your luck holds out, good for you. If it doesn't, bad for the one paying the engine bills.   Want to risk it? Want to bet $50K+ that those clouds won't hurt your engines? If so, then you're a wild and crazy guy and one with whom I prefer not to fly.

I know that none of us like to see the torque decrease as we extend the vanes. In fact, in the PT6A-20-powered A, B, and C90s, the vanes being extended can spell the difference sometimes between climbing and not climbing. I know; I've been there.

Thank goodness, folks, clouds usually don't extend over hundreds of miles. Rest assured that, given enough time, you'll break free of the clouds and be able to retract the vanes and continue the climb. Plus, for you pilots operating –21, -28, or –135/135A-powered 90s, enjoy the fact that even with your ice vanes extended you still have a whale of a lot more climb performance than those old – 20-powered models!

On nights with a bright moon, seeing upcoming clouds is easy. On a moonless night, it can be impossible. That is why you need to be more conscientious about ice vane usage when it's dark. As you probably know, you can get a better view of what's ahead by momentarily turning off the cockpit lights and leaning close to the windshield so as to block other stray light from the cabin. Unless that view shows clear sailing ahead, then there is indeed "doubt" and you need to "get 'em out."

The other advantage of ice vane extension is better FOD (Foreign Object Damage) protection on the ground. In the older models that have the chin-type cowl, not the pitot-cowl, it is quite difficult for the engine to ingest sand or gravel on the ground, even if one stays in Reverse at too low of a speed. That's because, since the back of the cowling is always open, that relatively heavy particle will likely take the straight path of least resistance and exit the cowling harmlessly instead of turning the corner and making it into the compressor. Thus, routine use of ice vanes on the ground is not necessary if you have the chin-type cowl.

However, if you operate a King Air with a pitot cowl – F90-1, C90As and later, 300-series – then it is best to use Engine Anti-Ice for all ground operations. Without the switch activated, now the back of the cowling is closed and once a particle crosses the cowling intake lip there's no other place for the foreign object to go except into the compressor.

The 300-series – due to their very flat propeller blade pitch on the ground and their relatively small propeller-tip-to-ground clearance – are the models most prone to FOD when Engine Anti-Ice is not used all the time on the ground. Although it is much less likely that a three-blade C90A model will suck up a piece of sand or gravel high enough such that it crosses the intake lip, why take the chance? You see, extending the vanes on the ground has virtually no downside risk! Does ITT go up? Not noticeably. Does oil cooling suffer? No. Does the engine start differently? No.

The only downside risk of ice vane usage on the ground is the fact that the cowling is now less efficient and achieving full takeoff torque will cause slightly higher N1 speeds and ITTs. Is this really a concern? I don't think so, because, once you are sure that you will be avoiding deep Beta or Reverse usage, then there is no need for ice vane extension. In other words, Engine Anti-Ice should be turned off when doing the runway lineup procedure. Of course, if it's a snow-covered runway and/or if icing conditions will exist soon after liftoff, then the vanes should stay down. If it is that cold outside, you'll have no problem making takeoff power even with the vanes extended!

Also realize that the amount of inefficiency caused by ice vane deployment depends on how much ram air is available…airspeed, in other words. The amount of torque drop you observe when extending the ice vanes in cruise will be much higher than the difference you would observe at lift-off and initial climb speed.

The cowling on the model 200-series is neither the chin-type nor the pitot-type. It's a middle-of-the-road design, even though it is still the cowling being used on the latest B200s and B200GTs. Here's my thoughts: If you operate a 200 with three-blade propellers, the ice vanes are not needed for routine ground operation. (But, as always, "If in doubt, get 'em out!") On the other hand, because of a flatter blade angle at the tip and a higher idle propeller speed, I strongly suggest that all 200-pilots with four-blade propellers use the vanes for all ground operations.

Unlike the pitot-cowl, however, there is a definite downside risk in using the 200's vanes on the ground…less air flow across the oil cooler. Because of this, early 200s had a limitation stating that ice vanes could not be used if the OAT was above 15°C. The later B200 POHs have this limitation removed – and the earlier book should be revised – and instead one will find the following limitation: "Ice vanes, left and right, shall be retracted for all takeoff and flight operations in ambient temperatures of above +15°C." In the Normal Procedures section of the POH, you will also find this: "Note: The engine ice vanes should be extended for all ground operations to minimize ingestion of ground debris. Turn engine anti-ice off, when required, to maintain oil temperature within limits."

I operate 200 models a lot out of various Valley-of-the-Sun airports here in the Phoenix area. It is very rare that I find the oil temperatures reaching the redline even on summer days. It only happens if I am conducting extensive high power ground runup checks. There is absolutely no worries about FOD during the rare times we need to retract the vanes due to oil temperature if – and it's an important *if* – we merely stay out of deep Beta/Reverse. It may mean we need a little more brake usage, but so be it.

*****

Here's another topic I want to ramble about: Gear and Flap operating speed limits. Although the airplane has certainly been tested at dive speeds well beyond VMO, such is not the case when it comes to gear and flap limits. I suggest that you plan ahead and start your deceleration process such that you can extend flaps and gear at speeds 20 knots or so below the limits. On the other hand, by not making it a habit to use the limits, it makes you feel better when you get yourself into a situation where you really need to put out the brakes at their highest speeds. Use the limits when you have to, but don't make it routine. (One of my friends who flew for a commuter airline in Beech 99s years ago reported a phenomenal decrease in gear maintenance problems when this technique was taught to and demanded of the pilots.)

*****

If I were to sit down in your cockpit today, how many annunciator or post light bulbs would I find inoperative? None, if any? Would the digital clock(s) have the correct time and date? If your answer is yes, I'll wager that you are a very conscientious pilot with a reasonable degree of obsessive-compulsive behavior that bodes well for a professional pilot. If the answer is no, I am not nearly as optimistic about your approach to flying. When little things are allowed to slide, bigger things tend to follow…at least that's my observation.

*****

When your Garmin 400- or 500-series navigator(s) is on a small enough map scale, is it cluttered with a lot of IFR intersections that you couldn't care less about? There's an easy fix. Hit the Menu key and select "Set Up Map." Now scroll and find the "Waypoints" section. Continue to find "Intersections" and then use the small knob to set both label and symbol to "Off." I suggest you do the same thing for "NDB" which you'll find right there too.

Another Garmin trick: When you hit the Direct-To key, I'll wager that most of us are only aware of the top line that is already highlighted with the cursor on. That's where we can type in the name of whatever point we want to head toward. There are two other selections on the Direct-To page that have merit, however. Take the big knob and move it clockwise to move the cursor down past the three top lines. Now you will find a "Flight Plan" box. Once it is highlighted, you can now take the small knob and find every waypoint that exists in the active flight plan. When ATC offers you a shortcut to a point further along in your plan, you don't have to hit the Flight Plan key to find that point. (Although you can, of course!) Instead, you can start by hitting Direct To, scrolling down to the Flight Plan box, finding the waypoint you want, then finish by hitting Enter twice. Overall, it is a few less operations to do it this way.

The second thing one can do after hitting Direct-To is to continue scrolling the cursor past the Flight Plan box to the last box on that page: Nearest. Once there, by use of the small knob, you can find and highlight any of the nearest airports. In an emergency, when you need to quickly find a place to get to now, you can start by hitting Direct To instead of going to the Nearest chapter.

***

Here's the last ramble for this month: Do you wish that your control wheel digital clocks displayed in 24-hour instead of 12-hour format? Get a screwdriver out and remove the clock from the wheel. Turn it over and you will find a hole in the metal housing. Often a piece of paper will be covering the hole. Remove the paper, take a little thing like a toothpick and slide the switch in that hole from one position to the other. Voila! Now you have it set in the 24-hour format. When I set the clock, I always use UTC time so that, when I listen to an ATIS report, it makes it easier to decide how old it is…but that's just ol' obsessive-compulsive Tom!

Be safe out there!

HOT WEATHER GROUND OPERATION

High temperature and long trouble-free engine life do not mix. One factor that helps to make an engine powerful and efficient – high internal temperature – is also a factor that contributes to its deterioration. Hence, any choice of cruise power settings for a turbine engine becomes a compromise between good performance and good engine health. If we want the engine to last indefinitely, we had better keep it in a sealed container and not put it on the wing of an airplane...which is not very realistic. It is also unrealistic to expect the engine to be trouble-free if we operate it at maximum ITT for significant periods of time.

(Let me interject a comment about the PT6A-21. This model's hot section is in fact identical to the –28 that has a 750°C redline, yet the –21's redline is only 695°. Why the difference? To keep the –21 from competing too strongly with the –28, and to make the early –21-powered C90s look worse on paper than the concurrently-manufactured E90s of that era. Knowing this, the –21 is the only model that I feel very comfortable operating at or near redline much of the time.)

If we accept the concept that high temperature and cycling temperature hasten engine deterioration – and should therefore be avoided, when *reasonable* to do so – what can we do? Here is where proper hot weather ground operation plays a big part.

Burning more fuel in an engine creates more temperature in the engine, right? Not necessarily. When we examine the effect of compressor speed (N1 or Ng) on interturbine temperature (ITT or T5), when other factors such as OAT and accessory load are held constant, we find this relationship:

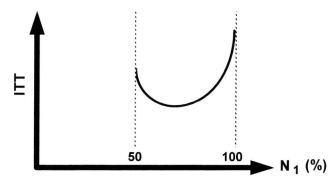

Fuel flow is increasing as compressor speed increases, but so also is total airflow. Since 75% or more of the engine's airflow is used for cooling, not combustion, it is understandable why ITT actually decreases as compressor speed increases (up to about 70%, or High Idle, speed)...the cooling effect of the air is greater than the heating effect of the fuel. This curve will shift upward on the graph when OAT, field elevation, generator load, or the amount of air bled from the engine increases. Recognizing this relationship and making it work for him or her is one of the best steps a pilot can take to promote engine health and longevity.

The cumulative effects of a high field elevation, hot outside air temperature, high accessory load – air conditioner running – and low compressor speed will guarantee that the ITT of any PT6 can exceed limits. (Remember that the Low Idle ITT limit is less than the takeoff limit that is "redlined" on the gauge, and varies from model to model. It may be as low as 660° or as high as 750°. Unfortunately, the Low Idle ITT limit is not shown on the cockpit gauge. One has to read the POM or POH to find it.) Once we have decided to operate at a particular airport, the field elevation and OAT are out of our control. The secret then to lower ground ITTs is the proper control of engine idle speed and accessory load.

An on-going point of argument concerning PT6s is this: At what N1 speed does the Low Idle limit cease to be a factor? Does the limit only apply at the lowest of the permissible Low Idle settings? Does the limit disappear only after the engine passes High Idle?

If anyone out there has a definitive answer about this, I would like to know. However, desiring to treat the engine as nicely as possible, I have concluded that I will treat the Low Idle limit as an *Idle Range* limit, doing all that I can to never exceed this limit while operating at any N1 speed I can select by use of the Condition lever.

There is one accessory that can be eliminated with the flip of a switch, and which will not be missed in any way…environmental bleed air. By keeping bleed air valves open for summer ground operation we are introducing warmer-than-ambient air into the cabin, making the air conditioner less effective. Although this bleed air is warming for us, it is cooling for the engine. Letting it remain in the engine will drop ITT anywhere from 5° to 20°. Thus we recommend that in the "After Landing" checklist that the bleed air valve switches be moved to the Closed or Envir Off position. Leave them there until runway lineup for your next takeoff. In fact, leaving bleed air off and turning the air conditioner off until after takeoff will always help in reducing ITT. You can turn them on after takeoff – with a 30 second or so delay between them to avoid an excessive pressurization bump – and get the air conditioner back on line then also.

Other significant accessory loads that we can control are those that the generator gives to the engine…specifically, the drag it imparts when helping with a generator-assisted start, when charging the battery right after starting, or when supplying current for the air conditioner's compressor motor as used on the 90–series and 100–series. During these high-load times it is imperative that the condition levers be positioned forward enough to sustain an elevated idle speed. All the way forward, to High Idle, will generally yield the coolest ITTs, with other factors constant. However, with the exception of generator-assisted starts, in which High Idle – or even more! – should always be used, the need to go *all* the way to High Idle usually arises only with an extreme combination of OAT and elevation…the "Hot day at Denver" situation. Hotter days at lower elevations can almost always be handled with no more than 60% N1. A conservative rule is this: **If in doubt, go to High Idle.**

That is, after starting, before turning on the second generator, have both engines at 70% N1. Then, after the second generator and air conditioner are turned on, and with the battery still charging, check the stabilized ITT. If it is comfortably below the idle limit, then try 65% on the condition levers. If still good, try 60%, etc. The airplane *is* noticeably quieter and easier to taxi at 60% than at 70% and that is why we avoid a blanket recommendation of High Idle on hot days, but if in doubt, you know what to do.

In the case of the 200–series and 300–series of King Airs, in which the air conditioner's compressor is driven mechanically by the right engine, the designers have ensured that the mechanical drive cannot even engage unless about 60% N1 exists. Under extreme cases of thin, hot, ambient air conditions, it is nearly impossible in early 200s to keep the right engine's ITT below the idle limit when operating the air conditioner. Try this: Turn off the right generator. By doing so, you allow the right engine to drive the compressor while the left engine drives the generator that is now supplying *all* of the electrical demands. Sometimes it is uncanny how nicely the ITTs match up by using this technique, with both sides now comfortably below the Low Idle limit. When conducting the runway lineup procedure, turn the generator back on…it's nice to have the redundancy of two as we leave dear Mother Earth.

What we have been discussing is the relationship between ITT and N1 during *steady state* ground operations. When the engine is *not* in a steady state, when it is changing from one speed to another, the ITT changes drastically. When power is advanced from idle, ITT zooms well above its final stabilized temperature because the fuel enters the combustion chamber before the engine accelerates and the compressor brings in more cooling airflow. Vice versa, as power is reduced, the ITT initially drops well below its final stabilized value. These transients, or spikes, are more pronounced when accelerating from Low Idle than at any other time. On hot days, they can become quite severe.

Although most pilots are careful to avoid huge spikes (by advancing the power lever and/or condition lever slowly when at Low Idle), there are two situations in which they are unwittingly spiking the engine with a vengeance. First, a spike occurs when they add power to make a tight turn into a parking space on the ramp. Since the pilot's attention is on the line person who is directing, or on the wing tip, the spike slips by unnoticed and then, to make matters worse, the engine is immediately shutdown without allowing time for the spiked temperature to cool and normalize.

Second, an unnoticed spike occurs whenever a landing is made with condition levers at Low Idle and then sufficient reverse power is selected to spool up, even a little, the N1. The cooler the OAT, the less will be the magnitude of these spikes. So, although it is always desirable to avoid spiked temperatures, on a cool day it may not be a big deal. However, on hot days, Wow! The solution? Don't operate on hot days with the condition levers at Low Idle. Expressed as a Do instead of a Don't – Do maintain an elevated idle speed with the condition levers when OAT is above 20°C.

All King Airs equipped with four-blade propellers – either installed as original factory equipment or retrofitted under STC approval – contain a new engine limit that does not apply to three-bladed aircraft. Namely, a minimum *propeller* idle speed is stated. To avoid the "reactionless mode" of propeller harmonic vibration, the prop must not be allowed to idle too slowly…unless it is feathered. Depending upon the model and the propeller, this new limit may be as low as 1,050 RPM or as high as 1,250 RPM.

To achieve the faster propeller idle speed, yet without requiring lots of brake usage to control taxi speed, a combination of two changes are made. First, the propeller's low pitch stop blade angle is flattened, causing less rotational resistance. Second, the Low Idle N1 speed is raised, causing the gas generator to drive the propeller with more "oomph."

Consequently, most of our discussion recommending elevated Low Idle speeds on hot days becomes a rather moot point if you have four-blade props. Your idles are already elevated! On the other hand, make certain that you have your maintenance people rig the blade angles and N1 speeds correctly so that the new minimum RPM limit is not being violated. In my experience, this is an area in which many violations are found, perhaps due to less overall familiarity with the four-blade airplanes.

The plane will land differently when the condition levers are not at Low Idle…it will tend to float a bit more. However, this can be easily handled with proper speed control and landing technique.

So here is how it should go on a hot day. After landing, you turn off the bleed air…ITT drops 10°. Now, when approaching the ramp, within a minute or so of shutdown, you turn off the air conditioner…the ITT drops another 30°! (You leave the vent blower on in low or high speed so the passengers and yourself will still have a cool breeze blowing.) With the condition levers set where they are (57 – 62%) you are able to glide through that tight turn into the parking slot by merely dropping both power levers over the gate to Idle, thus developing a bigger propeller blade angle, but without an acceleration of N1…ITT stays low. Finally, when shutting down, you pull the condition levers from their current setting all the way back into Cut-off in one smooth motion. There is nothing to be gained by stabilizing at Low Idle…the ITT will simply rise.

Some King Air Flight Manuals state a maximum ITT limit for the last minute prior to shutdown, such as 585° or 610°. Other manuals simply tell the pilot to achieve the "minimum" ITT during the last minute. The techniques recommended here – bleed air off on the ground, air conditioner off at least one minute before shutdown, condition levers kept up for an elevated idle speed until fuel cut-off – should guarantee that the shutdown ITT limit, if stated, can always be avoided.

COLD WEATHER GROUND OPERATION

Turbine engines *like* cold weather; there is not much to worry about. Nevertheless, here are a few ideas for your consideration. I hope they make winter operation easier and more comfortable...for you, your engines, and your airframe.

Electric Heater Operation

(Author's Note: This brief article was written well before the longer next one that begins on Page 247. In that later work, electric heater usage was the entire topic. Not only did it cover the heater found in the 90- and 100-series but also the ones in 200s and 300s. You may wish to skip the following "Electric Heater Operation" paragraphs since you will also be reading that next chapter.)

All models of the 100-series of King Airs, as well as all models of the 90-series except the 90, A90, and B90 members, have essentially the same heating and cooling system. Heat can come from two sources, engine bleed air and an electric heater. The heater is comprised of eight large coils – grids – of wire, divided into two identical halves with four grids each. One half is called Normal heat; the other is known as Ground Max heat.

In my experience, it wasn't until about 1977 that Beech got the bugs worked out of the Auto mode of cabin temperature control. For you operators of these "later" airplanes, I'll venture to say that you rarely use the Manual Heat or Manual Cool modes because Auto works so well. Right?

So how do we get the maximum heat available as soon as possible after engine start on those wintry mornings when the airplane has suffered through a freezing night outdoors?

Before operating all eight grids of electric heat be sure that the condition levers are set for at least 57 – 62% N1. Drawing this huge amount of electricity from the generators at Low Idle will exceed generator load limits and may make the engines accelerate very slowly, if at all, leading to big increases in ITT whenever power is advanced.

With generators on and condition levers set for about 60% N1, select Auto with the mode selector, put the Electric Heat switch to the Ground Max position, make sure the bleed air switches are in the Open position, and move the Vent Blower switch up to High. (In later serials, the blower goes to High speed automatically whenever any heater grids operate.)

Remember that all eight heater grids are rendered inoperative if windshield, propeller, or lip boot heat is selected on. If you cannot get the electric heat switch to stay in the Ground Max position after you take your finger away from it while on the ground, check to verify that all of these "heater lockout" items are off.

The King Air Book

As soon as the electric heat switch is in Ground Max, the four Ground Max grids start to provide heat. The four Normal grids will not join in until the Auto system has selected full bleed air heat. Although it may take as long as a minute for this to happen, usually it occurs almost immediately since the bleed air was probably in a relatively hot position prior to the last shutdown…unless you experienced one heckuva cold front passage overnight!

What's that smell? What's burning? It's all of the carpet lint and dust that has accumulated on the heat grids since they were used the last time! Relax. The smell will go away in a moment.

Operate the heater occasionally on those deadhead legs at altitude – using Manual Heat mode – if you want to save your passengers from the fright caused by the smell. Can you "burn off" the Ground Max grids in flight? Yes, by *holding* the electric heat switch to the Ground Max position. When you do that, with the landing gear retracted, the Ground Max grids come on while the Normal grids shut off. Weird, eh?

So now, as you near the departure end of the runway, everyone is starting to feel toasty and warm. What now? Well, if you do nothing, it's OK. As soon as the landing gear squat switch senses that the airplane is airborne, it de-energizes the electromagnet that has been holding the electric heat switch in Ground Max. Also, the Auto system will turn off the Normal heat grids whenever it decides they are not needed.

If you prefer to turn off Ground Max yourself, you may move the switch down to Normal before takeoff or – to save a reach over to the environmental panel – click windshield or prop heat on for a moment, causing the electromagnet to release, allowing the electric heat switch to drop down to Normal.

Glow Plugs in Cold Weather

With a cold-soaked airplane and *glow plug* ignitors, this next tip may help guarantee a successful first start.

When you would normally place the Ignition and Engine Start switch up, to begin spinning the engine, place the Engine Auto-ignition switch up instead. After a ten to twenty second delay, turn on the Ignition and Engine Start switch, turn off the Engine Auto-ignition, and proceed with your usual start procedure. What this technique achieves is a preheating period for the glow plugs before battery voltage has dropped because of the starter load.

The very first few King Air 90s, back in 1964, had this feature by design…the starter switch activated the glow plugs immediately, but the starter did not spin until about 5 seconds later. It did not take Beech long to realize the folly of this design, since too many pilots thought something was broken when the starter switch did not immediately activate the starter!

By the way, if you are still not successful in obtaining a light-off, then try the other engine…it may have stronger glow plugs or a better fuel nozzle spray pattern. Another interesting theory is that the battery will actually be stronger during the second attempt because it was warmed up by the heat generated during the first discharge.

After the other engine starts, you'll have a better chance of obtaining a lightoff on the first one you tried, since you now have a generator to provide an assist. And remember, you need to conduct the engine clearing procedure before you try the first one again.

Icy Ramps

When you just about bust your fanny shuffling to the airplane across an icy ramp, plan for a modification of your normal starting technique. High Idle can easily provide enough thrust to slide the airplane across the ice, with brakes locked, if the propeller is unfeathered. You have a couple of options here.

One is to start with the propeller levers in feather. It is a technique that many pilots have used successfully for years, even on dry ramps. It sure keeps the noise and wind down! (It has a couple of drawbacks, too, which we'll discuss in a future article.) With feathered propellers, insignificant taxi thrust exists, even at High Idle.

The other option is to use an external power unit to start both engines. By doing so, there will never be a need to select High Idle on the first engine, since its generator won't be assisting in the second start.

Taxi slowly and carefully. Even if you see no obvious snow piles, extend ice vanes. You may need to use some Reverse at low speed if it's so slippery that the brakes won't slow you down, and the extended ice vanes will improve the chance of avoiding FOD (Foreign Object Damage).

When shutting down, don't revert to the out-of-date technique of feathering the propellers while the engine is still running. That is a sure way to start a slide toward the hapless lineperson! Use the Condition Levers first, then pause until propeller speed has dropped below 600 RPM before pulling the propeller levers into feather.

ELECTRIC HEATER USAGE

Brrrr! It's cold outside! Now that winter is upon us, let's review how we can create maximum heating in the cabin after starting.

There are three distinctly different electric heating systems on King Airs, depending upon the model. The first system is used on the 90- and 100-series of models (except for the straight 90, A90, and B90 that use a Jet-A fueled combustion heater instead of an electric heater). This 90- and 100-series design uses a heater that is located beneath the avionics bay on the right side of the nose section. This is the world's biggest hair dryer! It contains eight identical heavy-duty electrical "grids," each of which flows about 36 amps of current. With the exception of the momentary demand of an engine starter, operation of the electric heater is the largest user of electric power in the airplane and can only be accommodated with a strong GPU connected or with both generators operating. The eight grids are divided into two groups of four: The four Normal grids and the four Ground Maximum grids. The two groups operate in different ways, as we shall see.

The second King Air electrical heating system is the one used on all of the 300-series as well as on B200s manufactured in 1993 and after. Here the heater is in two separate parts in two separate locations. The forward heater element resides under the cockpit floor and the second element is under the aft end of the cabin, ahead of the entrance door. Whereas the first system, on 90s and 100s, can operate either in flight or on the ground, this second system is definitely a ground-only proposition. Since the engines' bigger compressors on these models put out more bleed air heat at altitude, the likelihood of needing any extra heat in flight is slim. The smaller engines on the 90- and 100-series, on the other hand, sometimes – rarely, but sometimes – need a heating supplement in flight. When in a holding pattern or descent, with the power pulled back, the compressor is slowed down and bleed air is not as hot as normal. That's when it's nice to have supplemental electric heat available.

The third King Air electrical heating system is the one found on 200s and B200s from the first model in 1974 up though 1992. The engineers at Beech were under the misconception that bleed air heat would always be sufficient for these models with their bigger – bigger than 90- and 100-series – powerplants. In flight, at normal power settings, that assumption proved to be correct. But while idling on the ground? Or in flight during a low-power descent or a prolonged holding pattern? Oops! It was getting cold! So, at the last design minute, the engineers came up with a "quick and dirty" way of adding supplemental electric heat: They added radiant heat panels to the cabin headliner as an extra-cost option! Most all of these airplanes were manufactured with this option.

The King Air Book

Our discussion will focus on how to heat the cabin as quickly as possible on the ground after a cold day's start. Since the technique varies a bit, depending upon which of the three systems you have, we will discuss the three variations separately.

90- and 100-series

First, we will talk about the 90-series and 100-series: C90, C90-1, C90A, C90B, C90GT, E90, F90, F90-1, 100, A100, and B100. Before operating all eight grids of electric heat be sure that the condition levers are set for at least 57 – 62% N1. Drawing this huge amount of electricity (over 300 amps!) from the generators at a Low Idle speed near 50% Ng will exceed generator load limits and may make the engines accelerate very slowly, if at all, leading to big increases in ITT whenever power is advanced. For all of you who are operating King Airs with four-blade propellers, your normal Low Idle setting should already be in this 57 – 62% range. The idles are higher since the four-blade propellers must idle above a minimum speed value, whereas there is no minimum idle propeller speed limit on the three-blade models.

After that cold winter start – Wow, the engines sure put out a lot of white smoke (atomized fuel) you haven't seen on the summer days, didn't they?! – (1) Select Auto with the mode selector. (2) Move the bleed air switches to the Open position. (3) Put the Electric Heat switch to the Ground Max position. (4) Move the Vent Blower switch up to High. (In later serials, the blower goes to High speed automatically whenever any heater grids operate.)

I hope that all of my readers are now using the "new" improved method of leaving bleed air switches in the Closed position for all engine starts and shutdowns…regardless of what the slow-to-be-updated manufacturers' checklists may say. This procedure seems to really improve Bleed Air Flow Control Unit life expectancy by keeping engine oil from entering the "Paks" at this time, before the engines' labyrinth oil seals have sufficient air pressure to operate correctly. In the summer, bleed air is typically not turned on until Runway Lineup. For short field takeoffs, whenever power is ITT-limited, it should even remain off until climb!

On these cold days, however, don't forget switching on bleed air once the engine has reached idle speed. Yes, bleed air will not yet be blisteringly hot – since the compressors are only idling – but it will still be warmer than cabin air and can help in providing heat.

It is very tempting to also spin the Cabin Temp rheostat fully clockwise at this time, to the maximum temperature position. What does this really do? Not much! You see, if the cabin is currently at a chilly 25 degrees Fahrenheit and we ask for a temperature of 55, the heater is going to work just as hard initially as if we had asked for a temperature of 85! (Typically, the rheostat has a range of about 30 degrees, from somewhere in the 50s to somewhere in the 80s.) I know that, psychologically, it feels "right" to spin that sucker up! Realistically, however, all it really achieves is a need to turn it back down into the comfort zone after the cabin has eventually become *too* hot. My suggestion? Tweak it up a little, if you like, but don't move it too far away from the comfort zone that has worked well on previous flights.

Remember that all eight heater grids are rendered inoperative if windshield, propeller, or lip boot heat is selected on. (Lip boot heat went away with the introduction of the *Pitot Cowl*.) If you cannot get the electric heat switch to stay in the Ground Max position after you take your finger away from it while on the ground, check to verify that all of these "heater lockout" items are off. The designers made it such that the more critical *safety-of-flight* ice protection items that use significant electric power would never find themselves lacking electricity due to the demands of a *comfort* item such as supplemental heat.

Whether the Electric Heat switch is in the center, Normal, position or in the top, Ground Maximum, position, the four Normal heat grids operate identically. Namely, if the bleed air reaches its full hot setting – if the left and right bleed air bypass valves in the wing roots both move to the full hot position – then the Normal heater receives a command to operate.

Conversely, the four Ground Maximum grids receive their operating command in a totally different way. Their operation has nothing whatsoever to do with how much bleed air heat exists. Instead, they are simply told to operate when the Electric Heat switch is moved up to the top. Period.

I often teach that the Ground Max heat grids are like a heater that you can plug into an electrical outlet in your bathroom to supplement the furnace on a wintry morning. When you plug it in and turn it on, it works. It is totally independent of what the home's furnace may or may not be doing at this time.

Consequently, as soon as the electric heat switch is in Ground Max, the four Ground Max grids start to provide heat. The four Normal grids will not join in until the Auto system has selected full bleed air heat. Although it may take as long as one full minute for this to happen – the time required to run the bleed air bypass valves from a full-cold to a full-hot setting – usually it occurs almost immediately since the bleed air was probably in a relatively hot position prior to the last shutdown…unless you experienced one heckuva cold front passage overnight!

What's that smell? What's burning? It's all of the carpet lint and dust that has accumulated on the heat grids since they were used the last time! Relax. The smell will go away in a moment.

A good suggestion is to operate the heater occasionally on deadhead legs at altitude – using Manual Heat mode – if you want to save your passengers from the fright caused by the smell. Can you "burn off" the Ground Max grids in flight? Yes, by *holding* the electric heat switch to the Ground

The King Air Book

Max position. When you do that, with the landing gear retracted, the Ground Max grids come on while the Normal grids shut off. Weird, eh?

So now, as you near the departure end of the runway, everyone is starting to feel toasty and warm. What now? Well, if you do nothing, it's OK. As soon as the landing gear squat switch senses that the airplane is airborne, it de-energizes the electromagnet that has been holding the electric heat switch in Ground Max. Also, the Auto system will turn off the Normal heat grids whenever it decides they are not needed due to the amount of bleed air heat being experienced.

If you prefer to turn off Ground Max yourself, you may move the switch down to Normal before takeoff or – to save a reach over to the Environmental panel in front of the copilot's left knee – click windshield or prop heat on for a moment, causing the electromagnet to release, allowing the electric heat switch to drop down to Normal.

B200-series (1993 and after) and all 300-series

With the standard Low Idles set near 62% Ng, there should always be sufficient electric power with both generators on line to operate as much supplemental electric heat as desired. To get maximum ground heating, do the following: (1) Move both Bleed Air Valve switches from the center, Envir Off, position, to the top, Open, position. (2) Select Auto on the Cabin Temp Mode selector. (3) Move the Vent Blower switch up to the top, High, position. (4) Turn on the Aft Blower switch. (5) Turn on the Electric Heat switch.

Although operating forward and aft heater elements together –as is being done here – draws a heavy electrical load, it is not as great as the load consumed by the eight grids of a C90's heater and no *lock-out* items are provided. In other words, you can operate windshield heat and electric heat simultaneously, as desired.

Remember that the aft electric heat grid can only operate when the Aft Blower switch is on. (It wouldn't do much good to have a hot heater without air flowing across it to distribute the thermal energy around, eh?) Also realize that it's never a good idea to terminate a heater and its respective air circulation blower at the same time. When you decide to turn off the Electric Heat switch leave the forward and aft blowers on for *at least* 15 seconds more. We don't want that remaining thermal energy to stay in one place and get that location too hot. Use the air circulation to distribute it around!

Because these heater elements are powerful but not *super*-powerful, in most cases the Electric Heat switch will stay on until you are directed to turn it off during the Runway Lineup procedure. If you forget to do so – not following the ol' checklist too well today, hmmm? – it's actually not a big deal because the switch will lose its magnetic latch and turn itself off at rotation. (Not that you should be careless! The takeoff power charts are based on the assumption that your generators will not be working hard to supply the electric heat load during takeoff.)

One obscure fact that has left a few pilots of these models perplexed: Once you turn off the Electric Heat switch, it is usually impossible to get it back on! The heater elements have thermostats that will shut off the heater automatically if the outlet duct becomes too hot. Although I do not have the exact values available to me, what I know is that the temperature required to shut off the heater automatically is much higher than the temperature at which the heater is permitted to resume operation. The duct has to be relatively cool before the heater can *start* operation, although it must get overly hot before the thermostat causes the heater to automatically *cease* operation.

What's the point of this obscure fact? This: Don't be in a hurry to turn off the heater anytime before Runway Lineup. If you have an unanticipated further ground delay and want the heater to help out in keeping warm, there's a good chance that you won't be successful in activating it a second time.

200s and B200s (1992 and before)

Radiant heat panels in the headliner?! What a joke! They're better than no supplement heat at all, but not by much! The sad fact is that you really are not going to get warm and toasty until the engines are at high power pumping out the BTUs of bleed air energy. But hey, the Beech engineers deserve credit for coming out with a dandy replacement system in 1993, right?!

In a meager attempt to make you feel a little better about this not-so-impressive option, remember that there are three types of methods by which thermal energy is transferred from one body to another: Conduction, Convection, and Radiation. In the magic of radiation, the energy is not first absorbed by air; it only heats up the solid body it reaches. Put your head's bald spot under the radiant heat panel and it will get quite warm fairly quickly, yet the air is still chilly. Given enough time – like hours! – the air too will warm by convection as it flows over your now warm bald spot…and seats, and cabinets, and carpets. But it is a s-l-o-w process!

Since the cabin air remains chilly for so long, I strongly believe that having either forward or aft blowers on at this time is counter-productive. It just serves to increase the wind-chill factor! So how do we maximize ground heat on these models? (1) Move the Bleed Air Valve switches up to Open. (2) Turn on the Radiant Heat switch.

That's it; no more! Well, there is one more thing to do, but please do it only when stopped with the parking brake set: Go to High Idle to make your incoming bleed air a bit warmer.

There is no restriction on operation of Radiant Heat in flight but it is no longer needed once the engines start pumping out those welcome BTUs of warmth. Usually, either right before or after

The King Air Book

takeoff, it's a good idea to turn off the Radiant Heat switch and to move the Cabin Temp Mode selector from Off to Auto.

In the Auto mode of temperature control – the one you use 99% of the time, right? – remember that the cabin temperature sensor is in the ceiling. (Well, it's in the ceiling after serial number BB-55, if you want to be a stickler for accuracy.) What else is in the ceiling? That's right, the radiant heat panels. Guess what the sensor tends to feel when radiant heat is on: Hotter than normal temperatures, right? So what will be the automatic cabin temperature controller's response? It will start reducing the bleed air temperature to cool the cabin that it "thinks" is too hot…just what you don't want!

In the rare cases – prolonged low-power descent, prolonged holding pattern – in which you are getting cold in flight and want to use the Radiant Heat panels, it's best to move the Mode Selector from Auto to Manual Heat before doing so, and to use the Manual Temp Increase-Decrease switch as desired to affect cabin temperature.

Heating with a Ground Power Unit (GPU)

Regardless of which of the three supplemental electric heat systems you are operating, it can work fine on the ground using a GPU, prior to engine starting. Since no bleed air is yet available, go ahead and leave the Bleed Air Valve switches in the Closed or Envir Off position but set the other controls in the same positions as we have already suggested. Isn't that nice! The cabin can be all warm and comfortable before the passengers ever arrive.

No starting loads should ever be incurred while heater loads are still operating. Be sure to turn off the Environmental panel switches before starting the engines, then turn them back on after both generators are on line.

Even those nasty radiant heat panels work relatively well with ground power since they have plenty of time to function…presuming you plan far enough ahead.

Stay warm out there this winter!

COLLINS FCS–65 FLIGHT CONTROL SYSTEM

OVERVIEW

The Collins FCS–65 is probably the most common automatic flight control system – or "Autopilot" for us old-fashioned folks – on Super King Air B200s, 300s, and 350s from about 1984 to the present, and it is also found on almost all C90Bs. It is an excellent piece of equipment, with lots of state-of-the-art standard features. It can be ordered with any one of numerous flight director displays, including EFIS (Electronic Flight Instrument Systems), but except for size of the display and interfaces with various long-range navigation systems, they all work the same.

It is an integrated autopilot/flight director system, with one computer providing data to both the flight director command bars and to the autopilot servos. With the autopilot disengaged, the flight director shows the pilot how to accomplish the tasks asked of it by the movement of the command bars on the ADI (Attitude Director Indicator, a fancy artificial horizon or attitude indicator). The bars tip left and right, for example, showing how much to bank to follow an assigned heading. They also pitch up and down, showing how to adjust attitude to maintain an assigned altitude. When the autopilot is engaged, it merely provides the muscle to make the airplane follow the command bars.

Since the autopilot will always attempt to align the airplane with the bank attitude displayed on the flight director, be certain that you have manually maneuvered the airplane into good alignment with the commands before engaging the autopilot. That way, there will be no unexpected change in bank attitude when the autopilot takes control.

MODE CONTROL PANEL

Flight director commands are selected by push buttons on the mode control panel:

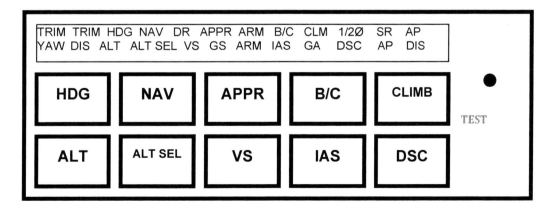

The King Air Book

The two rows of annunciator labels indicate the status of the various flight director and autopilot modes. A similar annunciator is located on the instrument panel, above the electro-mechanical style of ADI. With an Electronic ADI (EADI), the annunciators are displayed right on the indicator.

There are two rows of mode select buttons. The first four buttons on the top row control *lateral* modes, banking of the airplane. The last button on the top row and all the buttons on the bottom row control *vertical* modes, pitching of the airplane. (Some early models do not have the Climb and Descent modes. The buttons are there, but they are not labeled and are not functional.) The buttons are push-on, push-off type. This means that the first push of the button turns on that particular mode, but the next push of the button turns off that mode.

With a few exceptions, only one button in each row can be active at any one time. For example, pushing the ALT button cancels the IAS mode, selecting IAS cancels VS, HDG cancels NAV, etc. Some exceptions to this rule need to be noted, however. First, ALT SEL (Altitude Select) remains engaged no matter what other vertical mode is selected, until the flight director begins its flare maneuver to capture the selected altitude. Second, NAV, APPR, and B/C do not cancel HDG immediately. Instead, the HDG mode remains active until the system decides that it is time to stop following the selected heading and begin to track the navigational aid that is being intercepted – VOR, localizer, or Long Range Nav.

The DSC (Descent) mode is similar to VS (Vertical Speed) mode. When DSC is hit, the airplane will very smoothly nose over into a 1,500 fpm descent rate (1,200 fpm for some B200s and C90Bs). In systems with updated/later computers, ALT SEL is automatically activated whenever the altitude alerter is dialed to a new altitude. (That's a *great* feature!) In earlier systems, ALT SEL is not automatically selected by rotation of the altitude selector knob, but either DSC or CLIMB mode automatically selects it. It is not uncommon to see a pilot hit DSC and then ALT SEL. What he or she fails to initially note is that, since ALT SEL was already activated automatically, the hitting of the ALT SEL switch canceled it out! Check the annunciators carefully and often to know exactly what modes are active and what modes are armed. To avoid an altitude bust, I always try to force myself to point at the ALT SEL annunciator and verify it is on when I receive the "1,000 to go" call.

The CLIMB (Climb) mode is similar to IAS (Indicated Airspeed) mode. When CLIMB is hit, the airplane will very smoothly pitch (usually up) to achieve a speed – in the C90B – of 150 KIAS from Sea Level up to 10,000 feet. Starting at 10,000 feet, the speed begins to decrease by 2 knots for each 1,000 feet. Thus, by the time the airplane has reached 25,000 feet, the IAS is down to 120 knots. In the 200 and 300-series, the speed starts at 160 instead of 150, and above 25,000 feet the reduction becomes 1 knot per 1,000 feet instead of 2 knots per 1,000 feet.

FCS-65 FLIGHT CONTROL SYSTEM

These speeds are a good compromise between going forward and going up. The speeds are not as slow as most pilots tend to think, since an indicated 130 knots at 25,000 feet equates to a true airspeed of about 200 knots!

However, when better over-the-nose visibility is desired at lower altitudes, or when you need to keep the speed above 140 knots at higher altitudes while encountering icing conditions, or when you are fighting lots of headwind and want to climb at a shallower angle with more ground speed, then the CLIMB mode should be avoided or modified to a higher speed range, as we will discuss shortly.

There are three more vertical modes, but they do not contain push buttons on the mode controller.

There is a basic pitch hold mode that has no selection button at all. Instead, when there is no other vertical mode selected, the command bars merely direct the airplane to maintain the currently existing pitch attitude. This mode may be selected by canceling any other vertical mode the system is in. For example, if the ALT mode is on, and then the ALT button is pushed again, ALT will be disengaged and the system will revert to the basic pitch hold mode. The bars may be reset to any other reasonable pitch attitude by momentarily depressing the PITCH SYNC & CWS button on the airplane's control wheel. (CWS is the abbreviation for Control Wheel Steering, and we will tell more about this button's functions later. For now, it merely acts as a Pitch Sync button for the command bars when in basic pitch hold mode.)

The GA (Go Around) mode is selected with a push button on the left power lever. When the flight director goes into GA mode, *all* other modes are canceled and the command bars display a wings level, +7° pitch up attitude. If the autopilot is engaged, it disengages when GA is selected, but the yaw damper stays on.

The third and last vertical mode that does not have a button on the mode controller is GS mode – Glideslope. When the APPR mode (a lateral mode) is selected, the localizer has been intercepted, and the airplane is flown to intercept the glideslope of an ILS – capturing the glideslope from either below or above – then any other vertical mode will automatically be canceled and the GS mode will engage. The pitch commands will now direct the airplane to track the ILS glideslope.

Selecting a vertical mode will cause no command to be displayed unless a lateral mode (such as HDG) has already been selected to bring the V-bar into view.

For a localizer back course approach, the B/C mode should be selected while the HSI course needle is set to the ILS *front course* bearing. Now the system will turn toward the tail of the HSI course pointer – not the head – as the intercept occurs and use this as the zero-wind course datum. Remember that with an HSI one never needs to accommodate to a reversed course needle on an ILS

The King Air Book

back course. So long as the head of the needle is on the front course, the left-right needle will read correctly. The B/C button does not "reverse the needle," even though a lot of pilots still think it does.

For a VOR or RNAV/GPS approach, if you choose to couple to the desired track instead of just following your own selected headings, then hit the APPR button, not the NAV button. The command bars will continue following HDG until they "see" that the course is nearing interception. At that point, HDG will disengage automatically and the command bars will display computed commands to track the course and compensate for crosswind. In effect, APPR is just like NAV, but with a slight change in the sensitivity.

THE AUTOPILOT CONTROL PANEL

The controls used for engaging the autopilot and yaw damper, for selecting Soft Ride (SR) and Half Bank (1/2 Ø) modes of autopilot operation, and for directing the autopilot to change the pitch and roll of the airplane when not coupled to the flight director are all located on the autopilot control panel:

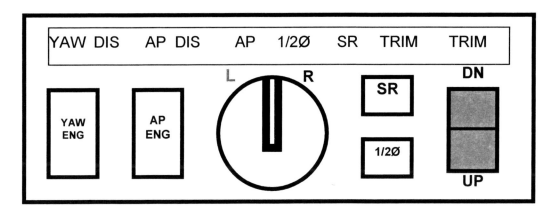

All buttons have a push-on, push-off type of operation, with the exception of the YAW ENG button that can be pushed to turn the yaw damper off only when the autopilot is *not* engaged. SR is good for use in turbulent air, since it provides less abrupt control response. The gain of the aileron servo on the majority of C90Bs seems to be, in my opinion, set too high, causing lots of unnecessary sawing/jerking of the control wheel left and right. I use SR a lot on these models and it seems to provide a more comfortable level of response. In smooth air, on the other hand, soft-ride usually makes the autopilot fly worse, allowing the airplane to drift around a bit too much. SR is automatically canceled in the APPR mode and whenever the autopilot is first engaged.

1/2 Ø (Half Bank) only works in the HDG mode, and is inoperative when the capture of a NAV, APPR, or B/C course has occurred. My experience is that controllers are not too happy with me if I have 1/2 Ø engaged while being vectored for an approach. Since the bank angle is halved, the

256

turns become quite slow and wide. Except for VFR sightseeing flights over, say, the Grand Canyon, where I'd like some big slow lazy turns to give everyone some good camera angles, I almost never use the 1/2 Ø mode.

Whenever the turn knob is moved out of its center detent, all flight director lateral modes (except APPR) are canceled and the autopilot merely holds the bank angle corresponding to the displacement of the turn knob. Full knob displacement commands about a 30° bank, one-third displacement commands 10°, etc.

In basic pitch hold mode (no other vertical command selected), each *momentary tap* of the Vertical Trim Switch, the one labeled "UP/DN" on the right side of the control panel, changes pitch attitude by 1/2 of a degree. If the switch is *held* in the Up or Down position, the pitch attitude is adjusted up or down by exactly 1° for each second the switch is held. Want to nose over exactly 3°? Then hold the switch down for exactly three seconds. (Love these digital systems! We're talking *precision* here!)

This vertical trim switch also provides very precise adjustment over the other vertical modes – ALT, VS and DSC, and IAS and CLIMB. Each *momentary tap* of the switch creates a corresponding change in the appropriate mode of exactly 25 feet, 200 fpm, or 1 knot. It is amazing how precise this system is! If the switch is *held* in the Up or Dn position for more than one second, all other vertical modes are canceled and the autopilot holds the commanded basic pitch attitude. (The vertical trim switch has no effect after a glideslope is captured.)

UNCOUPLED AUTOPILOT OPERATION

It is rare, but not unheard of, to operate the autopilot without a flight director mode selected. This is called "uncoupled" autopilot operation. Suppose you are climbing to altitude, flying without a copilot and without using the flight director, and you need to reach for something…the checklist slid down the aisle slightly out of reach.

If you simply press the AP engage button, the autopilot will take control of the airplane, holding the existing roll and pitch attitude. Now you can let go of everything as you stretch for the checklist, knowing that nothing unusual will happen to the airplane's attitude. Need to make a right turn to 060°? No problem. Simply twist the turn knob to the right to set up a medium bank. As the heading nears the assigned 060°, use the turn knob to roll the wings level.

Here's something nice to know if your airplane is equipped with the Collins MCS–65 Compass System. When the wings roll level, the autopilot reads what heading it is flying from the HSI and holds that heading. In other words, it is not merely a "wings leveler" but instead is holding an exact heading, even though the heading bug may not be on that heading. Consequently, there is no worry about the airplane drifting off the assigned heading, even if the rudder or ailerons are not perfectly trimmed. This is a nice feature!

If the compass system in your King Air is the C–14 or AHS–85, then your system does not have this heading hold feature – with wings level but without HDG depressed, the system merely maintains zero degree of bank. Misadjusted rudder trim will result in a slow turn.

The autopilot may also be operated in what we call a "half-coupled" mode. That is, it may be following the flight director's vertical modes only, while still holding the bank attitude commanded by the turn knob.

In the "half-coupled" mode, the V-bar is not in view even though a vertical mode (for example, IAS or ALT) is active.

For example, you are still flying your assigned 060° heading (because you rolled the wings level on that heading with the turn knob), but now you are asked to climb at 170 knots and level off at FL 230. One way of doing this is to hold the vertical trim switch until 170 knots is achieved, then push the IAS button on the mode controller. Now the pitch will be automatically adjusted to hold 170 knots, followed by leveling off and entering ALT mode at 23,000 feet.

In most cases, of course, the autopilot is operated fully coupled to the flight director modes. In the previous example, it would be more realistic to say that as 060° were assigned, the heading bug would have been placed on that value and then the HDG button would have been depressed. This would have made the autopilot adjust bank to steer 060° (or whatever new heading was selected by the bug), and would have made the flight director command bars come into view.

THE PITCH SYNC & CWS BUTTON

On the control wheel's outboard grip, activated by the flying-hand's thumb, is the PITCH SYNC & CWS (Control Wheel Steering) button.

With the autopilot engaged, following the flight director's lateral and vertical modes, the PITCH SYNC & CWS button, first of all, serves as an autopilot interrupt button. When held depressed, the roll and pitch servos disengage. Only the yaw axis, the yaw damper, remains engaged, continuing its job of improving ride comfort. Thus, you are now "steering" the airplane with the control wheel; the autopilot no longer has control.

One case in which this feature is beneficial is the sudden appearance of conflicting traffic nearby. In an instant, you can grab the wheel, press PITCH SYNC & CWS, and take evasive action without overpowering or disengaging the autopilot. When the traffic situation is resolved, you only need release the PITCH SYNC & CWS button and the autopilot will smoothly resume the *lateral* command – probably HDG or NAV – it had been following.

What about the *vertical* mode? The answer depends of the age/status of your system's computer. For the later systems, the vertical mode is not canceled but rather is *synchronized* to the condition existing when the button is released. For example, if you were in ALT mode and had gained 100 feet during the evasive maneuver, the newer computers will leave you in altitude hold mode, but holding an altitude 100 feet higher than before. For the earlier systems, pressing the PITCH SYNC & CWS button cancels other vertical modes and puts you in the basic pitch hold mode. Arguments can be made for whether canceling or synchronizing the vertical modes is preferable, but I tend to like the later, synchronizing, option. However, many pilots have made the mistake of using PITCH SYNC & CWS to start a descent by nosing over to a reasonable descent attitude while holding the button, then releasing it and expecting the autopilot to continue holding that descent attitude. This will work just fine in the earlier systems but all it will accomplish in the later ones is an immediate level-off a few feet lower than you were before! If you want to use this descent-initiating technique on the later systems, the ALT button would need to be depressed first to cancel the ALT mode.

Back to the situation of maneuvering around the unexpected traffic using PITCH SYNC & CWS…Since the vertical mode will not revert back to its last value, be sure that you regain the assigned altitude you had been holding before releasing PITCH SYNC & CWS. If you do not, then as PITCH SYNC & CWS is released the autopilot will turn back to the desired heading but will hold a new, incorrect, altitude. If necessary, hit the ALT button to reengage the mode.

For all installations, PITCH SYNC & CWS has no effect on a captured glideslope. When released, the airplane will return to the glideslope.

Remember the dropped checklist story? The one where you used the autopilot to "hold" the airplane, uncoupled to the flight director, while you reached elsewhere? Here is another case in which PITCH SYNC & CWS can be a nice aid. Need to climb a little steeper? Bank a little more in the turn? Easy! Just hold PITCH SYNC & CWS while you establish the new attitude manually, release the button, and "George" (the autopilot) comes back on and takes over holding this *new* attitude. Now want to roll out on 060°? OK, here's how. As you near the heading, hold PITCH SYNC & CWS, roll the wings about level, and release PITCH SYNC & CWS. As long as the bank was less than 5° when the button is released, the wings will continue to roll level.

PITCH SYNC & CWS will operate even when the turn knob is not in the center detent, however, upon release, the autopilot will resume the bank attitude commanded by the turn knob.

TYPICAL AUTOPILOT OPERATION

Remember that the modes we describe for autopilot operation are programmed and used just the same when the airplane is being manually flown to satisfy the flight director commands. When you engage the AP button, you are simply saying, in effect, "You take it, George, and keep on following those flight director bars."

For takeoff, depress HDG and ALT SEL, with the heading bug set on the runway heading and the altitude alerter set for the first assigned altitude. Unlike many other systems, in the FCS–65 system you cannot select GA *and* HDG for takeoff, since to do so will cancel GA and sync the V-bars to your current, level, attitude. (Actually, this is not a bad deal, since the +7° GA attitude is really not steep enough to maintain V2 with an engine out, especially in the 300–series.)

You should usually make the initial rotation attitude to about 10°, even 12 ° in a no-flap 300-series takeoff. Use the vertical trim switch to preset this attitude on the command bars. (If an engine failure occurs at this critical time, follow the bars – they will steer you to hold heading and your speed will be very close to V2.) After passing at least 400 feet AGL, with the airplane clean and without any engine problems, engage the autopilot – the yaw damper will come on also, of course – and move the heading bug to the various assigned or desired headings. When the autopilot engages, it will hold the existing pitch attitude. If you've been careful in following the bars that you had preset before takeoff, then the AP will also hold that angle. On the other hand, if you allowed the nose to pitch too high or sag too low, that's what will be held initially by the AP. Hence, it is a good idea to also engage CLIMB mode at this time.

The autopilot won't know which way to turn if it finds the heading bug 180° out of position with the current heading, and it may begin to reverse its roll direction. When you are making a 180° or greater turn, never move the heading bug past the 135° right or left relative bearing positions on the HSI (that are usually indicated by a small mark). After the airplane has turned 45° or more, then continue moving the bug as desired, but avoid crossing the 135° relative position.

During the climb, the CLIMB mode usually works very well. Remember that you may modify the climb speed schedule higher or lower by deliberate taps on the vertical trim switch or by use of PITCH SYNC & CWS on the later systems. If the air is quite turbulent, the AP may tend to overreact and work too hard in holding an exact climb speed. In that case, hold the vertical trim switch for more than one second to cancel the CLIMB mode and then, using the same switch, set a reasonable (5 – 10 degree) attitude and let the plane's speed and rate of climb wander with the turbulence.

Avoid using VS in the climb, since if you select too large a value the airplane can pitch up and slow down so much that a stall may be encountered!

When the airplane approaches the altitude set in the altitude alerter, the computer begins a flare maneuver to level off. The annunciator will change from ALT SEL to ALT as the level-off is completed. Don't use the vertical trim switch to help the airplane capture the selected altitude. Using this switch may cancel ALT SEL and cause the system to revert to basic pitch hold mode.

On the other hand, it is nice to know that when ATC gives you a higher altitude at the last instant, merely adjusting the pitch attitude with the vertical trim switch for more than one second will prevent an undesired level-off at the old altitude. As time permits, the new altitude can be set into the alerter and ALT SEL can be reengaged, if it hasn't armed itself automatically.

When you are cleared to a higher altitude, hit CLIMB, or begin the climb by using the vertical trim switch to set a proper climb attitude. Activation of the vertical trim switch for more than one second, remember, will cancel the old altitude being held.

For the enroute descent, similar to the climb, set the newly assigned altitude in the altitude alerter. This can be done immediately, even if you are waiting to begin the actual descent "at pilot's discretion." When ready to start down, depress DSC. Use either the vertical trim switch or the PITCH SYNC & CWS button to adjust the descent rate for a steeper or shallower angle, if needed.

For an ILS approach, use HDG and ALT or HDG and basic pitch hold mode to follow the radar vectors or published terminal routes until near the localizer. When you are close enough to the localizer to avoid receiving false signals (usually, within 30° of the localizer course), depress the APPR button. Keep using the heading bug to set up the proper intercept. At the correct time, HDG mode will automatically disengage as the localizer is captured. If we are below the glideslope, it will be automatically captured when it centers. On the other hand, if the approach controller (or our own poor planning) has put us above the glideslope, we must use PITCH SYNC & CWS or the vertical trim switch to set up a sufficient descent attitude that will dive us onto the glideslope. When that occurs, again the glideslope will be captured.

For a non-precision approach, IAS works exceedingly well to control the descents. Suppose you have just turned inbound from a procedure turn, clean configuration, indicating 160 knots, with ALT and HDG modes engaged, and APPR selected so that it is ready to capture the VOR or GPS course.

As the course comes alive and the capture occurs, you now want to descend to a new altitude, the one at which you will cross the FAF (Final Approach Fix). Dial the new altitude into the alerter, press IAS, and pull power back to your "magic number" for a 1,000 fpm descent rate. The autopilot will cause the airplane to smoothly nose over to hold 160 knots, and down you will come. IAS mode will cancel automatically as the new altitude is captured. Now extend Approach flaps, slow to your approach speed (120 to 140 knots, usually), and adjust power accordingly.

Put the next altitude (MDA or an intermediate step-down altitude) into the alerter. As you cross the FAF at your chosen speed knots, hit IAS, extend the gear, start the clock, and reduce power.

Down you will come, maintaining approach speed perfectly. Add power to level off as the new altitude is captured.

In the event of any missed approach, either from a precision or non-precision approach, hit the GA button on the left power lever as you add POWER. The autopilot will disengage and the command bars will show a wings-level, 7° pitch up attitude. Follow the command bars as you advance PROPS, and retract FLAPS and GEAR. (Power, Props, Flaps, Gear – there are our "Four Friends" again!) Now you may reengage the autopilot. When it comes on, GA will be automatically canceled, the wings will be rolled level (if they aren't already), and the existing pitch attitude will be maintained. In other words, the autopilot comes on in the uncoupled mode, wings level. You may now select the desired flight director modes – probably HDG and CLIMB – that will cause the autopilot to couple to them.

When you disconnect the autopilot and are maneuvering visually to the airport – we're not talking about 200 feet above touchdown on an ILS, but rather a few miles from the airport – we advocate getting rid of the command bars. When your attention should be directed more outside of the airplane, scanning for traffic and planning your arrival to the airport, it is a poor idea to waste effort in programming the command bars for various turns and descents. If the bars are not removed from view, there will be a good deal of time when disagreement exists between the bars and the airplane symbol. We believe it is a poor procedure to have the bars in view while intentionally ignoring them. (Someday, they might be telling you something very important – such as how to stay on the glide path – but you are so used to ignoring them that their significance goes unheeded.)

Unfortunately, we have not yet found a way to remove the bars from view without taking your hand off the power levers (unless you have a copilot; then it's easy.) You must hit the existing lateral mode to turn it off, and when no lateral mode is selected, the command bars will go away. But here is a hitch. If you have already hit GA, no lateral mode is on, but the GA mode causes the bars to still be in view. Consequently, you will have to hit HDG twice – once to turn it on (which cancels GA and syncs the bars to your attitude) and again to turn it off.

FINAL COMMENTS

Use of electric trim causes the autopilot to disengage but leaves the yaw damper on, so it is the preferred method for routinely turning off the autopilot.

Every time the autopilot is engaged, a 2-second pre-engagement test is performed. The red TRIM and AP lights illuminate during this test. If the test is successfully passed, those lights extinguish and the green AP and YD lights illuminate.

FCS-65 FLIGHT CONTROL SYSTEM

Sometimes, especially on 300s after serial number FA–38 and on all 350s, you will find that *two* hits of the AP ENG switch will be required to get the yaw damper or autopilot to work. The first hit clears faults that the system had previously detected, while the second hit turns it on.

If your airplane was ordered with the fancy Air Data Computer-driven electronic Airspeed Indicator, Altimeter, and Vertical Velocity Indicators on the pilot's side of the panel, then you have "bugs" that you may set for desired airspeeds and rates of climb or descent. When we talked about modifying IAS or VS modes, you have another, easier, option of merely dialing the bug to the value desired. Sweet!

The system annunciators are quite elaborate and complete. Observe them carefully and get used to what they are telling you.

The Test button on the Mode Control Panel provides a test of annunciator lights, but it also can be used for detailed diagnostic troubleshooting tests when used in conjunction with some of the mode buttons. The Pilot's Guide for the FCS–65 from Collins, as well as the installation and maintenance instructions, give details about test switch operation.

Reading and studying both the Pilot's Guide and the Airplane Flight Manual Supplement in the Pilot's Operating Handbook and FAA Approved Airplane Flight Manual are essential for complete system understanding. Use that airport waiting time to review these soon.

I can spot the pilots who utilize their APs fully…they're the one with calluses on their index fingers. The Collins FCS-65 system is a fantastic device that can make your flying considerably easier and safer. It's a winner! We know you'll enjoy it!

SPZ-200A AND SPZ-4000
FLIGHT CONTROL SYSTEMS

Overview

The Sperry SPZ-200A is probably the most common autopilot on King Air 200s, B100s, F90s, and E90s from about 1976 through 1984. (Sperry became Honeywell in 1988 and AlliedSignal and Honeywell have just announced a merger in 1999.) The SPZ-200A is a very fine piece of equipment, with lots of standard features that are optional on its major competitor of the time...the Collins AP-105 system. It can be mated with numerous flight director displays, but except for size of the display, location of the annunciators, and interfaces with various long-range navigation systems, they all work the same. Beginning in about 1985, the SPZ-200A was replaced by the SPZ-4000. Although the look, feel, and performance of the two units is very similar, the 4000 uses digital electronic architecture and can perform to a new standard of precision and smoothness. The following discussion emphasizes the more-numerous 200A, but significant changes in the 4000 will be presented at the end.

This is an integrated autopilot/flight director system, with one computer providing data to both the flight director command bars and to the autopilot servos. With the autopilot disengaged, the flight director shows you how to accomplish the tasks you ask of it by the movement of the command bars on the ADI (Attitude Director Indicator, a fancy artificial horizon or attitude indicator). The bars bank left and right, for example, showing you how much to turn to follow an assigned heading. They also pitch up and down, showing you how to adjust attitude to maintain an assigned altitude. When the autopilot is engaged, it merely provides the muscle to make the airplane follow the command bars.

Since the autopilot will always attempt to align the airplane with the attitude displayed on the flight director, be certain that you have manually maneuvered the airplane into good alignment with the commands before engaging the autopilot. That way, there will be no unexpected change in attitude when the autopilot takes control.

The Flight Director Display

The flight director commands may be presented either by a single cue or by double cues on the ADI. For many years, Sperry systems offered only a double cue or cross-pointer display, in which two bars operated independently...a horizontal bar providing pitch commands and a vertical bar for

The King Air Book

bank commands. The cross-pointer display has the advantage of being somewhat more precise than the single cue, V-bar display, and it also can provide pitch commands alone, without any bank commands, which can be handy while doing 45° bank steep turns in training. However, following the cross-pointer display is not as intuitive a task as following the V-bar, and most pilots seem to prefer the single cue commands. It wasn't long before Sperry bowed to its customers' requests and began offering both displays, and we would guess that the V-bar is the more popular display.

Also, the raw-data display of glide slope information may be presented on either the right or left side of the ADI and HSI, whichever the customer desires.

Flight Director Commands

Flight director commands are selected by push buttons on the mode controller that looks something like this:

HDG	NAV	APR	BC	VORAPR
ALT	ALTSEL	VS	IAS	SBY

The buttons on the top row control *lateral* modes, banking of the airplane. The bottom row buttons control *vertical* modes, pitching of the airplane. The buttons are push-on, push-off type. This means that the first push of the button turns on that particular mode, but the next push of the button turns off that mode. (There is one exception here. Namely, the SBY button, each time it is pressed, causes two things to happen. First, the command bars are removed from view, as the flight director goes into a Standby mode of operation. Second, all annunciators – both in these push button switches and on the flight director annunciator above the ADI – are illuminated to test their light bulbs.)

With a few exceptions, only one button in each row can be active at any one time. For example, pushing the ALT button cancels the IAS mode, selecting IAS cancels VS, HDG cancels APR, etc. Some exceptions to this rule need to be noted, however. First, ALTSEL (Altitude Select) remains engaged no matter what other vertical mode is selected, until the flight director begins its flare maneuver to capture the selected altitude. Second, NAV, APR, BC, and VORAPR do not cancel HDG immediately. Instead, the HDG mode remains active until the system decides that it is time to stop following the selected heading and begin to track the navigational aid that is being intercepted: VOR, localizer, or Long Range Nav.

There are three more vertical modes, but they do not contain push buttons on the mode controller.

SPZ-200A AND SPZ-4000 FLIGHT CONTROL SYSTEMS

There is a Pitch Attitude Hold (sometimes abbreviated PAT) mode, that has no selection button at all. Instead, when there is no other vertical mode selected, the command bars merely direct the airplane to maintain the currently existing pitch attitude. This mode may be selected by canceling any other vertical mode the system is in. For example, if the ALT mode is on, and then the ALT button is pushed again, ALT will be disengaged and the system will revert to the Pitch Attitude Hold mode. The bars may be reset to any other reasonable pitch attitude by momentarily depressing the TCS button on the airplane's control wheel. (TCS is the abbreviation for Touch Control Steering, and we will tell more about this button's functions later. For now, it merely acts as a Pitch Sync button for the command bars when in PAT mode.)

The GA (Go Around) mode is selected with a push button on the left power lever. When the flight director goes into GA mode, *all* other modes are canceled and the command bars display a wings level, +7° pitch up attitude. If the autopilot is engaged, it disengages when GA is selected, but the yaw damper stays on.

When the flight director comes on initially (whenever it has been off and then receives electric power again) it comes on in the GA mode. The command bars will not appear until the attitude gyro has erected properly and has pulled its flag from view, but the GA annunciator will always be illuminated during the initial power-up of the system.

The third and last vertical mode that does not have a button on the mode controller is GS mode, Glideslope. When the APR mode (a lateral mode) is selected, the localizer has been intercepted, and the airplane is flown to intercept the glideslope of an ILS – capturing the glideslope from either below or above – then any other vertical mode will automatically be canceled and the GS mode will engage. The pitch commands will now direct the airplane to track the ILS glideslope.

With a cross-pointer display, vertical modes may be selected and displayed without any lateral mode selected. For example, press ALT and the horizontal command bar will appear and give pitch commands to hold the altitude that existed when the button was hit. On the other hand, with a V-bar, single cue display, hitting ALT will cause no command to be displayed unless a lateral mode (such as HDG) has already been selected to bring the V-bar into view.

To track a localizer back course to the runway, the BC mode should be selected while the HSI course needle is set to the ILS's *front course* bearing.

For a VOR approach, if you choose to couple to the VOR course instead of just following your own selected headings, then hit the VORAPR button. The command bars will continue following HDG until they "see" that the VOR course is nearing interception. At that point, HDG will disengage automatically and the command bars will display computed commands to track the course and compensate for crosswind. In effect, VORAPR is just like NAV, but with a slight change in the

The King Air Book

sensitivity. In fact, the NAV annunciator also illuminates when VORAPR is selected. By the way, when an IFR approach approved GPS navigator is installed and is driving the HSI course needle, it has been my experience that VORAPR does not work properly. Instead, basic NAV should be used.

The Autopilot Controller

The controls used for engaging the autopilot and yaw damper, for selecting Soft Ride or Low Bank (if installed) modes of autopilot operation, for directing the autopilot to change the pitch and roll of the airplane when not coupled to the flight director, and for conducting a test procedure are all located on the autopilot controller. It looks like this:

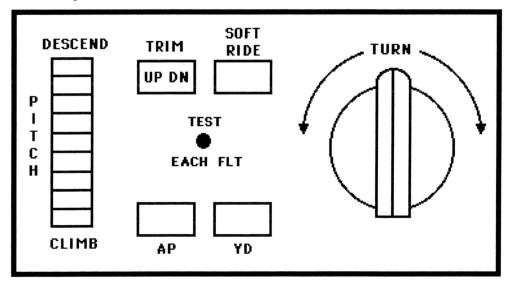

The soft-ride button (and low-bank button, if installed) has a push-on, push-off type of operation. Soft-ride is good for use in turbulent air, since it provides less abrupt control response. In smooth air, on the other hand, soft-ride usually makes the autopilot fly worse, allowing the airplane to drift around too much.

The autopilot and yaw damper engage buttons can only turn *on* their respective functions. A common frustration that newcomers to the system experience is trying to disengage the AP and YD by depressing these buttons...but nothing happens. Instead, you usually disconnect the AP and YD by depressing the red button on the pilot's or copilot's control wheel.

Whenever the turn knob is moved out of its center detent, all flight director lateral modes are canceled and the autopilot merely holds the bank angle corresponding to the displacement of the turn knob. Full knob displacement commands about a 30° bank, one-third displacement commands 10°, etc. Likewise, when the pitch command wheel is rotated, all vertical modes are canceled and the autopilot holds the pitch attitude appropriate to command wheel rotation. (This wheel has no internal

SPZ-200A and SPZ-4000 Flight Control Systems

stops. It actually can rotate right past 360°, but the computer limits maximum and minimum pitch angles to safe values.)

There is a small push button on the center of the controller label "Test Each Flight." This test button simulates an improper command to the autopilot servos. If their torque monitors are performing correctly, the autopilot should totally disengage shortly after the button is pushed. Do this check often, like the placard says. It is very simple…merely engage the autopilot, verify that all controls are stiff, then push the button and verify that the autopilot turns off and that all controls operate freely.

There are a couple of lights on the controller that we have not yet mentioned…Trim Up and Trim Down lights. Usually, these lights are part of what appears to be a "Trim" button – a button that appears exactly like the AP engage or Soft-Ride buttons. Although it looks like a button, it is only an annunciator…pushing it does nothing. (On later model controllers, the Up/Dn lights are housed right in the controller face, not in a separate button.) In a nutshell, if you observe a steady Up or Down light, then there is a malfunction in the autopilot's trim system and the autopilot should not be engaged. Momentary blinks of the light, as the autopilot trims out pitch control forces, are to be expected.

Uncoupled Autopilot Operation

It is rare, but not unheard of, to operate the autopilot without a flight director mode selected. This is called uncoupled autopilot operation. Suppose you are climbing to altitude, flying without a copilot and without using the flight director, and you need to reach for something – the boss wants the latest Wall Street Journal that accidentally fell between the copilot's seat and the sidewall.

If you simply press the AP engage button, the autopilot will take control of the airplane, rolling the wings level (if they aren't already) and holding the existing climb pitch attitude. Now you can let go of everything as you stretch for the newspaper, knowing that nothing unusual will happen to the airplane's attitude. Need to make a right turn to 060°? No problem. Simply twist the turn knob to the right to set up about a 20° to 30° bank. As the heading nears the assigned 060°, use the turn knob to roll the wings level.

Here's something nice to know. When the wings roll level, the autopilot reads what heading it is flying from the HSI (Horizontal Situation Indicator), and holds that heading. In other words, it is not merely a wing leveler but instead is holding an exact heading, even though the heading bug may not be on that heading. Consequently, there is no worry about the airplane drifting off the assigned heading, even if the rudder or ailerons are not perfectly trimmed. This is a nice feature!

The King Air Book

The autopilot may also be operated in what we call a "half-coupled" mode. That is, it may be following the flight director's vertical modes only, while still holding the bank attitude (or HSI heading) commanded by the turn knob. In the half-coupled mode, the V-bar is not in view even though a vertical mode (for example, IAS or ALT) is active.

For example, you are still flying your assigned 060° heading (because you rolled the wings level on that heading with the turn knob), but now you are asked to climb at 140 knots and level off at FL 230. One way of doing this is to rotate the pitch command wheel until 140 knots is achieved, then push the IAS and ALTSEL buttons on the mode controller. Now the pitch will be automatically adjusted to hold 140 knots, followed by leveling off and entering ALT mode at 23,000 feet.

In most cases, of course, the autopilot is operated fully coupled to the flight director modes. In the previous example, it would be more realistic to say that as the 060° heading was assigned, the heading bug would have been placed on that value and then the HDG button would have been depressed. This would have made the autopilot adjust bank to steer 060° (or whatever new heading was selected by the bug), and would have made the flight director command bars come into view.

The TCS Button

On the back of the control wheel's outboard grip, activated by the flying-hand's index finger, is the TCS button...Touch Control Steering. What a clever device this is! Get to understand and feel comfortable with this button, and you will really like its features.

The TCS button performs different functions, depending on whether the autopilot is on or off, coupled or uncoupled. We will talk about coupled operation first.

The TCS button will not operate unless the turn knob is in its center detent. Also, the autopilot will not engage initially, unless the knob is centered. If you are having trouble with TCS or autopilot engagement, check the turn knob...it probably got knocked out of position by accident.

With the autopilot engaged, following the flight director's lateral and vertical modes, the TCS button, first of all, serves as an autopilot interrupt button. When held depressed, the roll and pitch servos disengage and the AP Engage annunciator extinguishes. Only the yaw axis, the yaw damper, remains engaged, continuing its job of improving ride comfort. Thus, you are now "steering" the airplane with the control wheel; the autopilot no longer has control. (Is this how they came up with that strange name, TCS?) One case in which this feature is beneficial is the sudden appearance of conflicting traffic nearby. In an instant, you can grab the wheel, press TCS, and take evasive action without overpowering or disengaging the autopilot. When the traffic situation is resolved, you only need release the TCS button and the autopilot will smoothly resume the *lateral* command – probably HDG or NAV – it had been following.

What about the *vertical* mode? Well, this is another nice feature of TCS. TCS allows the vertical hold modes (attitude, altitude, indicated airspeed, and vertical speed) to be changed, or synchronized, to the value you have when the button is released. For example, the autopilot is holding altitude about 40 feet too low. Merely depress and hold TCS, manually fly the airplane up 40 feet and level it off, then release TCS. Voila! The correct altitude is held! Or, you are descending in the VS mode at 1,000 fpm and desire to steepen it up to 1,500 fpm. Simple: Hold TCS, nose over and obtain 1,500 fpm on the VVI, release TCS. Of course, you can also make vertical speed, indicated airspeed, and altitude changes using the pitch command wheel, but as soon as that wheel is moved the autopilot reverts to pitch attitude hold only, and any other vertical hold mode is canceled. Consequently, you must reengage the desired mode when the proper value is reached. Using TCS is often times easier.

TCS has no effect on a captured glideslope. When released, the airplane will return to the glideslope.

Back to the situation of maneuvering around the unexpected traffic using TCS: Since the vertical mode will not revert back to its last value, be sure that you regain the assigned altitude you had been holding before releasing TCS. If you do not, then as TCS is released the autopilot will turn back to the desired heading but will hold a new, incorrect, altitude.

Remember the Wall Street Journal story? The one where you used the autopilot to "hold" the airplane, uncoupled to the flight director, while you reached elsewhere? Here is another case in which TCS can be a nice aid. Need to climb a little steeper? Bank a little more in the turn? Easy! Just hold TCS while you establish the new attitude manually, release the button, and George (the autopilot) comes back on and takes over holding this *new* attitude. Now want to roll out on 060°? OK, here's how. As you near the heading, hold TCS, roll the wings about level, and release TCS. As long as the bank was less than 6° when the button is released, the wings will continue to roll level and the autopilot will begin following whatever heading the airplane is flying on the HSI.

Finally, what about when the autopilot is not engaged and the airplane is being hand-flown to follow the flight director commands? Now what does TCS do? Just as in the coupled mode, it has no effect on lateral modes but it changes or synchronizes vertical modes. It is a Pitch Sync button when attitude hold only is in use. With ALT, IAS, or VS, it is a means of synchronizing those modes to the airplane's current condition.

Typical Autopilot Operation

Remember that the modes we describe for autopilot operation are programmed and used just the same when the airplane is being *manually* flown to satisfy the flight director commands. When you engage the AP button, you are simply saying, in effect, "You take it, George, and keep on following those flight director bars."

For takeoff, depress GA (on the left power lever), HDG, and ALTSEL, with the heading bug set on runway heading and the altitude alerter set for the first assigned altitude. You should make the initial rotation attitude slightly higher than the GA attitude: usually about 10° , instead of the 7° setting of the command bars. After passing at least 400 feet AGL, with the airplane clean, align the pitch attitude into the command bars, engage the autopilot, and move the heading bug to the various assigned or desired headings.

The autopilot will not know which way to turn if it finds the heading bug 180° out of position with the current heading, and it may begin to reverse its roll direction. When you are making a 180° or greater turn, never move the heading bug past the 135° right or left relative bearing positions on the HSI (that are usually indicated by a small mark). After the airplane has turned 45° or more, then continue moving the bug as desired, but avoid crossing the 135° relative position.

When the airplane approaches the altitude set in the altitude alerter, the computer begins a flare maneuver to level off. The annunciator will change from ALT ARM to ALT CAP, then to ALT as the level-off is completed. When you are cleared to a higher altitude, set the altitude alerter to the assigned altitude, hit the ALTSEL button, and then begin the climb by using the pitch command wheel to set a proper climb attitude. Rotation of this wheel will cancel the old altitude being held. Be careful about changing the altitude alerter setting when the ALT CAP light is on. It is okay to change the setting with either ALT ARM or ALT illuminated. But the system doesn't appreciate your changing the game when it is already in the flare maneuver to a particular altitude!

Placing a new altitude in the altitude alerter and depressing ALTSEL will *not* cancel the current altitude being held. If you use TCS to set the pitch attitude to begin the climb, the aircraft will level off immediately when TCS is released, since all you have done is synchronize ALT to a slightly higher one. Thus, if you desire to use TCS to set the climb attitude, hit *both* the ALT and the ALTSEL buttons. That way, ALT will be canceled and ALTSEL will be armed.

For the enroute descent, just like the climb, set the newly assigned altitude in the altitude alerter and depress ALTSEL. (This can be done immediately, even if you are waiting to begin the actual descent at pilot's discretion.) When you are ready to start down, use either the pitch command wheel or the TCS button (remember to hit ALT to cancel it out, if you use TCS) to set the desired attitude. In smooth air, the VS mode may be useful, selecting it when the aircraft has stabilized at the desired vertical speed.

For an ILS approach, use HDG and ALT or HDG and PAT to follow the radar vectors or published terminal routes until near the localizer. When you are close enough to the localizer to avoid receiving false signals (usually, within 30° of the localizer course), depress the APR button. This is usually done on base leg, but could even be done on an extended downwind. Keep using the heading bug to set up the proper intercept. At the correct time, HDG mode will automatically disengage as the localizer is captured. If we are below the glideslope, it will be automatically captured when it centers. On the other hand, if the approach controller (or our own poor planning) has put us above the glideslope, we must use TCS or the pitch command wheel to set up a sufficient descent attitude that will dive us onto the glideslope. When that occurs, again the glideslope will be captured.

For a non-precision approach, alternating between ALTSEL and IAS works exceedingly well to control the descents, especially if the air is relatively smooth. Suppose you have just turned inbound from a procedure turn, clean configuration, indicating 160 knots, with ALT and HDG modes engaged, and VORAPR selected so that it is ready to capture the VOR course.

As the course comes alive and the capture occurs, you now want to descend to a new altitude, the one at which you will cross the FAF (Final Approach Fix). Dial the new altitude into the alerter and press ALTSEL (if you had not already done so), press IAS (which causes ALT to disengage), and pull power back to your magic number for a 1,000 fpm descent rate. The autopilot will cause the airplane to smoothly nose over to hold 160 knots, and down you will come. IAS mode will cancel automatically as the new altitude is captured. Now extend Approach flaps, slow to your approach speed, and adjust power accordingly.

Put the next altitude (MDA or an intermediate step-down altitude) into the alerter and press ALTSEL again. As you cross the FAF, at 120 knots say, hit IAS, extend the gear, start the clock, and reduce power. Down you will come, maintaining approach speed perfectly. Add power to level off as the new altitude is captured. When the air is choppy, the rate of descent may vary too much as the autopilot works diligently to hold IAS. In that case, revert back to a basic descent attitude by using the pitch command wheel to cancel the IAS mode.

In the event of any missed approach, either from a precision or non-precision approach, hit the GA button on the left power lever as you add POWER. The autopilot will disengage and the command bars will show a wings-level , 7° pitch up attitude. Follow the command bars as you advance PROPS, and retract FLAPS and GEAR. (Power, Props, Flaps, Gear…there are our "Four Friends" again!) Now you may reengage the autopilot. When it comes on, GA will be automatically canceled, the wings will be rolled level (if they aren't already), and the existing pitch attitude will be maintained. In other words, the autopilot comes on in the uncoupled mode. You may now select the desired flight director modes – probably HDG and ALTSEL – which will cause the autopilot to couple to them.

The King Air Book

When you disconnect the autopilot and are maneuvering visually to the airport – we're not talking about 200 feet above touchdown on an ILS, but rather a few miles from the airport – we advocate getting rid of the command bars. When your attention should be directed more outside of the airplane, scanning for traffic and planning your arrival to the airport, it is a poor idea to waste effort in programming the command bars for various turns and descents. If the bars are not removed from view, there will be a good deal of time when disagreement exists between the bars and the airplane symbol. We believe it is a poor procedure to have the bars in view while intentionally ignoring them. (Someday, they might be telling you something very important – such as how to stay on the glidepath – but you are so used to ignoring them that their significance goes unheeded.)

There are two easy ways to turn off the flight director, to remove the bars from view. First, have the copilot hit the SBY button. (Or do it yourself, but if you are going to do it yourself, you might as well use the second method.) Second, hit GA with the right thumb, and then TCS with the left forefinger. When GA is selected, all other modes turn off, the autopilot disengages but the yaw damper stays on. Now when you follow-up by hitting TCS, you are syncing the bars to…what? No lateral mode is on, and you have just canceled the only vertical mode. So, there is nothing left for the flight director to do and hence it turns off! That is a nifty way of clearing the display without ever taking your hands of the controls.

> Remember: GA first + TCS second = No Command Bars

Final Comments

Here are a few last comments, that didn't fit anywhere else. First, for the 100-series of King Airs, the autopilot does its trimming by using the aircraft's own Standby (horizontal stabilizer) Pitch Trim system. Since Main and Standby systems are not to be used simultaneously, whenever you activate the Main Trim switches on either the pilot's or copilot's control wheel, the autopilot disengages. The yaw damper stays on.

For the 90-series and 200-series, however, use of electric trim does not cause the autopilot to disengage. When you make a large power or configuration change quickly, such as lowering Approach flaps right at their limiting speed, you can help the autopilot avoid too much of a momentary altitude gain by trimming down with the control wheel switches. (You can also do this in the 100-series, but only if you depress TCS while using the trim switches.)

Using GA mode (and Main Trim in the 100-series) to turn off the autopilot has an annoying side-effect. Namely, the red AP DISC annunciator in the airplane's glareshield-mounted annunciator panel will illuminate. This annunciator illuminates to tell the pilot that the autopilot has disengaged for some reason *other than* the pilot himself turning it off with his disconnect button. If the autopilot's

274

own servo torque monitoring system detects a malfunction and turns off the autopilot, the annunciator tells the crew about it. If the *copilot* hits his disconnect button while the autopilot is engaged, the red light reminds the pilot about it. Finally, if GA is selected while the autopilot is on, the light illuminates to remind the crew that they are now flying, not the autopilot. To cancel this red annunciator, the pilot must depress his control wheel disconnect button (or, reengage the autopilot).

So, it doesn't do much good to routinely turn off the autopilot using any method other than the pilot's disconnect button, since you'll probably end up hitting it anyway to clear the annunciator.

The conclusion is this: There is no realistic way to turn off the autopilot without also turning off the yaw damper on the SPZ-200A. When you want to keep the yaw damper on – and we highly recommend that you do, right to short final – then hold down the YD button with a finger on your right hand while you hit the disconnect button with your left forefinger. It's messy, but it works. (This was corrected on the SPZ-4000. Both the autopilot's and the yaw damper's engage buttons are now push-on/push-off types.)

You know that red annunciators, including the AP DISC one, are accompanied by the master fault warning flasher. However, there is one case in which this is not true. In the midst of a go-around, the designers felt that the pilots should not be required to pay attention to the flasher, to cancel it out. Thus, the autopilot disconnect caused by activating GA mode *will* trigger the AP DISC annunciator but it *will not* trigger the flasher.

If any of our readers still have a Collins ANS-31 or ANS-31A Rnav system installed by Beech as part of the airplane's avionics package, you will find no switch for selecting between Enroute and Approach sensitivities of the HSI's course needle. (Full-scale course needle deviation represents a distance from the course centerline of 10 nm when Enroute is selected and 2 nm when Approach is selected. We are not talking about GPS sensitivity now, just that associated with the ANS-31 systems.) When trying to find a particular location, such as an airport, it is recommended that Approach sensitivity be used when within 10 nm of the point.

To select Approach sensitivity on the ANS-31 system, the VORAPR button on the Sperry mode controller must be activated. It follows that there is no way to remain in HDG mode while the Rnav is in Approach sensitivity...too bad for those who want to select their own headings instead of having the autopilot/ flight director do it for them.

A few installations of the SPZ-200A system have a VNAV (Vertical Navigation) option. This is an additional vertical mode, that allows the airplane to fly a constant descent angle so as to reach a new altitude at or near a selected waypoint or Vortac. With this option, the altitude alerter is upgraded. It contains an electronic digital display and has a knob with which to set various necessary parameters.

The King Air Book

To use VNAV, set in STA EL (Station Elevation, the elevation of the Vortac in use) in hundreds of feet in the altitude alerter display, to correct for slant range errors. If desired, select TO/FR and dial in a distance that indicates how much before (To) or after (From) the waypoint you want to arrive at the new altitude. (For example, if you are inbound to XYZ Vortac on the 220° radial and you are told to "descend at pilot's discretion so as to cross a point 30 miles southwest of XYZ at 10,000 feet," you would want to set 30nm TO.) Set the new ALT you have been assigned. Finally, select VANG (Vertical Angle) to see what angle is required from your present position to make good the crossing restriction. (Angles greater than 6° are not accepted.) When the VANG display shows a reasonable value – most typically, 3° – hit the VNAV button on the flight director mode controller. Now a glideslope needle will be displayed and the system will follow this phantom glidepath and level off at the new altitude.

Sometimes, these fancy digital displays also show exactly what IAS or VS value the system is following when in those vertical modes.

Changes for the SPZ-4000 System

If you are not sure which unit you have, SPZ-200A or SPZ-4000, look at the autopilot controller. If it is lacking the little "Test Each Flight" button, then yours is a 4000.

When the 4000 is engaged for a test prior to takeoff, the AP and YD lights flash, they are not illuminated steady. Not until the pilot has deliberately checked the ability to overpower the autopilot's servos in all three axes do the lights become steady. This is supposed to be done before each flight. Also, if the STBY button is depressed for a brief time, only an annunciator lamp test is conducted, but holding it down for more than five seconds leads into a deeper self-test of the system.

The TCS button will now operate even when the turn knob is not centered. Upon release of TCS, the bank selected by the turn knob will be resumed.

Hitting ALTSEL will immediately cancel the old altitude being held. I personally don't prefer this "improvement" over the previous system, but at least if the descent attitude is being set by use of TCS instead of by the pitch command wheel, you will never have the surprise of an immediate level off due to your forgetting to clear the previous altitude hold function.

As mentioned before, the AP and/or YD may be *disengaged* as well as engaged by merely pressing the appropriate button. Each successive push cycles the AP or YD from off to on and vice versa.

The Sperry designers have done a good job on these autopilots. You can be justifiably proud of your system. When the SPZ-200A was new, it was the premier autopilot offered on the King Air.

Even today, with more modern digital systems being installed, it can still hold its own against all challengers.

COLLINS AP-105 / FD-108 OR FD-109
AUTOPILOT/FLIGHT DIRECTOR SYSTEM

OVERVIEW

The Collins AP-105/FD-108 is one of the most popular autopilots on King Air A100's, B100's, and 200's from 1972 through about 1979. It was the first autopilot/flight director system to be installed and certified in the Super King Air 200, in 1974. Various versions of the FD-108 flight director had been produced for many years prior to 1972, and are often found on A90, B90, and 100 model King Airs, as well as on lots of airline and corporate "heavy iron." However, in the early days the flight director was separate from the autopilot, having its own control panel and computer. In King Airs, the flight director was often installed along with the Honeywell H-14 or Bendix M4C autopilot.

By mating the AP-105 autopilot with the FD-108 flight director, Collins made an integrated autopilot/flight director system, in which the same information can be provided to both the flight director command bars and to the autopilot servos. With the autopilot disengaged, the flight director shows you how to accomplish the tasks you ask of it by movement of the command bars on the ADI (Attitude Director Indicator, a fancy artificial horizon or attitude indicator). The bars bank left and right, for example, showing you how much to turn to follow an assigned heading. They also pitch up and down, showing you how to adjust attitude to maintain an assigned altitude. When the autopilot is engaged while the flight director is on, it merely provides the muscle to make the airplane follow the command bars.

Since the autopilot will attempt to align the airplane with the attitude displayed on the flight director, be certain that you have manually maneuvered the airplane into good alignment with the commands before engaging the autopilot. That way, there will be no unexpected change in attitude when the autopilot takes control.

THE FLIGHT DIRECTOR DISPLAY

The flight director display - the ADI, HSI (Horizontal Situation Indicator) and the system annunciators - are available in either a four-inch or five-inch version. The smaller one is called the FD-108 while the larger one is the FD-109. Also, various options - such as the presence of a rising runway symbol operated from the radar altimeter - determine the suffix letter. For example, the FD-

108Y differs from the FD-108Z in that the "Z" model contains airspeed hold and vertical speed hold modes in its computer while the "Y" model does not.

The flight director commands are presented by a single cue, V-bar, display on the ADI.

FLIGHT DIRECTOR COMMANDS

Flight director commands are selected by push buttons on the mode controller that looks something like this:

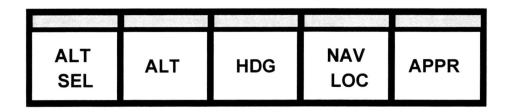

The HDG (Heading) and NAV/LOC (Navigation/Localizer) buttons control *lateral* modes, banking of the airplane. The ALT (Altitude) and ALTSEL (Altitude Select) buttons control *vertical* modes, pitching of the airplane. The APPR (Approach) button can control both bank and pitch (tracking both a localizer and a glideslope). The buttons are push-on, push-off type. This means that the first push of the button turns on that particular mode, but the next push of the button turns off that mode. When on, a green band appears at the top of the button. The *feel* of these buttons is excellent, with very positive engagement and disengagement clicks.

ALTSEL was an extra-cost option. Some airplanes do not contain that mode. Also, if the FD-108Z or 109Z is installed, you will find a second row of buttons that includes IAS (Indicated Airspeed) and VS (Vertical Speed) modes. (Some of the heavy iron installations include even more goodies, such as Mach number hold. In the King Air, there are some unused buttons on the second row.)

Usually, only one lateral and one vertical mode can be active at any one time. For example, pushing the ALT button cancels the IAS mode, selecting IAS cancels VS, HDG cancels APPR, etc. Some exceptions to this rule need to be noted, however. First, ALTSEL (Altitude Select) remains engaged even though IAS or VS is on. Second, depressing ALTSEL will not cancel ALT. (This is a nice feature. It allows you to set a new altitude into the altitude alerter and "arm" the autopilot for capture of that altitude, yet still keep holding the existing altitude until you decide to start the descent.) Last, NAV/LOC and APPR do not cancel HDG immediately. Instead, the HDG mode remains active until the system decides that it is time to stop following the selected heading and begin to track the navigational aid that is being intercepted: VOR, localizer, or some long range nav course.

COLLINS AP-105 / FD-108 OR FD-109 AP/FD SYSTEM

There are three more vertical modes, but they do not contain push buttons on the mode controller.

There is a Pitch Attitude Hold mode, that has no selection button at all. Instead, when there is no other vertical mode selected, the system maintains the currently existing pitch attitude. This mode may be selected by canceling any *other* vertical mode. For example, if the ALT mode is on, and then the ALT button is pushed again, ALT will be disengaged and the system will revert to the Pitch Attitude Hold mode. To change to a new attitude, the pitch command wheel is used when the autopilot *is* engaged, and the Pitch Sync button is used when the command bars are in view and the autopilot *is not* engaged.

The GA (Go Around) mode is selected with a push button, usually on the left power lever but sometimes on the pilot's control wheel. When the flight director goes into GA mode, ALL other modes are canceled and the command bars display a wings level, 7° pitch up attitude. If the autopilot is engaged, it disengages when GA is selected, but the yaw damper stays on.

We wish it were not so, but Collins does not permit ALTSEL to be active when the Go Around mode is on. If you are unable to make the ALTSEL button stay down (engaged) when you hit it, it is probably because the system is in GA mode. Disengage GA mode by hitting the Pitch Sync button and now ALTSEL should work fine.

The third and last vertical mode that does not have a button on the mode controller is GS mode: Glideslope. When the APPR mode (a lateral mode) is selected and the airplane is flown to intercept the glideslope of an ILS - capturing the glideslope from either below or above - then any other vertical mode will automatically be canceled and the GS mode will engage. The pitch commands will now direct the airplane to track the ILS glideslope.

It can be hazardous to descend on a glideslope unless you are established on the localizer, yet some models of this system permit GS capture before LOC capture. If a premature GS capture occurs, monitor altitude carefully and re-select ALT if it appears the airplane will go below the published glideslope intercept altitude before being established on the localizer.

With this V-bar, single cue display, selecting a vertical mode will cause no command to be displayed unless a lateral mode (such as HDG) has already been selected to bring the V-bar into view.

For a localizer back course approach, the APPR mode should be selected while the HSI course needle is set to the ILS's *front course* bearing. If your heading is closer to the back course bearing than the front course bearing as you fly toward the localizer, then the system will assume that you want to track the back course when you intercept. It will illuminate the BACK LOC annunciator and cause all displays to show proper, fly-to-the needle commands.

The King Air Book

In technical language, if your intercept angle is greater than 110° from the front course, the *back course* approach mode will be automatically selected by the APPR button.

For a VOR approach, if you choose to couple to the VOR course instead of just following your own selected headings, then use the APPR button. The command bars will continue following HDG until they "see" that the VOR course is nearing interception. At that point, HDG will disengage automatically and the command bars will display computed commands to track the course and compensate for crosswind. In effect, APPR is just like NAV/LOC here, but with a slight change in sensitivity.

THE AUTOPILOT CONTROLLER

The controls used for engaging the autopilot and yaw damper and for directing the autopilot to change the pitch and roll of the airplane when not coupled to the flight director are on the autopilot controller. It looks like this:

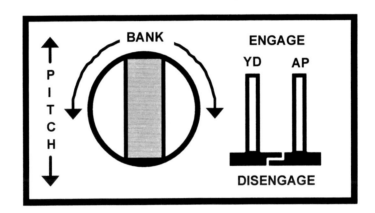

The autopilot and yaw damper are engaged and disengaged by moving the appropriate lever forward or aft. Depressing the red disconnect button on the pilot's or copilot's control wheel is another method of turning off the autopilot and/or the YD. Since the levers are spring-loaded to the aft position and held in the engaged position by a solenoid, they will spring back when the disconnect button is hit. Notice that the design prevents the autopilot from being engaged without also engaging the yaw damper, but the yaw damper can be used by itself.

The bank command wheel (or turn knob) is spring-loaded to its center position. It always returns to neutral when released. Whenever the turn knob is moved out of its center detent, all flight director lateral modes are canceled and the autopilot merely holds the bank angle existing when the knob is released. Continuing to hold the knob fully to right or left will command a bank that is limited to about 30°. Likewise, the pitch command wheel (or pitch knob) is also spring-loaded to its center position. When it is moved, all vertical modes except ALTSEL are canceled and the autopilot holds the pitch attitude existing when the knob is released. Again, the computer limits maximum and minimum pitch angles to safe values even if the knob is held fully forward or aft.

The rate at which the airplane rolls into and out of a bank and the rate it pitches up and down depend upon how far the bank and pitch knobs are moved from neutral. A slight displacement causes a slow change, a large displacement makes for a rapid change.

Also, small adjustments in pitch can be made by quickly hitting the pitch knob fully forward or aft and releasing it, as many times as required to affect the pitch change desired.

UNCOUPLED AUTOPILOT OPERATION

It is rare, but not unheard of, to operate the autopilot without a flight director mode selected. This is called "uncoupled" autopilot operation. Suppose you are climbing to altitude, flying without a copilot and without using the flight director, and you need to reach for something - the boss wants the latest Wall Street Journal that accidently fell between the copilot's seat and the sidewall.

If you simply bring the AP engage lever forward, the autopilot will take control of the airplane, holding the existing bank and pitch attitudes. Now you can let go of everything as you stretch for the newspaper, knowing that nothing unusual will happen to the airplane's attitude. Need to make a right turn to 060°? No problem. Simply hold the turn knob to the right to set up about a 20° bank, then release it. As the heading nears the assigned 060°, hold the turn knob to the left to roll the wings level.

Here's something nice to know. When the wings are within 2° of level, the autopilot reads what heading it is flying from the HSI (Horizontal Situation Indicator), and holds that heading. In other words, it is not merely a "wings leveler" but instead is holding an exact heading, even though the heading bug may not be on that heading. Consequently, there is no worry about the airplane drifting off the assigned heading, even if the rudder or ailerons are not perfectly trimmed. This is a nice feature!

The autopilot may also be operated in what we call a "half-coupled" mode. That is, it may be following the flight director's vertical modes only, while still holding the bank attitude commanded by the turn knob.

In the "half-coupled" mode, the V-bar is not in view even though a vertical mode (for example, IAS or ALT) is active.

For example, you are still flying your assigned 060° heading (because you rolled the wings level on that heading with the turn knob), but now you are asked to climb at 140 knots and level off at FL 230. One way of doing this is to set 23,000 feet in the altitude alerter and push ALTSEL, then use the pitch command knob to set an attitude that will achieve 140 knots, and continue adjusting pitch to hold 140. (With the "Z" model, simply select IAS when 140 is reached.) The airplane will level off automatically at 23,000 feet.

In most cases, of course, the autopilot is operated fully coupled to the flight director modes. In the previous example, it would be more realistic to say that as 060° were assigned, the heading bug would have been placed on that value and then the HDG button would have been depressed. This would have made the autopilot adjust bank to steer 060° (or whatever new heading was selected by the bug), and would have made the flight director V-bars come into view.

THE PITCH SYNC BUTTON

On the control wheel's outboard grip, activated by the flying-hand's thumb, is the Pitch Sync button - Pitch Synchronization. When this button is momentarily depressed while the command bars are in view, the bars synchronize to the airplane's existing pitch attitude, the vertical command becomes Pitch Attitude Hold, and ALT, IAS, and VS modes are canceled.

Pitch Sync has no effect when a glideslope is captured.

TYPICAL AUTOPILOT OPERATION

Remember that the modes we describe for autopilot operation are programmed and used just the same when the airplane is being *manually* flown to satisfy the flight director commands. When you engage the AP, you are simply saying, in effect, "You take it, George, and keep on following those flight director bars."

For takeoff, depress HDG and ALTSEL, with the heading bug set on runway heading and the altitude alerter set for the first assigned altitude. After you make the initial rotation (usually to about 10°) hit Pitch Sync to establish the bars at that attitude. After passing at least 400 feet AGL, with the airplane clean, set the desired cruise climb attitude, (usually about 7°) hit Pitch Sync, engage the autopilot, and move the heading bug to the various assigned or desired headings.

The autopilot won't know which way to turn if it finds the heading bug 180° out of position with the current heading, and it may begin to reverse its roll direction. When you are making a 180° or greater turn, never move the heading bug past the 135° right or left relative bearing positions on the HSI (that are usually indicated by a small mark). After the airplane has turned 45° or more, then continue moving the bug as desired, but avoid crossing the 135° relative position.

When the airplane approaches the altitude set in the altitude alerter, the computer begins a flare maneuver to level off. The ALT annunciator will illuminate as the flare maneuver begins. If you move the pitch command knob, hit the Pitch Sync button, or place a new altitude into the alerter during this flare, the system reverts to Pitch Attitude Hold mode, which ruins the level-off. Let the level-off progress without trying to "help" the system.

As each altitude is correctly captured, we recommend that you hit the ALT button, which will clear the ALTSEL mode. By so doing, you will be able to set the altitude alerter to any new value at any time you want, without the autopilot starting an immediate deviation toward the new altitude.

When you are cleared to a higher altitude, set the altitude alerter to the assigned altitude, hit the ALTSEL button, and then begin the climb by using the pitch command knob to set a proper climb attitude. Deflection of this knob will cancel the old altitude being held.

Placing a new altitude in the altitude alerter and depressing ALTSEL will *not* cancel the current altitude being held if the ALT button had been previously hit. On the other hand, if the system were holding altitude while still in the ALTSEL mode, as soon as a new number is put into the alerter, the system will begin moving to the new altitude at about 700 fpm.

If you decide to track VOR courses using NAV/LOC mode instead of HDG, you should be aware of the following facts. Unlike many less-expensive systems, you will find that the AP-105 does a rather good job of tracking VOR signals without a lot of unnecessary weaving back and forth. In the "zone of confusion" directly overhead a VOR, many less-sophisticated systems are almost worthless, but not this one.

As the VOR is approached and the needle begins to get very sensitive, the system computer, just like a good pilot, holds the current heading until station passage is completed. When on the other side of the station, with a steady signal once again being received, the system once more begins tracking the actual course instead of just holding a wind-corrected heading. This lateral mode is termed "Dead Reckoning" by Collins. The installations on later airplanes (that is, B-232 and after for A100's, BB-204 and after for 200's, and all B100's) annunciate this automatic selection of the Dead Reckoning mode near the VOR by having the green "N/L CAP" annunciator flash on and off.

Collins says that it is acceptable to make a course change over a VOR without ever leaving the NAV/LOC mode, only if the change will be small: 10° or less. For a bigger course change, select HDG, set up a proper intercept of the new course, then re-select NAV/LOC.

For the enroute descent, just like the climb, set the newly assigned altitude in the altitude alerter and depress ALTSEL. (This can be done immediately, even if you are waiting to begin the actual descent "at pilot's discretion.") When you are ready to start down, use the pitch command knob to set the desired attitude. In smooth air, the VS mode may be useful, if installed, selecting it when the aircraft has stabilized at the desired vertical speed.

For an ILS approach, use HDG and ALT or HDG and Pitch Attitude Hold to follow the radar vectors or published terminal routes until near the localizer. When you are close enough to the

The King Air Book

localizer to avoid receiving false signals (usually, within 30° of the localizer course), depress the APPR button. Keep using the heading bug to set up the proper intercept. At the correct time, HDG mode will automatically disengage as the localizer is captured. If we are below the glideslope, it will be automatically captured when it centers. On the other hand, if the approach controller (or our own poor planning) has put us above the glideslope, we must use the pitch command knob to set up a sufficient descent attitude that will dive us onto the glideslope. When that occurs, again the glideslope will be captured.

For a non-precision approach, alternating between ALTSEL and IAS, if available, works exceedingly well to control the descents. Suppose you have just turned inbound from a procedure turn, clean configuration, indicating 160 knots, with ALT and HDG modes engaged, and APPR selected (yes, APPR not NAV/LOC) so that it is ready to capture the VOR course.

As the course comes alive and the capture occurs, you now want to descend to a new altitude, the one at which you will cross the FAF (Final Approach Fix). Dial the new altitude into the alerter and press ALTSEL (if you had not already done so), press IAS (which causes ALT to disengage), and pull power back to your "magic number" for a 1,000 fpm descent rate. The autopilot will cause the airplane to smoothly nose over to hold 160 knots, and down you will come. IAS mode will cancel automatically as the new altitude is captured. Hit ALT as the level-off is completed. Now extend Approach flaps, slow to your approach speed (about 120 knots, usually), and adjust power accordingly.

Put the next altitude (MDA or an intermediate step-down altitude) into the alerter and press ALTSEL again. As you cross the FAF at 120 knots, hit IAS, extend the gear, start the clock, and reduce power. Down you will come, maintaining approach speed perfectly. Add power to level off as the new altitude is captured. (If your system does not have the IAS mode, make the descents by use of the pitch command knob, alternating between it and ALT or ALTSEL.)

In the event of any missed approach, either from a precision or non-precision approach, hit the GA button as you add POWER. The autopilot will disengage and the command bars will show a wings-level , 7° pitch up attitude. Follow the command bars as you advance PROPS, and retract FLAPS and GEAR. (Power, Props, Flaps, Gear...there it is again!) Now you may reengage the autopilot. When it comes on, it will be in the uncoupled mode, holding the existing bank and pitch attitudes. You may now select the desired flight director modes - probably HDG and ALTSEL - that will cause the autopilot to couple to them.

When you disconnect the autopilot and are maneuvering visually to the airport - we're not talking about 200 feet above touchdown on an ILS, but rather a few miles from the airport - we advocate getting rid of the command bars. When your attention should be directed more outside of the airplane, scanning for traffic and planning your arrival to the airport, it is a poor idea to waste effort in programming the command bars for various turns and descents. If the bars are not removed from view, there will be a good deal of time when disagreement exists between the bars and the airplane symbol. We believe it is a poor procedure to have the bars in view while intentionally ignoring them. (Someday, they might be telling you something very important - such as how to stay on the glidepath - but you are so used to ignoring them that their significance goes unheeded.)

There are two easy ways to turn off the flight director, to remove the bars from view. First, have the copilot hit the lateral button in use, such as HDG or APPR. (Or do it yourself, but if you are going to do it yourself, you might as well use the second method.) Second, hit GA followed by Pitch Sync. When GA is selected, all other modes turn off, the autopilot disengages but the yaw damper stays on. Now when you follow-up by hitting Pitch Sync, you are syncing the bars to . . . what? No lateral mode is on, and you have just canceled the only vertical mode. So, there is nothing left for the flight director to do and . . . it turns off! That is a nifty way of clearing the display without ever taking your hands off the controls.

> Remember: GA first + Pitch Sync second = No Command Bars

FINAL COMMENTS

Here are a few last comments, that didn't fit anywhere else. First, for the 100-series of King Airs, the autopilot does its trimming by using the aircraft's own Main (horizontal stabilizer) Pitch Trim system. Since Main and Standby systems are not to be used simultaneously, whenever you activate the Standby Trim switches on the pedestal the autopilot and yaw damper disengage. (This is true even when the Main trim master switch, not the Standby, is on!)

In both the 100-series and 200-series, when you make a large power or configuration change quickly, such as lowering Approach flaps right at their limiting speed, you can "help" the autopilot avoid too much of a momentary altitude gain by trimming down with the control wheel switches.

When in the APPR mode, test features for Nav, Marker Beacon, and Radio Altimeter are disabled. If you want to test Marker audio before your ILS, do so before APPR is selected.

The FD-108/AP-105 system installed in 200s and B200s has an extra circuit associated with the landing gear. This circuit causes the aileron servos to operate in a higher gain mode when both main landing gear legs are extended, which leads to a couple of odd quirks. First, you are not supposed to extend the gear with the autopilot engaged when above 15,000 feet. Second, when doing a manual extension of the gear with the autopilot engaged, invariably the autopilot kicks off right before the last green gear-down light illuminates. The autopilot can be reengaged immediately, but it is an annoying nuisance when this unexpected autopilot disconnect occurs.

The King Air Book

The system supplement in the Airplane Flight Manual should be read and studied, especially for the knowledge of how to conduct a thorough and complete test of the system. This supplement also discusses the fact that some installations contain an "AP CPLD" button on the mode controller. If this button is off, then the command bars can be in view even though the autopilot is still operating in the uncoupled mode. The button was very rarely installed.

Finally, a few A100's contain a "Control Wheel Steering" option, in which you will find a CWS button on the pilot's control wheel. When the autopilot is engaged and the CWS button is held, the pitch and roll servos disengage while the yaw damper stays on. Any realistic bank and pitch attitude can be set by manually maneuvering the airplane with the button depressed, and that attitude will be held when the button is released. In effect, you are doing the same thing as if you moved the bank and pitch knobs on the autopilot controller, but you never have to take your hands off of the control wheel. It is a handy feature.

RUDDER BOOST SYSTEMS

You will notice that the title of the article is "Rudder Boost *Systems.*" *Systems*, plural, not *System*, singular. There are actually three variations of this system that we will be discussing. My goal is to present the history of these systems, why they are required on some King Air models and not on others, how they function, how they are tested, and a few trivial tidbits I hope you find interesting.

The first Rudder Boost system appeared on the Super King Air 200 model. The prototype, BB-1, first flew in the Fall of 1972 and the model was issued its FAA Type Certificate in late 1973 with customer deliveries beginning the next year. Up until this time, the top-of-the-line King Air model was the A100. This model shares the same wing center section width as the 90-series, although its engines are rated at 680 SHP instead of the 550 SHP rating for the C90. The fuselage is longer than that of the 90-series, yielding a cabin length four feet greater. The A100 has quite benign engine-out characteristics since the extra horsepower is more than compensated for by the longer fuselage and bigger tail surface. VMCA is actually a few knots lower on the A100 than it is on the C90.

The 200 model, however, has 850 SHP engines that are located twenty-five inches further outboard from the fuselage's center, due to the 200's much wider wing center section. Why so wide? First, to provide sufficient clearance from the fuselage for the larger diameter propellers that the 200 has. Second, to make for a quieter cabin, by moving the propeller arc farther away from the occupants. The 200 design team at Beechcraft realized that extra power, further out on the wing, would definitely raise VMCA unless something was done to offset the increased engine-out yaw force.

Few people realize that the T-Tail configuration of the model 200 – the first Beechcraft to sport such a tail configuration – did not come about due to a designer's whim for a more modern look. No, instead the T-Tail was selected after lengthy theoretical and wind tunnel testing showed that this configuration was optimum for increasing rudder effectiveness at low speeds, for keeping VMCA down to reasonable levels. You see, since VMCA occurs at lower airspeeds, the airplane's angle-of-attack is high at this time. The conventional tail configuration of the C90 or A100 causes the airflow to the rudder to be impeded, or blocked, by the horizontal stabilizer, making the rudder less effective. By moving the horizontal tail up to the top, however, two benefits are realized: (1) The airflow to the rudder is no longer being blocked, and (2) the horizontal surface provides an *end-plate* effect that contributes to even more rudder effectiveness by not letting the air escape too readily off the top of the rudder surface.

The King Air Book

As a side note, moving the horizontal surface up to the top gives both added benefits as well as added problems. The two big benefits are (1) smoother flight operation, since the tail is no longer being subjected to as much of the disturbed airflow behind the wing and propellers, and (2) much less pitch trimming is required when the flaps extend or retract, since the airflow changes created by the flaps pass below the tall tail. On the other hand, the fuselage is now subject to more twisting stress since the forces generated by the horizontal surface are no longer acting right on the fuselage's centerline but instead are acting at a point many feet above the fuselage. (It took nearly twenty years before some unanticipated cracks starting showing up in the fuselage stringers that helped connect the tail to the cabin, leading to an AD requiring reinforcements at the aft pressure bulkhead.)

When the 200's design team finalized the T-Tail choice, they suspected that there was a good chance that a human pilot would not be able to provide sufficient rudder pedal input to move the big new rudder fully to the stop during VMCA testing. You see, the FAA rules require that no more than 150 pounds of rudder force may be "asked for" from a pilot. Furthermore, previous T-Tail airplanes at that time – primarily the Learjet and the Boeing 727 – had horrible stall characteristics that required both of them to be fitted with stick shaker and stick pusher systems. In anticipation of stall and VMCA certification hurdles, the prototype 200 flew with stick shaker, stick pusher, and rudder boost systems.

Well, happy days! As the flight test program progressed, all three of these extra systems were found to be unnecessary. Although there was very little pre-stall buffet – since the T-Tail did not feel much of the disturbed airflow burbling off the wing – nonetheless enough buffet was felt that the buffet and a conventional stall warning horn were sufficient to advise the pilot that a stall was imminent. Goodbye shaker. Second, a brisk forward movement of the control wheel always resulted in a reduction of the angle-of-attack, allowing the stall to be broken: No *Deep Stall* was ever encountered that could not be overcome by forward elevator. Goodbye pusher. Finally, the maximum rudder force required from the pilot was found to be 147 pounds…3 beneath the limit. Goodbye Rudder Boost.

But wait a minute! Three pounds under the limit?! I thought Beechcrafts were supposed to be the "Cadillacs of the Air." No? Surely, this massive leg input is not going to endear the engine-out characteristics of this new model to many of its pilots, right?

It was this type of thinking that led the design team to make the decision to provide Rudder Boost as standard, not optional, equipment on all of the 200-series of King Airs. On the other hand, the "Required Equipment List" shows that Rudder Boost is never required for any condition of certified flight: Day, Night, VFR, IFR, and Icing. That means that the Master Minimum Equipment List (MMEL) permits the system to be inoperative without operational restriction.

RUDDER BOOST SYSTEMS

Before we talk about how the system functions, allow me to summarize the application of the Rudder Boost system to other, later, members of the King Air family tree.

The F90 made its appearance in 1979. It was the next model developed after the 200 and it shared many of the 200's systems, including Rudder Boost. As with the 200, Rudder Boost was never required by regulations and its lack never yields a No-Go situation. The same is true for the F90-1, the follow-on to the F90, produced in 1983 to 1985.

The C90A, appearing in 1984, also got the Rudder Boost treatment. This continues on all of the C90 variants – C90SE, C90B, C90GT, C90GTi – right to the present day. No 65-90, A90, B90, C90, C90-1, E90, 100, A100, or B100 has ever had a Rudder Boost system.

(Allow me to add a side note. All of the 90-series of King Airs *need* Rudder Boost like a fish needs a bicycle. Any pilot who has passed a multi-engine flight test has probably experienced and used more rudder force than he or she ever will use in a 90-model King Air, even without any rudder assistance. Do you know the most common observation I make when conducting engine-out flight training on these models? It is not that too *little* rudder force is used, it's just the opposite: Too *much* "good side" rudder force is applied, as shown by the ball being displaced to the bad engine's side. Instead of "raising the dead," like we should, we are flying uncoordinated with the good engine raised. Why? Because the Rudder Boost is applying so much assistance that the pilot is required to add virtually none. Invariably, newcomers – and even some old pros – overdo it.

The presence of Rudder Boost on the 90-models gives Marketing another thing to crow about and it makes an engine failure in cruise – with Autofeather armed and the autopilot flying – a feet-on-the-floor, watch-it-happen, experience. Neat! But please keep an eye on the state of coordination as you start hand-flying and conducting an engine-out approach. It is very easy to be too aggressive on the good side's pedal, not realizing that Rudder Boost is doing all the work for you.

One other comment before we continue: The 147 pound rudder force figure that I mentioned was the worst-case scenario. That includes all the "baddies" that exist when VMCA is determined, including a windmilling propeller, a gear up configuration, and with no rudder trim input allowed. The mere act of getting the propeller feathered cuts the required rudder force in half! Trimming can now allow for feet-on-the-floor flying. In other words, in the real world, you will never come close to needing anything close to the 150 pound limit even if Rudder Boost were inoperative. Now back to our regularly scheduled article...)

Also first appearing in 1984 was the 300 model: a 200 on steroids! The 1,050 SHP engines and the large propellers they spun finally led to the fact that the 150 pound human pilot rudder force limit was indeed being exceeded without a helping hand...uh, helping foot. The same is true for the model B300 (known as the 350) that came out in 1990. The only King Air models in which the

MMEL will *not* allow for inoperative Rudder Boost are these 300-series members. For them, if Rudder Boost is inoperative, it is a No-Go situation.

So how does the system work? There are three variations.

For the 200-series, the F90-series, and the C90A-series (which includes the C90B and later models), Rudder Boost is basically identical in design and operation. It is an all-or-nothing aid that involves a pneumatic power-differential sensor, an electric control system, and a pneumatic source of rudder force. Let me explain further.

Since the need for rudder input depends on the difference in left and right thrust, some method must be devised to measure this thrust differential. Do you realize that engine power is not a perfect measure of thrust? Imagine that a big ugly wooden club were bolted onto the shaft in place of the propeller. Do you see how lots of power could be produced by the engine spinning that club and yet absolutely zero thrust would be developed? On the other hand, since both sides have identical propellers with identical efficiency characteristics, it makes sense to equate power differential with thrust differential....and this is what the Beech design engineers decided to do.

Shaft Horsepower, you will recall, is the product of Torque and Propeller Speed. To measure power accurately would involve a complicated process in which both Torque and Np inputs would be needed by some comparative computer. That would not only be complicated but expensive, too. So the question for the designers became this: How can we measure power differential conveniently, cheaply, and yet with sufficient accuracy to serve our purposes?

The solution that the designers hit upon was to use raw, unregulated compressor discharge pressure – our old friend P3 Air – as the substitute for power. At first glance, it appears to make sense: Developing more power generally implies more compressor speed and higher P3 air pressures. Furthermore, there already existed a location under the cabin floor in which both left and right side's raw P3 was available and could readily be accessed: The point, upstream of one-way checkvalves, just before the two sides join together and flow into the pressure regulator that reduces pressure down to about 18 psi above ambient. This reduced-pressure air is the well-known *Pneumatic Air* that inflates the deice boots and cabin door seal, among many other functions. It goes by a variety of names: *Instrument Air, Pneumatic Air,* and *Little P3.*

Tap-offs were installed in the left and right Little P3 lines under the floor and the raw P3 pressure was directed into a Differential Pressure (ΔP) switch. This ΔP switch contains a movable shuttle that is held near the center of the device by equal spring force on both sides. One side of the shuttle feels the P3 air from the left side while the other side gets the right P3 air. So long as the two air pressures are similar, the shuttle does not displace very far from its centered location. On the other hand, if one side's air pressure goes to near ambient – as it would with the engine shutdown – while the other side's pressure is high, then the shuttle moves sufficiently to cause an electric switch to make contact. When this occurs, power is sent to a normally-closed solenoid in the tail that now opens, allowing regulated air to enter a pneumatic servo and pull forward on the good engine's rudder cable.

It is probably obvious that the amount of desirable rudder assistance is not the same among all models with this style of Rudder Boost system. The big 200 is going to need more than the smaller C90A or F90. Also, the P3 pressures being developed by the compressor of a PT6A-42 and the compressor of a PT6A-21 are not the same for a given power output.

These individual variations, however, are quite easily handled by two things: First, by making the ΔP switch have differing pressure differentials required before the shuttle hits the stop. It takes nearly 60 psid before the shuttle travels completely in a 200, but less on a C90A or F90. Second, although an identical set of pneumatic servos, left and right, are used on all these models, the amount of force they apply to the rudder cable is changed by regulating the 18 psi pneumatic air down even further to give the force desired. It goes down to about 15 psi in the 200-series but closer to 13 psi in the 90-series. Clever, those engineers!

When the model 300 made its appearance – certified under the more restrictive requirements of Special FAR 41C – you will recall that we already stated that Rudder Boost became a requirement: nearly 180 pounds of rudder force would be demanded of the pilot in a worst-case scenario. Beech decided to take a totally new approach that would eliminate the "doubling up" of rudder servos.

To the best of my knowledge, there was only one (!) King Air 200 ever manufactured without a factory-installed autopilot. This single airplane, however, still had Rudder Boost since nothing in the Rudder Boost system relied on an autopilot. (It also used these same pneumatic servos to provide Yaw Damping…a requirement for flight in 200s above 17,000 feet.) Knowing that the likelihood of another end customer ever desiring a sans-autopilot airplane was nil, it was recognized that an opportunity existed to utilize the already-installed autopilot rudder servo to do double duty: Act as a Yaw Damper routinely, but stand by to be the Rudder Booster during one-engine-inoperative operation.

300s were offered with three different autopilots: the Collins FCS-65 system, the Honeywell (Sperry) SPZ-4000 system, and the Honeywell (King) KFC-400 system. All three of these manufacturers teamed with Beech to develop and certify the 300's Rudder Boost system as part of the autopilot system. Although there are minor differences in detail, all three systems share some commonalities.

The first of these commonalities is the fact that measuring *Little P3* is still the method by which power is measured. However, the ΔP switch has been eliminated. The raw P3 pressures are converted to electrical signals by pressure transducers and that information is fed to the autopilot computer. The computer, in turn, decides if enough P3 difference exists to warrant some left or right rudder help. If the help is warranted, then the autopilot's rudder servo – the third axis of a three-axis autopilot – applies the force desired.

The second commonality in the 300-style systems is that Rudder Boost is no longer an all-or-nothing proposition. The previous models – with a minimum ΔP value required to trigger the signal and with a fixed force helping on the rudder when the pneumatic servo activated – either applied the help or did not. On or off, nothing in between. The 300's autopilot computer, however, can direct the rudder servo to vary the rudder force being applied. As thrust differential increases – as sensed by P3 differential – the rudder force also increases.

There is one last commonality between the various autopilot manufacturers: The computer isn't capable of providing *both* Yaw Damping and Rudder Boosting at the same time. When the Rudder Boost starts to work, Yaw Damping takes a back seat. (Since a functioning Yaw Damper is a requirement for flight above 11,000 feet in a 300, does this mean it's against regulations to lose an engine above that altitude? Hmmm. I'll get back to you on that one, OK?)

All 300s as well as all models of the 200-series contain three-position Bleed Air Valve switches that permit shutting off Little P3 (Pneumatic Air, Instrument Air) in the event of a bleed air line leak or failure. Only members of the F90-series *that contain the optional Brake Deice system* also have the three-position switches. (F90s without Brake Deice as well as all C90As, C90Bs, etc have two-position switches and Pneumatic Air cannot be terminated when the engine is running.)

So there we are, sipping our coffee at FL250, when a Bleed Air Fail warning annunciator illuminates. Knowing that history tells us that this will more than likely be a false warning, nonetheless we follow the Abnormal Checklist procedure and move that side's Bleed Air Valve switch all the way down to the "Pneu and Envir Off" position. The other side's air flow should be sufficient to keep us fully pressurized with plenty of air also available for boots, door seal, etc. (Yes, it may get a little chilly up there eventually with only half the BTUs of heat energy being supplied to the cabin.)

Think about the effect experienced by the Rudder Boost system when that Little P3 air was terminated in this situation. Rudder Boost will immediately "think" that you've had an engine failure and will – if it weren't for what we are about to present – apply rudder force on the other side. Yet, both engines are running fine, so no rudder force is needed. Although the application of this rudder force would not be dangerous – it could easily be compensated by use of rudder trim – it would be unnecessary and a bit disconcerting to the crew and passengers to experience a sudden yaw until proper control inputs were applied.

RUDDER BOOST SYSTEMS

Well, those clever engineers anticipated this potential problem and wired the Rudder Boost control circuit through both left and right Bleed Air Valve switches. If either Bleed Air Valve switch is positioned all the way down – not just to the center, but to the bottom position – then the Rudder Boost control circuit is disabled. In other words, even though there will be enough difference in Little P3 to warrant Rudder Boost operation, no electric power will be available and hence no force will be applied to the rudder.

The bottom line is that there are three ways to electrically disable Rudder Boost: (1) Turn off the Rudder Boost switch on the pedestal. (2) Pull the Rudder Boost circuit breaker. (3) Move either Bleed Air Valve switch to the bottom position. Only if none of these actions has taken place does Rudder Boost have a chance of operating. (So, in a 300, since Rudder Boost is a required flight control, does this mean it's against regulations to experience a Bleed Air Failure and follow the checklist procedure? Hmmm. I'll get back to you on that one also, OK?)

We presented earlier in this article the comment that using P3 air pressure as a stand-in for engine power measurement offered convenience and frugality. We also stated that it offered "sufficient" accuracy. Well, yes and no.

The relationship between Shaft Horsepower, P3 pressure, and Ng speed is a complicated one with many variables. There is definitely not a linear, one-to-one, correlation. At 60% Ng idle speed do we have 60% power? No, of course not. Power is barely measurable at that idle speed. Is P3 air pressure at idle 60% of what it is at maximum Ng speed? Again, the answer is No. Typically, it is about 30 – 40% of its maximum value.

How does this affect the typical King Air pilot? It makes testing the Rudder Boost system before flight a sometimes difficult if not impossible situation. During the test, one merely leaves one engine at idle and advances the power lever on the opposite side until the distinctive forward kick on the high-power side's rudder pedal is felt. Remember, folks, that the ΔP switch must experience enough *differential* pressure to fully displace the shuttle. But, hey, the low power side is putting out quite a bit of P3 pressure since the engine is not shutdown but is turning at 50 – 60% Ng or more. So, to get enough *difference*, the high power side must really get with the program! On hot days at high altitudes, the ITT limit may be encountered before the rudder kicks. At lower altitudes, especially in B200s, sometimes the torque limit is reached first.

What to do? First, turn off the air conditioning and make sure you have the lowest possible idle setting on the low power side. If you can get back to 53% Ng or so – only permissible with three, not four-blade propellers – the test will occur much easier. Second, don't be afraid to go right to ITT or Torque limits on the high power side. It may be required to activate the system. (It has been my experience that some King Air simulators do a poor job of showing how difficult it can be to get a proper test.) Third, repeat the test without holding the Prop Gov Test switch. To save time and to eliminate one extra partial power cycle, the Rudder Boost test is combined with the Overspeed Governor test. Holding the test switch up resets the Overspeed Governor to a lower RPM. The lower RPM means that the torque limit will be reached at a lower power setting, lower Ng speed. Letting go of the switch and allowing the propeller RPM to reach redline will allow more Ng and higher P3 pressures to be attained before the torque limit is reached. Fourth, as a last resort, you may actually need to shut the low power engine down to get a proper test. This is extreme and unlikely, but it is a last resort.

Because it takes so darn much torque to do a proper test, most pilots tend to think that Rudder Boost will only operate in flight in extreme power situations. They believe it will help on a takeoff engine failure situation but may not help much during cruise. No, they're wrong. With an engine truly shutdown, now the P3 pressure goes basically to ambient and not very much Ng speed is required on the good side to trigger the ΔP switch. It has been my experience that, in a 200 or B200, it is common to see 2,000 ft-lbs of torque or more before the test occurs. With an engine actually shutdown in flight, however, usually Rudder Boost triggers closer to 1,300 – 1,600 ft-lbs.

In a typical single-engine ILS or visual approach, on the standard 3-degree glidepath with gear down and Approach flaps extended, with maximum speed (2,000 RPM) selected on the propeller, the torque required is typically about 1,300 ft-lbs, just below the threshold value at which Rudder Boost kicks in. If the air is gusty and you find yourself varying power significantly, it becomes aggravating because the rudder seems to have a mind of its own: The trim setting that was right a second ago is all wrong now! Of course, what is happening is that Rudder Boost is turning on and off with the power changes. Solution? Turn it off! Reach down on the pedestal and move that Rudder Boost switch aft! Remember, the system is there to *help* you. If it's not helping – and in this scenario it sure as heck is not! – kill it! If you do a Go Around – heaven forbid! – and face a prolonged single-engine climb, turn it back on if you so desire.

The last two paragraphs were written using the 200-series as the example, but they apply as well to the 90-series with appropriate lower torque numbers.

Everything we've discussed about this frustrating On-Off tendency does not apply to the 300, since it's rudder help varies with power, not an all-or-nothing proposition.

There is another case in which using P3 as a substitute for actual power measurement leads to problems. Think about how the system would react when the one-in-a-million catastrophic Reduction Gearbox (RGB) failure occurs. When the gearbox lets loose, the Power Turbine is no longer connected to the propeller. Without that connection, its speed is no longer being governed and PT blades start flying off the disk due to massive centrifugal force as the disk spins to zillions of RPMs.

RUDDER BOOST SYSTEMS

The blades hit the containment ring, break into little pieces, and start leaving a disconcerting trail of sparkling fireworks out the exhaust stacks. But in the few moments it takes the pilot to react – and before the engine runs out of oil – what is the compressor doing? It's just as happy as can be, still turning at the Ng speed the FCU was set for and still pumping out the same P3 pressure that it was before the gearbox let go. So what does Rudder Boost do? Absolutely nothing. It still "thinks" that all is fine, since the pressures across the ΔP switch are still about equal. So don't expect any Rudder Boost help until your shaky hand finds the Condition Lever on that exploded engine and pulls it into Fuel Cut-Off.

In summary, using P3 measurement as a substitute for power measurement means (1) that Rudder Boost will not always operate with a power loss – the broken RGB case, and (2) that what is seen during the test with an idling engine is far different than what is experienced with an actual engine shutdown.

The only King Air model that eliminates these two, relatively minor, concerns is the 350. The engineers finally recognized that a much better substitute for power was readily available…torque! By tapping into the existing torque transducers and providing that information to the autopilot computer, a much more accurate manner of determining the necessity of Rudder Boost was readily available. In the 350, the Rudder Boost test is always easy to accomplish because idling torque is miniscule, even at 62% idle speed. If an RGB ever blows up, Rudder Boost will still sense the resulting immediate loss of torque and function as it should. Lastly, the tie-in between the Bleed Air Valve switches and the Rudder Boost control circuit are eliminated, since shutting off Little P3 plays no role in the Rudder Boost system.

So there you have the three Rudder Boost system variations: (A) The All-or-Nothing, pneumatic servo system, using a ΔP switch as the trigger; (B) The variable system, using P3 as the power measuring substitute, and using the autopilot's rudder servo to do double duty; (C) The variable system, using Torque as the power measuring substitute, and using the autopilot's rudder servo to do double duty.

Version C is for the 350, Version B is the 300, and Version A applies to everything else.

Before we bring this long presentation to a close, there are two additional bits of arcane knowledge concerning the model 300 that I wish to review. Recall that Rudder Boost is a required item for all 300 operation. We can't satisfy that 150-pound rudder force FAA limit without it. And, class, what triggers Rudder Boost in the 300? That's right: Varying left and right P3 pressure values. An interesting phenomenon was found to occur at times on 300s that have the optional Brake Deice system. When Brake Deice is on, some of the raw Little P3 is being vented overboard through the piccolo tubes around the brakes. This results in the P3 value being sensed at the transducer being less

The King Air Book

than it would otherwise be. Since Rudder Boost force is variable depending upon the magnitude of the difference in the sensed P3 pressures, Rudder Boost will apply less force than it should. Uh-oh. "Not good," says the FAA.

"Well, we direct pilots to turn off Brake Deice for takeoff. It's written into the AFM supplement," says Beech. "Not good, " says the FAA, " you and I both know that pilots won't always read the fine print and, even if they do, they'll forget at times to turn off Brake Deice on the takeoff runway."

"Yeah, you got a point there," says Beech. So back to the designing boards they go to come up with a method that will guarantee Brake Deice will never be inadvertently left on during takeoff.

"Eureka! I've got it! We'll wire Brake Deice through the Autofeather circuit! When Autofeather arms on takeoff as the power levers are advanced, it'll be just as if some invisible hand reached down and turned off Brake Deice if it was inadvertently left on. Done deal!"

And that's why, children, you've got to turn off Autofeather when you want to cycle and test your Brake Deice system during descent in your 300.

The last bit of trivia is this. Suppose you are landing your 200 or F90 with an engine out on a short runway and you need/want to use maximum single-engine Reverse. (Why didn't you go to a longer runway, eh?!) As the good engine revs up to about 85% Ng in maximum reverse, what if that is sufficient to trigger Rudder Boost?

If you answered, "It will work backwards!" go to the head of the class. Yes indeed, although we usually think "Good foot, good engine; dead foot, dead engine," when we are using reverse thrust that memory aid is incorrect, just backwards. For example, with the left propeller feathered and Maximum Reverse on the right, the airplane will be pulled to the right and left rudder will be needed to keep it straight. Yet the Rudder Boost would be "helping" on the right, not left pedal. Oops!

So why isn't this mentioned more often? Why is Maximum single-engine Reverse power utilized in creating the Accelerate-Stop distances presented in the 200-series and F90-series performance charts?

Because, happily, 82 - 88% Ng – the proper Maximum Reverse value – should never create enough P3 differential to trigger the all-or-nothing system that these models contain.

However, when the 300 was being flight tested, with its variable Rudder Boost system, sure enough…the test pilots were feeling Rudder Boost working against them when Maximum Reverse was used during single engine landings. What to do? The answer was to not allow the actual selection of single-engine Reverse, but have the pilot stop going into the Beta range when Ng started to pick up. It was okay to use *Beta for Taxi,* in other words, but the pilot should avoid *Beta Plus Power.*

298

Here comes Mr. FAA guy again. "What?! You are going to require the pilot, during his single-engine landing, to divert his attention to the Ng gauge and/or the power quadrant, and stop moving the power lever back behind Idle when Ng starts increasing? Get real!"

And that, children, is why the 300-series was the first of the King Air line to have a hard power lever stop at the bottom of *Beta for Taxi,* the start of *Beta Plus Power.* With that *Ground Fine* stop separating Beta for Taxi – what is now simply known as *Beta* – from Beta Plus Power – now known simply as *Reverse* –we have the power quadrant as it appears on all of the current production models.

If you are using any Beta during rollout following a single-engine landing in a 300 or 350, remember to lift the power lever only once and stop at Ground Fine. Don't lift a second time and enter Reverse…if you do, you may be in for an interesting rudder experience!

CABIN AIR CIRCULATION AND TEMPERATURE BALANCE

I am often surprised to sit down in the cockpit of a King Air that I haven't flown before and find that the position of the defroster and vent air knobs don't make sense, at least not to me. Why isn't the defroster knob pulled on? Why are the pilot and copilot "Vent Air" knobs pulled? Let's spend some time discussing the purpose of these knobs and how we can use them to make the cockpit and cabin more comfortable for ourselves and for our passengers.

To begin, let's review how hot and cold air get introduced into the interior of a King Air. Hot air comes in the form of environmental bleed air that has been routed such that little if any of it has passed through the air-to-air heat exchangers in the wing center section. Since this bleed air has not been allowed to lose energy to the ambient air that is passing across the heat exchanger core, it has retained its thermal energy and has entered the airplane at a relatively hot temperature. This hot bleed air flows into the mixing plenum, or mixing chamber, that is under the cockpit floor beneath the copilot's rudder pedals. On most models, the bleed air heat can be supplemented by electric heat if needed. (This discussion will concentrate on the more modern King Airs, the ones that utilize bleed air for pressurization and heating. The old 90/A90/B90 system uses a fuel-fired heater, although the use of the air control knobs is virtually identical.)

Likewise, cold air – generated when cabin air flows across the cold coils of the Freon evaporator – is also directed to that same mixing chamber. Thus, regardless of whether we are in a heating or cooling mode of environmental operation, the air that we are relying on to feed the cabin and cockpit all originates from the mixing chamber below the copilot's rudder pedals.

(For the 300-series, hot and cold air may also be introduced elsewhere – namely, near the aft end of the cabin. Similarly, many models in the 200-series contain an aft air-conditioning evaporator. We will discuss the effect of these differences later in our article.)

The air that is in the mixing chamber gets distributed via four outlets: Defroster air, pilot's air, copilot's air, and cabin air. In most King Airs, all of these four outlets contain individual control valves linked to cockpit control knobs. In some models, however, the cabin air outlet does not contain a control valve. Instead, it is always fully open. How do you know which is correct for your individual King Air? Easy. Merely look to see if there is a push-pull control knob just to the left of and slightly below the copilot's control yoke. If a knob is there, then you have all four controls. If not, you are one of the few – C90s, E90s, A100s, and B100s – that have only three air flow control valves.

The King Air Book

Whenever you want to obtain the maximum amount of air from the mixing chamber into the cockpit and cabin, you want all valves fully open, so that air flow can freely exit the mixing chamber through all four outlets. It may seem logical that, to open all valves, one would pull all four knobs fully out, right? Logical? Yes. But is that the way the valves work? No! Let me explain.

I'll start with the easy one, the defroster control knob. For all King Airs, regardless of model type or year of manufacture, the defroster control valve opens when the knob is pulled and shuts off when the knob is pushed. The only difference worth mentioning is that later models have individually-controllable air outlets ("Wemacs") on each side attached to and beneath the glareshield. These outlets receive their air from the defroster duct. Unless the defroster knob is pulled, they are useless.

I am almost certain that some of you are now scratching your heads and saying, "Why would I want defroster air on in the summer? Wouldn't that primarily be used as an aid to windshield heat?"

That line of thinking is quite common and easily understandable, given how the knob is labeled and how we use the defroster in our automobiles. Unfortunately, it is totally wrong! Remember, the mixing chamber is the source for *all* normal cockpit and cabin airflow, both hot and cold. Instead of thinking of the defroster outlet as a Defroster – Even though that's what it's labeled! – try instead to consider it as merely one of three possible paths that "conditioned" air (hot or cold) can take to reach the cockpit. Although there is a time that it is beneficial to push the defroster knob in to shut off its flow – as will be discussed later in this article – realize that anytime you want more airflow into the cockpit, either hot *or* cold, you need to have the defroster knob pulled on.

We'll now discuss the other two paths that airflow can take to reach the cockpit. These are the pilot and copilot air outlets, the ones that allow conditioned air to enter the cockpit near the rudder pedals. In the 90, A90, B90, C90, C90-1, E90, 100, A100 and B100 – in other words, in all King Airs except the C90A, C90B, F90-, 200-, and 300-series – the knobs that control these outlets are beneath the instrument subpanel on the extreme outboard ends and are labeled "Vent Air – Push On." I have only two complaints about these knobs: How they are labeled and how they work.

Why does the label say *Vent* Air? When I hear the word "Vent," I think about air flowing in or out of some compartment: "The engineer needs to vent steam off the boiler to reduce the pressure," or "Let's open the window to vent those fumes from the kitchen." Yet these knobs only control the flow of circulating air *within* the pressure vessel. I wish "Vent" were eliminated and the knobs were simply labeled "Pilot Air" and "Copilot Air." Well, hallelujah, that is exactly what the label became on the C90A, C90B, F90-, 200-, and 300-series!

So why did the engineers design it so that to open this valve we *Push* the knob, just the opposite of how the Defroster knob works? There is, in fact, a reasonable explanation for this.

Namely, when maximum hot defrost air flow is required – for example, if windshield heat were inoperative in icing conditions – then the pilot should pull every air control knob he or she can reach on the panel. This action would pull *on* the defroster but pull *off* the pilot and copilot air outlets, and shut off the flow to the cabin also, if equipped with that fourth knob. With the other mixing chamber outlets now shut off, maximum flow would be directed toward the windshield.

As mentioned, the crew's air outlets got a new name and a new operating methodology with the C90A, C90B, F90-, 200-, and 300-series. Instead of being beneath the instrument subpanel, now the knobs are on the subpanel just outboard of and slightly below the control wheels and they are labeled "Pilot Air – Pull On" and "Copilot Air – Pull On."

Just as with the defroster, when you desire more flow of air into the cockpit – regardless of whether it's hotter air or colder air – have the crew air knobs in your airplane either pushed or pulled appropriately to open up the valves and allow the air to flow out near the rudder pedals.

How many of you are using your King Airs as cargo haulers, not passenger planes? I see. Not many. It's really only you cargo haulers who need to know about that fourth air valve control knob that is on most, but not all, King Airs. This is the one just to the left and slightly below the copilot's control wheel. If your model has this knob, it is probably labeled "Cabin Air – Pull Decrease." To make the operation of the knob more intuitive, the label was changed in the 300-series to read "Cabin/Cockpit Air – Pull Decrease Cabin/Increase Cockpit."

When this knob is pulled you are closing the valve on the last of the four mixing chamber outlets…the one that feeds every floor vent behind the cockpit. In other words, it's the line that feeds the entire *cabin*, or passenger area. Unless you are really angry with the passengers today and want to fry 'em when it's hot or freeze 'em when it's cold, it's best that you not pull this knob! With the knob pulled, the only conditioned air that they'll receive will be what drifts back to them from the open cockpit door. (Close the door to really mess 'em up!) Do you see why I said that cargo haulers may find this knob useful but not the rest of us? In fact, that's why Beech decided to eliminate the knob on some C90, E90, and 100-series models. However, they must have received enough complaints from some operators – Not from me! – that they concluded that reintroducing the knob was a wise move, and they did so.

The 200- and 300-series contain an annunciator labeled "Duct Overtemp." This yellow caution light is triggered very rarely but in almost every case when it does illuminate it is caused by the Cabin Air knob being pulled. Since heat cannot now freely flow out of the mixing chamber into the cabin, it is not uncommon for the trapped heat to raise the duct temperature sufficiently to activate the warning. The correct procedure to follow if the light comes on includes making certain that the Cabin Air knob is pushed in…another reason to never pull it during routine operation.

The King Air Book

Let's now focus on hot weather operation, down at lower altitudes when we want and need a good air-conditioning system. As you make your way from the cabin door up to the cockpit, it is beneficial to reach up and open all of the cabin overhead air vents. Passengers may always shut them off later as they desire, but by opening them now you are allowing the best flow of colder air into the cabin. The overhead outlets are fed by air that has been cooled by the air conditioning evaporator but that has been tapped off prior to reaching the mixing chamber. Hence, these outlets are always able to receive colder air regardless of how the cockpit air control valves are positioned.

Once in the cockpit, make sure that the defroster knob is pulled fully on, that the pilot and copilot air valves are open (knobs pushed for the earlier models and pulled for the later ones) and that the cabin air knob (if so equipped) is fully pushed in. By positioning the knobs in this manner, you will have achieved maximum airflow out of the mixing chamber into the cockpit and cabin.

Now if you are a real masochist and don't mind sweating a little for the benefit of the boss in back – Man, you need help! – then I suppose it would be better to shut off the pilot, copilot, and defroster outlets and hence force more cold airflow to the cabin. Not many crews do that but be my guest if you like the idea.

Although this article is aimed at discussing airflow circulation, not the entire Environmental system, it might be worth mentioning that keeping the bleed air switches Closed and using High blower speed would also be appropriate in optimizing ground cooling on hot days.

As the airplane climbs into colder air, the environmental system terminates the air-conditioner and starts introducing hotter bleed air into the mixing chamber. What I am about to describe is a common occurrence at cruise altitudes. It doesn't take a graduate degree in thermodynamics and heat transfer to realize that it is typical that the back seats in a King Air will now be colder than the front seats. Since the heat that is being distributed originates at the mixing chamber under the copilot's feet, there is a lot more chance of energy loss as the air wends its way all the way through the ducts to the farthest aft outlets.

That's why it is common for the passengers to ask for more heat when in cruise. The problem is this: As you turn the cabin temperature rheostat clockwise and get more heat, they get comfortable but now you get too hot! Combine the extra bleed air heat flowing into the cockpit with the radiant heat streaming in through the cockpit windows and it's easy to see why the crew is sweltering. Here's the solution! Shut off the cockpit heated air outlets!

How? Very easy: Shut off the defroster and crew air outlets. (Push or pull the knobs, as you've learned.) You may also find that it is better in some cases to only *partially* close one or more of the valves. Remember that they are totally adjustable, not just with Open and Shut choices. Also, since the overhead air vents always contain relatively cooler air, you may wish to make sure that the two in the cockpit are wide open. If you don't like the air blowing directly on yourself, direct your vent toward the power quadrant or side window.

As the descent begins into a warm climate, remember that eventually you will want to reopen the defroster and crew air outlets so that the cool air can once again flow into the cockpit.

When the Super King Air 300 made its appearance in 1984, it incorporated a simple yet profoundly advantageous improvement to cabin air circulation. For the first time, heated bleed air could now enter the airplane in two locations: The mixing chamber in front, as had always been the case, and the distribution ducts in the aft end of the cabin. Instead of having a single line proceeding forward from the junction where left and right bleed airs joined together beneath the cabin floor, now there was a new line added that plumbed this bleed air aft. This new line contains another air control valve. However, instead of being a manually-controlled valve with a knob, like the others we've discussed, this valve is a motor-driven electric valve controlled by a new switch on the copilot's left subpanel that is label "Aft Heat." I've often said that if the label had been "Aft *Bleed Air* Heat" it would be easier to teach and understand.

This will come as a shock to many, I am sure, but if you are flying a 300 or 350, I suggest that you go out now and flip the Aft Heat switch up to the On position and leave it there until you sell the airplane!

Just a couple of weeks ago I flew a nearly new 350 and, noticing that the Aft Heat switch was off, I positioned it to On before the flight began. After the flight, the owner commented to me that his wife had gone back to use the potty during the flight and came back rejoicing that, for the first time, the potty compartment wasn't freezing!

In my view, there is only one time that I'd ever turn off the Aft Heat switch in the 300-series: If the bleed air ever gets so weak that I am freezing in the cockpit, then I suppose I'd sacrifice the toilet and baggage areas to get more warmth in front. But, guess what? That's never happened to me! Also, realize that it costs nothing to leave that switch on between flights. There is no need to shut it off at shutdown, regardless of what the Raytheon checklist says. Why? Because the motor-driven valve only uses electric power when it is in the process of moving from open to closed or vice versa.

Does having the Aft Heat switch on cause our air-conditioning capability to suffer? Not at all. When we turn the bleed air on, its thermal energy has got to enter the pressure vessel someplace. Those BTUs of energy may as well be divvied up between front and back instead of all dumping into the front.

As an option in the 200-series and as standard equipment in 300-series there is an aft evaporator and an aft blower. Also, the 300-series and B200s after 1994 have an aft electric heat element embedded in the aft air distribution ductwork. Turn the Aft Blower switch on to utilize these great additions.

However, as the airplane climbs into cooler outside air and bleed air heat starts replacing the air-conditioner's cooling, there comes a time that the aft blower is counter-productive. You see, as the hotter bleed air starts flowing aft from the mixing chamber into the cabin it runs into a restriction of colder, re-circulated, cabin air coming from the aft blower. Depending on the OAT and how hot the cabin was initially, you should turn the Aft Blower switch off somewhere in the climb. If you haven't switched it off by FL180, that's a good time to do it.

In summary, I encourage you to experiment with your air distribution control knobs and don't be reluctant to change their positions as environmental conditions dictate. On the ground and at lower altitudes, having all valves open is the way to go for most of us. In cruise, however, shutting off the cockpit valves usually yields more uniform temperatures throughout the King Air interior.

THE LOST OPPORTUNITY

(WHAT YOU SHOULD DO WHILE YOUR PLANE
IS GETTING A NEW INTERIOR)

Time and time again when I fly with a client in his or her King Air, we discover that the airplane has developed humongous pressurization leaks. "Look! Up in the sky! It's a bird. It's a plane. No, it's a flying sieve!"

With two strong bleed air flow control units – Flow Paks – the cabin leak rate can be quite excessive and yet the airplane will still pressurize just fine in climb and cruise using the commensurate power settings. But watch out for low-power descents! When power is reduced, the ratio between air in and air out often cannot reach the level required to descend the cabin rapidly enough, and thus sometimes we "catch the cabin" in the descent and must make the rest of the descent unpressurized. We also find much worse-than-normal cabin climbs and dives as power is being reduced and re-applied.

Sometimes, especially in the 90 and 100-series with their infamous crossover ductwork in the nose, the leaks are relatively easy to find and remedy when the shop uses an air machine to blow up the cabin on the ground. On the other hand, sometimes the leaks are quite hard to find and, once found, are difficult to reach. Thus, the repair is either deferred to a later date or it requires a lot of maintenance hours.

The best time to find and remedy the leaks is when the interior is out of the airplane. At that time, virtually all of the pressure vessel surface is relatively accessible. **Don't schedule your airplane into the completion center for a new interior without budgeting a few extra days to attend to sealing the pressure vessel!** This may involve moving the airplane to a different shop after the interior has been removed if the first shop lacks the capabilities you seek.

So how do you, the pilot, go about determining the state of your airplane's leaks? How bad is bad? The Maintenance Manuals give guidance in this area, but here is a brief, quick-and-dirty, approach.

Merely takeoff on a deadhead flight and leave the pressurization controller set for a Sea Level cabin and climb until the cabin starts to climb also. This should occur when the Differential Pressure (ΔP) needle reaches the top of the green arc, but it may occur sooner if the inflow is weak and/or the outflow is excessive. When at the maximum attainable ΔP, level off and set your normal cruise power. Turn off the left (or right) Bleed Air Valve switch while watching the cabin Vertical Velocity

Indicator. It should rise to a peak value, then start a gradual reduction. Record what the peak value is. Turn that switch back on, wait for the Pak to reopen (as evidenced by a cabin dive) and for the ΔP to return to the highest attainable value, then repeat the check for the other side.

What *should* you have seen? The response you should have observed is a sharp, immediate cabin climb to 1,000 fpm or more. Ideally, the cabin would have then stopped climbing and descended back to maximum ΔP using the remaining Pak alone. Also, both sides should have responded about the same.

What *did* you see? Unfortunately, typical results usually indicate either one or two problems.

First, the two peak cabin climb values may have been quite different. For example, perhaps 400 fpm on one side and 2,000 fpm on the other side were recorded. Obviously, one Pak is much stronger than the other. Which one? The answer is, the one that caused the greater change when it was turned off. In other words, a 2,000 fpm value is a lot better than a 400 fpm value. See why? What if a Pak were totally dead, not supplying any air at all? The result observed when it was turned off would have been no change, or 0 fpm, since it was already "off."

The second problem typically observed is that neither Pak alone is able to descend the cabin back down to regain maximum ΔP. Either both Paks are very weak – a possible but unlikely scenario – or the airplane is a sieve.

After each Pak has been analyzed individually using the above procedure, turn them both back on, regain maximum ΔP, and then turn them both off together. (For you who have three-position Bleed Air Valve switches, be sure to go only to the center "Envir Off" position. Avoid using the bottom position because it causes the door seal to deflate.)

If the peak rate of climb value you observe now is over 4,000 fpm, you should find and repair some leaks while the interior is removed. Even 4,000 fpm is high according to Raytheon manuals, but there comes a time that the quest for perfection is not economically sensible.

There is another system that lends itself to repair when the interior is removed…the Static Air System. Remember that the normal static air source are the two "buttons" on either side of the aft fuselage (or a single button per side on earlier models). The alternate source is inside the unpressurized tail. We all have heard the stories during our initial pilot training about the static source(s) being obstructed with wax or tape, and the resulting errors. This scenario is still applicable to King Airs, but let me propose a more realistic and common one.

Namely, recall that these static sources get connected to the cockpit instruments – airspeed, altimeter, and vertical velocity indicators – via plastic tubes that must run almost the entire length of the pressure vessel, inside the pressurized volume. If one of these tubes develops a huge hole, then that static system basically senses cabin altitude instead of actual outside altitude and yields a huge and noticeable error. (This also occurs if the system drains behind the upholstered right side panel in the cockpit are open.) But what if just a little pinhole leak occurs? This may bias the static pressure just enough to introduce a small error that grows progressively worse as differential pressure increases.

Again, here is a quick check to make the next time you fly; you can even do this one with passengers onboard. If you are using the autopilot, put it in *attitude* hold, not *altitude* hold mode, to avoid a possible wild pitch excursion.

Now reach over and move the Pilot's Emergency Static Air Source selector lever to the Alternate position. What you *should* see is a slight increase in all three static air instruments, with the altimeter increasing perhaps 70 feet or so. If you have the dual static air system – two buttons, not one, on each side of the tail – only the pilot's side instruments should have been affected. (With the single system on older models, both sides should have responded the same.)

Wow! I have seen some strange unexpected results when I've done this test! For example, I've seen only the copilot's instruments respond…an indication of a definite reversed plumbing job. I have also seen situations in which the pilot's instruments went *down* a little instead of *up*…the normal and alternate lines had been reversed at the selector valve. And finally, I have seen cases in which the pilot's instruments descended tremendously when alternate air was selected…a pressurization leak into the alternate source's tubing.

If you do indeed suspect a pressurization leak into one or more of the static systems, get rid of the passengers, go to a safe altitude (a couple of thousand feet or so above the cabin), and dump the cabin. If any change shows up in the static instruments as the cabin suddenly depressurizes, you have confirmed the leak.

With the interior removed, access to the static tubing has been improved about a thousand percent! So find and fix the problem now!

To summarize, if ever your airplane is scheduled to have the interior removed, check the airplane's leak rate and the operation of the static systems before your interior work is started. If problems are found – as they likely will be! – don't let this great opportunity for repair slip through your fingers. "A penny saved is a penny earned." Lots of pennies and dollars can be saved seeing to these repairs during this lovely window of opportunity.

QUESTIONS AND ANSWERS

Quite often I receive email or telephone contact from King Air operators asking my input on a particular topic. Often these questions come from larger flight departments in which differing opinions among the pilots are very common. Here are a few of these that have been sanitized to protect the identity of the questioner.

Question #1

Another issue that is worth discussing is Engine Auto Ignition. For years we have armed the ignition as the Before Takeoff (final items) checklist calls for. Pilots returning from SimuFlite have brought home two theories on why you should not arm the Auto-Ignition for takeoff. I have inquired about this issue with our P&W and Raytheon field rep but to date no one has returned with an answer.

I understand Auto-ignition should be on for precipitation, icing, and turbulence. I have also found that pilots will fly around with the igniters clicking rather than plan their descent accordingly to stay above 17%, wearing out the igniters.

The first issue of concern is possible engine damage if the fire goes out and relights at 17%. In your opinion will enough fuel accumulate in the engine during the spool down to cause damage when the ignition comes on? Maybe you would be better off to let the fire go out and attempt a restart.

The second issue was of loss of control during the restart. They simulated this situation and ended up in a spin. Maybe not the best situation either.

To date I have not received any POH revisions that would change procedures regarding Auto-ignition.

Answer #1

Geez, you are giving me heartburn. So much misinformation is being promulgated!

"For years we have armed the ignition as the Before Takeoff (final items) checklist calls for." It does? Show me! Yes, in the F90 and some models of the 200 it did call for a blanket arming of Auto-Ignition before every takeoff. But that was "corrected" in the 300-series. Look at the POH Page 4-15. (I am still on Revision B8 in my 300 book.) Auto-Ignition is only mentioned under item #5, "Ice Protection," and this entire section 5 says "ON (if required)." So if there are no icing conditions around, then it's not to be armed for takeoff per the POH is it?! I never arm it unless there is cold, (less than 5 degrees C), visible moisture on the runway or within the first few thousand feet above it.

The King Air Book

"The first issue of concern is possible engine damage if the fire goes out and relights at 17%." The engine is still rotating, fer chrisake! The fuel that is still being injected – minimum fuel flow at that, since P3 decreases – blows harmlessly out the exhaust stacks. When the relight occurs, it always starts at minimum FF and then, as Ng and P3 increase, it smoothly increases to the fuel flow/power setting that existed before the flameout occurred. I have done this thousands of times in flight training and the manner in which power returns to what it was before – so smooth, so easy, without surging – is always impressive and eye-opening for those who haven't experienced it.

"The second issue was of loss of control during the restart. They simulated this situation and ended up in a spin. Maybe not the best situation either." Well, it must not have been realistic in any sense of the word! The engine merely restarts very easily and ends up at the power setting it was at before. If a pilot cannot handle this he/she shouldn't be flying any twin, much less a King Air.

The only time a PT6 in a King Air will flame out and need auto-ignition to relight it is if the pilot didn't extend the ice vanes in cold, visible, moisture. Period! Auto-Ignition is a fine back-up safeguard, but neither you nor any of your departmental pilots will ever see it function unless they screw up first by overlooking the Engine Anti-ice switches!

It's late and I'm in a foul mood, I guess. But, for goodness sake, don't take the word of what some wet-behind-the-ears Simuflite instructor says over what's in the POH. And read the POH carefully, darn it!

Question #2

We operate in conditions requiring ice protection about half the year. To follow up on the rest of those "if required" items, what procedure do you advocate for the so called Hot Five (Fuel vent, pitot heat, and stall warning) when icing conditions are not imminent? If icing conditions exist for takeoff when are you comfortable getting these heats on? In my opinion some pilots put these heats on prematurely considering they are final items.

And finally windshield heat, you leave 90° Miami for a four hour flight to a state in New England where the descent and approach will be in winter conditions. When will you put on the windshield heat? I know the descent check list calls for WSHLD Anti-ice as required. Is there any danger in warming a cold soaked windscreen?

Thanks Tom, I really appreciate your taking the time to answer my questions.

Answer #2

The "Hot Five" are fine to use "all the time" since they pull so little current. I think the Army starting teaching that years ago in U-21s and then in C-12s and it started getting quite popular, as it still is. This is a battle not worth fighting, so if anyone wants to make that a part of their routine

QUESTIONS AND ANSWERS

Runway Lineup procedure, so be it. As for me, it is still part of Ice Protection and I do not use them unless I am about to encounter "Visible Moisture in flight with OATs below 5 degrees C..." However, if I do get them on I tend to leave them on until 100% guaranteed cloud-free for the remainder of that leg. I see no advantage of cycling them, in other words, but when it is cloud-free all the way – and I guess we have more of those legs out here in the Southwest than you do – then I never use them.

(You know where this all came from, don't you? It all started with the Northwest Boeing 727 that departed from EWK or LGA with just the crew onboard back in the '70s, heading up to someplace in New England to pick up a sports team. They inadvertently left the pitot heat off when they were climbing through icy clouds, the pitot tubes iced up, the IAS kept rising as they climbed (since static air pressure kept decreasing but ram air pressure was trapped), all three crewmembers in the cockpit seemed to fixate on the high airspeed and they proceeded to pitch up something like 30 degrees and stalled the airplane. All were killed. The FAA came out with the requirement that pitot heat be on at all times in flight in jets, and they mandated annunciator lights to tell the crew if they forgot. That's what Beech copied for the 350.)

Since your department flies both 350s and 300s, it probably makes sense to use the pitot heats "all the time" for consistency, and if you're going to do that, then I'd be inclined to think "Why not add in the remaining Three of the Hot Five?"

Yes, I think enough cases have been recorded of windshields cracking right after heat was applied that I am very adverse to heating an already cold-soaked WS. I have "Windshield Anti-Ice – NORMAL" as part of my 10,000 foot checklist, but I would do it even earlier on cold winter days. Once it's on, I leave it on until the OAT gets above freezing in the descent. I don't like the slight distortion of clear vision it gives when on, so I almost always have it off before the landing.

(An Alaskan client of mine said they did a very careful heating procedure when the plane had sat outside for a long time in the winter. After start, they'd select WS heat on for, like, 10 seconds, then off for 10, then on for 20, off for 20, etc., until they finally had built up to a full minute. Maybe that's overkill but something to consider if you had to leave it outside overnight when it's truly frigid.)

I believe there are no statistics that show windshield life or delamination can be traced to usage techniques involving WS heat. Getting a proper installation of the WS and being sure that the "hump seal" is good and not abraded away in any section is critical, however.

While we are discussing, windshields, the best thing, I think, to use for cleaning them – and it's preferred by PPG, last I checked, the WS manufacturer – is a 50/50 blend of purified or distilled water and rubbing alcohol, with a couple of drops of dishwashing detergent added to the spray bottle.

313

The King Air Book

Spray it on liberally, use your hand to clean off the big stuff, spray again and then use a soft towel to wipe dry. Works like a charm and does not strip off the electrostatic coating.

Hope you find these ramblings useful. Thanks again for contacting me.

Question #3

It may be a simple question, hopefully a simple answer too.

In my piloting experience I have come across AFM, POH, POM, and most recently AOMs. Here we have the Pilots Operating Handbook and Manual for many of the King Airs. I don't really see or understand the difference between the Handbook and the Manual? I have seen both in use in the Aircraft before.

Which one should we give away with our Ground school program? What did *Flight Review* do?

Answer #3

Good questions!

The first many KA models came with a "Pilot's Operating Manual," or POM as it's been often abbreviated. It is, in fact, two books in one: The whole thing is the POM but certain sections comprise the "FAA Approved Aircraft Flight Manual," or AFM. Turns out that, for this light turboprop – a new class of machine, at the time of introduction – what was required by the FARs (actually, back then, CARs) to be in the AFM was rather limited. Beech, realizing that operators would probably want more – like Systems Descriptions and Cruise Performance – decided to make a bigger document, but one that would include within it both the required AFM and the required Weight and Balance information.

I happen to have an early C90 POM in front of me, but what I am about to say would be true for many other models. The very first page of the book, the one with the picture of the airplane on it and the title "Pilot's Operating Manual," states "This book is incomplete w/o a current FAA Flight Manual, P/N 90-590010-5C." Many of my students through the years have said, "Wait a minute! What does that mean? Isn't THIS the AFM?!"

Well, the AFM is in there, but it's not the entire POM. Certain tabs of this POM have "FAA" on them: e.g., "FAA Data," "FAA Revision Log," "FAA Limitations," etc. If we turn to that first tab with "FAA" on it – Lo and Behold! – here is another title page, with an airplane picture even, but the title is now "Airplane Flight Manual" and the referenced Part Number (P/N) shows up at the bottom. This AFM goes through Section 5, "FAA Airplane Flight Manual Supplements." After that section, Sections 6 through 10 now continue the POM, but are not in the AFM. There are even separate revision issuances and log of revision pages for the POM and the AFM contained therein!

314

One of the oddities that gets cleared up by the understanding of the POM is why there are three different sections of performance charts. "FAA Performance," Section 4, includes what the FAA mandated. But Section 6, "Performance," and Section 7, "Cruise Control," include lots of other good charts that are nice for the pilot to have, but are not FAA-required.

In about 1971, as I recall, GAMA (General Aviation Manufacturers Association) was formed to coordinate certain activities of all the competing light aircraft manufacturers. One of the first things they did was make and promulgate a standard for how all POMs should be created. The rationale behind this was so that a pilot who first learned in a, say, Piper Warrior, could transition into a Cessna 210 or a Beech Baron and find the POMs identical, in so far as section order and chapter contents were concerned. Thus was born the POH, Pilot's Operating Handbook, the name chosen for this new, standardized, format.

If one looks carefully at the POH's first page, the title page, notice it now says, "Pilot's Operating Handbook AND FAA Approved Airplane Flight Manual." Now the AFM is blended within the POH and no longer constitutes certain distinct sections.

I am a big supporter of the newer style manual and think GAMA did a very good thing here. However – There's always a "but," eh? – but now it is impossible for a reader of the POH to determine which performance charts are legally binding and which are not. For example, how does one know, from the book, that we need to comply with, for example, the "Minimum Takeoff Power" graph but that we may ignore the "Accelerate-Stop" distance one? (Not counting the 300-series, of course, that have different rules due to their weights above 12,500 pounds.)

As for what you should provide to your students, you should give the POM for the models that use that format and POHs for the rest. From memory – so I am probably overlooking one or two – the POMs would apply to the 90, A90, B90, C90 (LJ-502 - 667), E90, 100, and A100. Everything else would be new enough to have the POH format. In other words, the POHs would be for: C90 (LJ-668 and after), C90-1, C90A, C90B, C90GT, F90, F90-1, B100, 200, B200, B200GT, 300, and B300 (350). (Plus the occasional oddball like the B200T, the tip-tanked version.)

I hope that clarifies the situation. By the way, Beech went back soon after the GAMA POH format appeared and re-issued some older POMs in the new format. I think they did this for all Bonanza models, even the straight 35s dating from 1947 (!) as well as all the Baron series. Maybe they felt there weren't sufficient numbers of King Airs to justify this rewrite, but for whatever reason there has never been a re-issuance of any KA POM in POH format.

The King Air Book

Question #4

Hi Tom,

I will take you up on your offer to share your King Air expertise. As I explained previously I manage a small flight department with two aircraft and five pilots. We have a 300 and a 350. As you can imagine getting five independent thinkers on the same page can be a challenge.

I was fortunate to have attended SimCom several times. The rest of my crews attended Simuflite to get their type rating in a simulator. I have found that Simuflite teaches a very sterile by the book course, lacking any real world understanding of the operation of systems and engines. Courses are usually taught by a recently furloughed airline pilot. I know, I should not be so harsh.

I have read and passed on your many articles on King Air operations, they just make sense. I am currently trying to convince my crews to go straight to high idle on the first start and get the second generator on line before coming off high idle. The POH does not prescribe this method so they are resistant to do it.

Can you elaborate on the thermal cycle issue and the benefits of this procedure?

Does the increased engine speed benefit the start by way of additional bypass air?

Is there any point in allowing engine speed to stabilize at low idle before moving to high Idle?

I also have the issue of brake de-ice valves sticking now and then. My maintenance provider will occasionally squirt some lube into the valves which works for a while. We have contacted tech support for help in understanding these valves; they are not able to locate a diagram of the valve and say there is not any preventative or periodic maintenance that can be performed. Their only recommendation is to use the Brake de-ice regularly. The POH says to use the brake de-ice each flight. The problem is crews are hesitant to cycle the valves each leg because they are fearful one will stick. A friend suggested operating the brake de-ice each flight for a minute and a half to clean out any sticky residue.

Your thoughts on these issues are greatly appreciated.

Answer #4

First, let's look at exactly what the POH says about engine starting. I happen to have a 300 POH in front of me and it may not be 100% current. It's up through the B8 revision of July, 2000. I don't happen to have access to a 350 book here at my home office but I would be very surprised if its starting procedure differs significantly.

Here is an exact duplication of the Battery Starting procedure, as shown on Pages 4-8 and 4-9:

1. Right Ignition and Engine Start Switch – ON (R FUEL PRESSURE annunciator – EXTINGUISHED)
2. Right Condition Lever – LOW IDLE (after N1 indicates 12% minimum)
3. ITT and N1 – MONITOR (1000°C maximum)
4. Right Oil Pressure – CHECK
5. Right Condition Lever – HIGH IDLE
6. Right Ignition and Engine Start Switch – OFF (at 50% N1 or above)
7. Right Generator – RESET, then ON. Charge battery until loadmeter reads approximately 50%.
8. Left Ignition and Engine Start Switch – ON (L FUEL PRESSURE annunciator – EXTINGUISHED)
9. LEFT Condition Lever – LOW IDLE (after N1 indicates 12% minimum)
10. ITT and N1 – MONITOR (1000°C maximum)
11. LEFT Oil Pressure – CHECK
12. Left Ignition and Engine Start Switch – OFF (at 50% N1 or above)
13. Left Generator – RESET, then ON.
14. Right Condition Lever – REDUCE TO LOW IDLE

How in the world could anyone maintain that "getting the second generator on line before coming off high idle" is not prescribed by the POH?!

As the Limitations Section states (Page 2-6), the Maximum Generator Load at High Idle or more N1 is 100% but it's only 75% in the Low Idle to High Idle range. Although it is very rare (caused by a highly depleted NiCad battery) that the load will exceed 75% on one generator after the second start, it *could* happen and that's why Beech wants both generators sharing the load before bringing the first engine back to Low Idle.

Now allow me to address the "straight to High Idle" issue. Please reread steps 3, 4, 5, and 6 above. In my view, step 3 is quite nebulous. Don't we always monitor these gauges? If, not always, do we look at them now for – what? – one second? Five seconds? Five minutes? And step 4, how long does it take before oil pressure starts to rise and can be checked? By the time our eyes get to that gauge now it is usually in the green. Don't you agree? Now step 5: We go to High Idle. When? Well, for darn sure it's not *after* the start switch is turned off if we are following the POH procedure, is it?! Because that doesn't come until step 6! Granted, in step 6, we can turn the starter off "at 50% N1 or above" so we certainly don't have to *wait* for N1 to *stabilize* at High Idle, but we do need to have the Condition Lever up there already if we are true to the POH. How can anyone with reading comprehension disagree with this?!

The King Air Book

It's not worth fighting the "Straight to High Idle" suggestion for those who are reluctant to do it. In fact, on the 300-series, I don't do it! The Woodward FCUs on these engines act a bit differently from the Bendix FCUs on other PT6-powered King Airs and I am of the opinion that going straight to High Idle on a –60A does in fact elevate the starting ITT peak by a tiny but noticeable amount. (It does not do this on the other models.) So I go to Low Idle, monitor that N1 starts to increase within a few seconds, see ITT coming up, wait for the ITT to hit its peak, then immediately go to High Idle at that time before the ITT has decreased much, if at all, from the peak value.

If we allow the engine to stabilize at Low Idle, the ITT will fall to a much lower value than the starting peak, of course. If we now go to High Idle as a separate step, we get another, much smaller, ITT rise, peak, and fall, this time to a lower stabilized value than what we'd had at Low Idle. (As you probably know, the heating effect of the additional fuel is less than the cooling effect of the additional air, when we compare stabilized Low Idle and High Idle operation.) So not only do we give the engine two ITT "cycles" if we stabilize at Low Idle first before going to High Idle, but we also run the starter a lot longer than necessary/desirable. (Remember, if we are true to the POH, we don't turn the starter off until we've *selected* High Idle.)

Although it is stated nowhere in the POH, the Starter Limits on Page 2-6 (30 seconds on, 5 minutes off, 30 seconds on, 5 minutes off, 30 seconds on, then 30 minutes off) are in fact based on how much heat the starter generates when it *alone* is driving the engine without any exhaust gas helping. Thus, once we observe the light-off the starter time limits may be discarded, in my opinion. Nevertheless, for those who view the starter limits as ironclad, we are sure to violate them if we don't get to High Idle darn quickly!

I think I have addressed your starting questions except for the one that says: "Does the increased engine speed benefit the start by way of additional bypass air?" I don't know what "bypass air" means in this context. I guess the answer is "no."

Two more starting comments. First, yes, the POH says we can give it fuel anytime "after N1 indicates 12% minimum" but that surely does not tell us that we are *not permitted* to get as much N1 as the starter will give us. To get as much cooling airflow established as possible is very desirable, in my opinion, and does indeed lead to cooler starts. So I won't say someone is "wrong" if I see them slip that Condition Lever forward as the engine goes through 12% but I sure prefer that they wait until N1 stops its rise. Second, the "charging the battery to 50%" comment was written when the standard airplanes had NiCads and most experts think that 30% or so is a better figure for the lead-acid-equipped models. (As you have read in my past articles on Starting, doing between-start battery charging is unnecessary and wasteful of time, in my opinion, *except* when the battery is weak, as shown by the first engine's stabilized-on-the-starter N1 value not meeting our expectations.)

Now on to Brake Deice.

Yes, the valves are notoriously prone to sticking if not used regularly and, even then, there is no guarantee that they will always work properly. Since the Brake Deice System is not standard, we must go to the POH Supplements (Section 9, supplement number 101-590097-55 in my 300 POH) to find the official information.

You wrote: "The POH says to use the brake deice each flight." I may be overlooking the obvious, but I don't see that directive anywhere in the referenced Supplement. I believe the suggestion for regular cycling of the valves has indeed been promulgated by Beech – probably in one of the King Air Communique series – and I, for years, have advocated it. But here is the compromise position that I believe is best: Only conduct the brake deice exercise procedure as you begin descent to your home base on the last flight of the day. That way, if a valve sticks open, the likelihood of problems are almost zilch because (1) power will tend to be lower in the descent than in a climb or cruise situation, (2) the gear will be down some of the time, and (3) you won't be flying too much longer anyway. As you know, the 300 has the Autofeather "lock-out" of Brake Deice (unlike the 350) so the check must be done before Autofeather is Armed in the descent. (Or you've got to turn off Autofeather during the check, if you left it Armed.) Of course, the implication here is that there will be some days in which Brake Deice is not exercised because you never get back to home. So? Big deal. Doing it as I suggest has proven enough for me and the clients I have taught to do it this way.

(This is a little digression, but I also think it is darn ill-advised to conduct *all* the checks that you do at home when you are on the road. Ever had a Fuel Firewall Shutoff Valve stick closed during the fuel panel check? Want that to happen in Timbuktu?)

By the way, the Brake Deice Valves are indeed rather weird, combining both electrics and pneumatics to operate. When power is applied to the solenoid, it doesn't open the actual deice valve. It just opens a port that allows raw bleed air to enter so that pneumatics can slide open the valve. As you probably know, you can move the Brake Deice switch all you want with battery power on and generator bus ties closed in the hangar or on the ramp but until the engine is started – and with the respective Bleed Air Valve switch *not* in the bottom position – nothing happens that can be observed in the cockpit.

To me, your friend's "minute and a half" of using Brake Deice for exercising purposes is overkill. It's not going to harm anything, but all I do is turn on the switch while looking at the torque and ITT gauges, observe a tiny drop in torque and rise in ITT, (and if you have a third eye you will usually see a little rise in the cabin's vertical speed indicator), look for both Left and Right annunciators, then turn the switch off and look for everything to do the opposite. For the 300 only, a neat variation is to re-arm the Autofeather switch *before* you turn off the Brake Deice switch and see if Brake Deice turns off automatically, as it should. (Then go ahead and turn it off yourself, too.)

I hope you find this input helpful. I applaud your efforts to strive toward departmental-wide Standard Operating Practices! It's a great goal but a darn hard one to achieve… herding cats comes to mind!

PART 3

BONUS EXTRAS

90-SERIES HISTORY

I am often asked to give my opinions about various King Air models, based on the more than thirty-five years I have spent flying and instructing in them. Prospective buyers often ask, "What should I look for? What should I avoid? What options are worthwhile? What's your favorite model?"

I like all King Airs and I am quite sincere when I respond to the "What's your favorite King Air model?" query by stating, "The one I am flying today!" Variety is the spice of life, so they say, and I am fortunate to have the opportunity to fly many different models every month. It is certainly a joy to fly a nearly new model C90B, B200, or 350, but it is also fun to get in an older A90 and remind myself of what a nice flying machine it is.

The King Air "Family Tree," as I call it, is comprised of four branches…the 90-Series, the 100-Series, the 200-Series, and the 300-Series. Adding all of the members of these branches together, over twenty different variations of King Airs have been manufactured…and that does not count the many military models.

The purpose of this article is to describe the various models of the 90-Series, telling a bit about their history and highlighting the major differences between models.

It all began in 1964, when Beech decided to provide a pressurized version of the turbine-powered Queen Air model that they had developed for the U.S. Army. In a surprisingly short time, they had the first King Air flying and certified: the model 65-90, more commonly known as the "Straight 90." Serial number LJ-1 was the first King Air, and it not only was the factory prototype and test aircraft, but it went on to be sold and utilized as a corporate transport. (As of 2005, a fellow was trying to get sponsors and suppliers who would help him finish restoring this relatively low-time airplane for an around-the-world flight, each leg being crewed by a different pilot-celebrity.)

A mystery that our readers may be able to solve is this: How are the serial number letter prefixes chosen? "LJ." Golly, you'd think Bill Lear should have used that one instead of Olive Ann Beech! LJ for the straight 90 up through the C90B. LW as the prefix for the E90 serials. LA for the F90. BB for the 200-Series. In the years I worked for Beech Aircraft, and in all the years since, I have never found a single soul who could tell me what method was used for picking these letters. Either it is a deeply guarded secret or else I have been unlucky in asking the right person.

In the mid-60's, the straight 90 was quite the rage, since it was the first small corporate turboprop. The model 18-series, the immortal Twin Beech of Pratt & Whitney R-985 round motor and twin tail fame, was still being made at that time. In hindsight, however, the 90 left a lot to be desired. Its meager maximum differential pressure value of 3.1 psid meant that the airplane would need to fly at or below 19,000 feet if the cabin altitude would remain below 10,000 feet. The cockpit layout was anything but pretty, with switches, gauges, and indicator lights thrown in wherever they would fit. The propellers feathered, of course, but they didn't reverse. (Thank goodness for low landing speeds and good brakes.) The fuel and electrical systems were rather primitive, yet surprisingly complicated. On the other hand, the marvelous first version of the Pratt and Whitney PT6 – even though it would be quickly eclipsed by better versions – was a great asset. I believe that much of the credit for the King Air's success must be shared with P & W. The PT6A-6 that the 90 used was rated by P & W at 550 maximum shaft horsepower (SHP), but Beech only allowed a maximum of 500 SHP to be utilized. Thus the engine was "flat rated" to a small degree. Even so, when hot summer days rolled around, takeoff, climb, and cruise power decreased remarkably, much more so than pilots of supercharged piston engine powerplants were used to seeing.

Although many improvements were made during the two-year production run of the 90 – and many retrofit kits were made available later to update them – a very big change occurred in 1966 when the A90 replaced the straight 90. Although the two models looked and performed almost identically, the Beech engineers improved the A90 in hundreds of large and small ways. The maximum differential pressure became 4.6 psid, allowing a Sea Level cabin up to 10,000 feet and a 10,000 foot cabin up to 25,000 feet. The electrical system was simplified, improved, and made more reliable; likewise for the fuel system. The compressor that delivered air for pressurization was changed from a hydraulically driven supercharger to a mechanically driven one, which eliminated worry about the hydraulic pump, motor, and associated leaks. The PT6A-6 was replaced with the PT6A-20, offering a more reliable temperature sensing system and slightly better altitude performance. Reversing propellers were made available and, I think, every customer ordered them. Especially nice, for pilots, is that the cockpit was totally redesigned and came out much better from a human factors standpoint. Switches were organized according to function, warning and indicator lights were installed in a single Annunciator Panel perched atop the instrument panel's glareshield, circuit breakers were more accessible, and a larger pedestal beneath the power quadrant was added. With evolutionary variations, that cockpit design exists right to the present day.

1968 saw the B90 replace the A90. Systems and engines were nearly unchanged, although for the first time Beech used the full 550 SHP that the engine offered (even though it was available only for lower altitude, colder day takeoffs). The annunciator panel was now installed in, rather than on top of, the glareshield. The wingspan was increased by over four feet, due to longer wingtip extensions outboard of the ailerons, and the gross takeoff weight was brought up to 9,650 pounds, a 350 pound increase as compared to its 90 and A90 predecessors. Best of all, however, was the appearance of balanced ailerons and elevators. Compared to the 90 and A90, the B90 feels like it has power steering. Both the control forces and rates of response – in the roll axis especially – are noticeably improved. These balanced controls are still in use on current production C90Bs, as well they should be. The B90 "flies good!"

Later in the production run of the B90, some important options appeared. For the first time, a King Air could remain pressurized if the single supercharger failed or if the left engine had to be shut down for any reason. This was made possible by having a second source of air that was tapped, or bled, from the right engine's compressor. This "Bleed Air" robbed the right engine of noticeable power, and the cabin became hotter and noisier when it was used. Thus, it was only for use when the supercharger was inoperative. (Although, when the combustion heater failed at altitude – and notice I said "when" not "if" – many pilots and passengers were very willing to abide the extra *noise* to get the benefit of the *heat* provided by this compressed air!) Also, automatic propeller feathering was offered as an option. Many pilots did not trust Autofeather in its infancy and that included a lot of Beech factory pilots. "Real pilots feather their own darn props! They don't need no stinking automatic system!" seemed to be the prevalent philosophy. Well, thank goodness, Beech designed an absolute winner of a system when they made autofeather. Through the years, it has proven to be nearly faultless. And, with all of the designed-in safeguards, the worst that will happen if it *does* fail is that the pilot will have to feather the propeller manually just as if the option were not installed. Whereas back in the early '70s relatively few King Airs were ordered with the autofeather option, now rarely is a King Air made without it. The 150 horsepower Piper Apache that I used for my multiengine rating needed autofeather a lot more than a King Air did…but, since King Airs offer the option and Apaches don't, it is a truly wonderful aid to have. The sickening deceleration and yaw that usually results when an engine suddenly quits in a light twin are probably decreased by a factor of five or more with autofeather. Identifying, verifying, feathering…those steps are sure easy when the propeller is already feathered and stopped!

The next model was the C90, starting with serial number LJ-502 in 1971. Handling, performance, weight, size, flight controls…all were the same as the B90. The change – and it is an exceedingly worthwhile one! – is in the cabin's Temperature Control or Environmental system. Instead of the single supercharger driven by the left engine and the rudimentary bleed air back up option from the right engine, now both engines had identical, standard, bleed air Flow Control Packages. These "Flow Paks" are quite sophisticated metering and mixing devices that keep cabin inflow relatively constant over a wide range of power settings and mix ambient air with bleed air, varying the ratio based on ambient conditions. On hotter days, more ambient will be used, diluting and cooling the bleed air as well as decreasing the amount of bleed air that must be robbed from the

The King Air Book

engine. On colder days and at high altitude, the Flow Pak may exclude ambient air totally, as it always does when the airplane is on the ground. The King Air now offered the ability to maintain full pressurization on either engine alone with a quiet and comfortable system.

Of equal importance, the C90 replaced the combustion heater with an electric one. The combustion heater had been a weak link in the reliability chain – jet fuel doesn't want to burn as easily as gasoline, and the thin air at 22,000 feet doesn't support combustion very well either – but now with the amount of heat energy provided by the bleed air, a less energetic heater could be used. Unless it is extremely cold aloft, or unless one Flow Pak is inoperative or weak, or unless engine speed is reduced due to a low, holding pattern-type of power setting, the heater is not needed in flight. On the ground, when the engines are idling, is the time that a supplemental source of heat is needed. And, wow, does the electric heater put out the heat! Its "Ground Max" position can warm the coldest cabin up in no time!

There is, as you would expect, a negative associated with the electric heater. Namely, it pulls so much electric current – close to 300 amps to run all of it – that (1) both engines' idle speeds must be kept at near 60% on the ground to handle the high generator load, and (2) turning on windshield heat, propeller heat, or lip boot heat ice protection items "locks out" the heater totally. That's not a big problem, but occasionally you need to delay activating any of those items before takeoff until the heater has finished warming the cabin.

From 1971 through 1974 the C90 used the same engine as the A90 and B90, the good old – 20. (A few later serials used the PT6A-20A, which was a remanufactured –20 with an improved, simplified, propeller governor setup.) But partway through the 1975 model year, starting with serial number LJ-668, the C90 starting using the PT6A-21. In a nutshell, the –21 is a –28 (680 SHP) compressor mated to a –20 (550 SHP) reduction gearbox, and with a low enough ITT limit (695°C) so that it won't compete too strongly against its –28 brother with its higher limit (750°C). From the time this powerplant was introduced until the end of the 1981 model year, the manufacturer's cruise power settings remained virtually identical to those that had applied to the –20-powered C90s. Hence, book performance didn't change. However, the much more powerful compressor on this engine was "loafing" to produce this power, and ITTs tended to run close to 600° instead of 700° as they did in the –20-powered airplanes. To make the pilots feel more comfortable with this surprisingly low temperature, a cruise ITT limit of 635° was listed in the Pilot's Operating Handbook. Because the –21 engine was able to provide more climb power at altitude than the –20, and since higher power settings tend to have a destabilizing influence in the pitch axis, the –21-powered C90s have a 12-pound elevator bobweight installed behind the instrument panel to improve stability. Consequently, pulling the control wheel back during the landing flare requires more force than that needed on the earlier models.

In 1982, the C90-1 (pronounced "C90 Dash One") replaced the C90. The cabin door was changed to the beefed-up one from the 200-Series, maximum differential pressure increased from 4.6 to 5.0 psid, and the horizontal stabilizer spar was slightly strengthened. Published cruise speed at 20,000 feet on a standard day increased by 15 knots. Hmmmm… the same airframe, same engines, what makes it faster? Very simple: Beech published a higher set of cruise torque values based on a higher cruise ITT limit of 680°C.

Why didn't the 1975 through 1981 C90s offer this higher cruise ITT limit and better cruise performance? Because, to have done so, would have seen the C90 compete too aggressively with its E90 sister. Since the E90 went out of production in 1981, it was now "okay" to let the –21-powered C90 do what it had been capable of all along. (By the way, Raisbeck Engineering and at least one other company offer FAA-approved methods by which the earlier –21-powered airplanes can use the higher ITT limit. Also, history seems to be showing that the higher ITT value does not contribute to increased hot section inspection costs. In fact, there may even be a benefit to running the higher values…less compressor turbine blade sulfidation.)

Speaking of the E90, in 1972 Beech took a C90 from the assembly line, gave it to the experimental flight test department, and created the first E90. (A D90 had been planned – a lighter weight, shorter wing version of the C90 – but marketing studies concluded that it would not be worthwhile to produce.) The E90 used the same PT6A-28 engine as on the 100 and A100 King Air models. On those larger machines, Beech used the full rated 680 SHP, but flat rated the engine to 550 SHP on the E90. What great "high and hot" takeoff performance this change provided! And, at altitude, the E90 went 25 or so knots faster than the –20-powered C90. Gross takeoff weight was increased to 10,100 pounds, and an extra 90 gallons of usable fuel was provided. More importantly, however, the fuel system was "copied" from the A100, and was much, much, improved and simplified as compared to the fuel system of the LJ-series. Since the C90 would remain in production with the E90, a new set of serial numbers had to be chosen, and LW-1 was the designation applied to the first E90. In its ten-year production run, 347 E90s were made. It is a fine, fine, King Air, truly one of my favorites.

Starting in 1978, during the height of the '70s buying and building boom in aviation, three different versions of the 90-series were in production simultaneously: the C90, E90, and F90. The F90, sometimes called the Super 90, saw the designers reach into the King Air "parts bin" to create a unique airplane, with the serial number prefix "LA." The pressure vessel (cabin) was from the C90, but with the 200 door and double-pane side windows; maximum differential pressure was 5.0 psid.

The King Air Book

The T-tail from the 200 was used, but with a 1° angle of incidence change and a relocation of the tail strobe light. The wing was from the 100-series, giving it the same span as the straight 90 and A90, but with a pronounced leading edge droop in the center section. The main wing spar was actually a beefier design than that in the 100-series. The lower wing bolt bathtub fittings were integral with the lower spar cap itself instead of being separate pieces. It is sometimes referred to as the Super Spar. The landing gear was also from the 100-series, providing dual main tires and wheels and offering higher extension and retraction speeds. The standard size main tires could now be totally enclosed by the main gear doors, and the High Flotation Landing Gear (HFG) "fat tire" option was offered. (The large single main tire on other models of the 90-Series sticks out when fully retracted. "Look, Ma! I still can use the brakes after a gear up landing!") The cockpit was designed along the lines of the model 200, with the landing gear control on the pilot's instead of copilot's side, and the fuel system was similar to the E90 but with more automation. Engines were the Pratt and Whitney PT6A-135 model and their full 750 SHP rating was utilized. This engine has a slower-turning reduction gearbox, allowing propeller speed to be reduced by 300 RPM for takeoff and 200 RPM for cruise, as compared to C90s and E90s. The propeller was copied from the A100 model and was the first four-blade design used on a 90-Series model. The only system that wasn't retrieved from the parts bin, but was fully new on the F90, was the "Five Bus" electrical system that provides automatic load shedding in the event of dual generator failure. (That system became the standard for all models certified in later years, including the 300-series.)

20,000 feet, ISA, cruise speed was advertised as 259 knots, but a more-realistic power setting yields about 245. The F90 is a pilot's airplane: light on the controls, responsive, fun to fly, a little more challenging to land smoothly. But for passengers? The slower-turning, four-blade propellers are definitely smoother and quieter than in the C90 or E90 with their three-blade propellers, but the responsiveness that the pilot enjoys means less stability and more yaw for the passengers. Thank goodness for good electronic yaw dampers!

In 1983 the F90-1 replaced the F90, beginning with LA-202, 205 and after. Although there were minor engine and electrical system improvements, the most obvious change was in the engine cowling. Instead of the "chin scoop" cowl that had been used from the A90 onward (and which has been retrofitted to probably all straight 90s) now Beech used the "Pitot Cowl." A smaller intake scoop located closer to the propeller and a redesigned engine ice vane system provide for increased ram air potential at higher airspeeds. The inlet lip is heated by exhaust gases, instead of by an electrothermal boot. Realistic cruise speeds increased about ten knots. The last 11 F90-1s built, in 1985, have the electromechanical landing gear system changed to the "electrohydraulic" one that continues in all current production King Airs today. These 11 also have the new lower forward spar attach fitting.

In 1984, beginning with LJ-1063, the C90-1 was replaced by the C90A. The Pitot Cowl, the electrohydraulic landing gear, the five-bus electrical system, the landing gear handle on the pilot's side...these were the big changes made. Cruise ITT limit was again increased, this time to the 695° redline. A year later, starting with LJ-1085, 1088 and after, the C90A got the new Beech wing spar design. This is not the Super Spar such as on the F90, but instead offers a three element main spar and a lower forward wing bolt that is now under shear instead of tension loading.

In 1987, minor changes allowed the C90A to begin operating at the old E90 weight limit of 10,100 pounds. This began with LJ-1138.

Beginning in 1992, the C90A received a McCauley four-blade propeller as standard equipment and a lot of attention was given to improved cabin soundproofing with "tuning forks" and bagged insulation installed. The FAA type certificate still calls these airplanes C90As. However, in a clever marketing ploy, Beech calls them C90Bs.

The C90B has been selling well, and 1998 saw a special paint and interior package offered as the Jaguar Special Edition. With a Collins APS-65H digital autopilot system, EFIS, GPS...C90Bs are certainly well equipped, very capable, and exceedingly likable airplanes.

In 2006, taking a page from the Blackhawk conversion program, Beech starting putting PT6A-135A engines on the C90B, flat-rating them to 550 SHP, and thereby creating the C90GT, with about a 260 Knot cruise speed.

Place a 2006 C90GT next to a 1964 straight 90 and ask the non-aviation bystander to describe what he or she sees. The person will be hard-pressed to spot more than one or two differences. But beneath a very similar external appearance, the two airplanes are a study in contrasts, as we have seen. For over 34 years, involving about 1800 individual airplanes, the LJ-series had steadily improved and matured. In the 21st century, maybe it will be as immortal as its Twin Beech predecessor!

The table presented on the next two pages summarizes the various models that make up the 90-Series of King Airs.

First Year	Type	Serial Numbers	Engine; SHP	Remarks
1964	65-90	LJ-1 – 113 Except LJ-76	PT6A-6 500	9,300 lbs / 384 gal / 3.1 psid / 210 knots / Hydraulically-driven supercharger / Combustion heater / Many upgrades available
1966	A90	LJ-114 – 317 plus LJ-76	PT6A-20 500	9,300 lbs / 384 gal / 4.6 psid / 210 knots / Mechanically-driven supercharger / Combustion heater / Reversing propellers introduced / May be upgraded to nearly B90 status
1968	B90	LJ-318 – 501	PT6A-20 550	9,650 lbs / 384 gal / 4.6 psid / 210 knots / Mechanically-driven supercharger / Combustion heater / Balanced Controls introduced / Supplemental bleed air pressurization available on later serials
1971	C90	LJ-502 – 667, & 670	PT6A-20 550	9,650 lbs / 384 gal / 4.6 psid / 210 knots / Dual bleed air / Electric heater / Vertical engine instrument stack and nose baggage door introduced LJ-569 and after / LJ-586 and after may have PT6A-20A / Nose-mounted pitot tubes introduced LJ-625 and after
1972	E90	LW-1 – 347	PT6A-28 550	10,100 lbs / 474 gal / 4.6 psid / 230 knots / Dual bleed air / Electric heater / Simplified fuel system / Engine is flat-rated from 680 SHP
1975	C90	LJ-668 – 1010, except 670, 986, 996	PT6A-21 550	9,650 lbs / 384 gal / 4.6 psid / 210 knots / Dual bleed air / Electric heater / 635°C ITT cruise limit
1978	F90	LA-2 – 204 except 202	PT6A-135 750	10,950 lbs / 470 gal / 5.0 psid / 245 knots / Dual bleed air / Electric heater / T-tail / Super Spar / Main landing gear dual wheels with HFG option / 5-bus electrical system

1982	C90-1	LJ-1011 – 1062 plus 986, 996	PT6A-21 550	9,650 lbs / 384 gal / 5.0 psid / 225 knots / Dual bleed air / Electric heater / 680°C ITT cruise limit
1983	F90-1	LA-202, 205 - 236	PT6A-135A 750	Same as F90 but with Pitot Cowl, yielding about 255 knots typical cruise speed. LA-226 and after have the electrohydraulic landing gear system and the newest lower forward wing spar attach fitting.
1984	C90A	LJ-1063 – 1137, plus 1146	PT6A-21 550	9,650 lbs / 384 gal / 5.0 psid / 235 knots / Dual bleed air / Electric heater / Pitot-cowl / Hydraulically-operated landing gear / New wing spar design introduced LJ-1085, 1088 and after / 695°C ITT cruise limit
1987	C90A	LJ-1138 – 1299, Except 1146, 1288, 1295	PT6A-21 550	10,100 lbs / 384 gal / 5.0 psid / 235 knots / Dual bleed air / Electric heater / Pitot-cowl / Hydraulically-operated landing gear / New wing spar design / 695°C ITT cruise limit
1992	C90B	LJ-1288, 1295, 1300 and after	PT6A-21 550	10,100 lbs / 384 gal / 5.0 psid / 235 knots / Dual bleed air / Electric heater / Pitot-cowl / Hydraulically-operated landing gear / New wing spar design / 695°C ITT cruise limit / 4-blade propellers / better sound-proofing / 350-style interior / 3-position flaps / Some serials are less-expensive, more basic, C90SE models
2006	C90GT		PT6A-135A	Same as the C90B but with 750 SHP engines flat-rated to 550 SHP / 1,900 RPM for takeoff due to a gearbox with a higher reduction ratio / 260 knots

B100 Review and Commentary

The King Air B100 model is unique, as most of our readers know, in that it is the only production model in the King Air series that is *not* powered by a version of the Pratt and Whitney PT6 powerplant. Instead, it is fitted with the Garrett (now Honeywell) TPE331 turboprop engine, similar to those installed on lots of King Air competitors such as Turbo Commanders, MU-2s, Conquests IIs, etc. It is a fine engine with a large following of enthusiastic fans but it is very different in design and operation than the PT6. The intent of this article is to highlight those differences and to provide some operational tips for pilots of this rare model.

100-Series History

The King Air 100 model appeared on the market in 1969. The 100 was the first stretched King Air, with a cabin that is four feet longer than members of the 90-series. The wing, landing gear, and empennage for the 100 came from the Model 99, that had been developed a few years earlier. The 99 is the unpressurized, PT6-powered, commuter airliner that can carry up to 19 passengers. Its wing lacks the extended wingtip (that was introduced on the B90) giving it the same span as the wing on the 90 and A90. However, it has a pronounced droop in the leading edge of the center section that allows it to provide a lower stall speed for a given weight. It also has a large stall fence on each side midway out between the nacelle and tip. (Later, the F90 would use the same wing shape and size but without the stall fences.)

To accommodate the 19 passengers, the 99's fuselage is quite long and the tail needed to be designed to provide enough control and trim authority to handle a much larger CG envelope. Instead of trim tabs on the elevators, Beech went with a movable horizontal stabilizer…like that used on a Piper Cub or Cessna 180, for example. However, unlike the Cub and Skywagon, the stabilizer on the 99- and 100-series was so big that moving the jackscrew manually proved to be too difficult. Instead, a system was designed and certified that included both an electric Main and electric Standby trim motor that operate the stabilizer through a clutch/gearbox arrangement such that if one motor fails the other can still function. When one first flies a 100, it is a bit disconcerting to reach for the elevator trim wheel and find it missing! Normal trimming is accomplished through the use of dual switches on the outboard grip of the pilot's or copilot's control wheel. Standby trimming is achieved by use of two switches on the pedestal, accessible to both pilots. A trim-in-motion aural tone beep-beeps whenever the stabilizer moves. That, too, is unusual at first but soon becomes expected and almost unnoticed.

The King Air Book

The original "straight" 100 model had three-blade propellers, a maximum takeoff weight of 10,600 pounds, and fuel capacity was a rather paltry 374 gallons. B-2 through B-89, and B-93 are the 100 serial numbers.

In 1972 the A100 replaced the straight 100, beginning with serial number B-90. For the very first time, Beech installed a four-blade propeller as standard equipment. Fuel capacity went up to 470 gallons, with a highly-improved delivery system that, again for the first time, utilized an engine-driven boost pump. Maximum takeoff weight was increased to 11,500 pounds. The last A100, B-247, was built in 1979.

The very first 100, serial number B-1, has a fascinating history. After being the flight test vehicle used in certifying the 100, Beech kept the airplane at the factory in Wichita and used it for additional miscellaneous flight testing. It was next used as the prototype for the A100 certification program and remained at Beech in the flight test department. Finally, in 1976, Beech removed it from the Experimental category and re-certified it as a Normal category A100 and it was sold to the State of Kansas. N3100K is still shown in the FAA registry. Thus, B-1 was born as a straight 100 but became an A100!

All members of the 100-series exhibit a "big-airplane" feel. They are heavier on the controls than any 90, 200, or 300-series model. They tend to decelerate rapidly in the flare and finesse is required to make consistently satisfying landings. There's not much ground effect due to the short wings. Nevertheless, many pilots have come to prefer the solid, stable, feel of the 100, A100, and B100. It is a great instrument platform when hand-flying.

Origin of the B100

In the early 1970s, when the sales of new King Airs were setting records and production was at an all-time high rate, the Pratt & Whitney factory had a labor/management dispute that led to a long-lasting strike. The result of this protracted work stoppage was that the supply of PT6 engines virtually came to a halt. At one time, Beech had over 50 completed King Airs sitting in Wichita with paint, interior, and avionics all finished but with lead weights sitting on the engine mounts – to prevent them from tipping back onto their tails – since no engines were at hand. Needless to say, Beech had a severe cash-flow problem, with so much money tied up in those airplanes and no way to collect money from the customers since the airplanes could not yet be delivered.

Frank Hedrick, the president of Beech at the time, decided that it was too risky to have such a large component of the Beechcraft product line dependent upon one sole engine supplier and he instigated an effort to provide another engine supplier for the King Air series. The TPE331 was the obvious choice of powerplant, being about the only other game in town in light turboprop engines.

B100 Review and Commentary

About a year before the P & W strike, Beech had introduced the Super King Air 200 model. With the same cabin size as the A100 model – that had been the top-of-the-line King Air until the 200 came along – but offering a huge performance increase, most potential A100 buyers were being convinced to spend the extra dollars to order a 200 instead. Hence, Beech was seeing a dramatic reduction in the orders for A100s.

It was this fact that led Mr. Hedrick to decide that the 100-series would be the first to offer the new powerplant package. By doing so, perhaps some new interest and life could be breathed into this fine segment of the King Air model line. Eventually, however, Mr. Hedrick's plan was to offer the choice of PT6 or TPE331 engines across all branches of the King Air family tree existing at that time: the 90-series, the 100-series, and the 200-series.

By the time the TPE331-powered version of the A100 – given the designation B100, of course – was finally certificated and ready for customer deliveries, two years had elapsed and the flow of PT6s was back to its historically high abundance. Although the B100 found a ready market among die-hard TPE331 advocates, it never sold nearly as well as its big brother, the 200. A contributing factor to the lack of strong sales success for the B100, in my opinion, is that the King Air sales team had been so indoctrinated into the "PT6 good, 331 bad" school of thinking that many of the salesmen and saleswomen found it very difficult to sing the praises of this different engine to their prospective buyers.

The outcome of this lack of a strong B100 market is that Beech dropped the idea of offering the alternative powerplant across the board of King Air models. Although the factory did develop and conduct flight testing on a prototype TPE331-powered version of the F90 – it was to be known as the G90, and the prototype's serial number was LE-0, leading the factory pilots to refer to the plane as "Leo" – the program never evolved past the testing stage. I would be quite surprised to ever see another new King Air model that utilizes a version of the 331.

B100s were only delivered over an eight-year span, from 1976 through 1983. The prototype started life as an A100, serial number B-205, and was given the new SN of BE-1. The last one manufactured in 1983 was BE-137. All B100s were delivered with 715 SHP (shaft horsepower) TPE331-6-252B engines, all have a maximum gross takeoff weight of 11,800 pounds, with typical cruise speeds of about 250 knots. That speed is 15 to 20 knots faster than the realistic cruise speed of the 100 and A100. Because they have the short wingspan and the rather lowly 4.6 psid maximum differential pressure that is common to all of the 100-series, few B100s spend much time above FL220. Offering the same cabin dimensions of a 200 or 300, yet with significantly less fuel burn and rather good low-altitude speed performance, the B100 has proven to be a popular model among King

The King Air Book

Air charter operators. Also, it is much more commonly found in the Eastern rather than the Western portions of the USA due to its modest single-engine service ceiling.

Some B100s have been converted to the later-designed "Dash 10" version of the 331. These models exhibit increased climb and cruise performance as well as better availability of hot-section component parts.

As most of you know, the PT6 is a "free turbine" design wherein the Power Turbine (PT) that drives the propeller through the reduction gearbox is totally free and independent from the Compressor Turbine (CT) that drives the compressor. The TPE331, in contrast, is a "fixed shaft" turboprop, wherein all rotating components are fixed together and rotate simultaneously, although not necessarily at the same speed due to reduction gearing. The starter on a PT6 only turns the compressor and does not have to spin the mass of the propeller and gearbox. In contrast, the starter on the 331 must turn everything in the engine. That is why the PT6 gets by with a single battery but the B100 requires two of that same size. It also leads to huge differences in how the engines are started, operated, and shutdown.

If you do not fly a B100 and have no plans to do so, you may wish to stop reading now. For those of you who are currently operating the B100 or have plans to do so, please read on to discover operational suggestions about this unique and very fine model.

Engine Starting and Shutdown

Starting the 331 is a totally different process than starting a PT6. In fact, the pilot's left subpanel and the power quadrant are greatly changed between the A100 and B100 models. There are switches in the B100 that were never there before! Instead of *Power, Propeller,* and *Condition* levers, now we have *Power, Speed,* and *Fuel Cutoff & Feather* levers. Because it is relatively easy to harm the engine due to improper starting procedures – and I would opine that the PT6 is much more forgiving to bad technique than is the 331 – one needs to read the POH procedure thoroughly, practice it under the direction of an experienced instructor or operator, and take every care to do it properly.

For the newcomers, you need to practice the proper starting procedure thoroughly, with the battery switch off, until the steps are easy for you. It takes some coordination and practice for the fingers of the left hand to do their tasks well.

Here are a few points to consider:

1. If practical, park facing into the wind for starting. Allowing the wind to blow into the inlet and not the exhaust improves airflow and reduces ITT. If unable to park facing the wind, putting the flaps down will help keep the start cooler by partially blocking the wind from blowing up the exhaust pipe.

2. Remember the 300°C ITT residual temperature starting limit. If the ITT is above 300° before start, place the Start Select switch in the Crank position. Now initiate starter rotation by momentarily moving the Start/Stop switch up to Start. The ITT will rapidly fall as the starter spins the engine but with no fuel or ignition yet activated since we are in Crank mode. Once the speed reaches about 15% move the Start Select switch from Crank to Ground – which will bring on fuel and ignition – and proceed with normal start monitoring.

3. Move *only one* Engine Start/Stop switch from the Stop (bottom) position to the Run (center) position before the first engine's start. Why? Because by unlocking only one Engine Start/Stop switch before starting, accidental activation of both starters at the same time becomes impossible.

    Since this lever lock switch must be pulled over a detent to move out of the Stop position – A finger and thumb operation – it becomes difficult to do this when one finger is already devoted to holding up the NTS (Negative Torque Sensing) Test switch, a required starting step. Thus, unlocking the switch must be done before the start, before the NTS switch is activated.

    If a start ever needs to be aborted, moving the switch back down to Stop is proper procedure. This action should terminate the start sequence and close the fuel shutoff valve. Be aware, however, that electric power is required to close the fuel shutoff valve with this switch. So? Well, if ever *both* left and right starters are operating simultaneously (because someone unlocked both switches before start and accidentally hit both switches by mistake…yes , it has happened!) battery voltage may be lowered so severely that terminating the start with this switch becomes impossible! As stated above, if you unlock only one Engine Start/Stop switch at a time, accidental activation of both starters at the same time won't occur.

4. Since extremely low voltage prevents aborting with the Engine Start/Stop switch, the Fuel Cutoff & Feather lever is the back-up means of start termination. It closes the same fuel shutoff valve manually, instead of electrically. Periodically move this lever through its entire operating range before start to ensure that it is functional, with no binding. On every start (but especially

The King Air Book

following engine maintenance) be prepared to pull this handle if a start needs to be aborted but cannot be terminated with the Engine Start/Stop switch.

5. Start with the power levers at, or slightly behind, *Flight* Idle, not Ground Idle. Since the propeller blades are on the start locks, they cannot yet move to a larger blade angle, the angle that is being asked for when the power levers are near Flight Idle. However, there is nothing to prevent their moving to a negative angle as rotation begins creating oil pressure. If, by mistake, your Ground Idle setting was incorrectly adjusted such that it was calling for a slightly negative blade angle, and you started with the power levers at that Ground Idle position, more propeller rotational drag would tend to bog down the engine's acceleration during the start, leading to higher starting ITT.

    Also, by being certain that the blades stay on the locks until after a successful start is completed, it becomes impossible for them to go to feather. If ever the Fuel Cutoff & Feather lever is pulled to abort the start we *want* the fuel to be shutoff but we *don't want* the blades to feather. Instead, we want them to stay flat, on the locks, so that engine rotation – with its accompanying air cooling – is maximized.

    When you have observed the second ITT surge and as engine speed approaches the idle value of 65%, retard the power lever away from Flight Idle back to Ground Idle.

    However, do *not* retard to Ground Idle if you wish to conduct an Overspeed Governor check. This test should be conducted (1) when airstarts are to be made intentionally, (2) when engine control system adjustments have been performed, (3) when there is an indication of a malfunction, or (4) at least once every 200 hours. Do it during a start when the engine has already been operated recently and the oil temperature is still warm. Why? Remember the engine limitation: Oil temperature should be above 55°C when the engine is operated at Flight Idle or higher power settings.

6. The Negative Torque Sensing system is so important in the event of an engine failure that it should be checked during every start prior to flight. The fixed shaft engine exhibits lots more windmilling propeller drag than its free turbine counterpart. Although NTS is not a true automatic feathering system, it is similar. Without it, VMCA would be unreasonably high. It is a definite "No Go" if NTS is found to be inoperative.

The NTS system check involves these steps:

338

- Hold the NTS Test switch up before activating the start switch and confirm the annunciator light comes on.

- The light should extinguish at start initiation, just as the starter motor begins spinning the engine, providing negative torque.

- The light should reappear after lightoff at approximately 25 – 30% speed. When it does, the NTS test is completed and the test switch may be released.

The NTS annunciator lights are *only* for testing the system. When an engine fails in flight, the NTS light will *not* illuminate to help in your identification of the failed engine. This annunciator is only enabled when the unfeather pump's electric motor is powered.

What does the NTS Test switch really do? Very simply, it turns on the unfeather pump's motor. Want to know an amazing fact? The Unfeather Pump switch and the NTS Test switch are identical! Everything that one does the other does also. Why the duplication? I have been told it is because, after the new pilot's left subpanel was designed – changing from the A100 to the B100 set-up – the test pilots discovered that it was too big of a stretch for the fingers of one hand to activate the Unfeather Pump switch and the Engine Start/Stop simultaneously. Thus, they "threw in" duplicate switches right beside the Start/Stop ones.

When the unfeather pump is activated, it puts high pressure oil into the propeller dome. As the pressure in the dome increases, a high-pressure switch is activated that turns on the NTS Test annunciator. If the negative torque system works properly, it should open the feathering valve to release propeller oil pressure whenever it senses a tendency for the propeller to turn the compressor instead of vice versa. This *negative torque,* as it is called, can be created in two ways: First, when the propeller is windmilling in flight without the engine operating; Second, when the starter rotates the engine. Because the starter connects to the accessory gear box on the downstream side of the reduction gear box, the compressor experiences the same negative torque as if the propeller itself were driving the compressor.

The release of oil from the propeller back into the engine case – when the feathering valve opens due to the NTS system's action – causes the pressure to decrease, the pressure switch to deactivate, and hence power to be removed from the annunciator. In summary, when the pilot sees the NTS Test light extinguish as the start begins, he/she knows that NTS will start to feather the propeller if and when negative torque occurs in flight. Remember, as has been stated above, the propeller blades will not move to feather during this test time because the start locks have not yet been released.

Ignition should come on and fuel should be introduced automatically as the engine speed exceeds 10%. As the exhaust gases start to flow and drive the compressor, positive torque is being created. At some point, enough positive torque overcomes the negative torque being provided by the starter, meaning that the NTS system stops working. At that time, as the feathering valve closes, propeller dome oil pressure increases and the NTS Test light reappears. If the light comes back on too soon it indicates that too much negative torque must be experienced before NTS functions. In the opposite manner, if the light re-illuminates too late in the start the implication is that very little negative torque will trigger the system. Either one is bad. If the NTS only functions when negative torque is very high, one will not get the reduction in windmilling drag (and hence VMCA) for which the system was designed. On the other hand, if NTS functions even for a very minor amount of negative torque, it will tend to start feathering the blades during a low-power, high-speed descent. (This is felt as a pulsation in the airplane as the blades quickly increase and decrease their angle.)

Many pilots are not aware that the NTS test involves *more* than merely observing that the annunciator extinguishes as the starter engages. **No, the test is not completed until the annunciator *reappears* and it is important that the re-illumination occurs between about 25% to 30% speed.**

7. Don't over-prime. That is, don't hold the Engine Start/Stop switch up to Start too much, since it activates the SPR (Start Pressure Regulator) solenoid and sprays more fuel into the engine. The Engine Start/Stop switch should be held up on every normal, cold, start *until lightoff is observed* (ITT rises) to promote a more uniform spray pattern from the fuel nozzles. As soon as ITT rises, however, release the switch immediately and do not reactivate the prime function unless necessary – because engine speed stops increasing – and then *only* when above 25% RPM. So long as engine speed continues increasing, don't prime. Priming is necessary only if engine speed stagnates. Too much fuel entering the combustion chamber with too little air makes for high temperatures.

When the engine is already warm from recent operation – when the ITT starts out above 300°C – don't prime at all. It is unnecessary and tends to make for hotter start temperatures.

8. Releasing the propeller start locks merely requires that blade angle be momentarily reduced from the locked position. Before taxiing, lift the power levers up over the Ground Idle gate and move them slowly back toward Reverse until a small increase in ITT or torque is noted. That should do it. There is no need to pull any significant Reverse power and rock the plane back onto its tail!

There have been a few cases in which the blades of a propeller were not released from the locks and yet this mistake was not apparent during a short taxi period. If significant torque can be achieved, then the blade angle is no longer flat and the locks have been released. Especially on shorter runways, be certain that torque is increasing (500 ft-lbs or more) before releasing the brakes and beginning the takeoff roll.

9. Always observe the three minute cool down period to decrease the thermal stress that occurs following shutdown. Timing begins when the speed levers are retarded to low RPM after landing.

At engine shutdown, after moving the Engine Start/Stop switches to Stop, don't slam the power levers rapidly into full Reverse to engage to start locks. This won't hurt the engines or propellers, but it just about blows the unsuspecting line person standing out in front of you clear across the ramp!

Go into Reverse *gradually* as the engine speed slows down. As long as full Reverse is reached by about 30% RPM, the start locks will definitely be set. Bring the power levers forward to Flight Idle when RPM is below 15 – 20%. This action forces the blade onto the lock, leaving the propeller in a flat condition instead of reverse, and will tend to maximize windmilling time for improved engine cooling.

10. Service Bulletin #2177 introduced an Auto-Relight Ignition Kit (P/N 100-3019-1S) for the B100 to comply with AD 86-24-09 for improved in-flight ice protection. If the Man Fuel/Ign switch is left in the "Arm" position while attempting a normal shutdown, a clean shutdown cannot be accomplished. After the shutdown circuit is activated by placing the Engine Start/Stop switch in the Stop position, as torque pressure decreases to a value less than idle, a signal is sent to activate the ignitors and open the fuel shutoff valve causing the engine to spool-up until the torque pressure is above the idle value, then the shutdown circuit is completed once again and the engine cycles on and off. The consequence of this scenario is a gradual slowing down of the engine that provides less air flow for cooling and hence excessive

engine temperatures that *will cause engine damage!* Checklist procedure calls for turning the Man Fuel/Ign switches off before placing the Start/Stop switches to stop, and that is a *very* important step.

11. If an engine restart is to be accomplished within 45 minutes or so of shutdown, some vigorous rotation of the propeller by hand shortly after shutdown and again before entering the cockpit will significantly reduce residual ITT by forcing air through the engine. It will also decrease the tendency toward shaft bow.

Shaft bow refers to the bending of the main rotating group due to differential temperature. Since heat rises, the upper half of the group will be warmer than the lower half if it is allowed to remain in one position after shutdown. As the warmer metal expands and the cooler metal contracts relative to it, the shaft can develop a bow. In some cases, the bow is severe enough to cause rubbing against the case.

One other reason for hand rotation prior to start is to verify that no rubbing is occurring at this time.

12. The proper time to check engine oil level is within 20 minutes of shutdown. However, usually there is little if any change in readings when it is rechecked cold.

Flight Idle Fuel Flow Check

I have often discovered that the flare-for-landing characteristics of some B100s are less forgiving than desired because the Flight Idle Fuel Flow (FIFF) adjustment is set incorrectly. Perhaps in a misguided attempt to reduce engine starting temperatures, the FIFF is set too low, far below the setting desired by Beech or Garrett/Honeywell. The result is that the airplane "falls out of the sky" when power is reduced to flight idle. Here is how you, the pilot, can determine if your airplane is meeting the proper FIFF specifications.

Begin this check at 6,000 feet pressure altitude. Configure the airplane for landing…gear down, speed levers fully forward, flaps down. Trim the aircraft for 100 – 105 KIAS, and reduce power levers to flight idle.

Passing through 5000 feet, check for:

A. 1800 fpm descent rate. (Yes, it seems high but it's correct!)

B. No adverse yaw.

C. No Beta lights.

D. Approximately 180 pph fuel flow per engine.

Record the descent rate and the fuel flow that you observe, then add power and return to normal configuration.

If the FIFF needs to be adjusted, maintenance personnel should turn the adjusting screw on the rear of the fuel control unit clockwise to increase fuel flow (1 click = 2 pph). A *very* rough rule-of-thumb is that each 10 pph fuel flow change will make a 300 fpm rate-of-descent change. Realize that the Flight Idle Fuel Flow setting cannot be verified properly without a flight test being accomplished!

Engine Inlet Heat

When the Engine Inlet heat switches are turned on in flight, ITT will rise momentarily then drop to a lower value than originally set. The theory here is that the initial rise is caused by the reduction of cooling airflow as air is bled from the compressor and directed to the inlet, but that the subsequent decrease in ITT is caused by the P2/T2 sensor getting warmer and directing the fuel control unit to reduce fuel flow. If desired, the power levers may then be advanced to regain the original ITT. There is a trap waiting here for you. Namely, when you leave icing conditions and turn the switches off, ITT will eventually creep well above your original setting unless power levers are retarded. Therefore, monitor ITT carefully and reduce power enough to leave a comfortable margin below the cruise ITT setting when turning off Engine Inlet heat. Remember that +5°C OAT is the maximum value at which Engine Inlet heat may be used. Leaving it on too long when in warm air may lead to compressor rub in the engine!

Ballooning with Flaps

There is a *very* pronounced pitch-up, or ballooning, effect when flaps are lowered on *any* member of the 100-series, including the B100. Here are a few suggestions:

- When selecting Approach flaps while operating near the appropriate airspeed limit of 179 knots, holding the main trim switches in the nose-down direction for 3 or 4 "beeps" of the trim-in-motion aural indicator will nicely balance the pitch-up tendency.

- Another method when lowering flaps to Approach is to reduce power and let the airspeed drop well below the 179 knot limit without trimming, so that the nose is getting heavy, then lower the flaps. Presto! You are right back in trim!

- When changing from 30% to 100% flaps for landing, you may wish to do so in steps…60, 80, 100%. Instead of trimming forward (nose down) as they extend, stiff arm the control wheel to maintain the visual glide path and be patient. As the drag takes effect, airspeed will decrease and you will find yourself once again nicely trimmed. During this time do not rush to reduce power. The airspeed will very rapidly decay with full flaps if power is too low! The same torque that gave a stabilized ILS approach with 30% flaps will yield about the same descent angle with 100% flaps at landing speed.

Fuel Venting

Sometimes B100s (and E90s, F90s, A100s, 200-series and 300-series also, that have basically the same fuel system) have been known to vent an awful quantity of fuel onto an FBO's ramp or hangar floor. In most cases when this occurs, the cause is found to be a leaking check valve in the fuel vent plumbing. There is a step pilots can take to decrease the likelihood of this malfunction happening.

When fuel is being transferred from the auxiliary tank to the main tank, it transfers at a rate greater than the rate at which the engine is burning the fuel. Consequently, the main tank overfills and builds up enough pressure that a relief valve should vent excess fuel from the main tank back into the aux tank. (Although it *should* do that, sometimes a portion of the excess is vented overboard!) When auxiliary fuel transfers to an already-full main tank, that main tank becomes pressurized or overstuffed with fuel. If ever there is a time when a malfunctioning check valve will cause venting problems, this is it.

I suggest, therefore, that you delay turning on the Aux Transfer switches until leveling off at cruise altitude. Doing so will allow the main tanks to come down from their full condition and hence provide some room so that the aux fuel may now be accepted without causing an overstuffed condition.

When conducting wing-bending analyses, the designers assume that the main tanks will be full if the aux tanks contain fuel. That's why the Limitations tells you to fill the auxes last and use them first. Nonetheless, taking out one or two hundred pounds of fuel from the mains before transferring the auxes will not be enough to cause bending concerns unless perhaps you are loaded right up to the maximum zero fuel weight limit. In routine passenger-carrying operation, that is very rarely the case.

If your airplane *does* ever begin venting copious quantities of fuel one day – perhaps because another pilot wasn't using the delayed aux transfer technique – you might try jarring the malfunctioning check valve closed by some judicious pounding with a fist or mallet in three areas. One place to hit is under the wing tip, outboard of the main filler cap, near the vacuum relief vent opening. Another place is at the check valve upstream of the jet transfer pump in the top area of the main wheel well. Finally, (by now, the mechanics are on their way, right?) take off the oval plate atop the nacelle (lots of screws to remove here) and tap any valve you find beneath it. Good luck!

The C100

Bet you have never heard of this King Air model, have you? In 1976, Beech decided to add enough power to the A100 to have it perform as well or better than the B100. They accomplished this by replacing the 680 SHP PT6A-28 engines with the 750 SHP PT6A-135 engines, the same engine that was to be used on the F90. Since this was such a simple change – So they thought! – Beech began building C100s before the experimental flight testing was completed. BF-1 was the first and they built eight of them, through BF-8. Well, too much of a tendency toward tail flutter was uncovered at the higher speeds these engines provided. Rather than take the time and effort and money to redesign and strengthen the tail assembly, the decision was made to shelve the idea and to convert the eight undelivered C100s back into A100s. If one looks closely inside the cowl of the last eight A100s, one will find a "BF" serial number alongside the "B" number!

Summary

Fewer members of the 100-series branch of the King Air family tree have been produced than any of the other branches. Even the latest 100-series model is now over 25 years old. For those seeking the same large cabin of the 200 or 300 and yet for a price that is less than many used 90s, the 100-series has developed a devoted following. They are solid, pleasant-handling, fun flying machines.

FLYING TO EUROPE

In April of this year, 1998, my wife, Pam, and I, with three friends, flew Flight Review's King Air C90 to Italy. We stayed for a couple of weeks and then flew back. In sixty hours of flying, we never once painted a convective weather cell on the radar nor did we have to inflate the boots to remove ice. We enjoyed tailwinds on more than half of the legs we flew. The weather over the North Atlantic was delightful. We had a flat tire in Iceland. When we returned to the States, the East Coast weather was full of rain and low clouds, and we were forced to execute a missed approach following an NDB/GPS procedure and divert to another airport with an ILS. The trip was easy. If you are comfortable and proficient at IFR procedures and radio phraseology, you should try it.

Oh? Are you still here? What more do you want? That's the story. Details? Okay, I'll fill in some details. But I warned you, you already know the story.

I had previously crossed the Atlantic two times in King Airs, and the Pacific once. In 1985, I flew with one of my clients in his 1977 Super King Air 200 to the Paris Air Show and back, with numerous stops along the way, including Scandinavia, Switzerland, France, Ireland, and, of course, Canada and Iceland. In January of 1990, Pam and I delivered a BE-300 from Scottsdale to Rome in three days, and flew back on TWA. The BE-200 was equipped with a multi-chain Loran navigator and the BE-300 had a single-chain Loran and VOR/DME combination RNAV unit. Although we managed to find our way, there were numerous periods of dead-reaconing when the Loran signals were too weak to be received, mostly due to the precipitation static that resulted when we flew in clouds. Our ADF, tuned to some of the strong North Atlantic beacons, was a comforting back-up navigation system. On all of those trips, the airplane's range and the weather and winds encountered allowed us to over-fly Greenland; I had seen it from the air, but had never landed there.

With the encouragement of Dick and Earline, two pilot-friends from Monterrey, California, and with our friend Betty from my home town, New Castle, Indiana, also wanting to share the adventure, Pam and I decided to take our airplane "across the pond." We felt that this was a good opportunity for a "once in a lifetime" adventure, and I arranged to provide some King Air training for clients in Italy and Switzerland.

I should mention that Pam, too, is not a novice to Atlantic crossing and long-distance flying. Typed in the Learjet, Falcon 20, Falcon 50, and Citation 650-series, my wife is an accomplished corporate pilot with years of experience. She did the majority of the preparatory work such as obtaining the proper fuel credit cards and coordinating with FBOs for our various stops. Together, we pored over the Jeppesen charts for the route and planned each leg carefully. I made sure that our 1972 C90, LJ-542, N9442Q, was ready, with no scheduled maintenance due during this lengthy sojourn.

Dick and Earline arrived in Scottsdale in Earline's Cessna Skylane a couple of days before we left. On our departure day, Tuesday, April 14, the four of us departed at 7:00 a.m. local time for Beech Field in Wichita, Kansas. The Scottsdale-Wichita leg was an excellent omen of the easy nature our trip would prove to have—nearly a 100 knot tailwind! Our 200-knot true airspeed yielded a ground speed of over 300 a couple of times. Including climb and descent and vectoring around Wichita, we averaged over 260 knots. It took 2.9 hours for the 756 nautical miles. This is living!

I was a "Beechcrafter" in the '70s, but had not been back to my old stomping grounds for over five years and much had changed in that time. C. Don Cary, my old boss at the Beechcraft Training Center and now Raytheon's Director of Customer Relations, was gracious enough to meet us when we landed, treated us to lunch in the cafeteria, and then gave us an extensive tour of the facilities. If you haven't had the pleasure of a Raytheon Aircraft factory tour, plan to stop in and take one. It is interesting and educational. To me, it was quite exciting seeing Hawkers and Beechjets and the new Texan II military primary trainer being produced along with the King Airs I had been used to seeing.

Following the great factory tour, we took off for Indiana. With the previous tailwind, and good forecasts for much of the same, we didn't even need to add fuel. This leg took 2.4 hours. My cousin, Jim, picked us up at Sky Castle Airport, where I had first soloed on September 24, 1962. The Marlatt family still runs the place and they keep it in nice shape. We spent the night at the Raintree Motel and ate dinner in the good little restaurant there, with Betty now in our group. I even ran into a close high school classmate and her folks who were there dining. Her father had been a pilot and was excited about the trip…as were we!

Unfortunately, Sky Castle did not yet have jet fuel, so the next morning our first leg was a 15-mile hop to Richmond Municipal to top off with 339 gallons of Jet A. (The C90 holds 384 gallons, usable. The weather was fine.) Then it was on to KBTV, Burlington, Vermont, for fuel. On this leg, the winds had died down and our average ground speed was about 210 knots. Valet Air Services lent us their van and we drove a couple of miles to have a nice lunch at the Windjammer Restaurant. One of us was curious about a toggle switch installed in the van's ceiling, but we couldn't notice any difference regardless of switch position. That is, until we stepped out at the restaurant and noticed the yellow beacon rotating round-and-round on top of the van. No wonder the other vehicles were so courteous to us during our short drive! Our airport ramp alert beacon was probably mistaken for a fire or police signal. We kept the switch off during the return drive!

FLYING TO EUROPE

The relatively new Canadian Customs system – CANPASS – is slick. Pam had called their 800 number and told them of our planned ETA at Goose Bay, and gave them the particulars about crew and passengers. Upon arrival in Goose, CYYR, after our 3.9-hour leg, we merely called another toll-free number, received a release confirmation number, and never actually saw a customs official.

Pam and I alternated Pilot-in-Command duties, flying every other leg from the left seat, while Dick or Earline usually flew as copilot during the overland legs. Once we started over water, however, we shared cockpit duties as PIC and SIC. Most flights were at FL210 eastbound or FL220 westbound, which kept the cabin altitude under 8,000 feet. On the longest leg we flew, Inverness, Scotland to Reykjavik, Iceland, we went to FL240 for better range. (Even if headwinds increase quite a lot with altitude, a turboprop will usually increase range by flying higher. It takes more than a five-knot increase in headwind for each thousand-foot altitude increase, in the C90, before range is decreased by climbing.)

The last time I had passed through Goose Bay, one of the highlights was the excellent weather briefing service we had received from the meteorological department there. They provided weather for both the military flights and civilian flights operating from there. Unfortunately, the request I made to the two "met office" men this time was met with surprised and somewhat icy stares. "We don't give civilian briefings any more. We've been cutback and will soon be closed." Well, okay then, but where do I get the weather? "Use this 800 number to talk to St. Johns, Newfoundland."

It worked fine, and the St. Johns office faxed us a very complete packet at the requested time the next morning, that we picked up at the FBO. Still, there is nothing quite as good, in my opinion, as a face-to-face briefing from a professional who is familiar with the area, the routes, the procedures, and the typical weather patterns.

Two of the necessary skills to learn before flying to Europe are (1) being able to read the weather information with a good degree of accuracy, and (2) being able to correctly complete the International (ICAO) Flight Plan form.

If you have become familiar with the METAR and TAF formats that our government began using a few years ago, you will be quite familiar with these same reports. ("P6SM" is the same as "9999." "Visibility more than six statute miles" equates to "visibility more than ten kilometers." 9999, standing for 9,999 meters, is the shorthand for "greater than ten kilometers.") In addition, the weather briefing you receive often comes in a paper folder. This folder is preprinted with all of the pertinent abbreviations and symbols that you will find on the weather charts.

The ICAO Flight Plan procedures are described very well in the introduction pages of the European Jeppesen tripkit that you will order for your trip. Spend an evening or two reading about the form and filling out a few practice examples, and you'll have no problems with it. The tripkit coverage does *not* automatically include the high altitude enroute charts. Make sure you order them too if you'll be above 18,000 feet or so. You will also need the "North Atlantic Supplement" to cover Greenland, Iceland, etc. The entire package isn't cheap, but I found no way to order charts for only a few European airports. (But it is good to have all the approach plates since you never know when a diversion to an unexpected emergency landing field may be necessary.) We also bought the ONC visual charts through Sporty's mail order catalogue, and were glad we had them for flying the Greenland fiords, but were surprised to find they had not been updated since the 1980s, even though they were the latest version.

Our overnight stay in Goose Bay was uneventful, in a rather blah motel, but with clean rooms and decent food. I bought a book there about the history of the area, of the airfield particularly. It always amazes me how much we accomplished during WWII in such a short time! This was the jumping off spot for zillions of planes and crews heading to Europe during the war.

"Bluie West One," mentioned in some of Ernie Gann's books, was also built during the war as a refueling spot for Europe-bound planes who couldn't make Goose-Reykjavik nonstop. It is the infamous strip at the end of a long fiord near the southern tip of Greenland. It had no IFR approach and if a pilot found the runway socked in when at last it came into view, there was little room for a turn-around. Also, the chance of a successful IFR missed approach climb up the glacier and over the Greenland icecap was marginal. Passing by a beached derelict freighter told the olden-day crews that they were heading up the proper fiord. Today, the airport is still alive and well, even has an "NDB/DME" approach – with horribly high minimums – but is still a place not to take casually. It now goes by the name "Narsarsuaq," designated BGBW. (Anyone know what the "B" is for? All of the North Atlantic airport designators start with a B. G for Greenland, BW for Bluie West, that much I can figure out. But the B? Don't yet know.)

Being somewhat of a history buff, I hoped that great weather would allow us to refuel at Narsarsuaq as we flew between Goose and Reykjavik. However, guessing that chances of great weather were slim, we were prepared to go 300-some miles out of our way to refuel at Godthab, the capital of Greenland, that has an ILS approach to a paved but not-too-long runway.

Hallelujah! The weather-briefing packet contained nothing but good news! Clear skies all the way to Iceland. BGBW, here we come! This 676 NM leg took 3.8 hours, for an average speed of 178 knots. Not much help from the wind, and we took a lot of time oohing and aahing our way up the fiords before landing. Gosh it's beautiful! With the severe clear skies, a good VFR chart, unlimited visibility, and four pilots on board, you'd surely think we could have found the right fiord to start flying up, right? No way, Jose! After we had flown about 20 miles inland from the coast, it dawned on us that we were actually over the wrong fiord, and had to hop over to the next one to our north. Geez! Good thing they had the beached freighter for a checkpoint in WWII!

We landed on the single, up sloping, Narsarsuaq runway under calm, clear, and temperate skies, and found friendly Danes, quick and cheap jet fuel, and a reasonable cafeteria. A DeHavilland DHC-7 four-engine commuter plane was there, and a 737 landed while we were refueling there on our return flight. Leaving BGBW, we made a wide turn over the sparkling fiord until we had sufficient altitude to safely ascend up the glacier, that ran from the icecap down the valley toward the runway.

In foreign countries, the IFR rules can be a bit different, and one noticeable change in southern Greenland is that the airspace below FL195 (19,500 feet) is Glass G...uncontrolled. Thus, one never receives a clearance to make an instrument approach nor departure from BGBW. Your clearance only covers your flight when it is in controlled airspace. (Good thing there isn't a lot of traffic around there!) Also of interest is that very rarely do Flight Levels begin at 18,000 feet. Instead, the transition altitude is often low, perhaps 7,000 feet. It is at that low altitude that 29.92 inHg is set on the altimeters. When descending, the Transition Level may be FL80, meaning that the local altimeter setting replaces 29.92 only when descending below about 8,000 feet. Finally, be prepared to convert Inches of Mercury (inHg) into Hectopascals. Hecto-what?! It's what we used to call Millibars. If your altimeter does not have the ability to display Millibars, you'll need a copy of the handy table in the Jepp books, that allows you to convert them into Inches.

The stop at Reykjavik, the capital of Iceland, has always been a pleasure. The airport is right in the heart of town, and it is just a few steps from your airplane to the very nice Loftlieder Hotel. The hotel was built to accommodate the numerous Icelandair passengers in the days when that airline was known for its cheap European fares. Plenty long enough for DC-4s and DC-6s, the airport was bypassed by Icelandair and others at the advent of the jet age. Nevertheless, it has remained an exceedingly popular and helpful stop for international ferry and corporate flights.

The next day, after receiving a wonderfully complete weather package from the friendly folks at Reykjavik flight services, we were off to Aberdeen, Scotland. The 709 NM took 3.2 hours, for an average ground speed of 222 knots, thanks to a nice tailwind. (No, not all King Airs are 200-knot true airspeed airplanes. But the 1966 – 1974 A90, B90, and C90 ones, operated conservatively, are.)

Thanks to Pam's thorough planning, we did our trip without handlers. That is, we did not pay the extra charges for Universal Weather or Jeppesen to arrange our fuel stops for us. This is not necessarily the easiest or best way to go, but it is what we decided to do. A corporate airplane on a tight schedule would be, in my opinion, silly not to use professional handlers. However, if time is not a critical factor, then handling the fuel stops yourself is not an insurmountable task.

The King Air Book

After Scotland, Europe is your oyster. That is, the leg to any European destination is relatively short, or can be planned with an easy intermediate fuel stop. Flying IFR in Europe is very similar to flying IFR in the States. English is the universal language of ATC and all controllers were easy to understand. However, now is not the time for the usage of slang or non-professional terminology. Read the Aeronautical Information Manual (AIM) and use correct phraseology. Don't abbreviate your call sign unless ATC does so first. Always end your transmissions with your call sign, either "November" 9442Q or "King Air" 9442Q. Be precise on flight level terminology. If the transition altitude was 7,000 feet, then you are passing "Flight Level 124," not "one two thousand, four hundred feet." "Cleared to Flight Level One Hundred" is more correct than "Down to Ten." Be familiar with "QNH," "QNE," and "QFE" terminology. (QNH is the local altimeter setting, so that your altimeter reads field elevation at touchdown. QNE is the standard 29.92 inHg reference set into the Kollsman window. Lastly, QFE is the altimeter setting that makes the barometric altimeter read zero at touchdown…used almost never by civilian, non-airline, flyers.

From Aberdeen, we flew to Amsterdam and took a short train ride to Leiden, where the wonderful spring tulip festival is held. Then it was a short hop over the Alps to Florence, our ultimate destination. Golly, what a city! Even the two weeks we spent there were insufficient to totally grasp the art and history of this city.

The return flight was a retracing of our steps, but we changed Aberdeen for Inverness. Our longest leg was 4.1 hours, from Inverness to Reykjavik, and we went to FL240 for increased fuel reserves. This was my leg, and when we landed in Iceland, I felt a bad shimmy as the nose wheel was lowered to the runway. Although "Shimmy Damper" was the first thought through my mind, I quickly changed my diagnosis to a flat nose tire. I held the control wheel fully aft until we were nearly stopped, and inched off of the runway to a safe stopping spot. Sure enough, the nose tire, a tubeless one, was flat and mostly off of the wheel rim. Airport personnel came out quickly and we managed to get the nose wheel up onto a three-wheeled dolly for the slow tow to the ramp. The dolly, designed for single-engine airplanes, was being overtaxed by the weight of the King Air's nose, and the platform was rubbing on the tires. The only remedy was to get some weight off of the nose. While Pam stayed in the cockpit to use the brakes if needed, the remaining four of us crammed our bodies into the aft baggage compartment to get a lot of weight as far aft as possible. The twenty-minute tow to the ramp seemed like an eternity, with all of us wedged together like cordwood. Also, after the 4.1 hours in flight, visions of a bathroom were dancing rather heavily in all of our heads!

We had budgeted two nights in Reykjavik on the return, to enjoy more of marvelous Iceland, its scenery and people. The local maintenance facility had the proper tire in stock, and they found that the rim was undamaged. So our flat tire episode caused no unscheduled delay.

By the way, there seems to have been a rash of King Airs landing in Reykjavik, during their delivery flights to Europe, with flat nose tires! A French delivery pilot even drew a cartoon about it, that is on display in Sven's office at the flight service facility! I have no idea why this may be so, but if any reader can offer some insight, I will be grateful.

Although the challenges involved in such a flight are not inconsequential, they are not insurmountable, either. Yes, flying in Europe is more expensive than in the USA, and you will be paying fees long after you return. Nevertheless, we highly recommend this unique experience for those who have the desire and the ability to carry it off.

SPECIAL DELIVERY TO JAPAN

Lizard called a couple of days before Christmas, asking if I knew of any BE-300 rated pilots who could help him ferry some new Super King Air 350s to Japan. "How about me?" I asked. "That'll be great. I just assumed your time would already be booked up. Let's do it!" Thus began one of the most interesting long distance flights of my life…a special delivery to Japan.

Lizard – a nickname he earned during a tour of duty in Vietnam – is a good friend and excellent pilot. Over the course of many years I had the pleasure of providing King Air recurrent training for him and his colleagues when he was flying for an air ambulance operation in northern Arizona. After that operation shut its doors, he began working for Southern Cross Aviation, of Camarillo, California, a company that specializes in moving airplanes all over the world. The Japanese company that had sold a batch of new 350s to the Japanese Coast Guard had selected Southern Cross to provide the delivery service. It had taken Raytheon longer than anticipated to complete the certification process of the modifications for these special mission airplanes, and finally three of them were ready for the customer and everyone wanted to get them delivered as soon as possible. Hence, Lizard was looking for help on this three-airplane flight. A few BE-300 rated pilots I contacted were not available on such short notice during the holiday season, but Southern Cross found our third member, Mike Whitman, a Canadair Regional Jet captain for Mesa Airlines, who lives in Farmington, New Mexico. Mike had a lot of time in Mesa's Beech 1900 fleet before moving up to the jets. When he earned his BE-1900 type rating, the BE-300 rating was automatically included. That is how I had gotten a BE-1900 rating, along with my BE-300, although I had never flown a 1900! (This nice little loophole has since been closed.) The 350 is officially a Super King Air B300 and is covered by one's BE-300 type rating.

Late Wednesday morning, December 30, 1998, I left Flight Review's office on the Scottsdale airport and drove to the Phoenix Sky Harbor airport to catch an America West flight to Wichita. Having been given an E-ticket confirmation number, but not having a written confirmation in hand, I was told I couldn't check my bags curbside. What a long line inside due to the holiday travel! After waiting in line about thirty minutes to check two bags, I then spent nearly that long at the security checkpoint. Golly! I just love airline travel during busy seasons!

The plane was forty minutes late pushing back from the gate, but the flight was uneventful with no clouds all the way. Once my bag arrived, I took the hotel shuttle van to the Wichita Airport Hilton, that is just a couple of blocks away. A call to Raytheon Aircraft Services, the FBO at Wichita where the airplanes were located, failed to locate Lizard, who supposedly had arrived a day before to make a final pre-delivery inspection and acceptance flight on all three birds.

After a couple of hours at the hotel, Lizard called and we "Three Amigos" met for dinner at Legends, the nice restaurant in the hotel. It was the first time Lizard or I had met Mike, but our positive first impression certainly proved true…he was a great comrade during our trip.

After dinner, we met in Lizard's room to get our tripkits full of charts and computerized flight plan forms. We also got issued "Poopie Suits," the common name for our "Adult Immersion Suits," our protection if we had to survive in the icy waters or the frigid terrain of the far north. We were also provided with a handheld GPS navigator to back up the equipment in the airplanes, but the one for me was missing from the supply bag. This mistake made no difference since I had packed my old, trusty, Garmin 55 unit anyway.

"Say, Lizard, I think I know, but tell me why they are called 'Poopie Suits'?" I asked. Although we agreed that it probably had to do with certain necessary bodily functions after one had donned the darn thing, I liked Lizard's comment better: Namely, that it referred to what his fear would cause to happen *before* he put the suit on!

My excitement level was high awaiting tomorrow's start of our adventure, and I couldn't sleep at all well. After tossing and turning and checking the clock a few times every hour, I finally decided to give up the battle and get up. So, at 2:45 a.m., I was watching a little late-night TV, writing in my trip journal, and studying the charts and flight plans I had been given. At 4:45 I went down the hall to the Aviator's Club room and ate some microwave oatmeal, an apple, and herbal tea. Look out world, I'm ready!

After checking out of the hotel and taking the shuttle over to RAS, we found our airplanes in the nice warm hangar and were able to look them over carefully before they moved outside into the cold and wind. For Mike and me, it was out first glimpse of our "homes" for the next few days. What nice airplanes! Serial numbers FL-180, 188, and 191 were their official "names." For the purpose of the delivery flight, they were actually owned by Southern Cross and each carried a US registration, taped in durable numbers on the sides. I was assigned FL-188, N18297. It had 16.3 hours on the meter and had that new car smell we all like. To best serve in their special mission role for off-shore patrol and rescue duty in Japan, they had been modified extensively. In addition to the two crew seats, the cabin had ten forward-facing, commuter, seats that could be easily removed, and a large bench seat against the aft pressure bulkhead where the baggage compartment would normally be. Floor-to-ceiling observation windows had been installed on both sides of this baggage area so that observers would have unrestricted views in all directions. Each observer seat was provided with a radio/intercom panel for both internal and external communication. Just forward of the observer station was a large plug in the floor that could be removed when depressurized and used for air dropping life-saving equipment to survivors adrift at sea. (Right over the drop hatch was a *very* solid ring in the ceiling to which the airplane crewmen would attach a safety harness before working around the open hatch. Good idea!) Each airplane also had been fitted with a Forward Looking Infrared (FLIR) module that mounted near the nose gear wheel well and its presence forward on the airframe had necessitated the addition of large strakes or fins on the tail to provide the proper level of yaw stability. I was told there had been some last-minute snag in gaining export approval for this system, so the FLIR module was not installed for the delivery trip.

The cockpit, however, had not been modified in any remarkable way. Good! A Super King Air 350's cockpit is one of the nicer around, and these airplanes had all the whistles and bells typically found there: A three-tube Collins EFIS 85B system, a Collins APS-65 autopilot/flight director, dual coms, navs, and DMEs, an HF com radio, color airborne radar, and a Universal UNS-1C flight management system with VOR, DME, GPS, fuel flow, and air data computer inputs. This last whiz-bang unit made the trip a breeze; what a winner!

We all started up together in the early morning darkness and each of us struggled for a while in finding all of the dimming rheostats to get the cockpit lighting set to our satisfaction. Lizard went first on this leg, myself second, Mike third. When in a radar-controlled ATC system, we were able to depart with about a five minute interval between takeoffs. Later, in the non-radar environment of northern Canada and Russia, we usually were about thirty minutes apart. I started taxiing at 1227Z, or 6:27 a.m. Wichita time, and began my takeoff roll six minutes later at 1233. Our first leg was to Edmonton, Alberta, Canada, and the simple clearance was "N18297 is cleared to the Edmonton airport as filed. Maintain 5,000 feet. Expect Flight Level 260 ten minutes after departure. Departure control frequency will be 126.7. Squawk 1770." Lizard had filed us all "Direct," and that is the simple routing we flew.

The first thing I do when considering a long distance flight out of the country is to get my globe and look at the route. Only when viewed on a model of our actual orb does the shortest path become obvious. Lizard had told me that our stops would be Edmonton (CYEG), Anchorage (PANC), Nome (PAOM), Magadan (UHMM), Yuzhno Sakhalinsk (UHSS), and then Sendai, Japan (RJSS). Magadan and Yuzhno Sakhalinsk are both in Russia. Although the direct great circle route from Wichita to Sendai would have been slightly south of what we flew, our route was certainly a close approximation, and it involved short enough legs that additional fuel tanks did not need to be installed. Using the measuring scale on my globe, I eyeballed the individual legs at 1200, 1200, 470, 1260, 850, and 550 nautical miles, for a total of 5,530 nm. Knowing that 350s cruise typically at about 290 knots true airspeed, but making a guess about headwinds and possibly slower true

The King Air Book

airspeeds chosen for fuel conservation, I "guesstimated" that we would average 240 knots over the ground. Let's see here: 5,530 nm divided by 240 knots equals 23 hours. My guardian angel must have whispered that 240 knot estimate into my ear, because my plane's hour meter read 39.5 when we reached Sendai: 23.2 hours enroute.

Wichita departure control cleared me up to 15,000 feet before I had reached 5,000, and then Kansas City Center kept me climbing with assignments of FL220, 230, and then 260. The three of us had agreed to keep 122.75 tuned on the number two com radio, and we did lots of chatting and comparing of notes as we flew, which made the comfort level and fun factor much higher than if we had been truly alone. With a screw-up I made in setting up the radio panel, I had missed Kansas City's clearance to FL230, but Mike quickly passed it along on Com 2 and I got reconnected with Kansas City on Com 1.

The UNS-1C unit indicated a wind from 327 degrees at 69 knots, and it gave me only 227 knots of ground speed as I leveled in cruise. Because I was the middle airplane on this leg, ATC had me climb up 1,000 feet higher (FL270) to give proper traffic separation. As the winds picked up we made the decision to reduce power for a more fuel-efficient setting and our groundspeeds dipped below 200 for a while. However, the reduction of fuel flow more than offset the speed reduction, so we were better off. The UNS-1 provides instantaneous readouts of both air and ground Specific Range (nm/lb) and that made it easy to view the positive or negative effects of our power setting experimentation. This extremely capable navigation system also continually displayed the estimated fuel remaining upon arrival at the destination.

Outside air temperatures were only 1°C below standard (ISA-1°) on this last day of 1998. A bit later, I climbed on up to FL310 for better range, where the Indicated OAT was -39°C, still about 1° below standard. The cabin stayed warm and toasty using its bleed air heating system. The sun had come up shortly after departure, and I basked in comfort, sipping bottled water and snacking on jerky and an apple. This isn't bad at all!

Somewhere on this leg, Mike and I got a good laugh when I asked on 122.75 what the abbreviation "ESAD" meant, an acronym that showed up on some pages in the UNS. "Eat #$% and Die!" was Lizard's take on it, but we later concluded it actually meant "Equivalent Still Air Distance," or how far we would have flown after takeoff up to the present time in a no-wind condition.

My little Garmin 55 GPS was struggling to find enough satellites with which to navigate, while I experimented in placing its suction cup-mounted antenna on various different windows. When it did lock on, however, it was comforting that the distance and groundspeed it displayed were identical to the ones shown by its big, expensive, cousin, the UNS.

SPECIAL DELIVERY TO JAPAN

Kansas City center had passed us over to Denver, then Denver transferred us to Winnipeg, and finally Winnipeg sent us over to Edmonton. The ATIS: "Edmonton International Airport Information November. Time 1700Z. Wind 110 degrees at 16 knots. 3 statute miles visibility. Light snow and blowing snow. Ceiling 1,000 overcast. Temperature minus 17°C, dewpoint minus 21°C. Altimeter 29.79. ILS Runway 12 approach in use. Landing Runway 12."

I was cleared direct to the Edmonton VOR and to descend to 10,000 feet at my discretion. I started descent about 75 miles out, and received radar vectors for an easy ILS to a runway with lots of blowing snow a few inches above its surface, that yielded an optical illusion at times of excessive taxi speed. Touchdown was at 1812Z, and we stopped at 1820: 5.6 hours flight time and 5.9 block time.

We were on the ground in Edmonton for about an hour and a half getting fueled, clearing customs, and filing our next leg to Anchorage. I took off at 2010Z, or 1:10 p.m. local time, and climbed to FL310. The wind was shifting to the southwest, and ground speed was up to 256 knots for a while. The northern Alberta farm fields spread out below, with an overcast sky to the east and the early-setting sun shining through clear skies to the west. I tried FL350 for a while to see how the winds were, but decided that 310 was better so came back down. I was told not to exceed an indicated airspeed of 165 knots, to keep me from gaining on Lizard. ATC explained that we needed ten minutes of spacing as we entered an area without radar coverage.

As radar contact was lost, we began making IFR position reports, just like in the old days. PTA-ETA-NEXT. "18297 is over Eltex intersection at 2210Z, FL310. Estimating Deeja at 2338. Yakutat next." I'm about 50 miles behind Lizard and Mike is another 50 or so behind me. He got stuck at FL280 and cannot receive a climb clearance in this non-radar environment because of me. He's beginning to sweat his fuel status, and may have to land in Juneau or Cordova instead of making Anchorage non-stop.

The sun sets, it gets dark, but with a bright full moon to the east. A beautiful sight, with the moon and stars above and silvery clouds below. The air is smooth. Thank you, Lord, for letting me have this experience.

I pick up the Anchorage ATIS and find a special report of calm winds, one and one-half miles visibility in light snow and mist, a 1300 foot overcast ceiling, -7°C temperature and –8°C dewpoint, and 29.66 the altimeter setting. The ILS to Runway 6 Right is out of service, so the Localizer approach to Runway 6 Left is to be expected.

Being vectored for the localizer to 6L, the controller announces that the ILS to 6R is back up and clears me for that approach instead. Rush time! I quickly retune and identify the new localizer and set up for the ILS. The ceiling is about as advertised, and I pick up the approach lights about four miles out. During rollout, I am directed to cross the left runway and taxi to the base of the tower,

The King Air Book

where it is a slow wait for the customs official to arrive. However, once he is there, the process goes smoothly. Lizard and I heave a collective sigh of relief when Mike taxis in a little while later. He had been able to climb once he was back in radar contact with Anchorage center, and made it in OK without a fuel stop. My block time on this leg had been another 5.9 hours.

Once the customs paperwork was completed, we fired up and Lizard radioed as a "Flight of three" for permission to taxi to our FBO, the ERA Aviation Center. Mike and I followed Lizard, sometimes in almost whiteout conditions due to the snow his props blew back at us! Mike had a slow spool-up during his start after refueling in Edmonton, and it appeared that his battery was in need of a deep cycle, being rather puny in the cold weather. With that in mind, we stopped on the taxiway abeam the ERA ramp to provide sufficient time for the "Battery Charge" annunciator in Mike's airplane to extinguish. This took five minutes or more, and while we waited we were treated to some special entertainment provided by three ERA linemen. We later called it the "Line Dance." You see, these poor chaps thought we were confused about where to enter their ramp from the snowy taxiway, and so were standing atop a snow mound jumping up and down and waving their arms madly, trying to get our attention. In the darkness, they couldn't tell that we did in fact see them, and appreciated their fine efforts very much, thank you, but we just weren't quite ready to taxi in yet. We thought it best to blow the snow and make the noise on the taxiway, not on the ramp next to their hangar. Ah well. Even the "dancers" got a chuckle out of it when we explained the situation.

ERA lent us a Saturn station wagon in which "Parnelli" Whitman slipped and skidded us over to the Bartlett Inn on the other side of Anchorage International. After a fine halibut dinner with an adult beverage or two and a call to Pam at home to tell her where I was, bed felt splendid. I didn't stay awake to usher in the new year, and slept like a log until 9:00 a.m. on Friday, January 1. Happy New Year everyone!

We would lose a day when we crossed from Alaska into Russia as we crossed the International Date Line and west longitudes became east longitudes. The Japanese customers wanted the airplanes to arrive on Monday morning, January 4. Hence, we decided to spend two nights in Anchorage. Forecast weather conditions looked relatively good for our Siberian passage.

On New Year's Day, waking at 9:00 a.m., I showered, checked by Mike's and Lizard's doors to see if anyone was stirring (neither was), so I dressed warmly and walked about a quarter of a mile to Gwennie's Famous Alaskan Restaurant. This is one of my favorite breakfast spots in all the world and is not to be missed when in Anchorage.

I ate a delicious, huge, meal and leisurely read the newspaper and worked the crossword puzzles in it. Gwennie's always finds the friendliest servers; nice folks. It was cold, calm, and overcast with unlimited visibility giving a great view of the Chugach Mountains as I retraced my

360

steps back to the hotel. Lizard and Mike saw me coming up the sidewalk as they were having breakfast at the hotel restaurant and I was saved from a sneak snowball attack only by the fact I was inside before they could finalize their ambush plans. We drove over to the airport's international terminal to finish some customs forms and export approvals, drove around the Lake Hood portion of Anchorage International, which perhaps is the world's busiest ski-plane base in the winter and float-plane base in the summer. Mike had not been to Alaska before and was awed, like all first-timers, with the plethora of Beavers, Otters, Cessna 180s and 185s, and just about every other bush plane ever built! We stopped by ERA to check on the planes and to have their oxygen bottles topped up, and picked up some gallon jugs of water at a convenience store to take with us. After an afternoon nap, we met for dinner at the Regal Hotel just a block away from the Bartlett Inn, and watched the football Bowl games as we ate. Retired for the night early, with exciting anticipation of what tomorrow would bring. Russia!

I didn't need the alarm clock Saturday morning, January 2, 1999, since my excited internal clock woke me about an hour before wake up time. We met in the hotel lobby at 5:30 a.m. and drove the Saturn station wagon back to ERA. Lizard dealt with paying our fees to ERA, Mike checked weather, and I filed the flight plan from PANC to PAOM (Anchorage to Nome) for all three of us. This would be our shortest leg, only about 470 nm. We asked ERA to provide ground power for our starts, and all three planes started easily in the minus 3°C temperature. I brought up the rear position and taxied out last, a few minutes behind Mike. The Anchorage weather was 2½ miles visibility in light snow and mist, with a broken layer at 1,500 feet and an overcast at 2,600. Departures were off of Runway 32, which put us almost exactly in line to proceed straight out on course.

The snow had seemed more moderate to heavy, not light, as we had preflighted the airplanes, but the cold temperature and dry snow prevented it from adhering to the airframes. In fact, we had left the airplanes outside in Anchorage, with the thought that we would put them in the heated hangar Friday night to thaw them out for the Saturday morning departure, but they were totally snow and frost free when we had checked them on Friday. Hence, there was no need for the hangar.

Soon after liftoff I was in the clouds and turned off the strobe and beacon lights to eliminate the distracting light show they were providing. All twelve ice protection switches were activated and all systems were doing a good job of keeping the plane ice free. I kept the airspeed at about 180 in the initial climb, keeping in mind the 140 knot minimum speed for icing. However, as is so typical, just a light dusting of ice was found on the leading edges when I examined them using the wing ice inspection lights, and never once did I need to activate the deicing boots during the entire 23.2 hours of the delivery trip!

Coming through 12,000 feet, the sky began to lighten above, and I was surprised that dawn would begin to arrive at 7:45 a.m. local time at this time of year so far north. It wasn't the dawn! Nor was it the Northern Lights! Instead, at 13,000 feet, I burst out on top into a crystalline clear night sky…with the nearly full moon absolutely dead ahead of me! As I nosed over into cruise at FL260, the view was magnificent: A full moon directly ahead perhaps 20 degrees above the horizon, the flashing strobe lights of my two comrades clearly visible in the distance, and a moonlit winterscape of mountains, rivers, and clouds below. I'm a lucky guy.

The wind was now from the south at 43 knots and the groundspeed was up at 302 knots. It was 8 degrees Celsius below standard here at 260. I let the engine readings stabilize, and took the Engine Condition Trend Monitoring (ECTM) readings that we did on every leg. The engines were meeting book performance numbers easily as they purred through the arctic sky. Sitting in the comfort of my pressurized magic carpet with the autopilot doing the flying and the UNS-1C doing the navigating, I reflected on the role of the airplane in shaping Alaska and of the tremendous work and discomfort that the early bush pilots endured. Ellison, Wean, Reeve, and all your colleagues…my thanks to you all.

With calm winds, 4 miles visibility in light snow and mist, a 1,900 foot overcast ceiling and minus 17°C temperature, we all executed the ILS-1 approach to Runway 27 at Nome, landing one after the other in total darkness on the snow-covered but well lighted runway. Touchdown came at 9:31 a.m. local time, but it still looked like midnight. The hour meter had recorded 1.9; the block time was 2 hours and 10 minutes.

Two friendly and helpful Flight Service Station specialists helped us with the flight plans into Russian airspace as we got refueled. Southern Cross had utilized Jeppesen for help in the flight planning and in receiving overflight permission, and Lizard made a couple of phone calls from the Flight Service Station back to the Southern Cross home base to clarify a couple of questions. Everyone felt it was extremely important that each pilot knew his "CDS" number, both to enter in the "Remarks" section of the International Flight Plan form as well as to state on the radio when queried for it by the Russian ATC system. Boy, I had my number ready: FAS 94/1706/98! I was never queried about it by anyone, ever. Of course, if I had *not* had the number, you can bet it would have been requested!

The fellow in the weather office on the ground floor of the FSS building was also very accommodating, and made a weather packet for each of us. January in Siberia, yet the weather was forecast to be excellent for our entire route! What's wrong with *this* picture?!

We were on the ground about two hours in Nome, and had to depart with at least fifteen minutes of separation between us. Again, I was last to depart. Lizard always led the way so that he could start arranging for fuel for all of us when he landed. Mike went in the middle. I was last, so that just in case Mike's battery breathed its last during his start-up, I could give him a hand in getting started. Luckily, his battery, weak as it was, always came through for him. If ground power were not available, I had nightmares of pulling the battery out of my plane and installing it into Mike's long enough to get him started and to recharge the battery, then to switch the batteries back to their original locations. Geez, I'm glad it never came to that!

Dawn was beginning to break as we left Nome, with the GPS showing 1,236 nm to go to Magadan. Our flight plan was via the G212 airway most of the way ("Green 212") and I was "Cleared as Filed." I was above a little low scud layer soon after liftoff from Nome and when I told the controller that I could accept a VFR climb on course, he cleared me to "Flight Level 9,600 meters; maintain visual conditions until passing 6,000 feet." Lizard had briefed us well, and we knew that Russia and China were the last two countries in which altitude assignments were given in meters instead of in feet, distances in kilometers, and speed in kilometers per hour. We each carried a conversion table, and also knew that the factor was 3.2808 feet per meter. Multiplying 9,600 meters by 3.2808, I came up with 31,496 feet, so set the altitude alerter at 31,500. Anchorage Center bid me goodbye as I left US airspace and instructed me to contact Anadyr Control when over Valta intersection, which was about 16 minutes ahead. He gave me two frequencies: 119.3 Mhz for VHF, and 5,550 Khz for HF.

Eavesdropping on Lizard and Mike, I knew that Anadyr Control was not responding to their initial calls. A passing Continental airliner suggested another VHF frequency, 135.4, but that was also coming up a blank. However, my previous international flight experience told me that this was nothing new, probably just a little too far out yet for good line-of-sight communications. HF communication does not suffer a line-of-sight restriction, and I was able to hear Anadyr occasionally on 5,550 Mhz.

I hate to admit this, but none of us had yet figured out how to *transmit* on the fancy HF units we had on board! I know we *should* have, but the operator's manual for the unit was in one of the many tightly-packed boxes in the cabin that carried all of the airplane's "loose equipment" and spare parts. Furthermore, Lizard assured us that VHF communication would work well at our altitude...as it did, eventually. Later during this leg to Magadan, I did manage to figure out the HF transmitter operation, but by then it wasn't needed.

I made my ECTM readings and marveled at the view of the sun and moon both in view together. From my heading of about 250 degrees, I estimated that the sun was at about a 140 degree magnetic bearing from me (90° to my left) and the moon was at about a 315 degree bearing (65° to my right), both never very far above the horizon. Lizard, Mike, and I shared a lot of radio banter on

The King Air Book

122.75. I lost the last VOR and DME signals that I would have until arrival in Japan, and went to a squawk code of 2000, standard procedure in the international non-radar environment.

Lizard had regaled us in Anchorage with stories about his ferry flights through the middle east, and how he hated being "locked up" by fire control radar ready to launch a missile at him. The indication that a military weapon-aiming radar had locked on, he explained, was that the transponder's reply light flickered so fast that it remained on at all times.

Well, folks, Russia ain't got no radar turned on in Siberia now, at least not on the day we flew over! From shortly after leaving Alaska until arrival near Japan, I never saw my transponder reply light blink even once. Amazing! Being born in 1945 and raised in the height of the cold war, I found it hard to shake the feeling that Russia was a powerful and capable enemy…as well it might have been, and perhaps still is in some ways. But the part of Russia I saw engendered no feelings of awe at its military capability. Instead, it engendered feelings of sadness and of sympathy for the plight the needy Russian citizens find themselves in now.

Magadan, our first Russian stop, is a sister city of Anchorage, and friends living in Anchorage had told me of the numerous stories in the newspapers there about the horrible conditions in Magadan during this winter of 1998-1999. Heating fuel is scarce and not affordable to the average citizen. Heating of public buildings, including hospitals, could only be done for a few hours a day. The death rates among the very young and very old are astonishingly high. Pay is meager, if received at all, and the black market is thriving. Few people can afford to operate a vehicle and public transportation is limited.

How sad!

My very limited exposure to Russia showed me that these stories are probably true, at least in the eastern region, and I hope we Americans can expand our hearts and our pocketbooks in an effort to help these needy brothers and sisters who share our world.

Valta intersection came and went at 2118Z, then Abina at 2123, and Provid, and Provideniya Bay airport at 2132. At each of these reporting points I made my position report in the blind and never received a reply. Finally, at 2139, over Garos intersection, Anadyr Control read my transmission and I was in ATC contact again! The Russian controllers spoke easily understandable English, and I was thankful that my native language was the official international language of aviation. I asked to have a few transmissions repeated when there was confusion, but overall the controllers in Russia were helpful and clear in their communications.

OATs were now about ISA-7°C, and ground speed was holding at about 300 knots with a minor crosswind from the left. I was cleared to descend so as to cross 50 kilometers out of Magadan at 4,500 meters. Out came the calculator and 50 Km divided by 1.8520 Km/nm equated to 27 nm, while 4,500 meters times 3.2808 ft/meter gave about 14,800 feet. ATIS information was broadcast twice: First in Russian, then in English. It took several times listening to the transcribed information to get all the details, but it worked out to be clear skies, wind from 110° at 2 meters per second (4 knots), and a temperature of minus 22°C. The altimeter was reported as 988 hectopascals (millibars) or 721 millimeters of Mercury, and my handy chart from the Jepp book showed that to be 29.18 inches. (The altimeter in FL-188 had the ability to display either inches or millibars, a handy feature.)

Lizard clued us in on the fact that asking for a visual approach was fruitless, so we each crossed directly over the airport in plain sight below while proceeding out to a 10 nm teardrop turn to the ILS to Runway 10. It was bright and sunny (but oh so cold!) as I touched down at 0125Z with 700 pounds of fuel remaining. The flight had taken 4.8 hours; block time had been 5.0. I think the local time on this clear January 3rd in Russia was 12:25 p.m.

I pulled into the parking space designated by a marshaller, beside the other two 350s and next to a big, three-engine, Russian airliner, a Tupolev 154, I think. Lizard had told us to remain with the airplanes until the fueling was complete. After stepping out into the cold, seeing that the fuel truck was still working on the first plane, noticing that the three soldiers standing there in long, thick, black coats and fur hats seemed to be telling me to stay put, I went back into the plane to await the fuel truck. In Anchorage, we had stocked up on four cans of Prist, the anti-icing additive, for each airplane. At long last, when the truck came to me, I exited my warm cocoon to prepare the Prist cans for dispensing into the fuel.

Have you seen how this is done, at the fuel hose's nozzle? A vinyl tube gets connected to the aerosol can and is then clipped onto the fuel nozzle, so that the Prist will mix thoroughly with the fuel stream. Well, folks, the vinyl gets a little too brittle in the Russian winter. Snap! Snap! Snap! The tube broke every time I tried to position it. So, I climbed up on the fuel platform ladder with the woman who was doing the fueling, held the can in my gloved hand, and squirted the Prist into the fuel stream from her nozzle. Working together, but with an insurmountable language barrier, this woman communicated to me how tough her working conditions were. Her cotton gloves had holes; her canvas "tennis shoes" had been attacked by the kerosene such that there were gaping cracks in the soles that let in the frigid temperatures. My office manager, Kathleen, had packed a "goodie bag" of candy, ball point pens, cigarettes, playing cards, and even some old clothes, and I was happy that I could give these folks a little something.

The time I spent out in the cold was brutal. Even wearing good ski gloves, my fingers became numb and my toes joined them in their sensory defection. Svetlana, the attractive and English-speaking head of the servicing detail, had gone with Lizard to the distant buildings across the tarmac so that he could finalize our flight plans for the next leg and pay the airport charges. Mike and I stayed with our airplanes. Several times, I had offered the three soldiers to come onboard the 350, to get out of the cold, but they always politely declined…until Svetlana departed. Then -- wham! -- they came onboard in a flash. I chuckled at how they kept checking for the first sign of her return and as soon as her truck left the headquarters building a few hundred yards away, they quickly resumed their posts outside. Dressed in a lovely silver fox coat down to her ankles, she did not fit the stereotypical image I had of Russian women at all. She had told Lizard that the airport, her employer, had not paid her since April, eight months ago! She lived with her parents and had never been out of Magadan. "I'll be sent to jail if I don't show up for work," was her explanation of why she was still working there.

On the other hand, maybe she didn't need to get a salary; perhaps money came in from other sources. I say this because of how horribly expensive our Magadan stop proved to be. In Anchorage, Mike and I each received ten crisp hundred dollar bills from Lizard to use for personal expenses enroute, and as a down payment for our services. When he returned to the airplanes with Svetlana, obviously distraught, he sheepishly asked for the money back. He needed the cash! Although well-stocked with US currency – one of the few readily-accepted commodities everywhere – his stash would have been cut too low had he not borrowed back from us. The fee? $6,880. Although the fee covered everything, including landing fees, customs, etc., it worked out to about $5 per gallon! *(Author's note: Prices have come up astronomically since 1999, eh? $5 sounds pretty good now, ten years later.)* Magadan won't remain a popular stop for delivery flights at these prices.

About three hours after landing, all was ready for departure. Poor Mike's battery barely eked out enough speed for the start, and for a moment voltage went so low that all of his engine instruments quit! But the start was successful, and I followed him as he exited the ramp. Lizard was off at 12 past the hour, Mike at 23, and myself at 34. Our clearances were identical, and included a straight out climb to 1,000 meters and then a left turn direct to the BA nondirectional beacon. Departure control kept us climbing without restriction until we reached our assigned level of 7,800 meters, or 25,600 feet.

The low sun was slowly moving to the west, and for a while it was directly ahead, blindingly bright at its low angle above the horizon. An Air Canada and a United flight both chatted with us briefly, curious as to what we were doing so far from home. It was now 17°C below standard, with an indicated OAT of -42°C. As we droned along, making our position reports in the non-radar environment, the sun kept up its westward march until it finally went below the horizon, about 45° relative bearing to my right, at 0645Z, 2 hours and 11 minutes into the flight.

My engine instrument scan suddenly grabbed my attention. What's that right oil temperature doing? Whereas it had usually been averaging about 60°C, it was noticeably higher, and moving upward! Damn! I don't want engine problems over the Sea of Okhotsk! It kept rising until it was only about 10° below the start of the yellow arc, but then suddenly plunged down to the normal 60° value. This happened about three times. Oil Pressure and all other engine parameters remained steady. I concluded it wasn't anything to worry too much about, but it was hard to not be mesmerized by the now-suspect gauge. (The sharp Japanese maintenance technicians later theorized that the oil-to-fuel heat exchanger's diverter valve may have been hanging up.)

About twenty minutes after this worry, another crops up: The voltmeter is erratic, with the needle fluctuating a couple of volts up and down rapidly around the nominal 28V value. Come on airplane, let's be nice to each other! At least the winds are good; up to 312 knots ground speed now.

The battery ammeter is steady, panel lights are not flickering, and turning off each generator separately causes no change. "Got to be the voltmeter gauge," I say to myself, as indeed the technicians confirm in Japan. Poor little N18297 doesn't like the frigid temperatures aloft anymore than I liked them on the ground at Magadan, I guess.

The descent clearance arrives: "Descend so as to cross 30 kilometers from the PW beacon at Flight Level 4,500 meters." Out comes the calculator. Let's see now, that's 16 nm at 14,800 feet. I need to lose about 11,000 feet, which should require 36 miles, so I decide to start down when 52 nm from PW. (Thank goodness for the UNS-1C and its GPS receiver, since no DME came from PW.) Weather at Yuzhno is fine, clear and cold, and we all execute the ILS approach to Runway 1, following the published routing carefully over the mountainous terrain hidden below in the darkness. Touchdown for me comes at 0747Z, which is 6:47 p.m. local time: 3.2 hours flight time for the leg.

Once again comes the slow refueling saga, customs and general declaration forms, and then the long walk though the minus 6°C night to the terminal building, carrying our overnight bags. Dennis is the local Russian handling agent who is very helpful, is an old friend of Lizard's, and whose English language skill is excellent. We wait a long time in his chilly office on the second floor of the terminal while he finishes coordinating our paperwork. Lizard is playing a joke on Mike and me, and is bemoaning the sad state of the local hotels. Across the parking lot from Dennis' office, he points out the airport hotel and, well, I've seen better…in nightmares. We seriously consider spending the night on couches in an adjoining room in the terminal, but the building is really quite cold. After a couple of hours of waiting, we are finally done with the paperwork and Lizard says that he found available space in a local hotel, so Dennis calls for the crew bus to drive us there. Another wait. Finally, it arrives, looking like a 1940s school bus, but shorter. We slip and slide along the snowy, rutted roads into the city. Block after block of what appear to be apartment buildings line the city streets. Each is perhaps four or five stories high and nearly a block long. Yet, amazingly, perhaps only ten or fifteen windows are illuminated. It's after 9:00 p.m. local time. Are the people still at work?

The King Air Book

Out dining? Are the buildings nearly vacant? We don't know, but the unfamiliarity of it all gives me an uneasy feeling. A few citizens wait on street corners in the cold air for the few city buses that we see. I see not one neon sign, and the lights in the windows look like about 40-watters, max. We pass a couple of menacing looking compounds with razor wire atop tall fences, compounds that hold lots of automobiles. Few cars line the streets, and the ones there are covered with snow and look to be old clunkers. Lizard explains that the citizens with cars pay to keep them in these secure, guarded, parking lots, and some people have mile-long walks from the compounds to their apartments.

"Golly. What will this hotel be like?" is the recurring worry in my head. But what's this? Now the bus has passed though the city and is back in the countryside. It turns down a country lane that is surprisingly well-lighted with fancy street lamps in the snow. The guard at a closed gate says a few words to our driver, the gate opens, and we proceed. Wow! What's this?! It looks like the Scottsdale Hyatt, except covered with snow!

Lizard, you devil! What surprise is this? Well, it seems that oil is a hot commodity in Yuzhno-Sakhalinsk now, and many American and Japanese oil industry workers spend a lot of time there developing the oil fields. The Santa Resort Hotel is the joint-effort of a Russian and Japanese company, and stands in stark contrast to the area surrounding it. The lobby is full of marble with signs in Russian, Japanese, and English. The woman at the check-in counter speaks English perfectly, even with a hint of a British accent. The room I am assigned is clean, modern, and warm. The restaurant is bright and cheery with an extensive list of beers and a good menu. "Heaven. I'm in heaven. Tra la, tra la."

In bed at last, the television set receives a variety of Russian, Japanese, European, and American channels. Which American ones? Why CNN and CMT, of course! I watch the live launch of the Mars Polar Explorer, and fall asleep counting my blessings and being thankful that the USA and Russia are no longer enemies.

Our last leg is a short 2.1 hours from Yuzhno to Sendai. The bus arrives at 7:30 a.m. and we proceed back to Dennis' office in the terminal. All ATC clearances come "from Moscow," it appears, and that is the excuse given whenever a glitch occurs. We hoped to get off earlier, but aren't ready until shortly after 11:00 a.m. local time, which is 10:00 a.m. in Sendai. Dennis walks Mike and me through the bureaucratic maze upstairs in the terminal for filing our flight plans, getting the weather briefing, and also receiving a personal IFR departure procedure briefing.

All three planes start using battery power alone without problems in the -15°C temperature. With all three planes running, I get the middle slot this time and follow Lizard's takeoff about fifteen minutes later. The GPS shows 531 nm direct and the clearance, that will quickly put us in Japanese airspace, is for a climb to good ol' Flight Level 280. No more meters! Cruise airspeed is 293 knots, with a ground speed of 307. The right engine's oil temperature is running steady, but the airplane's voltmeter is still erratic. We provide ETAs for the Japanese border, and are soon talking to Sapporo Control, or "Beer Control" as Lizard says. (And they respond to his calls, with never a comment!)

Beer Control assigns a squawk code of 6175, and my transponder reply light starts blinking again, a sight I hadn't seen during the last 2,100 nm. Sendai's ATIS reports 14 knots of northwesterly wind, 10 km visibility, light snow, scattered clouds at 2,000 feet and broken clouds at 3,000 feet, with the ILS 27 approach in use. This approach comes in over the water to the runway's end that sits right on the shoreline. I receive easily-understood vectors to final, but a snow shower – little in size but heavy in strength – is sitting right on the ILS localizer path, so I don't sight the runway until a couple of miles out. All three airplanes join together at Parking Spot Number 1 at the very modern terminal building and we are met by a swarm of friendly and helpful people, representatives of the company that is the purchase agent for the planes as well as some who work for the company that will maintain them.

We are led through the customs and immigration process by Yugo, a friendly young woman, who makes the process quick and easy. Then the entire group have lunch – a noodle soup and sushi combination – at the terminal restaurant. What a contrast between Yuzhno and Sendai! Everything here is so clean, modern, bright and shining. The airport is humming with activity, and we watch lots of airliners come and go during lunch.

It takes nearly four hours for Customs to approve the airplanes and all the extra equipment that is being imported into Japan. While they do their work, we mark time in the terminal. I call Pam who is visiting our friends Dick and Earline in Monterey, California, and report that all is well. One of the terminal's display cases is full of hand-carved wooden dolls; we are told they are one of the specialties of the Sendai region.

When we get the word that Customs has completed their inspections, we return to the planes and taxi en masse to JAMCO, Japanese Aircraft Maintenance Company. What an impressive outfit! We are welcomed and ushered into a large briefing room where a slew of technicians attend to the official debriefing of us three pilots. We each list the discrepancies for our airplanes on the white board, and then answer probing questions from the staff that aid in their troubleshooting. They seem extremely knowledgeable, as well they should since they have maintained virtually all of the Coast Guard, Air Force, Navy, and turbine-training King Airs for many, many, years. Meanwhile, the 350s have been moved into a large hangar where other technicians unload them and make a meticulous listing of all contents that arrived. Looking at the swarm of activity, Lizard is reminded of "ants on a sugar cube," and indeed that is an apt metaphor. I gave away the remainder of my goodie "stash" to these willing workers and it is appreciated, especially the Snickers bars.

The King Air Book

We ride a comfortable bus to Hotel Metropolitan Sendai, check in, drop our bags and strip off our long underwear in our rooms, then meet in the lobby. "Tommy," one of our Japanese hosts, leads the way through a large, neat, open-air mall complex to our dinner restaurant…but he can't find it! After a few missed approaches, he finally locates the place and eventually ten of us gather for a most pleasant meal. Our Japanese hosts are extremely gracious and appear genuinely appreciative for the work we did in bringing the airplanes to their new home. We say "Sayonara" after dinner, and we three pilots head back to the hotel alone. Bed is most welcome at about 11:00 p.m. local time. Only Japanese stations are available on the TV.

I'm up the next morning, Tuesday, January 5, at 7:30 local time, which is 2230Z time and 1530 MST back in Scottsdale, but both of those places are still enjoying Monday, January 4. Weird! I have breakfast at the hotel – they offer both a Japanese and a western buffet – and Mike comes in about the time I'm finished. We agree to meet for checkout at 10:15, and all three of us lug our bags a couple of blocks to the Sendai train station. We say goodbye to Lizard. He is going back to the Sendai airport, catching a flight to Turkey via Bangkok, and probably picking up another BE-350 there to deliver to Paris. His nomadic life is somewhat glamorous and full of adventure, but what a schedule he keeps! I don't think that I could keep up his pace.

The language barrier is a challenge for me, and due to that Mike and I miss the train we hoped to take to Tokyo. Luckily, however, we get tickets for a slightly later one that connects through Tokyo's main station so as to arrive at Narita Airport at the originally-scheduled time. Whew! The "Bullet Train" proves to be as swift, smooth, and quiet as we had heard, and reminds me of an airliner – even with "flight" attendants pushing food carts up the aisles. The transfer in Tokyo is easy, and when we arrive at Narita to claim our reserved seats on Delta's flight 78 to Los Angeles, we are told, "So sorry, but Coach class is full. Would you mind moving up to Business class?" Oh, well, let me think about that a moment. Okay, we'll do it. (Yes!)

The big MD-11 departed at about 4:30 p.m. and arrived at LAX at 9:30 a.m. of the same day! I ate, read, and slept during the flight, and reflected on how much quicker the airliner was compared to our 350s. Clearing US customs was easy, and I said farewell to Mike as we each went our separate ways. A customer picked me up in a King Air C90B and flew me back to Scottsdale where we did some refresher training the next day.

Looking back now, a few weeks later, it seems unreal. Just five seemingly-brief days, and we made our deliveries to the far east and flew back. For me it will remain a very special delivery to Japan.

FLYING THE SOUTH PACIFIC

My wife, Pam, and I were blessed to have a once-in-a-lifetime flying experience in the fall of last year, 2001, when we flew Pat and Ashley Gallagher around the world in their Super King Air 200. The three-month trip started less than a month after 9/11 yet was completed in safety and comfort. We documented our journey with pictures from our digital cameras and stories written on our laptop computers. These we sent to our website administrator at our home base in Scottsdale, Arizona, who then kept the site up-to-date with our material, so that friends and family and other interested parties could follow our progress, almost in real time.

The website is still active: www.worldflight2001.com. If interested, please log on and spend some hours reliving the experience that we enjoyed. The following article is a modified, expanded, version describing a couple of the legs we flew. I hope you enjoy it.

December 14, 2001
Auckland, New Zealand (NZAA) to Nadi, Fiji Islands (NFFN)
Mother Nature Throws us a Punch

Our car and driver picks us up at Auckland's Ascot Metropolis Hotel at 7:30 a.m. for a planned 10:00 a.m. departure to Nadi, Fiji. Don't ask me why, because I don't know, but there are a lot of "n" sounds inserted into the words as they are spoken in Fiji and Samoa. Although they are spelled Nadi and Pago Pago, they are pronounced Nandi and Pango Pango.

The direct distance to Nadi is 1,164 nm, and we cannot tolerate very much headwind to make this flight with sufficient reserve fuel. We are flying N982GA, a 1976 Beechcraft Super King Air 200, serial number BB-149, equipped with standard tanks that hold 544 gallons of usable fuel. If the forecast winds look too strong, we will have to turn the flight into two legs by using Norfolk Island, Australia, for a fuel stop. We are using Universal Weather & Aviation, Inc., of Houston, Texas, for handling services. These services include outlook weather briefings and preliminary flight plans that are faxed to our hotel room the night before our departures, as well as final weather and flight plan packages that arrive the next morning. When Universal's fax arrives early in the morning, the forecast average wind component is minus 34 knots. 34 knots of headwind, in other words. Although worse than we hoped, this still allows the flight to be completed in one leg instead of two. Also, the computerized flight plan shows that the strongest headwinds come during the first half of the trip and then get less as we proceed north to Fiji. The winds never help, mind you, but they don't hurt us as much if the flight proceeds as projected.

Our superb on-site handling agents in Auckland, the ever-helpful and efficient Robin Leach (male) and Raynor Simich (female), of Air Center One, have things well in hand when we arrive. Catering, fueling, learning a bit more of the great store of South Pacific flying knowledge that Robin possesses...the time passes quickly; soon Ashley and Pat arrive. The helpful New Zealand Immigration agent is driven by Raynor over to Air Center One's facility so no time is lost traipsing through the corridors of the main terminal.

We are airborne at 10:14 a.m. local time, 2114Z. Today's flight is basically straight north but, for the first time during all of our World Flight 2001 legs, we go "backwards" one time zone. Hence, we gain an hour today instead of losing one. Our departure is from Runway 23L, a stone's throw from the hangar.

We have nice views of the Auckland area as we fly the simple departure procedure and our course takes us offshore on the east side of the North Island of NZ. ("En Zed" as they say here). We are handed from Auckland Departure to Auckland Center passing 12,000 feet and they ask for our estimate at "Kalag" intersection. Center offers us FL280 and we decide to accept, since the range for a turboprop is almost always improved by climbing higher. However, such is not the case today. Thanks to the wind readout we have in our avionics package, we can instantaneously see that the extra one thousand feet from 270 to 280 has brought us an additional twenty knots of headwind! Bad deal! At our request, Center quickly permits us to return to FL270.

We are now in clouds, with engine ice vanes deployed, and not having a smooth ride. Continuous light and occasionally moderate chop make the going uncomfortable for passengers and crew alike. Pam and I focus on the headwind and the groundspeed, and keep comparing our actual performance with what the computerized flight plan has predicted.

At Kalag, it is obvious that we are doing much worse than the projection. Since the winds are nearly twenty knots more than forecast now, there is always the hope that the improvement down the road will also be better than forecast. To bet on that, however, is very risky. If winds do not improve by an amount much more than forecast, then there is a very real possibility of not having enough fuel to make it to Nadi. I'd hate to need to test our Winslow life raft!

We are now using the temperamental HF (High Frequency) radio for contact with Center, and it is behaving itself well today. At 2230Z, the wind has increased to 80 knots, giving us a 76 knot headwind component. Our groundspeed dips under 160 knots for a time as we motor along with all ice protection devices activated.

To add another element of bad luck, our left fuel flow gauge is doing a weird thing: It is reading 180 degrees backwards! What I mean by that is that the needle on the gauge is pointing such that the big end is reading wrong but the little end is reading right. This year model King Air, 1976, still utilizes fuel flow gauges that are powered by Alternating Current, not Direct Current. The AC gauges, including the torque gauges, have the ability to operate in this backwards fashion.

I was never told of this by any other pilot or instructor or mechanic, but many years ago I stumbled across the phenomenon during a training flight that I was conducting. I could hardly believe my eyes, but there it was, a torque gauge working, but working 180 degrees out of phase. Being the curious guy that I am, I decided then to see if I could correct the problem and/or duplicate it.

There is a memory-aiding poem that says, "DC Dies but AC Lies." What this means, as applied to King Air AC and DC engine instruments, is that the loss of power to a DC-powered gauge will result in the gauge's reading going to zero. It dies, in other words. However, the loss of power to an AC-powered gauge will result in the gauge's reading remaining right where it is. In other words, the gauge needle lies still, and hence its value is telling a lie to the pilot.

I tried the following as I experimented with this phenomenon years ago. At idle, when the torque should be low, it was reading high. I pulled the torque circuit breaker and froze the torque gauge at that high, incorrect, value. Then I added power, using the Ng, fuel flow, and ITT gauges to guarantee that I didn't add too much power, until I had a lot of actual torque. I then reset the CB and – voila! – the needle jumped a minor amount to the correct reading and started working properly again.

Since that first time, I have found that this technique has always provided a successful fix to this rare problem. Later this day, it would repair our temporary malfunction.

At 2245Z, an hour and thirty-one minutes after takeoff, Pam and I agree that there is no point in continuing and I request a clearance from Center back to Auckland. At least the return will be quick, with so much tailwind. We receive the new clearance, south down the airway back to Auckland, and turn around. Immediately, our groundspeed picks up to 312 knots! Ashley and Pat understand that sometimes discretion truly is the better part of valor.

I ask Auckland to call Air Center One and advise them of our intentions, and soon I am able to talk to Robin directly on his frequency. He already is making plans for a re-route for us via Norfolk Island and is talking with NZ Customs about our change in plans. What a mind reader he is! In less than an hour after turning around, we are back where we started from. Two hours and thirty eight minutes after starting, we are shut down on the ramp outside of Air Center One's hangar.

Amazingly enough, with the wondrous help of Raynor and Robin, we are refueled, Customs' requirements are satisfied, a couple of new flight plan have been filed, and we are off again, this time heading to Norfolk Island, YSNF. Pam and I had discussed our duty hours, fatigue, and whether or not we should still try to continue to Nadi today. If it were not for the quick service provided in Auckland, our decision would have been "No." However, as it developed, we both felt good in pressing forward. We could, after all, spend a night on Norfolk Island if need be.

With these shorter legs, fuel is not the worry as it was earlier and hence we file for a lower altitude to make more speed. This also keeps the cabin altitude lower and provides more oxygen for our feeble brains. Our clearance is for FL220 and this puts us outside of controlled airspace for most of the way. Hence, our clearance is a clearance into uncontrolled airspace; it is not a clearance to YSNF. Odd, but typical here.

This time our route takes us right up the western shore of the North Island, with beautiful views of the beaches. We now have about 30 knots of headwind. The HF is working well, and from over 170 nm out we are hearing and talking to Norfolk clearly on VHF as well. The weather at Norfolk is fine. Pam is Pilot-Flying on this leg, as she was during the earlier aborted attempt, and she makes a visual right downwind entry into the traffic pattern for a landing to the east.

The small island is beautiful, green and lush, with lots of farm fields in view. Although I am no expert, the history of this place is fascinating. It is where many of the *Bounty's* mutineers were sent to as a penal colony after they were finally found living on Pitcairn Island. Today, many families on Norfolk still have the names of the famous crew: Christian, Adams, etc. Also, it is the home of the Norfolk Island Pine tree, and that species surely grows in abundance.

The flight takes two hours and forty-three minutes and our time on the ground for refueling takes a relatively short forty minutes. Now I am flying left seat. Upon departure, I stay low and give us a brief tour around the coastline of this pretty island before turning toward Fiji and climbing to altitude.

Now the HF decides to be stubborn again and it is hard to communicate with Auckland Center. "Pacific 910," a commercial flight, relays one report for us. Later, however, we talk to Nadi Control quite easily and clearly on the HF.

About an hour after takeoff we are out of all clouds and it is clear ahead. We notice cumulus buildups in the distance to our right, where we would have been had we flown straight from Auckland. The decision to reroute via YSNF seems better all of the time. The winds are now predominantly from the west and we are getting a minor help from them as we fly northeast.

Sunset in Nadi comes at 0640Z and the GPS says we will land at 0735, meaning it is going to be dark outside. The sun sets. Darkness falls. Nadi Approach clears us to an intersection about fifteen miles out for a straight-in ILS to Runway 02. We make a small right course correction to start heading to that point as Pam picks up the ATIS. What's that it says?! Heavy rain? Dang!

Actually, the ATIS is a bit old and the rain has moved away by the time we are setting up for the approach. We see the runway lights from ten miles out or so, but then the tower throws us a curve: "Turn left at the final approach fix and maneuver for visual right traffic to land on Runway 09." He is assigning this to us in order to allow an airliner to depart on Runway 20, heading right towards us as we land on the other end of the concrete strip, Runway 02. We see the airliner's landing lights ablaze between the twin row of runway lights as he sits waiting to takeoff.

"Uh, tower, I think we can slow it down and there'll be enough room to depart the airline traffic and we could still land on 02," I advise. "No, make a visual approach to 09. Noise abatement procedures in effect."

Noise abatement?! From a little ol' quiet BE-200? It reminds me of the old yarn about the Boeing 727 captain who complained to ATC vehemently after the controller had given him a 60-degree turn off course as he cruised at FL350. When the controller said that noise abatement was the reason for the turn, the captain exploded, "Noise abatement?! AT FL350?!" "Yes sir," says the controller. "Just think how loud it is if two airplanes hit each other at cruise speeds!"

Oh well, we tried for the straight-in. Night, circling approaches to unfamiliar runways, especially with little if any lights on the ground in the surrounding area, are hard to execute and, historically, have claimed the lives of too many pilots and passengers.

However, we decide to accept the controllers suggestion – They are always *suggestions*, not *commands*, in my opinion, until the Pilot-on-Command agrees to them – based on a number of favorable factors. First, the circle will be almost totally over the water of the bay. Even without local knowledge of the area, there won't be any hidden terrain to hit when we are over the sea. Second, visibility is good and winds are virtually non-existent. Third, the runway we are circling to is plenty long, well-lighted, and has a visual approach slope indicator (VASI). Fourth, we have GPS giving us distance to the airport and this vital information can help us execute a proper descent profile. Fifth, we have two experienced pilots crosschecking each other.

Thus, we do the circle, it all works just great, and we are on the ground parking at Bay #2 three hours and forty minutes after starting up in Norfolk. Local time is 7:38 p.m.

Our handling service here initially gives a less-than-stellar impression, but they improve during later encounters. Pat and Ashley and the baggage are off-loaded and moved into the terminal from Bay #2, then Pam and I must start up and taxi the airplane around the terminal building to the south side for long-term parking at Bay #15.

It's always the little stuff that gets you! As I taxi around the large, dark, ramp to the other side, the landing lights illuminate two large baggage trolleys that are sitting unattended and unlighted right on the ramp. How sad it would be to execute a flawless circling approach at night and then to ding the airplane severely hitting some nasty little ground obstacle! Vigilance pays!

We secure the airplane but the exhaust stacks and cowling inlet lips are still too hot to allow installation of the vinyl covers. "No problem!" says the handler, a man of Indian descent. "We will do it for you later when they cool!" Two days later, when we return to the airport to refuel, the covers are still sitting uninstalled, as we left them.

This same fellow now drives Pam and me back to Bay 2 and we find our employers waiting in the baggage claim area. We have to complete our immigration forms. We look a little worse for wear at the end of this long day as we sit on the edge of the unused baggage carousel in the dimly-lit building as we fill out the papers. The two-man crew of a Twin Otter that arrived just after us is doing the same thing.

Finally, out we go, pushing our airport carts full of luggage, including golf bags. A friendly gentleman, Kalam, another Indian, has been waiting for us for over five hours, having never been told of our change in arrival plans due to our unexpected return to Auckland. Although the vehicle is a Toyota Land Cruiser, we think it will be impossible to fit all of the luggage and all of us into it. Kalam proves us wrong! He does a superb job of packing, and we fit with room to spare.

We drive through the dark roads of Nadi, about a twenty-minute drive, across a small bridge onto the man-made island of Denerau, where we are booked into the Sheraton Royal Resort. I think we are all somewhat in a daze, finding it hard to believe that we really made it here on the scheduled day, just a few hours later than planned. Pam and I have a late dinner at one of the resort's restaurants…overlooking the beach, thatched roof, tiki torches blazing, the sea breezes cooling.

Mother Nature threw us a good shot today. We regrouped, found another way around her challenges, and persevered. The adventure continues.

December 17 & 18, 2001
Nadi, Fiji Islands (NFFN) to Bora Bora, Tahiti (NTTB)
A long day with lots of stops

We have done numerous communications with Universal Weather & Aviation in Houston via e-mail and telephone due to the complexity of the flying we are about to do today. Thanks to Robin Leach's inputs in Auckland, we have decided to modify our original plans. Pat Gallagher, in the trip planning that resulted from his extensive research, had us making two stops today on our way to Bora Bora in Tahiti. The first was going to be at Pago Pago in American Samoa, and the next at Papeete,

Tahiti, where we would clear Customs and Immigration and refuel before making the short hop to the island of Bora Bora.

Robin strongly suggested that we avoid Pago Pago if possible. He verified the stories we had heard: That the runway surface was in a poor state of repair and that the services there left much to be desired. He suggested two alternatives. First, substitute Apia, in Western Samoa, in place of Pago Pago. Second, take a more southerly and marginally shorter route, but one that required an extra stop. If we decided to use Apia, the leg from there to Papeete would become even longer than the already long leg from Pago Pago to Papeete. On the other hand, if we went the southern route via Tonga and Rarotonga, each leg would be shorter and we would have more fuel reserve and more alternates in case of emergency. The only disadvantage of this was the extra time consumed in one more stop.

Raynor and Robin, our handlers in Auckland, had also contacted Bora Bora directly, requesting a special permit that would allow us to arrive as late as 7:30 p.m. local time, and Bora Bora had faxed back a reply saying that this was approved. Remember, Robin and Raynor were doing all of this before we left Auckland. They were planning ahead in their routine, excellent, fashion. Bora Bora's airport normally closes at 5:30 p.m.

We estimated the flight times for the various legs of our new plan, factored in guesses for times on the ground at the refueling stops and for clearing Customs and Immigration in Tahiti, added them up and subtracted them from our 7:30 p.m. arrival time in Bora Bora. The conclusion was that we would need to takeoff from Nadi at 6:00 a.m. local time.

Complicating all of this was the International Date Line that we would be crossing. Although we would be leaving Fiji on Tuesday, December 18, we would be arriving in Bora Bora on Monday, December 17!

My method for trying to keep track of the times is to use Greenwich Mean Time and date for all calculations and then convert the various ETAs and ETDs back into the local time and date. Our Universal handlers, like everyone, struggled with the time conversions and we had more than one telephone conversation helping them get the plans straight. After we had gone to bed early on Monday night, we were awakened by one more call from Houston trying to clarify the times. Tuesday morning, after we awoke at 3:00 a.m. to start getting ready, we got another call from our Universal handling team in Texas, this time expressing their worry that Bora Bora closed at 5:30 p.m. and saying they were not convinced that we had permission for a later arrival. We assured them that we did.

It is dark and still as we pack and checkout of the hotel at the unseemly early hour so that we could meet our van and driver at 4:30 a.m. At the Nadi airport, the handling service is fine, although things move a little slower than we hoped they would. Although we think that loading up and departing from our parking area would make the most sense, the Fijians had us scheduled to depart from Bay 2 and, by God, that's what we were going to do! So, after Pam returns from a lengthy visit upstairs with Air Terminal Services, she and I go to the airplane at Bay 15 while our passengers accompany the luggage to Bay 2. We preflight the airplane, start up, and taxi back around the terminal to Bay 2. We had returned to the airport from the hotel and refueled yesterday morning so did not have to waste time for that now.

Soon we are loaded and starting up again for departure. The handlers had suggested the 4:30 a.m. pick up at the hotel and I must admit they knew what they were doing: Our taxi out time was precisely at 6:00 a.m., as scheduled!

Universal had prefiled our flight plan using our routine FL270, even though I had asked them to use FL210 for this leg. Air Traffic Control, however, quickly approves my request for 210. We decide to stay lower to go a little faster and to keep the cabin altitude lower, and hence have less fatigue during this long day. The HF radio contact with Nadi starts out fine. The early morning sun is directly in our eyes, so we have our sun visors and charts hanging in the windshield to keep from getting blinded.

The forecast slight tailwind is not materializing. In fact, the wind is showing 0 knots quite often on the Garmin GNS 530 readouts where the Shadin ADC 2000 data is visible. Fiji is comprised of over 300 islands and we see some very lovely ones as we cruise in smooth air. We had ordered some catered sandwiches from the airport handlers, for lunch, as well as a fruit and cheese plate from the hotel, for breakfast on board. As we left the hotel, we discover that Ashley also thought ahead and ordered food to go, so we are in fat city as far as edibles are concerned! We munch our way across the South Pacific ocean.

Our destination on this first leg is the Kingdom of Tonga. The island is Nuku' Alofa and the airport is called Fua' Amoto, identifier NFTF. About an hour and a half into the flight, the Avidyne Flightmax 850 multifunction display screen, in the Map mode, starts showing blue where black has been for the last couple of months. We realize that we have finally returned into the coverage of its installed database, so now we have ground detail again. In this case, maybe I should say "ocean detail," which isn't much! Since our GNS 530s have current databases, we haven't missed the Avidyne display in this mode at all, but it is still nice to have it back.

We land and are in the chocks two hours after taxi out. Due to the lack of tailwinds, we are about fifteen minutes behind schedule, but are hopeful the ground stop will take less than the forty-five minutes we had estimated. It is not to be!

We are on "island time" and things don't move very quickly. When the fuelers come, they are using an underground system installed in the tarmac, not the more typical truck. The hose cannot reach to our filler caps. With the help of some friendly local pilots of a Twin Otter parked beside us – Raj and Moses – as well as some ground handling crew, we manage to push the airplane back so the hose reaches the first side. Later, we have to again man-power the airplane back and then forward, while Pam steers in the cockpit, to allow the hose to reach the other side. All told, our ground stop consumes an hour and three minutes, putting us thirty-five minutes behind our plan.

I fly this leg at FL250. It is uneventful, except for so-so HF coverage. More than once we call on 123.45, the oceanic air-to-air frequency, as well as on 121.5, the VHF emergency frequency, to see if any other airplanes or ground stations receive us. No reply. We are in a vast expanse of airspace, all alone.

From over 160 miles out, we establish good VHF communication with Rarotonga Tower, and make a straight-in approach, landing to the east. This is a part of the Cook Islands, that is administered by New Zealand, and the controller as well as Paul, our handling agent, speak "Kiwi." We land at 0027Z, still running about a half hour behind schedule. The ground time is about what we had allotted, an hour. It would have been shorter, but the fuelers show up with a single-point rig first and have to go back and get the over-wing truck. We are airborne once again at 0126Z.

Up we go to FL270 for this leg, and, finally, we do get some minor but welcome tailwinds. On all of the legs today the outside air temperature is very warm, about 15 to 18 degrees Celsius above standard temperatures for our altitudes. Although we have trouble talking to Auckland oceanic on the HF, we can communicate relatively well with Tahiti control on HF as we get into their airspace. We enter clouds now and with the ice vanes deployed we lose speed. Tahiti Control reads our request on HF and clears us to FL210 in an attempt to get underneath the clouds, but we are still in IMC. Our hopes of getting to Bora Bora before closing time are dwindling. We may have to spend a night in Papeete.

Our autopilot system, a King KFC-300 unit, has a pitch trim switch located on the pedestal that allows minor altitude corrections to be made when in Altitude Hold mode as well as changes in pitch attitude to be made when in Attitude Hold mode. I discover that the switch has decided to stop working in the Up direction. Down, no problem, but nothing results when selecting the switch Up. No big deal, but we keep watching it and hope it is a momentary glitch.

The airport in Papeete goes by the name of Faaa. Since each vowel and consonant is pronounced in the Polynesian tongues, I guess it sounds like Fa-ah-ah. We again are fortunate to make a straight-in approach and are on the blocks two hours and fifty-three minutes after taxiing out at Rarotonga. It is 6:15 p.m., local. Can we get to Bora Bora in an hour and fifteen minutes? Veronique is the first person who greets us and she is an angel of speediness. Air Tahiti is our handling agent here, arranged for by Universal. They know of our desire to get to Bora Bora before

The King Air Book

7:30 p.m. and go out of their way to help it happen. Our passports are collected, the Immigration cards are provided to be completed by us, and I go with Veronique to the Operations office where I am told that I must call Universal, urgent!

Universal, overall, has provided great service for us during World Flight 2001. Yet there have been a few times when they drive us nuts. This is one of them. When I get through to them, there is confusion. "Did we call you? Why are you calling us?" Finally, someone seems to indicate that the entire gist of this urgent message is to, for one more @#$% time, tell us that they have not received permission for a late Bora Bora arrival. Yet, here at the Operation Office, I have just been handed a copy of the fax with our approval! Yuck!

When I get back to the plane, Veronique is escorting Pam, Pat, and Ashley back to it also and we are told that we can leave immediately. One great factor that helped here is not needing to refuel, since it is only a forty-five minute hop ahead. Still, I think all of us have been thinking that we will likely spend a night here, since there is little likelihood of a fast enough ground stop to make our deadline. Now, however, we are stoked with new enthusiasm and rekindled hope!

We are airborne a mere thirty-six minutes after landing, and I take an intersection departure off of the long runway, making an immediate left turn to our first fix on the IFR plan we are following. It is dark, now, with scattered to broken clouds. We have been assigned FL160 and I keep the deck angle low and the speed high as I climb. Excellent VHF coverage exists, both with Tahiti Control and with Bora Bora tower.

I make the descent a little earlier than normal to attain as high a ground speed for as long as possible. As we start to break out of the clouds at 3,000 – 4,000 feet, we can see the lights of some nearby islands and now we can see the Runway End Identifier Lights and the Runway lights for Bora Bora's Runway 29. The wind is reported as 040 degrees at 10 knots, and I decide to accept a slight tailwind component and have Pam request a straight-in landing on Runway 29, to save additional time.

The female tower operator tells us that she will approve that request but that we should know that the PAPI (Precision Approach Path Indicator) lights for that runway are inoperative. Pam immediately expresses her preference to circle to the other end, Runway 11, which I heartily agree is the better course of action, and we are approved to do so and told to report on final.

Remember my talking about the hazards of night circling approaches, in conjunction with our landing at Nadi? Well, here we go again, but to an even greater extent than before. Except for the runway lights, there is absolutely nothing to see. The sky and sea and land are all totally black. No other lights are installed on this stretch of the atoll. We are fatigued after this long day and, during the descent, the autopilot would disconnect whenever I attempted to use that quirky attitude adjustment switch, so I have been flying by hand since leaving 16,000 feet. Do the initials JFK, Jr., ring a bell?

Unlike JFK, Jr., however, we are instrument-rated and current and know of the hazards we face. I ask Pam to follow the instruments closely and to set the radar altimeter's DH bug to 500 feet and to advise if the light comes on, indicating that we are closer than 500 feet to the ocean, before we turn final. I must alternate my attention from my set of instruments to the visual contact I maintain with the runway lights as we fly a left downwind to base and final. We have the GPSs set for the airport, and the OBS mode allows us to see an extension of the runway's centerline and we can monitor both our distance to the airport and lateral offset from the centerline easily.

It works out very, very, well, as evidenced by the PAPI showing two red and two white lights as I turn from base leg to final. The landing lights finally pick up the dark runway. Now is not a time for finesse. I tell Pat and Ashley that this landing would likely be firm, since I was going to get it down and stopped without any fanfare. "At least you have an excuse this time," was Pat's clever comeback over the intercom! (We have a Garmin GMA 340 audio panel installed with a six-place intercom, so the passengers can listen-in and talk when they desire. We also can play CDs for musical entertainment. Pretty neat!)

We cross the threshold, I close the power levers to idle, do a minimum of flare, and we arrive. The time? 7:29 p.m. I think we are all in a little state of shock that we made it before the deadline...one whole minute early! To depart Fiji eleven and a half hours before and to arrive right on time, including three intermediate stops...wow! God smiled on us again today.

We park on the corner of the small ramp. No one is around. Pam and Pat proceed to the terminal to see what they can find while Ashley and I remain with 982GA. We discover a multitude of crabs on the tarmac, some quite sizeable. The ramp is wet from recent rain. In fact, I have decided to add an epithet to our trip's name. Now, maybe we should be known not just as "World Flight 2001" but instead as "World Flight 2001 – The Rain Maker." It seems that everywhere we have been since Perth, Australia, we have had clouds and rain! Need a little water for your local crops? Want to end the drought? Just call "WF2001 – The Rain Maker" and we can solve your problem!

Just about the time Ashley and I decide to see what's taking so long at the terminal, we see Pat and Pam coming, pushing a baggage cart across the ramp. As we are about to finish unloading the plane we hear a loud clunk and suddenly are plunged into total darkness...all runway and ramp lights have been turned off! We use flashlights – torches, for you English speakers – to find our way to the terminal that, fortunately, remains lighted.

The road from "town" to the terminal isn't a road. It is a waterway. On the opposite side of the terminal from the ramp, the lagoon comes right up to the loading dock. The Hotel Bora Bora, where Pat & Ashley are booked, had been notified of our arrival by the tower and are sending a water taxi for us. Pam and I are staying at the Sofitel Marara and they have advised that we can take a regular taxi to that hotel after we leave the water taxi at Hotel Bora Bora.

We sit on the deserted docks, the only people around. The warm tropic air is still. No bugs bother us. After twenty or thirty minutes, we see and hear the launch approaching. It has a powerful floodlight atop the cabin to help find its way through the night waters. Our mutton-chopped, French-speaking, boatman helps us load and then we zip through the smooth waters to the hotel, with occasional bursts of rain pounding the boat's windscreen.

Pam and I feel a bit guilty getting the royal welcome treatment at Hotel Bora Bora. ("No, no! Forget the leis and fruit juice drinks! We aren't really guests here!") John is the English hotel manager who greets us with his staff. Small, small, world…he has managed both the Hyatt in Perth as well as the Burj al Arab in Dubai, places we have been on WF2001!

While waiting for our taxi to the Marara, all four of us enjoy a libation at the bar and relive our day's miraculous adventure. We are all rethinking our plans for the coming flight to Hawaii. That day, as it is planned now, is even longer than this one, and now we have been shown again what a hard grind it can be as darkness and fatigue raise strikes against us. Maybe we will have to overnight in Papeete or Kona and break the day up into smaller segments. We'll see…

(Check out www.worldflight2001.com for the story of the complete three-month trip.)

EARLY FLYING MEMORIES

I believe that a love of flying is something that is firmly fixed into some of our little souls at birth. Maybe we were birds in some previous incarnation? Be that as it may, I can never remember a time that I didn't need to look up and search for the plane I heard overhead. Born in 1945, I grew up in New Castle, Indiana, right under the airway that went between Indianapolis and Dayton. Almost every clear day, the distinctive straight trailing edge, swept leading edge, profile of DC-3s could be viewed as they would pass over our town eastbound or westbound. I loved that sight!

My dad traveled a lot on the airlines for business and we sometimes flew as a family on Piedmont from Dayton down to Raleigh-Durham to visit relatives. There is a picture of my brother and me standing beside an early Lockheed twin-tail, ready to board, in our Sunday finery. It was a big deal to fly back then and everyone dressed properly for the occasion. Later we rode on DC-3s on this local route, making a few stops along the way. Want in on a secret? I always got sick! Plus, I remember one time horrible pain – A nail going into my head! – every time we descended on this flight when I had a bad head cold. Yet, I loved it. How can that be? It's crazy! On every leg, once I upchucked, then the air sickness went away and all was well in the flying world.

My great uncle, Claud Stanley, was a local car dealer and bank owner who got bitten by the flying bug. He lived right next door and, when his wife was at their summer cottage in Michigan, he ate breakfast with us every day she was gone. How I enjoyed hearing him talk about their travel…in his new, shiny, red and silver Cessna 170A. (The one that I used to own, that is now Don Lindholm's – an Oshkosh winner, no less! – looks exactly as I remember Uncle Claud's.) Due to his age – or maybe he was just a lousy pilot! – Uncle Claud never flew alone but always was piloted by the owner/operator of one of the three (!) little airports that New Castle had. This military veteran had the great name of Emerson Western. Now isn't that right out of central casting for a thin-mustachioed pilot type?! My first flight in a small plane was in the 170A with Emerson, going on some little jaunt to pick up Uncle Claud or Aunt Deedie. Ah…that row of piano key switches. How fascinating they were!

Not long after, the 170A got traded in on a yellow and silver 195B. Geez, that Jacobs radial engine sounded sweet! I couldn't see much out the front, but I rode with Emerson on a trip to and from northern Michigan in it. My great uncle died in the late '50s. I later was told that he had a new Piper Apache on order at the time of his unexpected death.

The King Air Book

Emerson taught ground school in the little line-shack at his grass field. When I was fourteen, I peddled my bike the four miles out there on two or three evenings a week and joined with three or four older guys, all taking our Private Pilot ground school together. There wasn't much room at the table when we all spread-out our charts! The thing I remember most about this class was that Emerson loved having us draw wind triangles on clean blank sheets of paper, using them to calculate our ground speed and wind correction angles. (Timid Virgins Make Dull Companions, and all that.) He insisted that we use the hand-cranked pencil sharpener after each exercise so that the pencil point would be as thin as possible and hence the WCAs could be determined with increased accuracy!

(Okay, for the newcomers: True Course plus or minus Variation equals Magnetic Course plus or minus Deviation equals Compass Course. TVMDC... Timid Virgins Make Dull Companions was the memory aid.)

When I was seventeen, between my Junior and Senior years of High School, I started taking lessons at another of the New Castle airports, Sky Castle, run by the Marlatt family on their farm. (It is the only one that survives today.) They had two 1956 172s for training...serials numbers 19 and 21, I think. My first lesson was on August 4, I soloed on September 15, and got my ticket on December 24...a very nice Christmas present from my folks. Larry Barker, from Muncie, was my instructor. The rate for the 172 back then? $12 per hour...solo or dual! Sectionals cost 25 cents. Fuel? I don't remember, but probably less than 50 cents a gallon.

I never planned to have a career in aviation. I was quite near-sighted, wore glasses, and knew military and airline flying were not to be. (Lasik surgery seven years ago is one of the true miracles in my life!) That I would end up having a long career in the corporate flying world, specializing in King Air training, would have been a complete surprise back when I got my license.

One last recollection to share: In the spring of 1962, prior to starting my flight training that summer, I was going to Washington, D.C., alone, to participate in the U.S. Senate Youth Program. Unbeknownst to me, after I boarded the American Airlines' Douglas DC-6 in Indianapolis, my dad spoke to the Captain and told him what a nut I was for aviation and that I'd be taking lessons soon. Before we got underway, the Stewardess – back then, that's what she was called – came back and asked me to come forward with her. Not knowing why, of course I did as requested. She ushered me to the cockpit and introduced me to the three cockpit crewmembers. I'll never forget what happened next: The Captain, after shaking my hand, before he'd taken his seat, looked at me with a serious expressions and said, "Tom, have you ever told a lie?"

"Well," I stammered, "Yeah, I have." "Good," he answered, "because if anyone ever asks you if you were in the cockpit during flight, you're gonna lie again and say No!" With that, he turned and closed the cockpit door, pulled down the jump seat, and one amazed and delighted seventeen year old kid stayed in that magnificent cockpit all the way to the gate at National airport. God! What a thrill! Captain, whoever you were, thank you from the bottom of my heart. You'll never know how much difference your act of kindness made in this life! After that ride, I knew that I wanted to be at home in the front of a complex airplane.

Thanks for coming along with me on this short journey of remembrance.

TOM CLEMENTS' DVDS

Flying the King Air

Want to know more about operating your King Air correctly? Tom has created a professional, one-of-a-kind, instructional video that you will find enjoyable and enlightening. Six strategically-located cameras were used simultaneously in the actual cockpit for creating the raw footage and then that footage was carefully edited into the final fantastic product. It's as if you are in the cockpit, looking over the shoulder of a pilot going through an entire Initial flight training session. Starting, taxiing, takeoffs and landings, single-engine work, autopilot/flight director utilization, RMI usage, IFR approaches…these are but a few of the more than twenty topics covered in this exceptional two-hour presentation. Filmed in *Flight Review's* C90, but significant differences that apply to other models are discussed throughout the video. **$40 includes shipping and handling!**

Using the KLN-90B GPS

Tired of trying to read the huge Bendix/King manual? Too many things to think about? Frustrated that you can't make this GPS do more? Tom has created a unique instructional video on one of his favorite GPS navigators, an oldie but a goodie. The first half of this two-hour presentation is devoted to the basics: what does each chapter and page do, how do you call up waypoints, how do you go Direct, etc. The second half deals with Flight Plans, SIDs, STARs, and, most importantly, GPS approaches. At your own pace you can watch this detailed and enjoyable presentation and learn from a master. If you cannot do a proper GPS approach after viewing this video a few times, if you don't pick up on at last three things you didn't know before about this great unit, your money will be gladly refunded! **$20 includes shipping and handling!**

FOR AN EVEN BETTER BARGAIN, ORDER BOTH FOR $50…SAVE 20%!

ORDER AT WWW.FLIGHTREVIEW.NET